Research Strategies in Historical Archeology

STUDIES IN ARCHEOLOGY

Consulting Editor: Stuart Struever

Department of Anthropology
Northwestern University
Evanston, Illinois

Charles R. McGimsey III. **Public Archeology**

Lewis R. Binford. **An Archaeological Perspective**

Muriel Porter Weaver. **The Aztecs, Maya, and Their Predecessors: Archaeology of Mesoamerica**

Joseph W. Michels. **Dating Methods in Archaeology**

C. Garth Sampson. **The Stone Age Archaeology of Southern Africa**

Fred T. Plog. **The Study of Prehistoric Change**

Patty Jo Watson (Ed.). **Archeology of the Mammoth Cave Area**

George C. Frison (Ed.). **The Casper Site: A Hell Gap Bison Kill on the High Plains**

W. Raymond Wood and R. Bruce McMillan (Eds.). **Prehistoric Man and His Environments: A Case Study in the Ozark Highland**

Kent V. Flannery (Ed.). **The Early Mesoamerican Village**

Charles E. Cleland (Ed.). **Cultural Change and Continuity: Essays in Honor of James Bennett Griffin**

Michael B. Schiffer. **Behavioral Archeology**

Fred Wendorf and Romuald Schild. **Prehistory of the Nile Valley**

Michael A. Jochim. **Hunter-Gatherer Subsistence and Settlement: A Predictive Model**

Stanley South. **Method and Theory in Historical Archeology**

Timothy K. Earle and Jonathon E. Ericson (Eds.). **Exchange Systems in Prehistory**

Stanley South (Ed.). **Research Strategies in Historical Archeology**

in preparation

Lewis R. Binford (Ed.). **For Theory Building in Archaeology: Essays on Faunal Remains, Aquatic Resources, Spatial Analysis, and Systemic Modeling**

John E. Yellen. **Archaeological Approaches to the Present: Models for Reconstructing the Past**

James N. Hill and Joel Gunn (Eds.). **The Individual in Prehistory: Studies of Variability in Style in Prehistoric Technologies**

Michael B. Schiffer and George J. Gumerman (Eds.). **Conservation Archaeology: A Guide for Cultural Resource Management Studies**

Research Strategies in Historical Archeology

Edited by
Stanley South

Institute of Archeology and Anthropology
University of South Carolina
Columbia, South Carolina

ACADEMIC PRESS New York San Francisco London
A Subsidiary of Harcourt Brace Jovanovich Publishers

ACADEMIC PRESS, INC.
111 Fifth Avenue, New York, New York 10003

United Kingdom Edition published by
ACADEMIC PRESS, INC. (LONDON) LTD.
24/28 Oval Road, London NW1

Library of Congress Cataloging in Publication Data

Main entry under title:

Research strategies in historical archeology.

(Studies in archeology series)
Includes bibliographies.
1. United States–Antiquities–Addresses, essays, lectures. 2. Archeology–Methodology–Addresses, essays, lectures. I. South, Stanley A.
E159.5.R47 930′.1′028 76-43377
ISBN 0–12–655760–8

PRINTED IN THE UNITED STATES OF AMERICA

To those who religiously believe that
the archeological record reveals far more than
merely what happened, when, and to whom.

Contents

List of Figures and Tables

FIGURES

TABLES

List of Contributors

Numbers in parentheses indicate the pages on which the authors' contributions begin.

Ronald C. Carlisle (287), Department of Anthropology, University of Pittsburgh, Pittsburgh, Pennsylvania

Richard F. Carrillo (73), Institute of Archeology and Anthropology, University of South Carolina, Columbia, South Carolina

Leland G. Ferguson (41), Institute of Archeology and Anthropology, University of South Carolina, Columbia, South Carolina

Albert C. Goodyear III (203), Institute of Archeology and Anthropology, University of South Carolina, Columbia, South Carolina

Joel Gunn (287), Division of Social Sciences, University of Texas at San Antonio, San Antonio, Texas

John H. House (241), Institute of Archeology and Anthropology, University of South Carolina, Columbia, South Carolina

Kenneth E. Lewis (151), Institute of Archeology and Anthropology, University of South Carolina, Columbia, South Carolina

Michael McCarthy (261), Le Projet du Garbage, Department of Anthropology, University of Arizona, Tucson, Arizona

John Solomon Otto (91),* Department of Anthropology, University of Florida, Gainesville, Florida

William L. Rathje (261), Le Project du Garbage, Department of Anthropology, University of Arizona, Tucson, Arizona

Michael B. Schiffer (13), Department of Anthropology, University of Arizona, Tucson, Arizona

* Present address: 1320 Lark Court, Titusville, Florida

Stanley South (1, 119), Institute of Archeology and Anthropology, University of South Carolina, Columbia, South Carolina

Robert L. Stephenson (307), Institute of Archeology and Anthropology, University of South Carolina, Columbia, South Carolina

Randolph Widmer (119),† Institute of Archeology and Anthropology, University of South Carolina, Columbia, South Carolina

†Present address: Department of Anthropology, Pennsylvania State University, State College, Pennsylvania

Foreword

This book is intended as a serious effort to renovate and redirect historical archaeology. In order to do that, its contributors have successfully welded their enterprise to anthropological archaeology. There is now no doubt that these people and their work are allied to the best contributions and better minds of the new archaeology and all the self-conscious efforts at self-improvement that that movement meant at its height. Further, they have accomplished all this without the disruptive polemic once associated with the parent movement. These essays fulfill all their own claims and expectations; they also provide analyses of data fascinating in their own right. This is of course as it should be, but besides this there are a number of other advantages to be derived from this book that are not so expectable and which come as delightful surprises. Among them we are given a tacit reappraisal of what archaeology is all about.

A historical archaeology which is fully competent intellectually, which is what we see in this volume, shows us two extraordinarily important developments. Archaeology is no longer dealing with the deep and irretrievable past and it is no longer dealing with the ultimately unknowable "other." It is dealing with us. The implications of this are as startling as the development itself.

These essays deal with modern society or with its direct historical foundations. With a rare exception they are not about the long dead past; they are about people and places and processes tied up with the Industrial Revolution, the founding of the modern English-speaking world, or directly with modern Americans. Not only are we not faced with the prehistoric, we are not particularly concerned with the cross-cultural.

We as archaeologists have always been clear about the reasons for studying the past, for reconstructing past lifeways, discovering cultural processes, and writing history in general. Knowledge of the past has never been valued as an end in itself within the domain of social science and sometimes not even within the discipline of history. As archaeologists we have always been aware at some level that all our knowledge of the past is derived from the present. We have long understood that, while the past is fascinating, the value of the fascination stems from what we can tell about our present and possibly our future state from it. The past has, rightly or otherwise, been regarded as the base from which calculations could be made, projections given, and lessons of a type thought to prevent the repetition of mistakes learned.

This generalizing rationale has motivated the archaeology we have all done and is the reason behind our mutual affiliation with cross-cultural research, hypothesis testing, the positivist logic of Carl Hempel, and the body of social theory we inherit as anthropologists. We are then unabashedly concerned with ourselves, and our concern with objectivity in studying others, whether they lived in the past or the present, has been to eliminate the ethnocentric bias we all recognize lies behind our research. We have always been aware of the inherent tautology that the model we find in our data is us. Now, however, we are faced with studying ourselves directly, not through the predictive and reflexive mirrors of the past or the living other. Consequently much of the care we took to eliminate ourselves from our own research so that we could utilize its results reliably can now be turned to discovering ourselves in it. Our concern with accuracy can be reoriented.

The main trend represented by this volume is not greater accuracy in knowing the past, nor massive technical sophistication; it is, rather the logical fulfillment of the insights Lewis Binford brought to prehistoric archaeology fifteen years ago. Binford, using an understanding of Marx derived from Leslie White, reasoned that if society produced something, that thing—a concrete object or set of them—should encompass and encode all the elements of society that produced it. If one worked with this assumption then an object, or better, an artifact could be turned into an index of all the production processes responsible for it. This included social and other nonmaterial factors. That logic and the talent of its proponents produced most of the best work done in archaeology in the last fifteen years. They renovated the discipline and its spirit.

When this logic and spirit entered historical archaeology it produced efforts such as this book, whose major intended effect is to place historical archaeology squarely inside anthropology. In its own terms this book is successful, and, by comparison with what we think of as the best products of the past fifteen years, it is yet more successful. In order to shift historical archaeology from its particularistic to a scientific or anthropological foundation, a large batch of methods and techniques have been used by these authors, sometimes with awesome sophistication. These include many already familiar to archaeologists like statistics, hypothesis testing, and systems theory. To provide a more sound epistemological base for historical archaeology, the use of written evidence has been carefully segregated from archaeological evidence in measuring variables so that the two sets of data appear to test and corroborate each other independently. The ethnography of modern and early modern technology and the careful observation of living processes which are tied directly to forming the archaeological record are also utilized by historical archaeology. Most of this enormous technical and methodological virtuosity is presented as an effort to understand the archeological record better. This is true even when the discoveries about the living present are novel and inherently valuable *per se*. All this virtuosity has been used to produce constructions of the past considered more accurate and trustworthy. Further, it has been done so that the past may be used more creatively in the service of understanding the nature of culture change, differentiation, and process. The reason for this circles back to understanding how the present came to take on its current form since that form stems from processual changes which link the past to the present and both to the future.

My own opinion is that historical archaeology is far closer to a radical reorientation to anthropological aims than even most of the authors in this volume think. Reason this way: Marx produced an analytical system which allowed us to see the dialectical or dynamic relationship between the parts of living society. One of the key insights in his analytical system was that production includes not only things but virtually the whole of society. Individuals, relations between them, and the concept of the individual self, in addition to the concrete items of manufacture, are productions of society. Further, things take on symbolic or use value, as they function within the various levels or structures of society. Binford translated this into primary and secondary function. But in Marx's system all function—i.e., value—stems from the symbolic or cultural value (i.e., meaning) an item has as it is used inside its society. But it is the initial insight into the realities of production, rather than a deduction from it useful to prehistorians who have only the material remains of a society, that is directing historical archaeologists inevitably to analysis of the present—always the point of looking at the past anyway. By nature we as archaeologists examine material productions; by recent inclination we see objects as social productions. By theoretical bent we choose to view these as commentary on process and now that they are readily open to our understanding since we or our immediate forebears made them, we can use material culture not to rebuild dead societies but, together with written and verbal data, to analyze the production of society in the fullest sense.

Henri Lefebvre (1968) in his *Everyday Life in the Modern World* shows us Marx's intention.

> Production is not merely the making of products: the term signifies on the one hand "spiritual" production, that is to say creations (including

> time and space), and on the other, material production or the making of things, it also signifies the self-production of a "human-being" in the process of historical self-development, which involves the production of social relations. Finally, taken in its fullest sense, the term embraces *re-production,* not only biological . . . , but the material reproduction of the tools of production, of technical instruments and of social relations into the bargain . . . [pp. 30–31].

Although Marx invented a system of analysis he thought was valid for understanding all society, he intended it primarily for use on modern nations. And certainly it is on these that his insights have been most valuable. Marx nonetheless intended to operate cross-culturally and did not have to face the enormous philosophical problems attendant on any system intending to be universally applicable. The fall of logical positivism that is latent in Freud and explicit with Wittgenstein was in front of him but in back of us. He did not see it, but we cannot ignore it. It is that fall and the fall of all absolutely certain knowledge with it that has bedeviled archaeology for most of its modern life. However, when we as archaeologists use the developments in this book as our marker, that fall is in back of us in two senses. True it has happened and we cannot continue to ignore its implications as we have been doing, but we now face an archaeology oriented to us, a subject which is obscure to be sure, but at least philosophically accessible. With one stroke we have attained a modern position epistemologically. Further, it allows us to utilize Marx's insights into production directly rather than in some convoluted and ultimately debilitating way. We can study productions directly, not as indices to what society was, but as measures of what society is. Rathje has come closest to doing this in this volume and he sees in what he calls a new kind of social science what Marx saw a century and more ago: a way of reading society through its productions. Stephenson sees an archaeological profession—in the sense of one that solves practical problems for society on a responsible business-like footing. And Schiffer sees in disposal processes part of what Marx saw in analyzing production. Schiffer and Rathje are analyzing the part of production that necessarily involves consumption. "Cultural formation processes" may be corollaries to uniformitarianism, but they are certainly illustrations of the changing "use value" of productions. Garbage as Rathje uses it is material production measured against social and ideological productions to illustrate the inevitable discrepancies between these levels. As such Rathje allows us to pierce the misconceptions—better, misrecognitions—that protect the process of production from clear and unsettling view. Marx saw more clearly what these men intuit: The system of production and reproduction encompasses a basic understanding of how a whole society operates.

Historical archaeology as it is to be seen in this book has been searching for a home in anthropology and clearly has found one. It is also conducting a search for a worthy set of problems. It understands that it possesses a powerful set of data, but it does not yet understand how powerful and comprehensive the data are. Potentially, it has a special way of analyzing our society. This is its true contribution, one it begins to make in this book. As Rathje shows, historical archaeology, regardless of what it is called, encompasses an entire level of reality: all the objects we create as well as their patterned uses. When contrasted to other levels of reality, i.e., verbal information about ideal and supposed behavior, archaeology as practiced in this book allows us to spot the full range of variability, contradiction, and negation modern society is composed of. Indeed material culture is the only coherent universe we possess which can comment on, measure, and contradict verbal reality.

I have chosen to find a certain kind of potential in this book and in historical archaeology. Some of these authors might agree with what I have seen and others, although I think they would be a minority, would not. My use of Marx's ideas on production are not meant to be political or polemical; they are useful because he provides the clearest ideas we possess of what an object is, and objects—at least the three-dimensional kind (as opposed to relationships which are objectified to make them seem inherently true when they are actually arbitrary)—are the common-denominator substance of archaeology. There are other productions which are of course not so obviously material: social structures or social relations and ideology. Everything we call culture is ultimately a production and as such is the domain of anthropology in general. Since our domain as archaeologists is so consistent and complementary to the rest of anthropology—insofar as it covers not the past, but rather the material productions of society—we are in a natural position to discover and expose the contrasts and contradictions between the levels of society. It is these that produce society's internal dynamic (or dialectic) and which in turn explain many of the surface changes we are aware of all around us.

Mark P. Leone

Department of Anthropology
University of Maryland
College Park, Maryland

Preface

The reader familiar with the field of historical archeology may be surprised to find that this volume is composed primarily of research by archeologists not typically associated with the field. Most of the contributors are products of anthropology graduate schools of the 1970s. They are colleagues whose work is oriented toward using strategies that link empirical data to current theory. The conceptual base of these colleagues is that of evolutionary and systems theory basic to contemporary archeological and anthropological thought. A qualitative pattern easily recognized in these chapters is the nomothetic paradigm of archeological science. The strategies employ both the inductive and hypothetico-deductive methodology necessary to complete the scientific cycle.

The strategies demonstrated here linking empirical data to theory reflect the revolution in archeological thought in the 1960s, as well as older concepts basic to archeological science. Using the broadened data base of historical archeology, these strategies are more revealing of the promise of historical archeology, as a mirror of its becoming, than a reflection of its past or a portrait of its present.

This volume is aimed at those colleagues involved in research on sites of the historic period and those not yet enjoying the variable-control advantage of this broader data base for theory building. It is especially aimed at those students and young archeologists who are questioning the relevance of particularistic strategies as research ends in themselves and who need models anchored in theoretical constructs as guides to fulfill this intellectual hunger in their own research. This volume is composed of such empirical guides toward the development of a science of archeology.

Stanley South

Acknowledgments

This volume owes its existence primarily to those of my colleagues whose research is included within it. The conceptual and methodological unity found herein results from shared goals, and from the ideas we are using to achieve them.

I want to thank Mark Leone for writing the foreword, and Susan Jackson for proofreading the manuscript. I am grateful also to Robert L. Stephenson for his role in contributing to a climate conducive to scientific research. I particularly want to acknowledge a debt I owe to a sage philosopher and friend who was a great inspiration during my formative years, David R. Hodgin. Maryjane Rhett has also assisted in many ways.

In acknowledging the help of those who have contributed to the compilation of a book such as this, the conceptual obligations are sometimes found to lie deep within past experience. In the introductory chapter I emphasize the importance of a frame of mind conducive to the synthesizing, nomothetic demands of archeological science. Such a frame of mind is not always acquired as the outcome of a course in graduate school. Sometimes it results from the gentle bending of the mind as a twig by those totally unaware of the germinal process of which they were a vital spark. I would like to acknowledge such a spark in my own life relating to my concern as an archeologist for transforming detail into synthesized pattern, synthesis into empirical laws, and laws into explanations of cultural systems and how they work. The minding process resulting in this bias came not only from sage philosophers, anthropologists, and archeological scientists, but primarily from my grandmother, Laura Elizabeth Gunlock Casey. She never lost her childlike enthusiasm for creatively interpreting patterned human behavior from the fragments of ceramics, glass, foundation stones, and flower beds she and I discovered in our Sunday expeditions to search for the old home places she loved to explore. I do not know why the challenge of discovering the size of the house that once stood around a lone stone chimney, or following the weed-covered path to the spring, or retracing the outline of the flower beds, the garden plot, or the place where "piggy" was kept appealed so to her. I do know that her delight did not end simply with the discovery of these features. As each was found she would relate, with an air of mystery as if unfolding an ancient saga, the tale of the people who once lived at this place. She made a game of finding specific features, reminding me of the "rules" whereby they could be found. "Remember, there are always two paths, one down-slope to the spring in the crotch of the hill, and another to the privy downstream of that or on the other side of the house." When we found the spring she would clean it out, being careful not to cut her hand on the broken tumblers, glass jars, milk crocks, and other containers we have come to expect there. As she brought these out of the icy water, she would relate how they had come to be there. Often these tales were filled with exciting accounts of dramatic events and people as she creatively reconstructed past lifeways. She never emphasized the things themselves, but the story they revealed in their relationship to one another. She saw artifacts as a means for interpreting, albeit imaginatively, lifeways in a past cultural system. She saw pattern in each ruined home place, and she took great pleasure in seeing the predictions she based on the pattern realized.

Only recently did I relate these childhood explorations to the context of my conceptual roots in archeology. Once the connection was made I was amazed to discover this wellspring of thought heretofore unrecognized and unacknowledged. I present this somewhat lengthy acknowledgment of a personal indebtedness because it illustrates the fact that sets of ideas compatible with nomothetic science and sets of ideas focused on particularistic goals are not simply focal points of a philosophy based on the rational activities of the human mind; they also constitute contrasting ways of viewing the world.

The world view reflected here in the work of my colleagues is clearly that of nomothetic science, emphasizing the generation of hypotheses and explanations of lawlike phenomena. I feel sure that the contributors to this volume join me in acknowledging their indebtedness to the ideas that serve as a generative force, allowing empirical data to be transformed into explanations of cultural systems. The secret of this generative power for understanding may emerge from long years of training and exposure to an empirical data base; it may come from devouring volumes on the philosophy of science; or it may be discovered within the minding process of a grandmother, a poet, or a sage. Whatever the source, the archeological scientist is indebted to those processes that have contributed to his or her particular bias toward understanding.

Acknowledgment is made for permission to quote from the following sources:

p. xiii: From Lefebvre, Henri, *Everyday life in the modern world* (translated by Sacha Rabinovitch), New York: Harper Torchbooks, 1971, Pp. 30–31.

p. 50: From Hume, Ivor Noël, *A guide to artifacts of Colonial America,* New York: Knopf, 1970, P. 114.

p. 55: From Peterson, Harold L., *The book of the continental soldier,* Harrisburg, Pa.: Stackpole Books, 1968, P. 150.

p. 75: From Binford, Lewis R., Archaeology as anthropology, *American Antiquity* 1962, *28:*218; 218–219. Reproduced by permission of the Society for American Archaeology.

p. 76: From Glassie, Henry, Structure and function, folklore, and the artifact, *Semiotica* 1970, *7* (No. 4):329.

pp. 153–157: From Casagrande, Joseph B., Stephen I. Thompson, and Philip D. Young, Colonization as a research frontier, in *Process and pattern in culture, essays in honor of Julian H. Steward,* edited by Robert A. Manners, Chicago: Aldine, 1964, Pp. 281–325.

p. 162: From Wallerstein, Immanuel, *The modern world system, capitalist agriculture and the origins of the world-economy in the sixteenth century,* New York: Academic, 1974, P. 302.

Figure 7.3, p. 174: From "A plan of the town of Camden," Craven County, South Carolina, John Heard, Deputy Surveyor, Original Manuscript Act. No. 1702 (1789), South Carolina Department of Archives and History.

Research Strategies in Historical Archeology

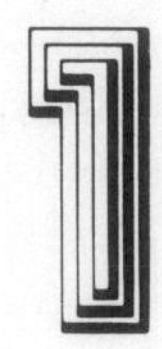

Research Strategies in Historical Archeology: The Scientific Paradigm

STANLEY SOUTH

The title of this book is a paradox in its implication that the research strategies demonstrated herein are uniquely characteristic of historical archeology. They are not. It is doubly paradoxical in that it also suggests that historical archeology is different from other kinds of archeology. It is not.

In planning sessions with those colleagues whose research is included here, this paradox was a major point of discussion. The theme of the dialog was that theory, method, and research strategies in archeological science do not vary simply because the trowel reveals, for example, musket balls from the British colonial system rather than Indian lithics from a tribal system or tin cans from a twentieth century American cultural system. Neither do the basic principles of archeological research vary as the data base is broadened to include ethnographic or historical data. The discussion over the paradox of the title clearly revealed that among these researchers there was no data bias, nor was there a prejudice favoring the remains of one cultural system over another. Their open attitude reflects instead an overt bias toward the development of a science of archeology.

There was therefore some concern that the qualifier *historical* implied a different kind of archeology. Nevertheless, there was also a recognition that the cultural processes within archeology since the 1950s have resulted in the use of the term *historical archeology* to designate archeological research on sites of the historic time period in which the broader base provided by ethnographic and historical data is used. Realizing this fact, my colleagues and I accepted *Research Strategies in Historical*

Archeology as the best compromise among those alternatives for designating the research contained in this book.

This ambivalence regarding the book title resulted also from an awareness of the particularistic orientation that has come to characterize the work of many of those using a combined historical and archeological data base. This phenomenon of particularism has been especially frustrating to those of us working with the broader data base who have emphasized a nomothetic thrust against what has often appeared as an overwhelming particularistic tide of resistance flowing in the opposite direction. Understandably, we are reluctant to be burdened with a particularistic label.

In my book, *Method and Theory in Historical Archeology* (South 1977), I have reviewed the development of thought and practice in this area of archeological research. This study revealed a dominant particularistic involvement with description and recognition of qualitative surface pattern, contrasted with a less prevalent nomothetic approach intent on quantitatively delineating deep patterning within the surviving material by-products of past cultural systems. This study also revealed that the search for deep-pattern recognition through archeological science is only now beginning to build a nomothetic levee against the particularistic sea within historical archeology.

The contrast between surface pattern with a historical–descriptive emphasis on qualitatively derived pattern and deep pattern based on quantitative analysis is illustrated in Figure 1.1. Qualitatively derived pattern is only the tip of the iceberg. In order to recognize deeper culture pattern, the archeologist must quantitatively explore the empirical data base using the methods of archeological science. The transformation from surface pattern recognition to deep pattern recognition depends on the organized integration of the empirical data base. The goal is the explanation of human behavior through a study of cultural systems. Past cultural systems are examined through archeological methods of pattern recognition. From delineated patterns, behavioral laws are formulated to describe the observed regularity. The explanation of why these laws exist within the past cultural system is the process of theory building. Testing theories about past cultural systems to build better theories is the major goal of archeology.

In order to define increasingly deeper pattern, one must organize the empirical data in ever-increasing levels of integration, from the level of idiosyncratic attributes through type, class, and group on an intra-and intersite basis (Figure 1.1). The depth of present research in historical archeology is represented by the Carolina Artifact Pattern, the Frontier Artifact Pattern, and the Kitchen Artifact Pattern, which reflect cultural pattern in the British colonial system (South 1977). The transformation to the next level would involve data reflecting indigenous territorial patterns plus the associated colonial territorial patterns. Such patterns would result from combining archeological data from Great Britain, for

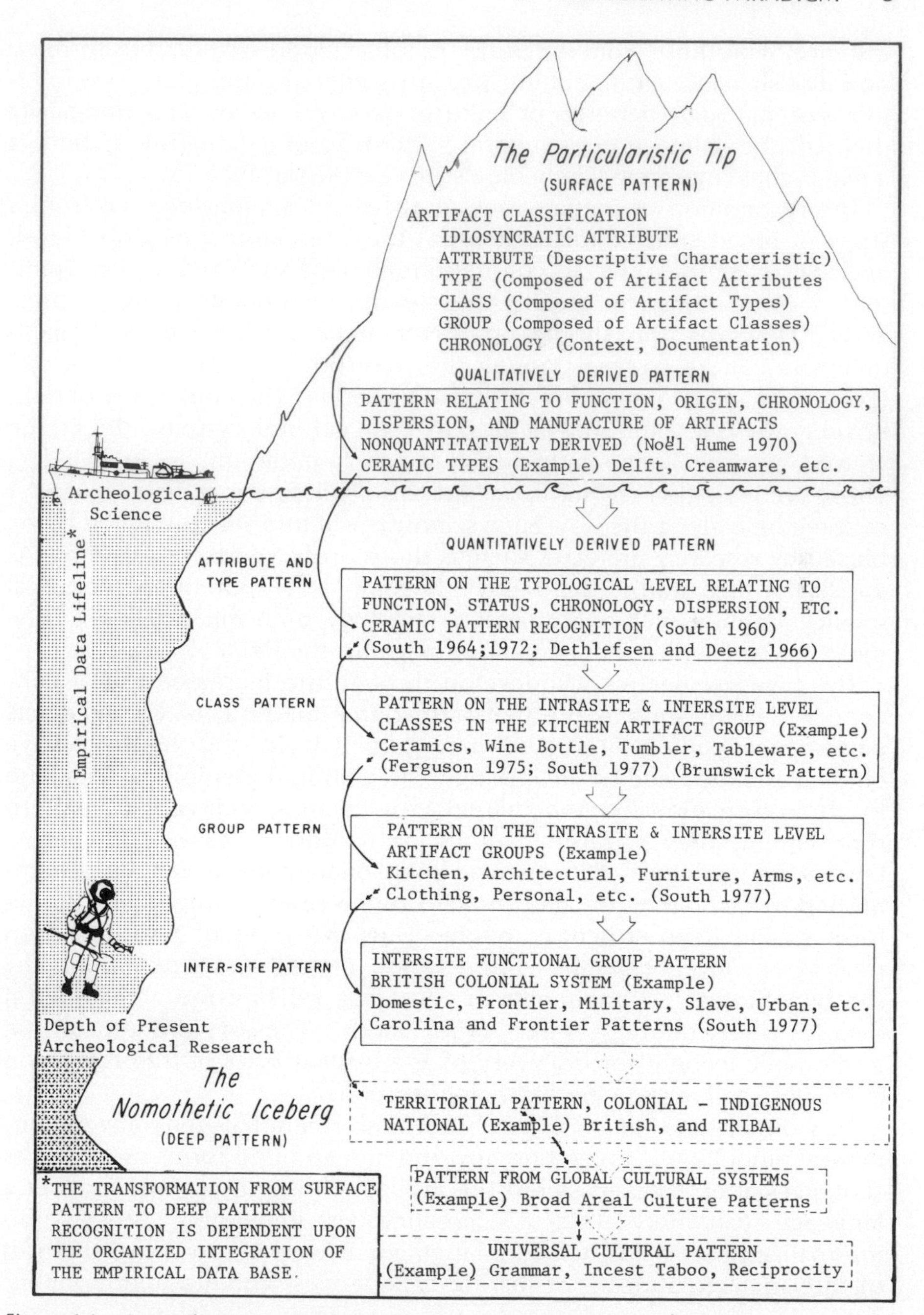

Figure 1.1. A transformational method for archeological pattern recognition.

instance, with those from the British colonial world system, thus forming new British nationalistic culture patterns reflecting the global exploitative system. Such patterns of culture have yet to be archeologically defined; the delineation of cultural patterns from nationalistic systems is a major challenge facing archeologists today (White 1975:158).

The recognition of pattern such as that which might emerge from a study of broad areal culture systems at the international or global level, and that reflecting universal cultural phenomena such as universal grammar, incest taboos, reciprocity, and so on, is certainly some distance away.[1] However, this should not deter archeologists from striving to delineate culture pattern through the transformation process from one level of organized integration of data to another. The complexity of delineating variables and regularities in past cultural systems should be viewed as a challenge rather than as an impediment to knowledge. Those archeologists willing to accept this challenge may find Figure 1.1 of some help along the way. Such scientists will find that the trail is being blazed by research strategies such as those presented in this volume. As a result of such studies the trail will become an avenue of archeological science opened within historical archeology and will provide a new direction, and with it a needed new image for the field.

This new perspective will develop through the increased use of conceptual designs such as the transformational method for archeological pattern recognition illustrated in Figure 1.1. In this figure I have emphasized the need for increasingly integrating the empirical data base by a transformational method aimed at delineating archeological pattern representing deep patterning within past cultural systems. The integration of archeological data for mapping deep pattern can be accomplished by combining the data in many different ways, depending on the form of the deep structure sought. Thus the rules of transformation relating one level of organized integration to another are determined by the hypotheses and arguments of relevance relating the archeological data to the cultural system under study. The exploration of the nomothetic iceberg for discovery of the explicit rules of transformation is a major challenge facing archeologists today.

As I understand Noam Chomsky's transformational–generative grammatical model, he is suggesting how the human mind forms or perceives sentences after it has mastered the available linguistic components of a language (Chomsky 1972). A creating or generating process, an internalized model for handling language, is working to afford the user of the language a means of sharing experiences, insights, and thoughts.

[1] The use of the terms *surface pattern* and *deep pattern* here was inspired by Noam Chomsky's *surface grammar* and *deep grammar* in transformational–generative linguistics (1972). As used here the concept is methodological, not explanatory.

Applied to archeology, this approach invites a frame of mind that generates hypotheses and sets of descriptions that relate to archeological science as a discipline concerned with sharing its findings with the general public as well as with archeologists. The position I have emphasized elsewhere (1977), and which is demonstrated by this volume, is that archeologists involved in the study of past cultural systems must have a useful idea-set as well as an appropriate methodology for generating hypotheses and explanations. Historical archeology has suffered for want of a frame of mind of sufficient scope to allow for the transformation of the bits and pieces surviving from the past into explanations addressed to the causal cultural system. I have emphasized the need for first, recognizing pattern in the archeological record, then constructing hypotheses to explain that pattern in terms of the past cultural system, and finally testing these ideas with new data. Before pattern can be recognized, however, an appropriate attitude of mind, a theory, must be deeply internalized to serve as a generative force for the transformation of empirical data into creative ideas for explaining patterned phenomena in terms of cultural systems. Without such a generative perception, the archeologist is severely limited in the depth to which he can go in his search for understanding.

The task of delineating pattern within past cultural systems is certainly not easy when data from historic, recent, and contemporary systems are involved. However, with the addition of a new dimension provided by documentation, ethnography, ecology, folklore, interviews, and observation of contemporary society, the archeologist has at his command a potential far greater than that provided by data for which no such control independent of the archeological data is available. The more archeologists come to realize the tremendous potential available in this broadened data base the more they will turn to the use of sites of the historic period to test ideas about past cultural systems. The more we understand about cultural systems for which we have some documented control of variables the more confident we can become about explanations of those phenomena operating in prehistoric systems for which no documentation is extant. I have made this point elsewhere (1977), and will continue to stress it, since it is in the field of historical archeology that the great proving ground for archeological, anthropological, and culturological theory and method is to be found toward the development of a science of archeology.

The chapters in this book reveal a common concern for pattern recognition as a necessay step "Toward a Unified Science of the Cultural Past," expressed by Michael Schiffer's chapter title. In numerous articles, and most recently in his book, *Behavioral Archeology* (1976), Schiffer has emphasized the importance of laws relating to the formation processes of the archeological record. He urges a more rigorous use of the surviving historical and archeological evidence toward a unified science of the cultural past. In this volume he addresses himself to the relationship between the systemic and the archeological contexts. In so doing he provides a methodological framework relevant to the research strategies demonstrated in the chapters to follow.

Leland Ferguson's study of artifact dispersion and density at the Revolutionary War battle site of Fort Watson is a good example of the use of quantitative analysis and historical documentation to derive the most interpretive value through masterful use of both data bases. His ceramic analysis reveals different behavioral implications regarding the consumption of food in a section of the site other than that on which the tea ceremony was performed. These data also have implications regarding military status—officers and enlisted men. Through skillful use of historical documentation, archeological artifacts, and statistical manipulation of quantitative data, Ferguson demonstrates the presence of annular pearlware in America a decade prior to its previously known occurrence. This finding is of considerable significance in the interpretation of sites of the period of the American Revolution (Ferguson 1975:2-28).

In addition to these results, the Fort Watson data revealed the kinds of weapons used by both British and American forces during the battle; it also revealed the location of a rifle tower constructed by the Americans, and provided information as to the military strategy used by the Americans to capture the fort. All this information was unknown prior to the Ferguson study.

Ferguson uses, as a basic means of interpreting past behavior, the variability in the archeological record resulting from accidental loss of objects and intentional discard of secondary and primary refuse as the by-product of different activities. Ferguson's background within archeology had been with prehistoric data. The study presented here is his first use of the broader data base provided by historical archeology. His work at Fort Watson is an excellent example of the maxim that with a scientific paradigm and skillful use of method, explanation of archeological phenomena in terms of the past cultural system can be accomplished without having to spend many years developing an expertise in handling data from the historic period. The critical factor making this possible is the generative power produced by theory, continually transforming the empirical data base into ideas probing cultural systems.

This vital minding, sciencing process (White 1938, 1949), when applied to any type of data base, be it history, folklore, pattern recognition in contemporary society, or archeology, is an essential, generative source in the growth of any contemporary inquiry. This attitude toward data can be applied to archeological projects at any level of sampling from a nationalistic system—to a region, to a site, to small areas of sites—for idea testing. Small areas of archeological sites contain patterned variability and regularity reflective of both site-specific behavioral activity and broader cultural patterns. Statements such as this can be made on the basis of demonstrated empirical patterning (South 1977) based on theory that links regularities and variability (pattern) in the archeological record with behavioral processes in the cultural system (Binford 1962). Such theory in relation to empirical patterning is an assumption underlying the chapters in this volume.

An example of the examination of small areas is seen in the chapter by Richard Carrillo. Often small areas are of concern primarily for the chronological and artifactual data they may reveal. However, Carrillo abstracts pattern in small areas at two sites; he links this pattern to disposal patterns, to other formation processes, and eventually to broader cultural variables.

Under a different paradigm Carrillo could have described the nineteenth century fragments as being singularly unimpressive. He could have provided an occupation date using the historical documents, and he could have dismissed the twentieth century whiskey-bottle fragments as being of little interest. However, he chose to test the small areas involved to determine the extent of the variability in the archeological record, with the view that patterned behavior would leave a patterned archeological record only revealed through quantification analysis. In so doing, he turned what might have been merely another mundane descriptive report of little value into an example of pattern recognition within a small excavation area. This study demonstrates that the archeological record is subject to revealing more than simply the first step in the archeological process, the questions as to what it was, who made it, where, and when.

Since dramatic differences in status are a characteristic of many cultural systems, it would seem that archeologists excavating sites of the historic period would long ago have devised a means of reliably making statements about status from an examination of the archeological record. However, such has not been the case beyond such obvious observations that a large manor house foundation is not likely to have been from the dwelling of an owner who was the slave of someone else. Many speculations based on subjective evaluation of artifacts have been made, such as the argument that it is "logical" that the upper classes would have used porcelain. A demonstration of historic site artifacts as status indicators was not accomplished until John Solomon Otto conducted a study of the question. His results appear in the chapter entitled "Artifacts and Status Differences—A Comparison of Ceramics from Planter, Overseer, and Slave Sites on an Antebellum Plantation." By using the control provided by historical documentation, and projecting against this the quantitative variability of the archeological record, Otto demonstrated a number of impressive patterns. He compared data from ruins of homes of planter, overseer, and slave, and found that ceramics were clearly a reflector of status. As more quantitative analyses of this type are conducted, using the historical record as a means of independent control, other status indicators will surely be discovered through such pattern recognition.

In our chapter, "A Subsurface Sampling Strategy for Archeological Reconnaissance," I demonstrate, with the assistance of Randolph Widmer, the results of a strategy using a standard posthole digger. This core-sampling strategy revealed, through a synagraphic computer mapping program, interpolations of the distribution of cultural materials. By this means, the location of occupation areas on the site were defined. The areas of major Indian activity involving the use of tidal resources, as well as specific activity areas resulting from short occupation, were located. Through this method of quantitatively mapping the distribution and density of the cultural materials within the research frame, we pinpointed the Civil War period military occupation and twentieth century occupation. Independent control over the location of these occupation areas was made possible through surviving surface indications plus documentation. The synagraphic computer mapping program (SYMAP) based on core samples taken at 100-foot intervals produced a map of the areas of occupation of the site in remarkable conformity to known areas of occupation. The usefulness of this core sampling method was dramatically demonstrated in the study.

Beyond the goal of testing the ability of subsurface core sampling as a discovery tool for interpolating site-occupation areas, the miniscule amount of data recovered from this sampling scheme was examined quantitatively to test the degree of fit of the nineteenth century military occupation debris with the Carolina and Frontier patterns (South 1977). The quantitative pattern was found to fit extraordinarily well with the Frontier Pattern. The implications of this discovery are that the patterns in the archeological record are sometimes remarkably regular on some levels as a result of the regularity of the behavioral pattern in the past cultural system.

The sampling strategy was also employed by Kenneth Lewis in his chapter and was designed to provide a stratified random sample of the eighteenth century frontier town of Camden, South Carolina. The study was made not only to sample the town, but also to sample the archeological frontier within a framework of a world cultural system. This broad perspective with a focus on colonization within a regional model is the kind of structure that will demonstrably allow historical archeology to grow into a study of cultural systems rather than a study of cultural particulars.

The SYMAP interpolations from over 180 five-foot squares, representing only 1% of the area of the town of Camden, dramatically revealed the location of the various structures in the frontier town as shown on a surviving document of the period. Using the 1% sample of this entire community, Lewis found that the quantitative relationship between artifact groups was consistent with that predicted by the Carolina Pattern (South 1977). Lewis revealed the mean ceramic date to be only 2 years from the known documented median date for the occupation of Camden. This study, representing the only such stratified random sample yet made of an entire community, has demonstrated the value of such a sampling approach at the discovery or reconnaissance phase of the archeological process. Lewis has explored method and delineated pattern toward seeking explanations to phenomena of frontier change rather than merely describing them.

Albert Goodyear's chapter is also oriented toward the understanding of past societies as functionally adaptive cultural systems. He used an ecological approach to examine one set of techno-environmental subsystems related to groups existing during the protohistoric period in the Lower Sonoran Desert region of southern Arizona. The analysis focused on a distinctive thin brown ware, which was demonstrated to have a unique temporal and environmental distribution within his mountain study area. Through rigorous application of archeological, botanical, and statistical methods, Goodyear was able to explicate subtle but important patterns surrounding the surface scatters of this thin brown ware. Such patterns would ordinarily be unperceived using traditional "stylistic" approaches to ceramic analysis. The fact that he was able to identify successfully a subsystem of the larger regional settlement–subsistence system is vindication in itself of the theoretical value of taking a systems approach to the study of now static archeological remains.

Goodyear's strategy combined archeological research with written ethnographic and historic records. He used anthropological documents as sources of relevant hypotheses, which were then tested against independent archeological data. He also demonstrated archeological patterns that are purely archeological in nature, having no written counterpart. This study made use of the unique plant ecology of the Sonoran Desert mountains, and is instructive in its implications for the use of environmental data in conjunction with archeological data in other areas. Historical geographers are beginning to exploit this potential in studies oriented toward man's use of the land and environment during the historic period. Historical archeologists should also begin to explore the link between the cultural system and the ecosystem to determine the nature and relative strength of this linkage in high-energy societies contrasted with that found in tribal societies.

Whether the archeological data at hand are thin brown ware made for use in cactus gathering, Colono-Indian pottery made for sale to customers of lower socioeconomic status, or British teaware discarded by upper-status army officers, the primary question is whether the research strategy efficiently exploits the behavioral ramifications of the archeological variables in question. Goodyear effectively develops the cultural and ecological implications of the thin brown ware by demonstrating that its patterning is in fact reflective of larger regional and temporal changes among the late prehistoric, protohistoric, and nineteenth through twentieth century periods.

In his chapter, John House points to the growing interest in regional data bases in historical archeology paralleling the increased involvement of both prehistoric and historical archeologists in cultural resource management. House demonstrates both theoretically and empirically that documentary sources cannot be assumed to provide an adequate picture of the human geography of past cultural systems. He presents technical, methodological, and theoretical suggestions for putting into operation a multistage regional research strategy in which frontier societies of the central Mississippi valley area are viewed in their behavioral diversity and in their ecological setting. This regional perspective parallels that used by Kenneth Lewis in its concern for using archeological data to answer questions on a far broader scope than the site-specific or artifact-specific level.

Through their study, "Regularity and Variability in Contemporary Garbage," William Rathje and Michael McCarthy are witness to the patterns found in refuse from an ongoing cultural system. Their concern is with testing traditional methods of archeological interpretation and delineating patterns relating to family size, income level, and ethnic affiliation. Their strategy is to examine patterns resulting from garbage disposal in relation to those emerging from interview surveys. Through the use of Monte Carlo simulations and data on nutritive values in canned goods, indices are derived for use in determining estimated nutritive values represented by archeologically recovered tin can refuse. The exciting aspect of the Rathje and McCarthy study is their use of documentation, interviews, and contemporary garbage to construct quantitative models of adaptive strategies operating in the past and the present. This study clearly reveals that in a science of archeology there is no place for prejudice based on the temporal period represented by the data.

In their study of idiosyncratic trait clusters within experimentally produced sets of nails wrought by five blacksmiths, Ronald Carlisle and Joel Gunn are working toward extracting new dimensions of knowledge from excavated artifacts. This study uses discriminant function analysis to determine which attributes were most discriminatory of 10 traits studied. The sets of experimental nails were then combined to simulate archeological data. Hypotheses as to the range of variability between experienced craftsmen and neophytes were tested, with a narrow range of variability projected for experienced craftsmen.

Such experimental studies of trait clusters idiosyncratically produced should help in distinguishing such behavior from the broader cultural patterns most often of interest to archeologists. In this regard, it is interesting to note that Carlisle and Gunn point out that there are few one-to-one correlations between such technical patterns and wider cultural patterns. In addition to the knowledge gained from such research for understanding idiosyncratic versus patterned behavior, this nail study might well be used in relative dating of structures based on the recognition of idiosyncratic traits of nails made by a single blacksmith.

Each research strategy in this volume was conducted under one of the "strategies for getting the job done" discussed by Robert Stephenson in the final chapter. Stephenson stresses the importance of full-time institutionally based research facilities if we are to make progress toward the development of archeological science and the fulfillment of the archeologist's role in cultural resource management. He emphasizes the welding of the institutional and business strategies to produce a climate within which archeological research can best be done. This chapter provides a broad perspective of the various research climates within which archeological research can be conducted and points the way most conducive to the development of archeological science. It should be noted that the studies discussed in the chapters by Carrillo, Ferguson, Goodyear, House, Lewis, South, and perhaps others were conducted under contract in the interest of cultural resource management.

The studies in this volume are aimed at a better understanding of cultural systems and how they work. The strategies are a mechanism for putting current theory into operation and laying groundwork for new theories. This process of theory building is the goal of archeology. Research strategies are the linking process between the empirical data base and theory building. This book, then, is not *about* theory. Rather, it dramatically demonstrates the dependent relationship between archeological method and theory. The chapters are empirically based, quantitative studies directed at pattern recognition delineating the variability and regularity in the archeological record. This fact reflects the emphasis now present in the field of American archeology, an emphasis oriented toward bridging the gap between ideas and the material remains of cultural systems through explicitly demonstrated research.

These contributors to this volume are explorers; they are not merely *willing* to risk the insecurity of the nomothetic depths of the iceberg to delineate deep pattern—instead they feel they *must* do so to fulfill the obligation and responsibility they have toward the development of archeological science. They are not content to remain safely on the surface exploring the details of the particularistic tip knowing the depths of pattern yet to be explored. They are not content merely to snorkle around on the surface intuitively recognizing an occasional pattern, nor are they satisfied by an implicitly scientific shallow dive from time to time to bring up a percentage to make a point. They recognize that they must put on the restrictive and often cumbersome methodological suit of antiquated design from the new-fledged vessel of archeological science, and, sustained by the lifeline of empirical data, descend to the depth necessary to delineate deep pattern within the remains of a cultural system. Eventually, through efforts such as those demonstrated in this volume, a less antiquated diving suit can be developed. In the decades to come, streamlined, flexible, highly mobile methodological diving systems will be developed within archeology to supersede the experimental models now current. Such progress will develop from research strategies now being used in archeology, just as those in this book are replacing those of yesterday.

ACKNOWLEDGMENTS

I would like to thank my colleagues contributing to this volume for reading Chapter 1 and offering their comments. I would especially like to thank John L. Idol, Jr., and Randolph Widmer for their assistance with the concepts shown in Figure 1.1. Thanks also go to Ralph Wilbanks for supplying illustrative models for the research vessel and diver shown in the figure, and to Darby Erd for drawing these parts of the figure.

REFERENCES

Binford, Lewis R.
1962 Archaeology as anthropology. *American Antiquity* **28:**217–225.
Chomsky, Noam
1972 *Language and mind.* New York: Harcourt.
Dethlefsen, Edwin, and James Deetz
1966 Death's Heads, Cherubs, and Willow Trees: Experimental Archaeology in Colonial Cemeteries. *American Antiquity* **31:** (No. 4):502–510.
Ferguson, Leland G.
1975 Analysis of ceramic materials from Fort Watson, December 1780–April 1781. *The Conference on Historic Site Archaeology Papers* **8:**2–28. Institute of Archeology and Anthropology, Univ. of South Carolina, Columbia.
Noël Hume, Ivor
1970 *A guide to artifacts of Colonial America.* New York: Knopf.
Schiffer, Michael B.
1976 *Behavioral archeology.* New York: Academic Press.
South, Stanley
1960 The Ceramic Types at Brunswick Town, North Carolina (1962). *Southeastern Archaeological Conference Newsletter* **9** (No. 1):1–5.
1972 Evolution and Horizon as Revealed in Ceramic Analysis in Historical Archeology. *The Conference on Historic Site Archaeology Papers 1971* **6:**71–116.
1977 *Method and theory in historical archeology.* New York: Academic Press.
White, Leslie A.
1938 Science is sciencing. *Philosophy of Science* **5:**369–389.
1949 Mind is minding. *The science of culture.* New York: Farrar, Straus. pp. 49–54.
1975 *The concept of cultural systems.* New York: Columbia Univ. Press.

Toward a Unified Science of the Cultural Past[1]

MICHAEL B. SCHIFFER

The study of the past is a remarkable pretension. The past no longer exists as part of the phenomenological world, yet we claim to know it. Archeology shares this pretension with history, paleontology, geology, and astronomy. Our ability to know the past is based on one faith and one fact. The *faith* is that the processes found operating in the universe today also operated in the past. Investigation of these observable processes provides students of cultural dynamics, psychology, functional anatomy, ecology, geophysics, and astrophysics with the principles that in part condition knowledge of the past. The *fact* is that aspects of the past are preserved in materials that exist in the present. Sherds and lithics, documents, fossils, soils, rocks, and the pockmarked face of Mercury were *formed* in the past but can be examined today.

The study of the past—whether it be the adoption of agriculture, the reign of King Henry VIII, the evolution of multicellular organisms, the formation of the continents, or the origin of the solar system—depends on establishing connections between observations of present phenomena and past events and processes. This connection problem inevitably involves consideration of other processes, *formation processes*—specific to each domain—that cause the varied trajectories of materials through time and ultimately the formation of evidence of the past. An understanding of the *deposition and modification* of archeological materials, the *circulation, assembly, and storage* of documents and other objects, the *deposition and preservation* of biological remains,

[1] An earlier version of this chapter was read at the Eighth Annual Meeting of the Society for Historical Archaeology, Charleston, South Carolina, January 1975.

the *laying down and alteration* of geological deposits, and the *preservation* of materials formed early in the life of the solar system is what permits the originating and testing of historical hypotheses. Of necessity, then, the central concern of any historical discipline should be to identify and investigate thoroughly the processes responsible for forming its evidence of the past. In geology and astronomy these processes have been of focal interest. In paleontology processes of fossil-bed formation and alteration comprise the important study area known as *taphonomy* (Efremov 1940). But in history, and especially archeology, research on formation processes has barely begun. Remarkably, archeologists have pursued the past with little conscious regard for the fact that their primary evidence—the archeological record—is not itself a past sociocultural system, but in part represents materials transformed from that system by numerous processes. Explicit recognition of this fact and the elaboration of its implications have indeed been slow in coming.

The purpose of this chapter is to treat in one general framework the diverse processes that form evidence of the cultural past. These are known as *cultural formation processes* (Schiffer 1972, 1976a). Although noncultural formation processes of the archeological record, such as geological deposition, rodent activity, and decay, have important effects on the nature of remains from the past, they will not be further discussed (see Reid *et al.* 1975; Schiffer and Rathje 1973). Nor will this discussion cover the many uses to which an understanding of cultural formation processes can be put. These topics, which include explanation of archeological variability, sampling, construction of classifications, testing of analytic techniques, designation of proveniences, and selection of relevant analytic units, are treated at length elsewhere (e.g., Reid 1973; Reid and Schiffer n.d.; Reid *et al.* 1975; Schiffer 1975a–e, 1976a; Schiffer and Rathje 1973).

Evidence of the cultural past falls naturally into two categories. The first form of evidence, called the *historical record,* consists of materials—written records and other objects—within an ongoing sociocultural system. The second form of evidence, consisting of materials in archeological deposits, is known as the *archeological record*.

On the surface this distinction poses no difficult challenges to traditional dichotomies based on written versus unwritten evidence; yet by the foregoing definitions a clay tablet at Babylon is part of the archeological record but a museum's nineteenth century locomotive is part of the historical record. These examples, far from being anomalies that are not readily handled in the present framework, emphasize the need to develop a unified science of the cultural past based on the recognition that the evidence we study in our respective disciplines has been formed in part by a coherent domain of cultural processes subject to the same laws. Because the distinction between kinds of evidence applies only at one point in time, any object may alternate during its existence between the historical and archeological records. Thus the neat correspondence some would see between scholarly disciplines and types of evidence (i.e., historians study the historical record; archeologists study the archeological record) ultimately breaks down, for the historian *is* interested in the clay tablets at Babylon just as the industrial archeologist *is* interested in the nineteenth century locomotive. The historian, then, needs to consider not only what is written on the tablets, but also the processes by which they were deposited and recovered archeologically; the industrial archeologist must inquire similarly as to how the locomotive came to its present resting place. Because sound interpretations of evidence require that formation processes be identified and taken into account, and because many investigations of the cultural past involve consideration of evidence that is or was both historical and archeological, a basis exists—at least on one level—for unifying the study of the cultural past.

Although we can scarcely expect the practitioners of traditionally defined disciplines to embrace each other warmly on all occasions, or even to be concerned with the same range of substantive historical questions, the common processes underlying the formation of our evidence would seem to suggest a need for developing a sustained and fruitful dialog on cultural formation processes. It is precisely in the field of historical archeology that we might expect to see the initial stirrings of a unified science; for, understandably, the historical archeologist possesses a particular sensitivity to the complexity of both kinds of evidence, and has important contributions to make toward illuminating the laws of cultural formation processes. It remains in this chapter to begin identifying major varieties of cultural formation processes, delimiting what is known (and especially what is unknown), and indicating promising avenues for future research. The following discussion is written from the standpoint of a prehistorical archeologist. Even so, it should provide a basis for examining further—in both general and specific inquiries—the nature of evidence of the cultural past.

CULTURAL FORMATION PROCESSES

Before one can understand the formation of archeological and historical evidence, it is necessary to distinguish rigorously between the two principal states of material objects. The distinguishing feature of the archeological record is that the materials that comprise it—artifacts, features, and residues—*no longer* are participating in a behavioral system. This nonbehavioral state of cultural materials is known as *archeological context* (Schiffer 1972, 1976a). In contrast, materials within an ongoing behavioral system—they are handled or observed—are said to be in *systemic context* (Schiffer 1972, 1976a).

Under some circumstances it is tempting to use *archeological context* and *systemic context* in other ways. With respect to the archeological record, for example, the systemic context is both inferentially derived and distant in time, whereas the archeological context can be observed directly in the present. Thus, some would use *systemic context* to mean "past" or "inferred," and *archeological context* to mean "present" or "observable." These usages are perfectly acceptable, although one must recognize their basis in convenience and epistemological shortcomings. For instance, in studies of modern material culture, experimental research, ethnoarcheology (the study of human behavior and material culture in ongoing sociocultural systems), and the historical record, the systemic context is both presently existing and observable. In the rest of this chapter I will adhere to the original, strict definition of the two contexts based on behavioral criteria (Schiffer 1972). Less rigorous usages do have their functions, but for proper understanding of the cultural formation processes the behavioral–nonbehavioral dichotomy is fundamental.

To summarize, the archeological record consists of materials in archeological context (prior to excavation by the archeologist). The historical record is defined simply as those items in systemic context that can supply information about prior system states.

It is very difficult to construct a definition of cultural formation processes that is narrow enough to exclude cultural activities not of interest and broad enough to encompass all the phenomena directly affecting the formation of the archeological and historical records. Instead of attempting such a definition, I will define the four major types of cultural formation process.

The first type of process corresponds roughly to what many archeologists recognize as *cultural deposition* (Willey and McGimsey 1954), that is, the laying down of cultural deposits. In sociocultural systems many of the activities carried out, such as discard, abandonment, and loss, result in contributions of material to the archeological record. These activities exemplify the type of cultural formation process primarily responsible for the archeological record, whereby materials are transformed from systemic context to archeological context. They are known as S–A processes.

Although S–A processes constitute the dominant factor shaping the archeological record, when attention is focused on the archeological record itself it will be seen that still other processes of a cultural nature must be considered when providing explanations for its structure and content. Activities such as scavenging, collecting, pothunting, and even archeological excavation remove and modify deposited materials. These activities, which comprise the second, or A–S, type of cultural formation process, *transform materials from archeological context back to systemic context.*

A lesser number of processes, which nevertheless are markedly affecting deposits in many parts of the world, *transform materials from state to state within archeological context* (A–A processes). Examples include the excavation of pits, plowing, land leveling, channelization, and other activities that *disturb* culturally deposited items. Although A–A processes cause materials briefly to enter systemic context, the materials do not really participate in a behavioral system.

Together S–A, A–S, and A–A processes account for many properties of the archeological record; yet they do not exhaust the domain. To interpret correctly some aspects of the archeological record, it is necessary to understand processes entirely internal to the past sociocultural system, those that do not result in cultural deposition or in modification of extant deposits. This type of process is also primarily responsible for formation of the historical record. That is, because some items do not leave systemic context (immediately), they can provide information about earlier system states even though they may still be in use. As the reader may have already guessed, the processes by which *materials are transformed through successive system states* are termed S–S processes. Chipped-stone bifaces, trade pottery, paintings, jewelry, books, documents, structures, and a host of other items may persist through many system states by changes in form, use, transfers from owner to owner, and by deposit in entities such as shrines, museums, libraries, and archives.

Clearly, it is difficult to delimit S–S processes precisely; their definition depends on the minimal change that an investigator deems necessary to constitute a new systemic state. Fortunately, a somewhat arbitrary, object-centered definition can resolve this problem productively. For any object, an S–S process has occurred if, after some period of use, there is a change in the social unit of use (user) or the activity of use. For example, when Aunt Marti gives away her darling old lamp, when that lamp is used as a table leg, when a lawn mover is bought at a swap meet, when that lawn mower is stolen 2 weeks later, and when a house is sold to permit a family to move into a "crime-free" neighborhood, S–S processes have taken place. Other types of *reuse,* more widely appreciated (e.g., recycling), are also S–S processes.

Cultural formation processes, regardless of type, consist of activities. The laws describing regularities in those activities are known as *c-transforms* (Schiffer 1976a; Schiffer and Rathje 1973). Because we aim to infer the past systemic context of materials in the archeological and historical records we must naturally be concerned with discovering these laws. Along with other principles and information, c-transforms allow the investigator to gain historical knowledge by modeling the processes that have transformed the objects of study from the past to the present. All who use the archeological and historical records are obliged to understand the nature and effects of cultural formation processes.

ACQUISITION OF C-TRANSFORMS

The nature and status of laws in archeology is presently a topic of sometimes lively discussion and debate. For some investigators this debate represents a nonissue left in the wake of the new archeology's unsuccessful forays into the philosophy of science; for others, it embodies the most fundamental, unresolved questions regarding human culture and society. My position in this matter is that regardless of whether determinism operates in human affairs the interpretation of archeological (and historical) evidence always involves the use of lawlike statements—but mostly they have been employed implicitly. Recent discussions have properly emphasized the need to bring processes of law discovery and use into the open. These pleas for an explicitly scientific (i.e., law-seeking, law-using) archeology (Watson, LeBlanc, and Redman 1971) are welcome, even if much of the accompanying conceptual baggage is not, for such developments are bound to hasten the long-overdue testing of lawlike principles and lead eventually to the cumulative growth of archeological theory.

Archeologists have acquired and continue to acquire laws in a variety of ways. The most venerable but least overt approach is to invest them as they are needed in the context of a specific substantive investigation. In the writings of investigators who have tried to draw inferences from archeological evidence, one will frequently encounter lawlike principles apparently invented ad hoc to facilitate reconstructions and explanations. These principles are being reinvented constantly but they are seldom tested. Nevertheless, if, after repeated use, such laws do not lead to substantial contradictions or anomalies, they will gradually acquire an aura of truth. Laws obtained in this manner form an important methodological resource and, because they abound in the literature, can be easily systematized and formalized (for example, see Schiffer 1976a).

Ethnoarcheology provides another approach to deriving laws. Unfortunately, most ethnoarcheologists have not, until recently, asked the kinds of general questions that might lead to the discovery of laws. Even so, many such laws, with varying degrees of empirical support, can be found in the literature and need only to be identified and examined critically in a wider range of appropriate sociocultural systems. Several ethnoarcheological projects now underway or recently completed have striven to find laws (see Schiffer 1976a), and it seems that the field is now evolving rapidly toward nomothetic goals (Gould n.d.).

A third major strategy for law acquisition is experimental archeology. In such endeavors the investigator artificially constructs a system that replicates a process of interest so that relevant variables can be controlled, manipulated, and their interactions recorded. To date, experimental research has concentrated on a limited range of questions, most of which concern artifact manufacture and use, and noncultural formation processes (Coles 1973). Even so, careful scrutiny of the large and growing literature will disclose numerous lawlike statements. Experimental archeology is burgeoning and, like ethnoarcheology, is finally developing a solid nomothetic orientation (cf. Schiffer 1974).

A final line of inquiry that has been used to uncover regularities is cross-cultural study and other uses of the ethnographic literature. Expectably, these studies, which must rely on data of uneven quality gathered inevitably for nonarcheological problems, have been less than fully satisfactory—though much has been learned (e.g., Baumhoff 1963; Binford 1971; Schwartz 1970; Wilmsen 1973). The concerted study of ethnographic reports, in which much potentially useful data lie obscured, may be expected to yield some nomothetic dividends.

In the following survey of cultural formation processes I indicate the approaches to law acquisition that have proved useful for particular lines of investigation and which, although untapped, appear promising.

S–A PROCESSES

S–A processes are broadly divisible into two types: *normal* and *abandonment*. Normal processes are those that operate during the use of an activity area. The three major kinds of normal S–A process are *discard, disposal of the dead,* and *loss*. Abandonment processes begin operation when activity areas are being abandoned.

Discard

When objects break, wear out, or become obsolete, and when useless waste products are produced, the materials, if not reused, will be discarded—perhaps in one or more specialized activity areas known as *dumps* or *middens*. If trash is discarded at its location of use it forms *primary refuse;* if away from its location of use, *secondary refuse* (Schiffer 1972). Thus an olla, used and broken inside a dwelling, is discarded as secondary refuse in the dump at the edge of the village, but dull flakes used for skinning a rabbit in the plaza may be discarded there casually as primary refuse. Additional varieties of refuse could be defined based on other dimensions of variation in discard processes.

Some descriptive information on discard processes is available in the ethnographic literature; unfortunately, it is widely scattered and borders on being inaccessible. In many monographs one finds passing reference to the customary way that this or that object or waste product is discarded, but rarely has the investigator looked at discard processes systematically. Because information on discard is so dispersed and uneven (not even Murdock 1950 has tried to deal with it), it cannot readily play a role in generating and testing c-transforms. Although some useful knowledge may result from a concerted effort to comb ethnographies for these tantalizing archeological morsels, I suspect that the returns might not repay the effort. Archeologists have resolved this difficulty by invention and ethnoarcheology.

Invention has yielded a not-insignificant quantity of c-transforms. For example, many of the reconstructions of dietary and population variables from shell midden data (Ambrose 1967; Ascher 1959; Cook 1972a; Heizer and Cook 1956) are based on (usually implicit) quantitative c-transforms. I have approximated several of these laws in a recent study (Schiffer 1976a). One basic principle is this:

$$T_D = \frac{St}{L}$$

where T_D is the total number of discarded elements (instances of an artifact type), S is the number of elements normally in use, t is the period of element use, and L is the use-life of the element. Many similar quantitative c-transforms await general formulation (a good place to begin is Cook 1972a,b).

Fauna have been treated with increasing sophistication recently, and there seems little doubt that quantitative c-transforms can be acquired from the literature with little effort (good starting points would be Chaplin 1971; Medlock 1975; Read 1971; Ziegler 1973). Many *potentially* quantifiable c-transforms pertaining to the discard of faunal remains are also to be found. The *Schlepp effect,* a well-known example of such a principle, states that the more butchering of an animal that occurs at a kill site, the greater will be the quantity of its bones discarded at the kill site. The amount of butchering performed is directly related to the animal's size and the distance it must be transported to the place of consumption (adapted from Daly 1969:149). This principle could easily be quantified, as could Thomas's (1971) ideas on how to distinguish naturally from culturally deposited bone.

Other c-transforms have been invented to account for differential discard activities. For example, I have hypothesized that the larger the population of an activity area, and the greater the intensity of occupation, the larger the ratio of secondary to primary refuse produced (adapted from Schiffer 1972). Although this c-transform still awaits testing (but see Yellen 1974), like others that have been invented, it does make intelligible (without introducing appreciable anomalies) a realm of archeological variability not previously understood.

Secondary-refuse deposits exhibit considerable variability that ought to receive serious explanatory efforts. Little systematic ethnoarcheology or experimental work has been carried out on this type of deposit, despite the fact that it provides the bulk of data for the study of most cultural systems. In sedentary communities, for example, secondary-refuse deposits are likely to form in any natural or man-made pit or depression that is not being used in other ways (Green 1961b). (Although pits are sometimes dug for the express purpose of refuse disposal, I suspect that "refuse" pits occur less frequently than one would gather from the archeological literature.) One of the major problems in using secondary refuse is identifying the activity areas from which the material was derived. Green (1961a) offers some hypotheses on determining the direction of dumping from the nature of the stratification, and I have considered the problem at a more abstract level when stratification is undetectable or unrecorded (Schiffer 1975b). The questions of how rapidly a deposit accumulated and in what season(s) have received some attention (e.g., Darlington 1969; Green 1961a; Hole and Heizer 1973; Wheeler 1954), but we still are some distance away from reliable c-transforms.

Even in those instances where secondary-refuse disposal systems are functioning efficiently, some materials are likely to become discarded, often inadvertently, at their locations of use. One hypothesis on the determinants of primary-refuse formation under these conditions has been tested recently on ethnoarcheological data. McKellar (1973), who observed discard behavior on the campus of the University of Arizona, discovered that object size has an effect on the probability that an item will become primary refuse (see also Green 1961a,b; Wall 1973). Small items (less than 4 inches in overall dimensions) are discarded almost independently of the location of trash cans (thus becoming primary refuse), whereas larger items find their way into trash cans if the latter are handy. Clearly, more variables need to be considered in future studies (cf. Schiffer 1976a), but McKellar's research illustrates neatly how c-transforms of discard behavior can be obtained from studying ongoing sociocultural systems. Several other ethnoarcheological studies have paid cursory attention to discard activities, although the absence of relevant questions and hypotheses somewhat diminishes the usefulness of these investigations (e.g., Robbins 1973). Richard Gould and Lewis R. Binford, among other investigators, are conducting promising ethnoarcheological research on discard processes.

Disposal of the Dead

Activities involved with disposal of the dead comprise another major type of normal process. Even though burial practices have been a serious area of archeological study for centuries, it is remarkable how few explicit and reliable c-transforms are presently available. Burial practices are sometimes well described ethnographically, and a systematic review of that literature would reward the investigator with a wealth of useful material. Invention has been fruitfully applied to burial practices. Howells (1960), a physical anthropologist, devised a quantitative c-transform that relates population variables of a community and duration of activity to the size of the burial population (see also Collins and Fenwick n.d.; Longacre n.d.). Although most archeologists recognize that basic elements of social organization in some way determine major patterns of grave good accompaniment, only recently have any appropriate c-transforms been explicitly framed (see Binford 1962; Brown 1971; Rathje 1970, 1973; Ucko 1969). One of the earliest c-transforms in the domain, long used for a variety of purposes, is Worsaae's law (Rowe 1962). This law states that objects placed together in the same grave were in contemporary use. Rowe (1962) amended Worsaae's law to include the provision, probably unjustified, that items deposited together in a grave were also manufactured at the same time. Another c-transform, rarely made explicit, is used often to infer the nature of a society's status system from burial artifacts. The principle states that only in societies with ascribed status will one find infants and children disposed of with all the accoutrements of a high-status adult. I anticipate that the domain of c-transforms related to burial practices will soon develop into a large body of genuinely predictive principles.

Loss

A third major type of normal S–A process consists of loss activities. It would be the height of understatement to suggest that no one has ever looked at loss as a regular process. To propose, as I do, that there are laws of loss is tantamount to contradicting oneself—or is it? Although individual instances of artifact loss are certainly random and probably unpredictable, when such activities are viewed in the aggregate, regularities should be readily discernible. I now offer a few thoughts on how one might begin to acquire the laws of loss.

Some c-transforms of loss processes, applicable to object types having similar (but presently unspecifiable) behavioral and morphological properties, might be expressed as loss probabilities. The loss probability for any such object type is simply the ratio of the number of items lost to the number transformed by all normal S–A processes. By studying the loss probabilities for object types within and between systems, an investigator may uncover significant patterns. For example, I suggest that loss probability varies inversely with an object's mass, (all other variables constant). Another hypothesis might be that loss probability varies directly with portability or transportability (again, all other variables constant). Given these two hypothetical c-transforms one could predict that although ships are large they will have higher loss probabilities than might otherwise be expected, because they are seldom stationary. Shipwrecks, an important source of archeological data, would then come under the purview of general principles of archeological record formation (see Schiffer and Rathje 1973).

Regularities of loss processes will be found not only in loss probabilities, but also in the kinds of loci where loss occurs. For example, if an object of a certain size is dropped to the ground, what is the probability that it can be picked up? That probability will vary among the set of activity areas in which the object type is used. Thus coins dropped on a linoleum floor, sidewalk, lawn, sand, sewer grating, and privy will be differentially retrieved with decreasing frequency. These hypothetical examples illustrate the important concept of *permeability*. That is, we must recognize that human occupations occur on variable, not rigid, surfaces that differ in the degree to which they resist the upward or downward movement of objects with respect to various forces. When loci are compared within and between systems, certain artifact "traps," consisting of highly permeable surfaces, will be discovered. These traps, containing a disproportionate amount of objects generated by loss processes, will be identifiable by common variables related to physical properties and conditions of use. Privies and wells, for example, are notorious artifact traps. Fehon and Scholtz (n.d.) have expressed these hypothetical c-transforms in their most general form as statements of conditional probability and have defined important varieties of loss behavior.

As our appreciation for the nature of loss processes increases, we will be able to make better use of our archeological data. For example, if one excavates the remains of a log cabin in the hope of inferring past behavior there, it makes a good deal of difference whether the material found resting on the original ground surface arrived there through the loss processes of the cabin's inhabitants or the discard processes of a previous use of the area. The same holds true for the materials recovered from a privy; some will have resulted from loss, and others from discard processes. For many research problems it is imperative to identify the process(es) responsible for deposition of the material under study.

Abandonment

When activity areas are abandoned, another set of S–A processes is put in motion. The most important of these is *de facto refuse* production. De facto refuse consists of the tools, facilities, and other cultural materials that, although still usable, are abandoned within an activity area. The nature of de facto refuse in an activity area should relate not only to what was used there, but also to the conditions under which abandonment took place, available means of transport, and distances to the next occupied activity area (Schiffer 1972). Knowledge of c-transforms pertaining to de facto refuse production is limited at present. The ethnographic literature contains scattered observations, but such information has yet to be synthesized, systematized, and *tested*. Some ethnoarcheological observations are available (Binford 1973, n.d.; Bonnichsen 1973; Longacre and Ayres 1968), and a few potential c-transforms have even been proffered. For example, during a planned and gradual abandonment of a community (when no return is anticipated), few portable objects that are still usable will be abandoned (adapted from Lange and Rydberg 1972: 430).

Abandonment of an activity area results not only in de facto refuse production but sometimes in the modification of other S–A processes. For example, if abandonment is anticipated by a group, they may begin to accumulate refuse in areas like house interiors that usually would have been kept relatively free of debris (Green 1961b). Such materials might be called primary refuse but they are really formed by an abandonment, not normal process. Naturally, serious errors could creep into one's interpretations if the correct process is not identified.

Other Processes

Discard, disposal of the dead, loss, and abandonment constitute the four major types of S–A process. These processes most certainly do not exhaust the variety of activities that transform materials to archeological context during the founding, use, and abandonment of an activity area. For example, caches of various sorts, including time capsules, are produced by normal and abandonment processes and also deserve attention (cf. Baker n.d.). In addition, objects are sometimes deposited to dedicate an activity area or structure at the time of its founding; such *dedicatory offerings* perhaps constitute a distinguishable process (Saile 1976). Reluctantly, I leave the identification of additional processes for future occasions.

A–S PROCESSES

The second major type of cultural formation process is responsible for transforming materials from archeological context back to systemic context. Even though A–S processes are poorly understood, we can still find examples of recurrent activities, subject to laws, that may eventually be classed as distinct types.

Ascher (1968), in carrying out an ethnoarcheological study of the Seri, observed that in unoccupied areas of a community previously abandoned items were removed (or *scavenged*) for use by the remaining inhabitants. Scavenging behavior probably occurs to some extent in every community that is differentially abandoned. It is necessary to note, however, that this type of scavenging involves an A–S transformation of de facto refuse. When materials produced by various normal A–S processes, such as primary refuse or burials, undergo A–S transformations, other types of scavenging behavior have occurred. I shall restrain myself and not name these important varieties of scavenging—although names will be required eventually so that we can avoid cumbersome constructions.

To this point attention has been directed at A–S transformation of *materials;* some A–S processes act on the *deposits* themselves as a unit. In Mesoamerica, for example, deposits of primary and secondary refuse were scooped up and used as a fill material in the construction of monumental architecture. Clearly, when an A–S process operates on a deposit as opposed to an artifact, a qualitatively different type of activity has taken place. Again, I defer to others in the task of describing and defining varieties of this type of A–S process. Let us simply keep in mind their existence and the fact that their operation has important effects on the nature of the archeological record.

Archeological excavation itself comprises a major kind of A–S process. And, though that fact is sufficiently obvious, its implications may not be. In the first place, the archeologist must be aware of effects on a site of previous archeological work. J. Jefferson Reid informed me (personal communication, 1973) that during investigations at the Grasshopper Ruin (Reid 1974; Thompson and Longacre 1966) Longacre attempted to test the hypothesis that certain surface modifications resulted from the excavation of rooms by Walter Hough in the early years of this century. Although the hypothesis tested negatively, the example does suggest how knowledge of such formation processes could lead to sound interpretations of the archeological record and to the design of appropriate data-gathering strategies (see Reid *et al.* 1975). In the second place, when one attempts to assess the archeologist's uses of the data, it is necessary to view the activities as cultural formation processes. For example, the extent to which counts of artifact types in a report correspond to artifact type counts in the original deposits depends on the nature of recovery and processing activities. It is a healthy sign that archeological procedures are now being considered as a process having tangible and predictable effects on the archeological record as it is described by the archeologist (e.g., Collins 1975; Daniels 1972; Wilcox n.d.). Despite the chronic variability in archeological procedures, I remain convinced that the behavior of archeologists is characterized by some regularities. One might expect, for example, that within a certain range, recovery probabilities vary directly with artifact size. Clearly, systematic investigations are needed to examine this and other potential c-transforms.

If the archeologist's activities are A–S processes, then so too are pothunting and collecting behavior. Pothunting, like all cultural formation processes, exhibits certain regularities. In general, it can be stated that pothunters seek graves where valuable, whole, or restorable objects are likely to be found. In the American Southwest, for example, the first areas dug in "pristine" pueblo sites are extramural secondary-refuse deposits where graves, and thus grave goods, frequently occur. In sites with severely disturbed secondary-refuse areas or no obvious extramural deposits, rooms will be dug in search of de facto refuse. I have observed these processes over a 4-year peiod in the Hay Hollow Valley of east-central Arizona. I suspect that my observations can be generalized beyond the borders of the Southwest, but additional data are required. One should also bear in mind when formulating c-transforms that prehistoric and ethnographic groups as well as modern ones engaged systematically in pothunting (see Bascom 1971; Hole and Heizer 1973; Schuyler 1968).

Surface collecting also affects the archeological record at a site. Some information on the nature of collecting behavior is beginning to accumulate, although it is not yet in the form of general, fully tested c-transforms. It is certain, however, that collecting activity is characterized by some regularities; for example, the items usually collected are finished, whole tools in which a considerable amount of effort was invested during manufacture (Claassen 1976). The artifacts are sometimes collected for resale, especially in parts of the Mississippi Valley (House and Schiffer 1975; Morse 1973, 1975).

In the face of widespread damage to and destruction of archeological sites all over the globe, it may seem peculiar for an archeologist to suggest that we begin to study seriously the nature and effects of pothunting and collecting processes. Nevertheless, there are compelling reasons for doing so. In some areas of the United States, almost all known sites have been affected by a variety of A–S processes. Thus, in future years, unless these processes decrease in intensity—an unlikely prospect—most sites to be scientifically investigated will have been already altered by collecting and pothunting. Even if that gloomy future fails to arrive many modified sites will be excavated. It thus becomes a practical necessity when using data from such sites to consider the nature and effects of collecting and pothunting. To do this effectively requires one to understand the regularities of these processes.

A–S processes are diverse and affect in important ways the structure and content of sites and our descriptions of them. In the near future I expect to witness a considerable expansion of research effort to uncover regularities.

A–A PROCESSES

Other activities of modern society (and prehistoric ones as well) are viewed as A–A processes. Activities such as constructing hearths, digging pits, building dams, chaining junipers, channelization, suburban sprawl, farming, and oil exploration either directly modify the archeological record or bring into operation various noncultural processes that do. In most A–A processes one must consider both cultural and noncultural factors. For example, plowing and disking not only damage and disperse archeological materials and deposits, but they also subject once-buried items to a wider range of noncultural processes, such as alternate freezing and thawing, oxidation, and erosion, which further affect the structure and content of sites. As another example, dam building disturbs sites in the areas where construction activities occur. But once a dam begins to impound water, the dynamic (usually noncultural) processes that operate in large bodies of water, such as currents, fluctuating levels, and siltation have other effects on archeological remains (Garrison 1975). For instance, sites located in the active zone of a reservoir—that area between high water and low water—will be severely modified and deflated by wave action (Garrison 1975).

One of the better known archeological principles, pertaining to A–A processes, describes the effects that mechanical activities have on culturally deposited materials. It has been found, in well-documented cases, that disturbance of a deposit, as by digging a pit or leveling the ground, brings up previously deposited (hence earlier) objects and residues and distributes them on a later occupation surface (Drucker 1972; Matthews 1965; Medford 1972). This principle, the generality and truth of which are widely assumed, may be termed the Law of Upward Migration—if it is taken that *upward* means through time and not always vertically through space. Daniels (1972:207–208) suggested that vertical-migration effects caused by a variety of processes may be considered fruitfully within the framework of probabilistic models.

Another widespread A–A process is *trampling,* the action of human (and animal) feet on archeological deposits. McPherron (1967) hypothesized that trampling results in a progressive reduction of sherd size; it would seem that this hypothesis is almost certainly applicable to other frangible materials, such as bone. In addition, Tringham *et al.* (1974:192) have shown that trampling of chipped-stone flakes produces a distinctive pattern of edge damage that differs from use wear. In a simple but definitive experimental study, Stockton (1973) was able to demonstrate that trampled artifacts are displaced vertically in sandy deposits. His results, obtained from excavating six arbitrary levels in an artificial deposit containing broken glass that was trampled for a day, indicate that large objects tend to be displaced upward and small objects are pressed downward. Explanations for these findings were offered in terms of the horizontal (scuffage) and vertical (treadage) actions of the human foot during walking (Stockton 1973:116–117). Clearly, much can be learned about A–A processes from such ingenious, yet inexpensive, experiments. Ascher (1968) assessed the long-term effects of foot traffic and other activities on the smearing and blending of formerly discrete artifact distributions in a Seri Indian community.

In another creative study, Baker (1974) attempted to determine whether plowing can laterally displace artifacts in a site. Although Redman and Watson (1970:280) believe that such effects are likely to be trivial, Baker found that gravels deposited on the surface of a dirt farm-road and been moved appreciably by plowing along the direction of the furrows. Significantly, he also observed that smaller gravels were displaced a greater distance than larger ones, although the latter sustained more damage (Baker 1974:46). I suspect that future investigations will reveal that the relationship between object size and lateral displacement by plowing need not be linear; it may be a stepped function with distinct thresholds that are affected markedly by the shape and size of the plow or disk. Other studies have been carried out to determine the large-scale effects of various agricultural practices on archeological sites, but the conclusions are not yet in general form (e.g., Ford and Rolingson 1972; Medford 1972; Schiffer and House 1975).

Only in recent years have archeologists, under the impetus of federal and state environmental legislation, begun to study systematically the regularities in A–A processes, especially those associated with massive land-modification schemes. When called upon to assess the direct and indirect impacts of a proposed project on the archeological resources investigators must use these all-too-scarce c-transforms (and *n-transforms*—laws of noncultural formation processes) to make predictions. It is now clear that if cultural resource managers are to provide sound predictions, a stepped-up program is needed for studying A–A processes (Schiffer and Gumerman n.d.). Research, for example, is now planned or in progress to examine processes operative in reservoirs (Calvin Cummings, personal communication, 1976; Garrison 1975; see also Neal 1974; Neal and Mayo n.d.; Prewitt and Lawson 1972). In order to provide sound information for managing U.S. Forest Service lands, DeBloois *et al.* (n.d.) conducted an exemplary experimental study of the impacts of juniper–pinyon chaining on surface lithic sites. This kind of knowledge is useful beyond the confines of conservation archeology, for, again, many investigators will scientifically study sites subjected to one or more of these processes. Though some effects may be readily apparent upon excavation, such as mixing of levels, deflation, and sedimentation, others, like chemical changes in the soil, artifact breakage, and horizontal artifact displacement, are more subtle. If archeologists are to succeed in approximating aspects of the past systemic context of such sites, then much more refined knowledge will have to be forthcoming from experimental, ethnoarcheological, and other types of research.

The varieties of A–A processes enumerated here serve only to illustrate the diversity of this domain. By and large, A–A processes are poorly studied—although that is beginning to change. I believe we have a clear practical mandate, as well as a demonstrable scientific need, to investigate in detail all the cultural processes that act on a site following (and even during) the original deposition.

S–S PROCESSES

The last basic type of cultural formation process, S–S, results in a material's transformation from state to state within systemic context. An appreciation for S–S processes affects the interpretation of both the archeological and the historical record. Before delving into the major types of S–S process, I want to emphasize the dualistic perspective required to appreciate their nature and significance. The archeological record of a systemic state and subsequent systemic states is involved. This is, in order to infer aspects of a sociocultural system as it existed at one point in time—the task of the archeologist, historian, and historical archeologist—it is necessary to use evidence that endures from that system into the present. This evidence (1) may be in the form of materials placed in the archeological record through S–A processes of that system or (2) may consist of objects transmitted through time within systemic context. An understanding of S–S processes affects the interpretation of both kinds of evidence.

First, an understanding of S–S processes facilitates explanation of what is and what is not subject to S–A processes, and under what conditions. For example, an archeologist of the twenty-second century working only in secondary refuse and cemeteries from a modern city would erroneously conclude, were he ignorant of S–S processes, that jewelry made of precious gems was not in widespread use—as indicated by its rare occurrence in the excavated samples. Of course, should this archeologist encounter a fashion magazine a distinct anomaly would present itself. Naturally, to interpret this archeological evidence properly one would need to know or infer correctly that jewelry incorporating precious gems was endlessly circulated, spiraling through time in systemic context from individual to individual by gift, sale, inheritance, or theft.

Second, if one had a particular question in mind, such as the range of designs used for jewelry in the late nineteenth century for a given city, it would be necessary to understand the nature of presently obtainable evidence of those manufacturing practices. Several lines of evidence come to mind readily: museums, where actual specimens and perhaps manufacturing equipment are stored; antique shops and jewelers, where specimens are available; libraries, where books may be found in which artisans or their contemporaries set down their observations or designs and where periodicals with advertisting may be found; manufacturing companies still in existence, where records and samples may be kept; and, of course, individuals, who may have heirloom jewelry from that time period. How one *finds and interprets* each line of evidence depends on the specific question being asked *and* on knowledge of the S–S processes that resulted in the preservation of these materials in systemic context.

For example, let us assume that we wish to learn the range of styles and materials used in wedding bands worn during the late nineteenth century by individuals in the middle and lower socioeconomic classes. Quite clearly, each form of evidence will provide information that varies in its relevance to the question being posed. Jewelers, for instance, might be expected to possess examples of more expensive or unusual items, probably related to the upper classes. This is based on the possible c-transform that, all other variables constant, the probability of an item's appearance in the present retail sales network is directly related to its initial purchase price. Whether or not this c-transform is true is less important than the fact that it illustrates the role that it or others can and must play in the selection, identification, and interpretation of historical evidence. It is likely that any particular question will have to be answered by careful sifting and evaluation of information provided through these multiple channels of material flow from the past. Although it is not recognized explicitly, this evaluative process, often cited as a hallmark of critical historical scholarship (Barzun and Graff 1970), includes consideration of the nature and effects of S–S processes.

Questions one might ask about those processes include these: Of the variety of rings made in this city during that time period, which are likely to end up in museums, in antique shops, or as privately owned heirlooms? Which rings are most likely to have been remanufactured into other jewelry? Which types would have been advertised in periodicals and which periodicals? Of those periodicals containing relevant information, which would be preserved in libraries or other archives? Which companies or individuals would have kept detailed records of designs? And of those records, which would have been maintained until the present time? These examples should illustrate just a few of the relevant questions that can orient the study of S–S processes.

Having just considered why the study of S–S processes is important to investigations of both the archeological and historical records, it is now necessary for me to define and describe these processes in more detail. Once again, this listing is by no means exhaustive; its purpose is merely to focus inquiry on the myriad unanswered questions that typify this domain. It is fair to state that few archeologists have ever considered S–S processes when making interpretations and fewer still have offered generalizations approaching the status of a c-transform. Nevertheless it is possible to delineate several major types of S–S process.

Recycling

"One variety of widely known S–S process is recycling. Recycling is . . . an activity whereby a secondary material is introduced as a raw material into an industrial process in which it is transformed into a new product in such a manner that its original identity as a product is lost [Darnay and Franklin 1972:2]." Secondary materials are those that (1) have fulfilled their useful function and cannot be used further in their present form or composition and (2) occur as waste from the manufacturing or conversion of products (Darnay and Franklin 1972:3).

Major varieties of recycling exist (see Darnay and Franklin 1972 for some definitions), but completely general types useful for archeological purposes remain to be defined. Recycling may or may not involve a change in the user of the item (although in modern definitions that is usually implied). For example, there are many archeological instances of recycling where the original user, remanufacturer, and final user are the same (e.g., a dull bifacially chipped knife is modified into a spokeshave; a sherd is ground up for use as temper in other pottery; a mano becomes part of a mealing bin). There are few explicit principles relating to recycling processes, at least in archeology. One interesting study by David (1971) deals with recycling (and secondary use) of structures and suggests some possible c-transforms. Economists and environmentalists have begun to study recycling, and perhaps some concepts and principles can be borrowed from them (e.g., Smith 1972).

Secondary Use

Often, an object need not be modified to make it suitable for its new use. The latter type of process is termed *secondary use* (Darnay and Franklin 1972:3). Familiar examples include the use of a metate as a wall stone, the use of an exhausted core as a hammerstone, and the use of a storage pit as a repository for secondary refuse. Secondary use processes, like recycling, may or may not involve a change in the user.

There appear to be several significant dimensions along which recycling and secondary use processes vary; variables within these dimensions should eventually permit isolation of general types of recycling and secondary use relevant for archeological and historical research. Quite clearly, a major aim of future studies should be the designation of significant varieties and the explanation of their differential occurrence within and between systems.

Lateral Cycling

Another major type of S–S process is known as *lateral cycling* (Schiffer 1972, 1976a). Lateral cycling occurs when an object is transferred, without modification or change in use, from one user to another. Some repair or maintenance may of course take place between episodes of use. Lateral cycling includes the many processes by which usable, but used, objects circulate within a sociocultural system and persist in time. In modern industrial sociocultural systems used material culture circulates by means of two major kinds of lateral cycling mechanisms: *formal* and *informal*. Formal mechanisms include auctions, thrift shops, real estate agents, and various retail and wholesale handlers of more limited ranges of material culture (see Young and Young 1973). Formal mechanisms are characterized by sustained activity and sanctioning, via taxation, by local, state, and federal governments.

Informal mechanisms are those that occur beyond the periphery of sanctioned economic activity; records of transactions are seldom kept, locations of transactions are transient. Often, lateral cycling occurs simply by barter or gift. Examples of informal lateral cycling mechanisms include patio and garage sales, rummage sales, swap meets, theft, and gifts within and between various social units.

Claassen (n.d.) has shown that some mechanisms (formal and informal), that simply facilitate transfers in the ownership of used objects also involve items that are recycled or secondarily used. Perhaps *reuse mechanism* is the most appropriate designation for the general class of activities.

Explicit c-transforms of lateral cycling processes are scarce. However, a number of my students have examined some types of reuse mechanisms; both formal and informal, in order to begin generating c-transforms, and especially to begin formulating relevant general questions (Schiffer 1973; 1976a). For example, Kassander (1973) found that as the social distance increases between the individuals or groups that give and receive laterally cycled goods, there is a greater likelihood that formal mechanisms with middlemen, such as secondhand stores and thrift shops, will facilitate the activity. Another hypothesis is that lateral cycling seems to deal mostly with items having relatively long use-lives (Brown and Johnson 1973; Kassander 1973; Wood 1973; Young 1973). These provocative studies have raised many important research questions and have provided numerous interesting hypotheses. For example, is lateral cycling a phenomenon only of systems characterized by considerable social mobility? What determines when a given type of reuse mechanism will come into existence? And what are the relationships between types of reuse mechanisms and the socioeconomic status of the participants?

These and related questions have given rise to the Reuse Project, a long-term program of ethnoarcheological investigations in Tucson, Arizona, begun in the spring of 1976 (Schiffer 1976b). In the first stage of the project a sample of Tucson households was interviewed in order to determine basic socioeconomic and demographic variables, as well as patterns of acquiring and disposing of used material culture. Household inventories were obtained for one major kind of item, furniture and appliances. Year and mode of acquisition and other variables relevant to testing the hypotheses were also ascertained. It is hoped that principles useful for the study of the past will emerge from these efforts.

Conservatory Processes

It should be apparent that the continuous operation in a system of S–A processes and recycling will tend to bring about the modification or deposition of most cultural items. Although lateral cycling processes can postpone the transformation of articles to archeological context, they cannot entirely prevent such occurrences; eventually, all objects will break, wear out, be damaged beyond usability, or be lost. In part, concern for the preservation of past remains has led to the development, especially in state-level systems, of processes that counteract the normal tendency of materials to enter the archeological record. For example, libraries and archives concentrate manuscripts and books; museums accumulate all sorts of material culture; and individuals and private institutions collect everything from toy trains to beer cans. A general definition of what I call *conservatory processes* can be provided. A conservatory process is one that brings about a change in the function (but not form) of an object such that permanent preservation is intended. Usually the change in function is accompanied by a change in the social unit of use, and is marked by obvious storage or display.

In the long run, even conservatory processes must be viewed as stopgap measures, which, although serving to make materials from the past temporarily accessible to antiquarians and scholars, do not prevent the ultimate transition to archeological context (as a librarian from first century Alexandria could readily testify). The attraction of the archeological record is an inexorable force that few objects can resist indefinitely. Even Lenin will be buried someday.

No one has yet suggested that any marked regularities inhere in conservatory processes, although clearly they must. As with other cultural formation processes, conservatory processes are not widely appreciated as an important domain of unified phenomena worthy of scientific study. To be sure, in order to carry out effective historical research one must know the kinds of material collected by various institutions (Winks 1969:xvii–xviii). But that level of information, casually acquired during scholarly training and research, is based on descriptive information and not on the comparison of variables that underlie the processes operating. Comparative investigation of private and public conservatory processes among varied sociocultural systems would doubtlessly disclose significant and useful regularities.

The processes just discussed—recycling, secondary use, lateral cycling, and conservatory processes—do not cover entirely the S–S domain. It would not be profitable, however, to continue subdividing and naming processes until after additional empirical research is undertaken. I have developed the present discussion only to the point of indicating some broad areas of study. Such research should strive explicitly to generate and test c-transforms.

CONCLUSION

Whether we consider ourselves to be historians, archeologists, or historical archeologists, our substantive research is likely to involve consideration of both historical and archeological evidence. If we are to achieve our particular research goals, then we need to consider the general processes that form evidence of the cultural past. That there is no one-to-one relationship between history and historical evidence and between archeology and archeological evidence requires the emergence of a unified science of the past built upon the investigation of cultural formation processes.

In this chapter I have tried to describe the nature of cultural formation processes and suggest ways that they might be fruitfully investigated. They are the link between a past behavioral system and the records of that system existing today—archeological and historical. The primary task of all investigators, if they aim to "read" those records, is to understand the lawful nature and effects of cultural formation processes. Development of additional c-transforms will not, however, bring the past closer to the present, although they will allow us to make more rigorous use of the evidence that persists from the past. The past is not distant or ephemeral. It is gone. The past is not perceived through casual ruminations or insightful glimpses. It is scientifically inferred. These simple facts, faced long ago by other historical disciplines, must lead now to an examination of the relationships between the cultural past and the remnants of it we observe today. Such relationships can be established only with the laws of cultural formation processes.

REFERENCES

Ambrose, W. R.

1967 Archaeology and shell middens. *Archaeology and Physical Anthropology in Oceania* **2:**169–187.

Ascher, Robert

1959 A prehistoric population estimate using midden analysis and two population models. *Southwestern Journal of Anthropology* **15:**168–178.

1968 Time's arrow and the archaeology of contemporary community. In *Settlement archaeology,* edited by K. C. Chang. Palo Alto, California: National Press Books. Pp. 43–52.

Baker, Charles M.

1974 A preliminary archeological field study of the Chicot Watershed, Chicot County, Arkansas. Manuscript on deposit, Arkansas Archeological Survey, Fayetteville.

n.d. Site abandonment and the archeological record: An empirical case for anticipated return. *Arkansas Academy of Science, Proceedings* (in press).

Barzun, Jacques, and Henry F. Graff

1970 *The modern researcher.* New York: Harcourt.

Bascom, Willard

1971 Deep-water archeology. *Science* **174:**261–269.

Baumhoff, Martin A.

1963 Ecological determinants of aboriginal California populations. *University of California, Publications in American Archaeology and Ethnology* **49:**155–236.

Binford, Lewis R.

1962 Archaeology as anthropology. *American Antiquity* **28:**217–225.

1971 Mortuary practices: Their study and their potential. In Approaches to the social dimensions of mortuary practices, edited by James A. Brown. *Society for American Archaeology, Memoirs* **25:**6–29.

1973 Interassemblage variability—The Mousterian and the "functional" argument. In *The explanation of culture change: Models in prehistory,* edited by C. Renfrew. London: G. Duckworth.

n.d. 47 trips: A case study in the character of some archaeological formation processes (in press).

Bonnichsen, Robson

1973 Millie's Camp: An experiment in archaeology. *World Archaeology* **4:**277–291.

Brown, Charles S., and Lane P. Johnson

1973 The secret use-life of a mayonnaise jar . . . or, how I learned to love lateral cycling. Manuscript on deposit, Arizona State Museum Library. Xerox.

Brown, James A. (editor)

1971 Approaches to the social dimensions of mortuary practices. *Society for American Archaeology, Memoirs* 25.

Chaplin, R. E.

1971 *The study of animal bones from archaeological sites.* New York: Seminar Press.

Claassen, Cheryl

1976 Cultural formation processes of the archaeological record in the Aleutian Islands. Paper read at the New England–New York Graduate Student Conference, Storrs, Connecticut.

n.d. Antiques—Objects of lateral cycling? *Arkansas Academy of Science, Proceedings* (in press).

Coles, John

1973 *Archaeology by experiment.* New York: Scribner.

Collins, Michael B.

1975 The sources of bias in processual data: An appraisal. In *Sampling in archaeology,* edited by James W. Mueller. Tucson: Univ. of Arizona Press. Pp. 26–32.

Collins, Michael B, and Jason M. Fenwick

n.d. Population growth rate estimates, Grasshopper Pueblo. In Multi-disciplinary research at the Grasshopper Ruin, edited by W. A. Longacre. *University of Arizona, Anthropological Papers* (in press).

Cook, Sherburne F.

1972a Prehistoric demography. *Addison-Wesley Modular Publications in Anthropology* **16**.

1972b Can pottery residues be used as an index to population? In Miscellaneous papers on archaeology. *Contributions of the University of California Archaeological Research Facility* **14:**17–39.

Daly, Patricia

1969 Approaches to faunal analysis in archaeology. *American Antiquity* **34:**146–153.

Daniels, S. G. H.

1972 Research design models. In *Models in archaeology,* edited by David L. Clarke. London: Methuen. Pp. 201–229.

Darlington, Arnold

1969 *Ecology of refuse tips.* London: Heinemann Educational Books.

Darnay, Arsen, and William E. Franklin

1972 *Salvage markets for materials in solid wastes.* Washington, D.C.: U.S. Environmental Protection Agency.

David, Nicholas

1971 The Fulani compound and the archeologist. *World Archaeology* **3:**111–131.

DeBloois, Evan, Dee Green, and Henry Wylie

n.d. *A test of the impact of pinyon–juniper chaining of archeological sites.* U.S.D.A. Forest Service, Laboratory of Archeology, Ogden, Utah.

Drucker, Philip

1972 Stratigraphy in archaeology: An introduction. *Addison-Wesley Modular Publications in Anthropology* **30**.

Efremov, J. A.

1940 Taphonomy: A new branch of paleontology. *Pan American Geologist* **74:**81–93.

Fehon, Jacqueline R., and Sandra C. Scholtz

n.d. A conceptual framework for the study of artifact loss. Arkansas Archeological Survey, Fayetteville, manuscript.

Ford, Janet L., and Martha A. Rolingson

1972 Site destruction due to agricultural practices in southeast Arkansas. *Arkansas Archeological Survey, Research Series* **3:**1–40.

Garrison, E. G.

1975 A qualitative model for inundation studies in archeological research and resource conservation: An example for Arkansas. *Plains Anthropologist* **20:**279–296.

Gould, Richard A. (editor)

n.d. *The vestigial image—Explorations in ethnoarchaeology.* Albuquerque: Univ. of New Mexico Press. (in press)

Green, H. J. M.
1961a An analysis of archaeological rubbish deposits. *Archaeological News Letter* 7(3):51–54.
1961b An analysis of archaeological rubbish deposits: Part two. *Archaeological News Letter* 7(4):91–93, 95.
Heizer, Robert F., and Sherburne F. Cook
1956 Some aspects of the quantitative approach in archaeology. *Southwestern Journal of Anthropology* **12:**229–248.
Hole, Frank, and Robert F. Heizer
1973 *An introduction to prehistoric archeology.* New York: Holt.
House, John H., and Michael B. Schiffer
1975 Significance of the archeological resources of the Cache River Basin. In The Cache River archeological project: An experiment in contract archeology, assembled by Michael B. Schiffer and John H. House. *Arkansas Archeology Survey, Research Series* **8:**163–186.
Howells, W. W.
1960 Estimating population numbers through archaeological and skeletal remains. In The application of quantitative methods in archaeology, edited by R. F. Heizer and S. F. Cook. *Viking Fund Publications in Anthropology* **28:**158–180.
Kassander, Helen
1973 Second hand rose, or lateral cycling: A study in behavioral archaeology. Manuscript on deposit, Arizona State Museum Library.
Lange, Frederick W., and Charles R. Rydberg
1972 Abandonment and post-abandonment behavior at a rural Central American house-site. *American Antiquity* **37:**419–432.
Longacre, William A.
n.d. Population dynamics at the Grasshopper Pueblo. In *Anthropological approaches to demography,* edited by Ezra Zubrow. Albuquerque: Univ. of New Mexico Press. (in press).
Longacre, William A., and James A. Ayres
1968 Archeological lessons from an Apache wickiup. In *New perspectives in archeology,* edited by Sally R. Binford and Lewis R. Binford. Chicago: Aldine. Pp. 151–159.
Matthews, J. M.
1965 Stratigraphic disturbance: The human element. *Antiquity* **39:**295–298.
McKellar, Judith
1973 Correlations and the explanation of distributions. Manuscript on deposit, Arizona State Museum Library.
McPherron, Alan
1967 The Juntunen site and the Late Woodland prehistory of the Upper Great Lakes area. *University of Michigan, Museum of Anthropology, Anthropological Papers* **30**.
Medford, Larry D.
1972 Agricultural destruction of archeological sites in northeast Arkansas. *Arkansas Archeological Survey, Research Series* **3:**41–82.
Medlock, Raymond C.
1975 Faunal analysis. In The Cache River archeological project: An experiment in contract archeology, assembled by Michael B. Schiffer and John H. House. *Arkansas Archeological Survey, Research Series* **8:**223–242.
Morse, Dan F.
1973 Natives and anthropologists in Arkansas. In Anthropology beyond the university, edited by Alden Redfield. *Southern Anthropological Society, Proceedings* **7:**26–39.
1975 Paleo-Indian in the land of opportunity: Preliminary report on the excavation at

the Sloan site (3GE94). In The Cache River archeological project: An experiment in contract archeology, assembled by Michael B. Schiffer and John H. House. *Arkansas Archeological Survey, Research Series* **8:**135–143.

Murdock, George P., et al.
1950 Outline of cultural materials. New Haven, Connecticutt:Human Relations Area Files, Inc.

Neal, Larry
1974 A resurvey of the prehistoric resources of Tenkiller Ferry Lake. *University of Oklahoma, Oklahoma River Basin Survey Project, General Survey Report* **13**·

Neal, Larry, and Michael B. Mayo
n.d. *A preliminary report on a resurvey of Wister Lake.* Oklahoma River Basin Survey, Univ. of Oklahoma, Norman. Manuscript.

Prewitt, Elton R., and Douglas A. Lawson
1972 An assessment of the archeological and paleontological resources of Lake Texoma, Texas–Oklahoma. *Texas Archeological Salvage Project, Survey Reports* 10.

Rathje, William L.
1970 Socio-political implications of lowland Maya burials: Methodology and tentative hypotheses. *World Archaeology* **1:**359–374.
1973 Models for mobile Maya: A variety of constraints. In *The explanation of culture change: Models in prehistory,* edited by Colin Renfrew. London: G. Duckworth. Pp. 731–757.

Read, Catherine E.
1971 Animal bones and human behavior. Ph.D. dissertation, UCLA, University Microfilms, Ann Arbor, Michigan.

Redman, Charles L., and Patty Jo Watson
1970 Systematic, intensive surface collection. *American Antiquity* **35:**279–291.

Reid, J. Jefferson
1973 Growth and response to stress at Grasshopper Pueblo, Arizona. Ph.D. dissertation, Univ. of Arizona, University Microfilms, Ann Arbor, Michigan.
1974 (editor) Behavioral archaeology at the Grasshopper Ruin. *The Kiva* **40:**1–112.

Reid, J. Jefferson, and Michael B. Schiffer
n.d. Toward a behavioral archaeology. In preparation.

Reid, J. Jefferson, Michael B. Schiffer, and Jeffrey M. Neff
1975 Archaeological considerations of intrasite sampling. In *Sampling in archaeology,* edited by James W. Mueller. Tucson: Univ. of Arizona Press. Pp. 209–224.

Robbins, L. H.
1973 Turkana material culture viewed from an archaeological perspective. *World Archaeology* **5:**209–214.

Rowe, John H.
1962 Worsaae's Law and the use of grave lots for archaeological dating. *American Antiquity* **28:**129–137.

Saile, David
1976 Pueblo building rituals. Ms. submitted for publication.

Schiffer, Michael B.
1972 Archaeological context and systemic context. *American Antiquity* **37:**156–165.
1973 Cultural formation processes of the archaeological record: Applications at the Joint Site, east-central Arizona. Ph.D. dissertation, Univ. of Arizona, University Microfilms, Ann Arbor, Michigan.
1974 Nomothetic aspects of chipped-stone experiments. *Newsletter of Lithic Technology* **3:**46–50.
1975a Archaeology as behavioral science. *American Anthropologist* **77:**836–848.
1975b Factors and "toolkits": Evaluating multivariate analyses in archaeology. *Plains Anthropologist* **20:**61–70.

1975c Behavioral chain analysis: Activities, organization, and the use of space. In Chapters in the prehistory of eastern Arizona, IV. *Fieldiana: Anthropology* **65:**103–119.

1975d Classification of chipped-stone tool use. In The Cache River archeological project: An experiment in contract archeology, assembled by Michael B. Schiffer and John H. House. *Arkansas Archeological Survey, Research Series* **8:**249–251.

1975e The effects of occupation span on site content. In the Cache River archeological project: An experiment in contract archeology, assembled by Michael B. Schiffer and John H. House. *Arkansas Archeological Survey, Research Series* **8:**265–269.

1976a *Behavioral archeology.* New York: Academic Press.

1976b Prospects for the archeological study of reuse processes in modern America. Ms. on deposit, Arizona State Museum, Tucson.

n.d. Methodological issues in ethnoarchaeology. In *The vestigial image—explorations in ethnoarchaeology,* edited by Richard A. Gould. Albuquerque: Univ. of New Mexico Press. (in press)

Schiffer, Michael B., and George J. Gumerman (editors)

n.d. *Conservation archaeology: A guide for cultural resource management.* New York: Academic Press. (in press)

Schiffer, Michael B., and John H. House

1975 Indirect impacts of the channelization project on the archeological resources. In The Cache River archeological project: An experiment in contract archeology, assembled by Michael B. Schiffer and John H. House. *Arkansas Archeological Survey, Research Series* **8:**277–282.

Schiffer, Michael B., and William L. Rathje

1973 Efficient exploitation of the archeological record: Penetrating problems. In *Research and theory in current archeology,* edited by Charles L. Redman. New York: Wiley. Pp. 169–179.

Schuyler, Robert L.

1968 Aboriginal "archaeologists." *Antiquity* **42:**57–58.

Schwartz, Douglas W.

1970 The postmigration culture: A base for archaeological inference. In *Reconstructing prehistoric pueblo societies,* edited by William A. Longacre. Albuquerque: Univ. of New Mexico Press. Pp. 175–193.

Smith, Vernon L.

1972 Dynamics of waste accumulation: Disposal vs. recycling. *The Quarterly Journal of Economics* **86:**600–616.

Stockton, Eugene D.

1973 Shaw's Creek Shelter: Human displacement of artifacts and its significance. *Mankind* **9:**112–117.

Thomas, David H.

1971 On distinguishing natural from cultural bone in archaeological sites. *American Antiquity* **36:**366–371.

Thompson, Raymond H., and William A. Longacre

1966 The University of Arizona Archaeological Field School at Grasshopper, east-central Arizona. *The Kiva* **31:**255–275.

Tringham, Ruth, Glenn Cooper, George Odell, Barbara Voytek, and Anne Whitman

1974 Experimentation in the formation of edge damage: A new approach to lithic analysis. *Journal of Field Archaeology* **1:**171–196.

Ucko, P. J.

1969 Ethnography and archaeological interpretation of funerary remains. *World Archaeology* **1:**262–280.

Wall, Kathy

1973 Primary and secondary refuse at the KOA campground. Ms. on file, Arizona State Museum Library, Univ. of Arizona, Tucson.

Watson, Patty Jo, Steven A. LeBlanc, and Charles L. Redman
1971 *Explanation in archeology.* New York: Columbia Univ. Press.
Wheeler, Sir Mortimer
1954 *Archaeology from the Earth.* Oxford: Clarenden Press.
Wilcox, David R.
n.d. Sampling pueblos: The implications of room-set additions at Grasshopper Pueblo. In Multi-disciplinary research at the Grasshopper Ruin, edited by William A. Longacre. *University of Arizona, Anthropological Papers* (in press).
Willey, Gordon R., and Charles R. McGimsey
1954 The Monagrillo culture of Panama. *Papers of the Peabody Museum* **49**.
Wilmsen, Edwin N.
1973 Interaction, spacing behavior, and the organization of hunting bands. *Journal of Anthropological Research* **29**:1–31.
Winks, Robin W.
1969 Introduction. In *The historian as detective,* edited by Robin W. Winks. New York: Harper. Pp. xiii–xxiv.
Wood, Patrick
1973 Survey of artifact distributions at a swap meet through time. Manuscript on deposit, Arizona State Museum Library.
Yellen, John E.
1974 The !Kung settlement pattern: An archaeological perspective. Unpublished Ph.D. dissertation, Harvard Univ.
Young, Ellen
1973 Lateral cycling of clothing within the nuclear family unit. Manuscript on deposit, Arizona State Museum Library.
Young, Jean, and Jim Young
1973 *The garage sale manual: Alternate economics for the people.* New York: Praeger.
Ziegler, Alan C.
1973 Inference from prehistoric faunal remains. *Addison-Wesley Modular Publications in Anthropology* **43**.

An Archeological–Historical Analysis of Fort Watson: December 1780–April 1781

LELAND G. FERGUSON

In December or early January of 1780–1781, Colonel John Watson of the British army constructed a fort on the summit of an abandoned Indian mound about half a mile from the Santee River in present Clarendon County, South Carolina. In a letter after the war, Watson (n.d.) commented that "having found a place, supposed to have been the burying Ground of their Indian Chiefs in former times, resembling the Barrows of this country [England]; we scarp'd it, stockaded it at Top, abattis'd it at bottom, and rendered it as strong as the materials we could collect, and the only utensils we had, our Tomahawks would admit." After completion, Fort Watson served to control traffic on the Santee River and on the road from Charleston to Camden, which also passed nearby. Proximity to these two Low Country arteries probably meant that Fort Watson was visited by many detachments of the British occupation forces.

After the battle of Guilford Courthouse on March 15, 1781, General Nathanael Greene sent Lieutenant Colonel "Light Horse" Harry Lee to assist Brigadier General Francis Marion in his harassment of the British in occupied South Carolina. As part of this campaign Marion and Lee set siege to Fort Watson on April 15, 1781. Eight days later, on April 23, 1781, Lieutenant James McKay, commander of the garrison, surrendered and the fort was destroyed by the Americans. Thus, Fort Watson came to an end approximately 4 months after its establishment (Gibbes 1853; Johnson 1822; Lee 1812; McKay n.d.; Watson n.d.).

Supplies and men enroute to Camden from Georgetown and Charleston passed by this fort, but it was simply a way station between the important terminals of the southern campaign. The historical record is not replete with descriptions, diagrams, and records concerning Fort Watson. In the frame of contemporary military activities this fort was not particularly important. Yet the artifacts and their distribution are representative of the cultural variables at work in the British colonial army. Thus, the challenge of this site is to exploit a special-activity cultural time capsule to help solve appropriate problems concerning eighteenth century culture.

This chapter conveys only a portion of the archeological-historical analysis of Fort Watson—the portion centering around the important analyses relating to ceramics and lead balls. These two artifact classes provided the cornerstone of the interpretation of the occupation of the fort prior to the battle in the case of ceramics and during the battle in the case of lead balls. Using these materials, this study demonstrates how historical documents, the archeological record, and the behavioral principles that create the archeological record have been used to interpret the events that took place at this fort in the swampland of South Carolina. More complete discussions of the materials recovered and other aspects of the analyses have been presented elsewhere (Ferguson 1973, 1975a, 1975b).

THE HISTORICAL RECORD

Aside from Watson's casual comment about the construction of his fort, historical references to this small garrison speak primarily to the most significant event of the day—the battle. We have specific descriptions of the battle from three officers: Lieutenant James McKay, commandant of the garrison; Brigadier General Francis Marion of the South Carolina Militia; and Lieutenant Colonel "Light Horse" Harry Lee of the Continental Army. Lieutenant McKay (n.d.) kept a brief daily journal of the events, and General Marion wrote a letter to Major General Nathanael Greene on the evening of the surrender describing the action (Gibbes 1853:57). These two accounts are perhaps the most reliable. Colonel Lee's story of the battle came many years (1812) after the war and therefore is perhaps the least reliable of the accounts. The following historical sketch is a general statement drawn from the most consistent portions of the written record.

After the conflict at Guilford Courthouse, General Greene sent Lieutenant Colonel Lee with his command to join General Marion and his partisans. Their mission was to harass British occupation troops in the South Carolina coastal plain. Together Lee and Marion decided to lay siege to Fort Watson. On the fifteenth of April they had "some riflemen and continentals [Gibbes 1853:57]" cut the British off from Scott's Lake, an old oxbow south of the fort used as a water source. Although they hoped for a quick capitulation, the Americans were to be disappointed. The British dug a well inside the fortifications; and since the Americans had insufficient trenching tools and no artillery, a stalemate resulted.

After more than a week of the siege the Americans, at the suggestion of Major Maham of the militia, constructed a firing tower that could command at least a portion of the interior of the stockade atop the 23-foot-tall mound. Marksmen were stationed in this tower, and others prepared for a ground assault. Lieutenant McKay tried to protect his fort by raising a traverse and deepening interior ditches. However, these defensive measures were not adequate. Under cover of fire from the tower two soldiers successfully pulled away a portion of the abatis at the foot of the mound, and the British surrendered (Gibbes 1853:57; McKay n.d.).

Although these historical records are very important in our understanding of Fort Watson, important information is missing. The lifeways of the men in this fort are lost to history. Furthermore, the accounts do not include a plan of the fort, nor the disposition of any of the activity areas within the fort. Tied to this lack of knowledge of the plan is a general lack of information concerning any aspects of orientation during the battle. The only references to orientation given relate to the beginning of the siege: Marion (Gibbes 1853:57) mentioned that they cut the British off from Scott's Lake and McKay (n.d.) referred to the initial attack as having come from his "front." As for the final attack, we have no information concerning the direction of the American ground assault, the location of the tower, or the placement of the British traverse. The archeological record is the only potential source for this missing information.

THE ARCHEOLOGICAL RECORD

During the summers of 1972 and 1973, as a representative of the Institute of Archeology and Anthropology of the University of South Carolina, I conducted exploratory archeology at the Scott's Lake site, of which Fort Watson is a component. Observation, local history, and tests indicated that there had been little disturbance to the main portion of the site since abandonment during the Revolution. The southern edge of the site had been eroded by wave action from Lake Marion, but the mound and most of the environs were not disturbed, and there had not been any significant vandalism. Thus, artifact location, even in the topsoil, was presumed to represent the pattern of original deposition. These distribution data were reckoned to be vital on this particular site, since most of the structures had been temporary; and, in many cases, I expected that identification of activity areas would rely totally on the pattern of deposition of artifacts. As a result, undisturbed areas on this site were excavated using a tightly controlled grid system and all the topsoil was sifted. The excavation units of concern (I and II), included the mound summit where the stockade was located as well as the area at the base on the eastern side of the mound (Figure 3.1).

The excavation of approximately 4000 square feet on the mound summit was sufficient to expose the entire stockade (Figure 3.2). The plan of this structure included a wall of upright logs with a 12-foot opening or gate facing Scott's Lake. Inside the wall was an interior ditch, two earthen platforms, and several pits. One of the pits (Feature 6) was used as the source of soil for the platforms, the others (Features 7 and 13) appear to have been used as trash pits and probably latrines during the siege. Excavation of approximately 4000 additional square feet on the eastern side of the mound revealed a portion of a fortification ditch and evidence of the abatis.

During the excavations numerous artifacts from the Revolutionary War occupation were recovered. These artifacts included ceramics, nails, glass, buttons, buckles, broken eating utensils, pipestems, lead balls,

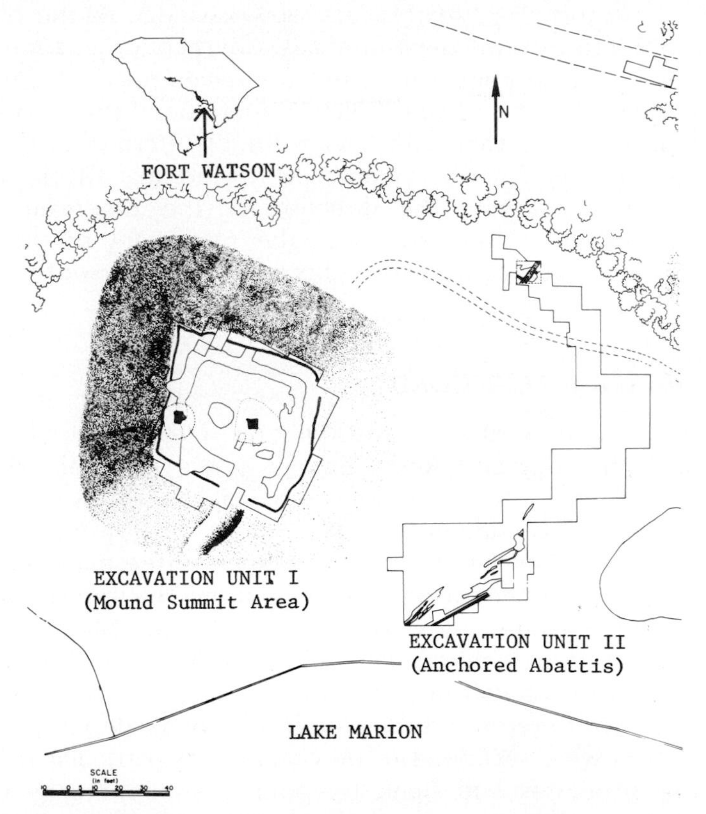

Figure 3.1. Scott's Lake site (38 CR1). Fort Watson-Santee Indian Mound 1972–1973 excavations. (Modern Lake Marion covered Scott's Lake which was 300 feet southeast of the mound.)

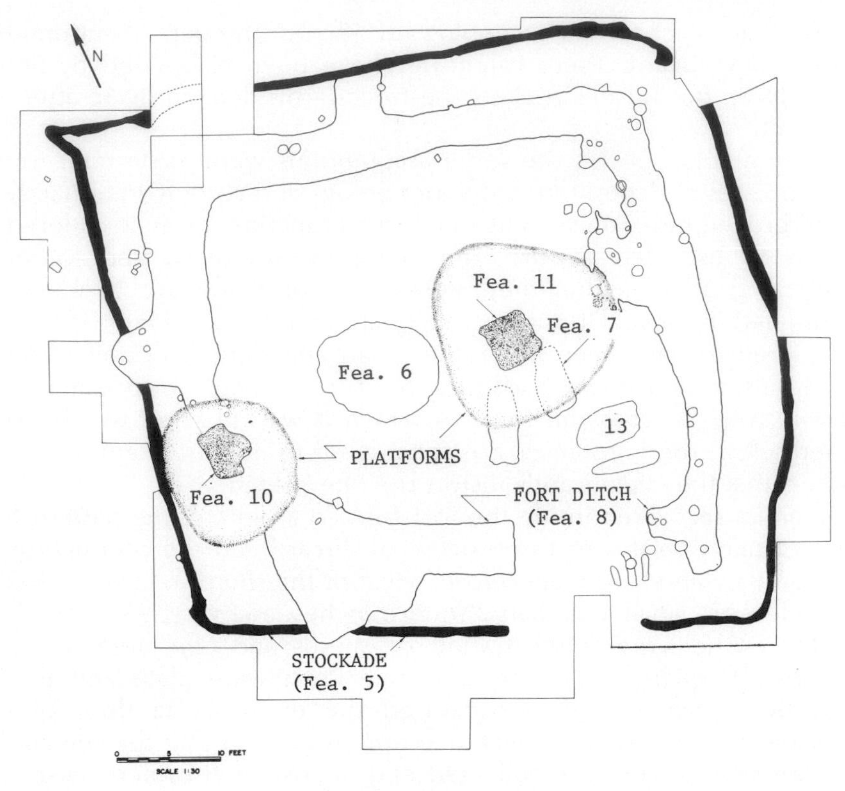

Figure 3.2. Mound summit stockade, Fort Watson (Mound A). (38 CR1)

musket parts, whirlygigs, Jew's-harps, a coin, and furniture hardware. Adequate analysis and interpretation of these artifacts required a consideration of how they were deposited as well as what they were. To this end, the processes by which this archeological record was formed were carefully considered and integrated into the study.

In recent publications Schiffer (1972, and this volume) has specifically and rigorously outlined the importance of cultural formation processes as well as the differences in the kinds of refuse produced by these various processes. There are many general processes that may result in archeological materials, and two of the most important are discard and loss. These two processes appear to account for most of the artifacts from this site. A small amount of the materials from this site may have resulted from abandonment, another process operating to create the archeological record. The processes of discard and abandonment produce refuse and Schiffer (1972) has likewise explicitly defined three important types of refuse—*primary, secondary,* and *de facto.* Primary refuse is that material discarded at its location of use, whereas secondary refuse is discarded away from the use location. De facto refuse is that refuse that reaches the archeological record through abandonment rather than discard. These categories have been elaborated by South (1975, 1977), but for this analysis the basic terms defined by Schiffer are sufficient.

In the analysis of this site some assumptions were made concerning the processes of deposition in the archeological record. If an artifact was found broken beyond use in its intentional function it was considered to have been discarded. On the other hand, when artifacts were found in perfectly good condition they were considered to have been either abandoned or lost. Of these, small, apparently valuable items were considered to have been lost rather than abandoned. Certainly, there could be some error in this assumption. For instance, a buckle might be thrown away because the strap to which it was attached was broken. Nevertheless, these instances are considered to be infrequent, and I do not feel that they significantly distort the interpretation.

Ceramics recovered inside the fort formed an interesting pattern that most certainly relates to the process of discard and the production of both primary and secondary refuse. Most of the sherds recovered in the stockade were small, less than 2 square inches, and very few of them fit together. One large concentration of sherds and one large sherd of perhaps 10 square inches were from a creamware plate and platter respectively. Since we had excavated the entire living floor of the stockade, this scatter of unrelated sherds suggested that the remainder of these vessels had been collected and deposited elsewhere as secondary refuse. Outside the stockade, sherds were generally larger. In one case on the western side of the mound about three-quarters of a creamware bowl was recovered. The evidence firmly suggests that the small sherds from the interior of the fort represent debris of such small size the soldiers did not bother cleaning it up. Therefore these sherds represent primary refuse.

During the excavations, lead balls were also frequently recovered. Initially, all these balls were thought to be primary refuse resulting from the Americans firing into the fort. During analysis, the picture changed somewhat. Though some of the balls were indeed those fired into the fort, others were apparently lost by the British protectors. The basis for these artifact divisions will be outlined later as they are used in the analysis of the final battle of the siege of Fort Watson.

CERAMICS AND TIME

Analysis of the ceramics from Fort Watson began with typological identification and an evaluation of the temporal position of the types. Ceramic types identified are presented in Table 3.1.

TABLE 3.1
Ceramic Types at Fort Watson

Type	Number of sherds			Reference
	Stockade	Other	Total	
Annular pearlware	119	13	132	Noël Hume (1970:131)
Marble slip pearlware	1	0	1	South (personal communication)
Underglazed blue hand-painted pearlware	1	0	1	Noël Hume (1970:128–129)
Creamware, lighter yellow	15	1	16	Noël Hume (1970:126–128)
Creamware, deeper yellow	278	80	358	Noël Hume (1970:126–128)
Creamware, S.C. made	48	1	49	South (1971:175–176)
Nottingham ware	19	0	19	Noël Hume (1970:114)
Salt-glazed stoneware, white	2	10	12	Noël Hume (1970:115–117)
Salt-glazed stoneware, brown	0	3	3	Noël Hume (1970:112–114)
Delftware, plain white	6	1	7	Noël Hume (1970:109)
English porcelain	2	2	4	Noël Hume (1970:137)
Oriental porcelain	12	8	20	Noël Hume (1970:258, 261)
Lead-glazed earthenware, yellow combed	0	1	1	Noël Hume (1970:107, 134–136)
Lead-glazed earthenware[a]		1	1	
Totals	503	121	624	

[a] Possibly locally made.

One of the first steps in the ceramic analysis was the insertion of these data into the Mean Ceramic Date Formula derived by South (1972). Application of the formula to these ceramics produced a date of 1778.2, quite an acceptable approximation of the date of occupation. However, one of the ceramic types, annular pearlware, has an initial appearance date of 1790 on South's temporal chart; the *terminus post quem* implications of this date appear to be serious for a site supposed to have been occupied during 1780 and 1781. Also, the occurrence of lighter colored creamware and Royal and Feather-edged patterns tends to make American historical archeologists examining the collection estimate a date from 1790 to 1805. There are obviously two possible reasons for this difference:

1. There is contamination of the historic component on the site.
2. Annular pearlware and the newest styles of creamware were in the colonies earlier than the date given by South's chart and earlier than they are now known to appear on American sites.

Contamination does not appear to be the case. The majority of the collection of historic artifacts divides neatly into two distinct categories—late eighteenth century and twentieth century. There were no glazed ceramics from the later context. The non-twentieth century artifacts invariably fall into a reasonable Revolutionary War period collection.

Furthermore, the general distribution of these artifacts within the mound summit stockade coincides with the distribution of creamware and pearlware tea-service fragments (Figures 3.3–3.5). Most of the items seem to come from the eastern half of the fort and tend to cluster in the northeastern quadrant.

Annular decoration was a technique being used on creamware during the 1770s (Godden 1966:Plate 341). The coining of the name *pearlware* by Josiah Wedgwood has been historically documented by Noël Hume as occurring in 1779 (Noël Hume 1969). Noël Hume (1969:395) states that "at the outset, pearlware was decorated with the same, often elaborate and mechanical, devices used on creamware, such as engine-turned checker patterns cutting through underglaze blue, green, or red-brown." Although "at the outset" in this sentence may mean as many as 20 years, in consideration of the total span of the production of pearlware, the tenor of this statement is that creamware decorative tech-

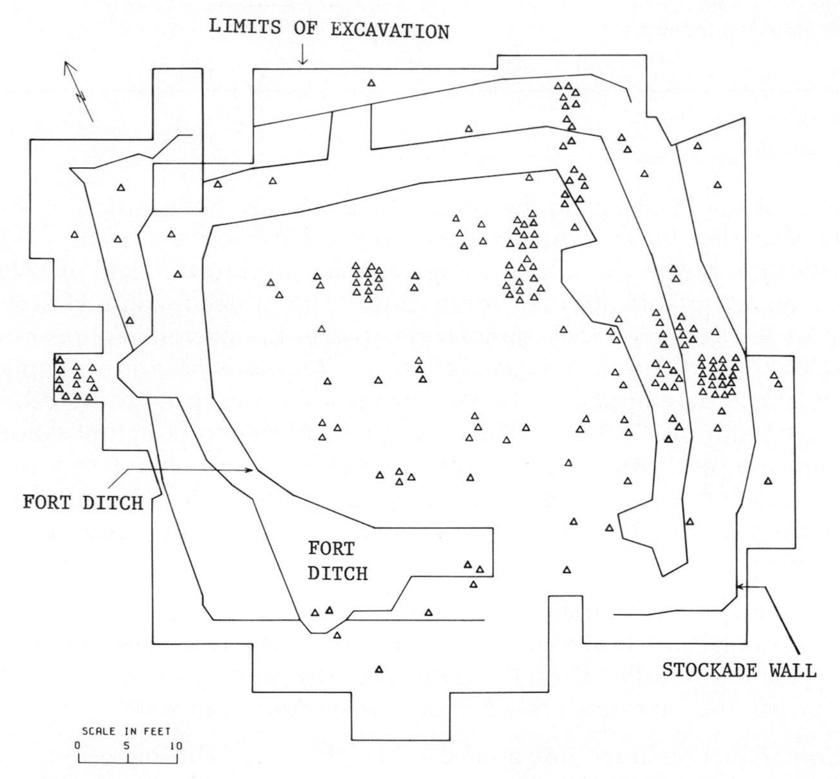

Figure 3.3. Distribution of creamware (tea service), mound summit, Fort Watson (38 CR1). Δ = 1 sherd.

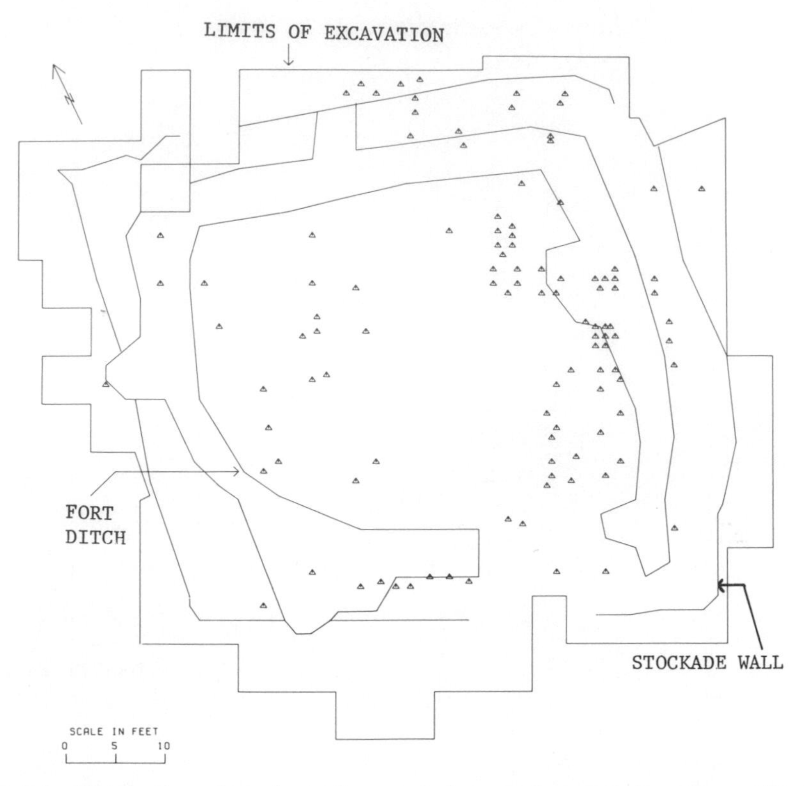

Figure 3.4. Distribution of pearlware (tea service), mound summit, Fort Watson (38 CR1). Δ = 1 sherd.

niques prevalent at the time of the invention of pearlware were probably used on pearlware. The ceramics from Fort Watson support such a contention.

South's temporal chart of historic ceramic production was constructed in conference with Noël Hume on the basis of archeological and historical documentation. Conservatism in assigning an early date to annular pearlware for use with the Mean Ceramic Date Formula was due to the expected lag of imports from England (Noël Hume 1969:394) and the fact that this type had not been historically documented or found on archeological sites in an early (ca. 1780) context in North America. South (personal communication) says that one of the problems regarding such identification was the fact that, assuming a 1790 date for pearlware, archeologists excavating sites of the Revolutionary War period would automatically assume a post-1790 intrusion was involved when pearlware was present, thus such sites would invariably be dated too late.

Fort Watson represents an early North American occurrence of annular pearlware and lighter colored creamware with the Royal and

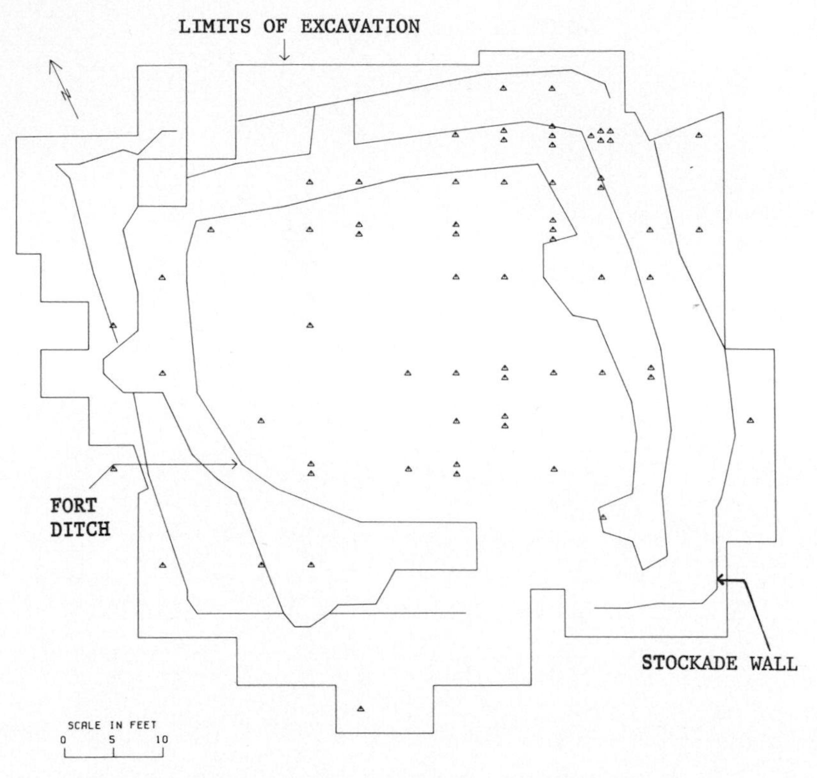

Figure 3.5. Incidental personal items, mound summit, Fort Watson (38 CR1). Δ = 1 item. Items include buttons, buckles, pipestems, whirlygigs, Jew's-harps, a coin, a pewter spoon, a chest escutcheon, cut musket balls, "lead pencils," two pieces of uniform jewelry, and a fragment of cooking pot.

Feather-edged pattern. Essentially, this site seems to be a reflection of the special nature of British sites during the Revolution. The difference in this type of site and domestic American sites may be similar to an interpretation by Noël Hume concerning stoneware mugs:

> It is safe to say that all English mottled brown stoneware mugs found on American domestic sites date between 1690 and 1775. Exceptions are likely to be found in New York, which continued to receive British military exports during the Revolutionary War years, and on British military sites to which the troops brought their own supplies undeterred by American boycotts [1970:114].

Although the case with these mugs represents the retention on the continent of an older type, the same characteristic of British occupation sites should relate to new types of ceramics produced in England during the war years. The two types of pearlware and the latest patterns of creamware may not appear on American domestic sites during the Revolution, but the living sites of British soldiers are quite a different situation.

Thus, on the basis of historical and archeological information from Fort Watson, I feel that annular pearlware was produced in England as early as 1780, and that it was being used as early as 1781, along with the newest styles of creamware, by the British army in the Colonies. Corroboration of this fact should be forthcoming from other Revolutionary War sites.

Of course, changing this ceramic information has changed the input for computation in South's formula. Altering the period of production of this type to ca. 1780–1820 and the median date to 1800, and placing the new information into the Mean Ceramic Date Formula provide a date of 1777, approximately 3½ years before the documented date of occupation.

DISHES AND GARRISON LIFE

South stresses, in the presentation of the Mean Ceramic Date Formula, that empirical testing has demonstrated that the spread of ceramics in the eighteenth and early nineteenth centuries was so well cast across geographical and cultural boundaries that the formula seems to work as well for Indian houses on the frontier as for metropolitan and rural sites on the Eastern Seaboard. The data from Fort Watson support this contention. However, when the data were divided into two obvious units and the ceramic formula applied to these separate collections an important difference was noted. The material from the stockade produced a date of 1778.4 while that from outside the stockade at the base of the mound produced an earlier date of 1771.6. In conjunction with the dating it was noticed that salt-glazed stoneware, one of the types on the site with the earliest median date came primarily from the non-stockade provenience. On the other hand pearlware, a recently introduced type, came primarily from the stockade on the mound.

The differences in the ceramic formula dates and this difference in the distribution of early and late ceramics immediately led to the hypothesis that as far as the culinary activities were concerned, there may be a significant difference between the stockaded and nonstockaded areas of Fort Watson.

From this point in the analysis, vessel form was considered in order to refine the data on the differences between the two collections. All sherds that were fragments of cups, saucers, slop bowls, or teapots, or that were delicate enough to have come from such forms were placed in a category termed *teaware.* All other sherds, including those of plates, bowls, platters, and jugs, as well as all sherds judged to have come from such forms, were classified as *heavyware.* Results showed that the highest relative percentage of teaware to heavyware ceramics was collected from the mound summit, whereas the highest relative percentage of heavyware to teaware ceramics came from the area away from the mound (Table 3.2). Thus, the concentration of teaware was primarily responsible for the date of 1778.4, but the concentration of heavyware was primarily responsible for the earlier date of 1771.6.

There seem to be four possibilities for the distribution:

1. The distribution is fortuitous and is not related to cultural phenomena.
2. The distribution is a function of variables operating within the British army as a result of combat.
3. The distribution is a function of the activities of the American militia and the Continental Army after the capture of Fort Watson.
4. The distribution is a function of variables operating within the British colonial army prior to combat.

That the distribution is fortuitous can be ruled out from the beginning. We have two variables, age and form of ceramics, that correlate in this distribution. Furthermore, chi-square statistics (Table 3.3), indicate that the distributions are not by chance ($p < .05$) for the two areas excavated (stockaded and nonstockaded), and I have confidence that this trend will continue as more of the nonstockaded area is excavated.

The key to understanding the meaning of this ceramic distribution seems to be in examining the nature of refuse inside and outside the fort closely, in light of history and the activities that would have been responsible for this refuse. We know from the historical record that the siege was set up quickly and that the British did not have time to secure provisions before being closed in the stockade. Had they had time to secure provisions before entering the stockade, dishes would probably not have been very high on the priority list. Therefore, dishes were probably in the stockade prior to the siege. Of course, some Americans might counter this conclusion and suggest that a British soldier and gentleman might well carry his tea service and no other provisions into a

TABLE 3.2
Teaware and Heavyware

	Teaware		Heavyware	
Area	Quantity	Percentage	Quantity	Percentage
Stockade	331	76.80	100	23.20
Other	52	48.15	56	51.85

TABLE 3.3

Distribution of Teaware and Heavyware: Counts and Chi-Square Values[a,b]

Area	Teaware	Heavyware	Totals
Stockade	O = 331 E = 306.26	O = 100 E = 124.74	431
Other	O = 52 E = 76.74	O = 56 E = 31.26	108
Totals	383	156	539

[a] O = observed; E = expected.

[b] Null hypothesis, H_0: There is no significant difference in ceramic class between the stockaded area and the nonstockaded area. $\chi^2 = 4.54$, $df = 1$, $p < .05$. Therefore H_0 should be rejected.

stockade to prepare for a siege. Fortunately, we do not have to rely entirely on guessing the kinds of items that a British soldier might have carried into a fort for a siege. Analysis of the archeological materials helps us significantly with this problem.

The pattern of ceramic refuse provides important information about the time and activity engaged in when the ceramics were deposited. As outlined in Table 3.4, the ceramic debris located within the stockade could have been deposited from activity engaged in before, during, or after the siege; each of these periods implies different activities and constraints on activities. Different activities and constraints in turn imply different patterns of use and discard and these differences should be reflected in the archeological record.

Had ceramic vessels been used, broken, and discarded prior to the battle they probably would have been cleaned up and placed in a secondary-refuse dump away from the activity area. Small unobtrusive sherds would probably have remained in the sand underfoot, and these are just the kinds of sherds most often found during the excavations.

Another possibility is that these vessels were used and broken during the siege. In this case there would perhaps be less tendency to clean up the materials. Nevertheless, if policing did occur the larger sherds would have been placed in secondary-refuse dumps and the smaller sherds left on the floor. The siege established severe constraints on the men in the stockade, limiting the location of secondary-refuse dumps. The narrow pits found in the stockade appear to have been refuse pits and latrines used during the siege; and although secondary ceramic refuse could have been thrown over the side of the stockade, we would expect some to have been deposited in these pits. Only a few small sherds of Nottingham ware were found in the excavation of two of these pits. These data imply that the majority of the ceramic refuse was not discarded during the siege.

TABLE 3.4
Archeological Evaluation of Ceramic Refuse

Time	Activity	Archeological implications	Test results and comments	Conclusions
Prior to battle	Culinary	Broken dishes	Broken dishes were recovered.	Most probable
	Policing area	Removal of refuse to secondary locations outside stockade	A variety of small sherds seldom fitting together were found.	Most probable
During battle	Culinary	Broken dishes	Broken dishes were recovered.	
	Policing area	Removal of refuse to secondary locations near stockade	Only a few small sherds were found in the fort ditch or in the pits used during the battle.	Improbable
After battle	Destruction	Broken whole vessels	No vessels or large fragments of vessels were recovered.	Improbable
	Looting	No de facto ceramic refuse	No whole vessels were found.	Probable

After the siege the Americans took over the fort. Activities would have included destruction and looting. Destruction would probably have left large portions of vessels—none were found. On the other hand, looting would have eliminated any de facto ceramic refuse. Since obvious de facto refuse was not found we must expect that perhaps looting did take place.

Thus, the archeological evidence implies that the sherds excavated at Fort Watson represent primary refuse from which larger sherds and fragments of vessels had been selected for deposition as secondary refuse. Failure to find any secondary refuse in the known secondary-refuse deposits used during the battle indicates that these sherds most probably represent fragments of vessels discarded prior to the siege.

One of the most striking facts revealed by the distributional maps (Figures 3.3–3.5) is that ceramics correlate well with incidental personal items. All these items are small. Many of them, such as pipestems, lead toys, and broken items, were probably discarded as primary refuse. Other items, such as a coin and buttons, were probably lost. Together all these items suggest that the area was an activity area prior to the battle, and the teaware suggests it was a location of social activity. Thus, we are able to see the mound summit prior to the battle as being a place where activity involving eating, taking tea, and smoking may have taken place. All these activities may also have taken place away from the stockade, but there is not as much evidence for the taking of tea outside as in the interior. If we accept this interpretation of the distribution of ceramics then the implications can be narrowed to three:

1. The distribution is related to some socioeconomic factor.
2. The distribution is related to a functional factor.
3. The distribution may be related to a combination of (1) and (2).

Since military groups are strictly stratified, a socioeconomic explanation of the distribution is appealing. The greatest difference would have been between officers and enlisted men, and it is tempting to assume that the difference was that the officers were in possession of teaware and heavyware while the noncommissioned soldiers had only heavyware. However, the historic data suggest that in field situations officers were probably the only people in possession of any ceramics. For the enlisted men of the Continental Army, Peterson (1968:150) mentions wooden trenchers; pewter spoons, knives, and forks; and horn cups as having been the primary personal items of culinary ware. With respect to the horn cups, Peterson has pointed out that they were "much less fragile than the costlier ceramic drinking vessels." Also,

> Higher ranking officers fared much better. Washington for instance, carried an elaborate mess chest with him in the field. Compactly designed,

> it included four kettles with detachable wooden handles, a folding grill, eight bottles for spirits, six pewter plates and three platters, containers for seasonings, two knives and four forks, and two tinder boxes [Peterson 1968:150].

In addition to this general information, we know that the officers at Fort Watson were able to acquire special items during their field duty. In a March 1781 letter to a Georgetown merchant, Colonel Watson related,

> The officers would be extremely obliged if you could send them an intelligent man who would inform them of the proper people to send to, to get those little supplies all troops must want who have been in the field for three months, such as wine, &c., &c. [Gibbes 1853:47].

Thus, we are aware of Watson's officers purchasing gentlemanly furnishings. In addition to the wine mentioned in the letter these officers would probably have been ordering tea services, dishes, bottles of gin or scotch and other "necessities" of a gentleman.

If the officers were the only people on the site with ceramics, and this seems to be a good assumption, then the difference probably reflects either a socioeconomic or a functional aspect of the officer's activities. The data suggest that eating took place in both areas but that in one area, the stockade on the mound, taking tea also took place. If the difference is socioeconomic then I would think that the tea taking area was more probably the activity area of the senior officers rather than the junior officers. However, this hypothesis does not seem to be testable with the available data.

Functional factors responsible for the distribution might include differences in food preparation, eating, tea drinking, or disposal patterns. These possibilities may be tested through a more complete study of the remaining artifacts as well as further excavation recovering hearths, pits, and other features. To complicate matters further, a combination of functional factors with socioeconomic factors may well be present. Presently, the data do not seem to be available to separate these factors if they are combined.

Beyond the distributional data collected for the stockaded and nonstockaded areas, specialized distributions were found within the stockade. Materials of all types seem to be concentrated in the eastern and northeastern portion of this area, and they seem to have a distribution that generally follows the interior fortification ditch. The area near the northeastern corner of the ditch has the heaviest concentration of artifacts of any location within the stockade. Here we found concentrations of ceramics as well as personal items, gun parts, nails, and postholes. The nails and the postholes suggest a structure in this vicinity. The most obvious differential distribution on the summit of the mound is again between teaware and heavyware. Heavyware has a wide distribution in the northwestern corner and another smaller distribution in the northeastern corner of the stockade (Figure 3.6). Teaware, on the other hand, is most strongly concentrated in the eastern to northeastern section of the stockade (Figure 3.7). These ceramic data together with the data from other artifacts suggest that the eastern and northeastern portions of the stockade were a general living area, whereas the northwestern quadrant of the stockade seems to have been primarily associated with either eating or preparing food.

LEAD BALLS AND COMBAT

In the process of analysis and interpretation of the archeological materials, ceramics proved an important key to understanding a portion of the activity in the fort prior to the battle. Not surprisingly, the lead balls frequently found during the excavations seem to have held the key to a better understanding of the battle. These lead balls were measured

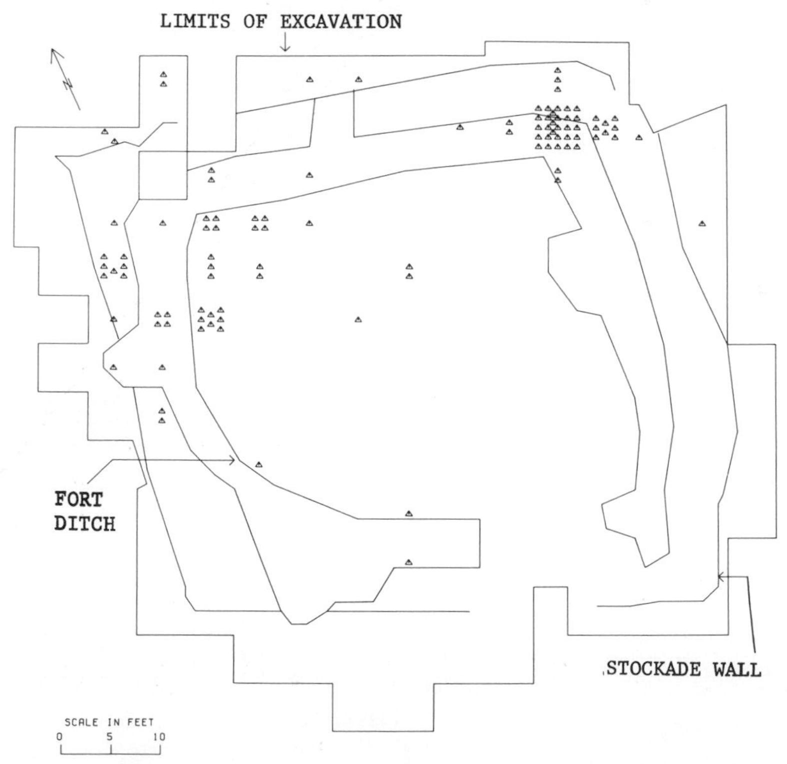

Figure 3.6. Distribution of heavyware, mound summit, Fort Watson (38 CR1). Δ = 1 sherd.

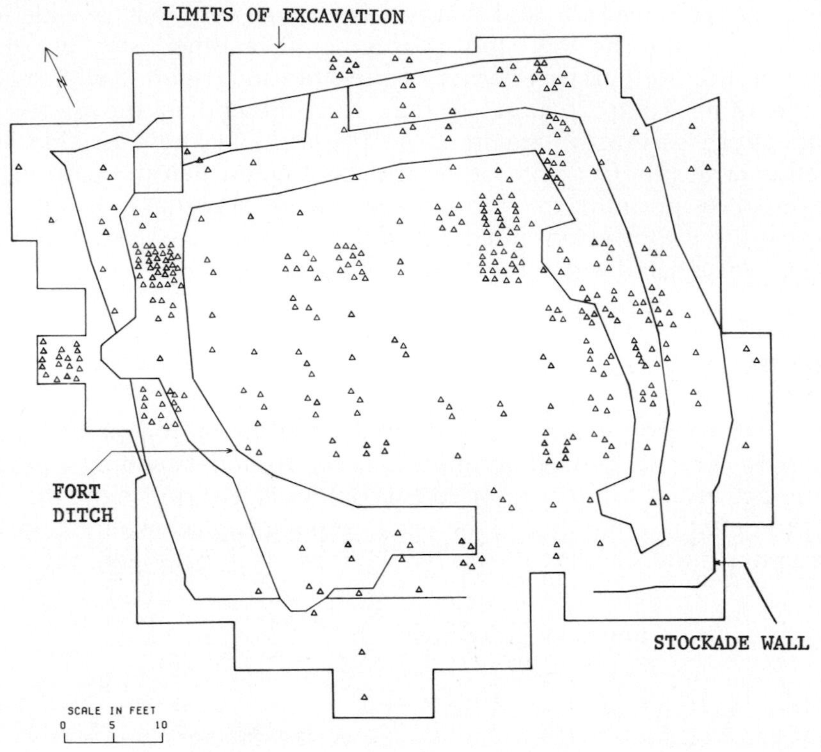

Figure 3.7. Distribution of teaware, mound summit, Fort Watson (38 CR1). Δ = 1 sherd.

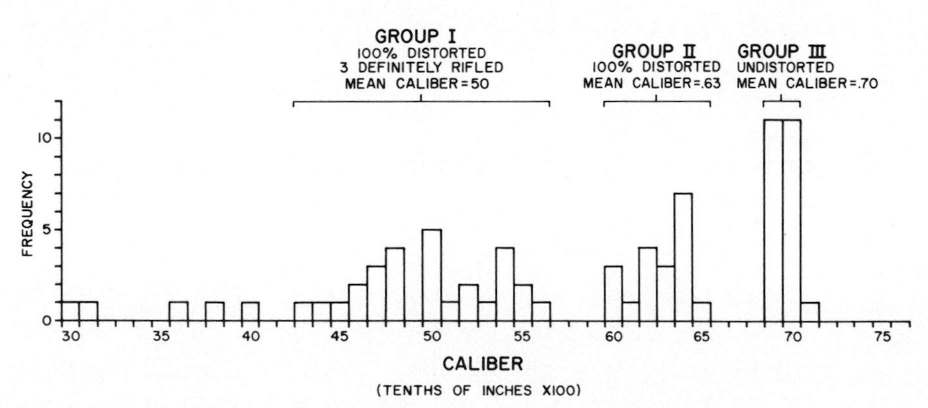

Figure 3.8. Distribution of lead balls, mound summit, Fort Watson.

to determine caliber (computed by weight for distorted balls). Graphic representation of these measurements (Figure 3.8) produced three distinct groups with a few small extraneous items representing "swan shot" or perhaps fragments of larger balls broken on impact. All the specimens from Groups I and II were distorted as a result of impact. Group I has a .50 caliber mean with a range from .43 to .56 caliber, and Group II has a mean caliber of .63 and a range from .60 to .66. Specimens from Group III are all undistorted. They have a mean caliber of .70 and a smaller variation from the mean than the other groups, ranging from .69 to .71 caliber. The obvious differences of Group III from Groups I and II combined with historical sources identifying the fort as British lead to the postulation that the first two groups were fired by the attacking Americans and that the third, undistorted group was left by the British defenders.

Association of the undistorted balls with the British is supported by the statistics for British ordnance. The bore size of the Brown Bess musket carried by most Royal troops was approximately .75 (Peterson 1956:165; 1968:68), and the ball size was much smaller, at about .69 (Peterson 1968:60) or .70 caliber (Greener 1858:344). South (1974:206) points out that the difference between bore and ball size indicates a wide windage tolerance for these muskets. The mean caliber of .70 with a very small variation implies that all these archeologically recovered balls were ammunition designed for use in a British Brown Bess musket of approximately .75 caliber. Thus, ordnance statistics support the historical documentation and the archeological information leaving little doubt that these undistorted balls are those deposited by the British soldiers at Fort Watson.

Once established that the undistorted balls are British, the second major question concerns the means by which they were deposited in the archeological context. All the balls are in finished form with all traces of flash removed, and there are no obvious flaws in the balls. Thus, they appear to have been deposited in good, serviceable condition. This observation leads to the conclusion that the balls were lost rather than discarded. If this conclusion of loss is correct, then these balls represent a special kind of cultural formation process and should be interpreted in light of this process (Schiffer, this volume).

The systemic process of loss is one of the most important factors responsible for the archeological record, yet it is a factor that is difficult to deal with in comparison to the process of discard. Discarding is directly related to the refuse outputs and disposal mechanisms of the specific activity responsible for creating the archeological materials, for example, the chips resulting from chopping a log in half or from making an arrowhead. Furthermore, if the material discarded is left at the locus of the activity in the form of *primary refuse* the spatial pattern of the artifacts is usually quite closely related to the activity being performed. Loss, on the other hand, is not usually so directly related to the activities performed with the artifact. Since it is an unintentional process, the loss of a valued object has more "random noise" about it than does discard. And since loss is a chance process, it may often be related to unusual variables. For instance, tripping over the same root may have caused several soldiers to stumble and drop musket balls at the same place; however, there is only slight systemic relationship between the location of this root and the deposition of musket balls in the archeological record. Quite clearly, any analysis of items deposited in the archeological record through the process of loss must proceed with caution.

In evaluating loss in the present archeological situation, time is one of the most fundamental considerations. The undistorted musket balls of Group III could have been lost before, during, or after the battle. Obviously, time of loss could be important in an interpretation of the battle. Of the three time periods, the historical and archeological evidence suggest that during the battle is the most probable time of loss (Table 3.5). The battle was a time of stress as well as a time of intense involvement with arms. Both factors seem likely to have increased the probability of loss. Loss prior to the battle is contrary to independent archeological interpretation of the domestic materials found in the stockade. Previous analyses suggest the mound summit to have been officers' quarters prior to the battle, leading to the assumption that activities involving ordinary musketry would probably have taken place elsewhere. After the battle the fort was "destroyed" and abandoned, so it is unlikely that the balls were lost then. Thus, although musket balls could have been deposited in the stockade at any time it seems most likely that the majority were lost during the battle.

The functional association of musket balls with other items of ordnance suggests that the lost balls should be associated with other items used in combat. Examination of Figure 3.9, which shows the distribution of all artifacts identified as ordnance, suggests an association between musket balls and these other related artifacts. Fisher's exact test (Siegel 1956) calculated for both the northern and southern halves of the stockade and the eastern and western halves indicates that there is no significant difference at this gross spatial level between the distribution of undistorted musket balls and all other forms of ordnance (Table 3.6).

A closer examination of Figure 3.9 shows that there is a similarity between the distribution of musket balls and the distribution of lead flash. Both items cluster on the eastern side of the stockade. A portion of the musket balls were probably lost in the process of manufacturing; or, alternatively, perhaps some flash was packed with ammunition and this flash was deposited when ammunition packages were opened.

TABLE 3.5

Archeological Evaluation of Loss Process for .70 Caliber Musket Balls

Time	Activity	Archeological Implications	Test results and comments	Conclusions
Prior to battle	Production of balls	Associated with lead flash or sprue	Inspection revealed only slight association (Figure 3.9).	Slight probability
	General activities	Associated with other loss items of similar size	Inspection revealed only slight association.	Slight probability
	Unknown	Look for unsuspected associations.		
During battle	Production of balls	Associated with lead flash or sprue	Inspection revealed only slight association (Figure 3.9).	Most probable
	Fighting	Associated with lost or discarded ordnance	Fisher's exact test showed no significant difference for northern and southern, eastern and western halves of the fort.	Most probable
	General activities	Associated with other loss items of similar size	Inspection revealed only slight association.	Probable
	Unknown	Look for unsuspected associations.		
After battle	General activities	Associated with loss items of similar size (perhaps American)	Inspection revealed only slight association.	Least probable
	Unknown	Look for unsuspected associations	Only one identifiable American artifact was found.	

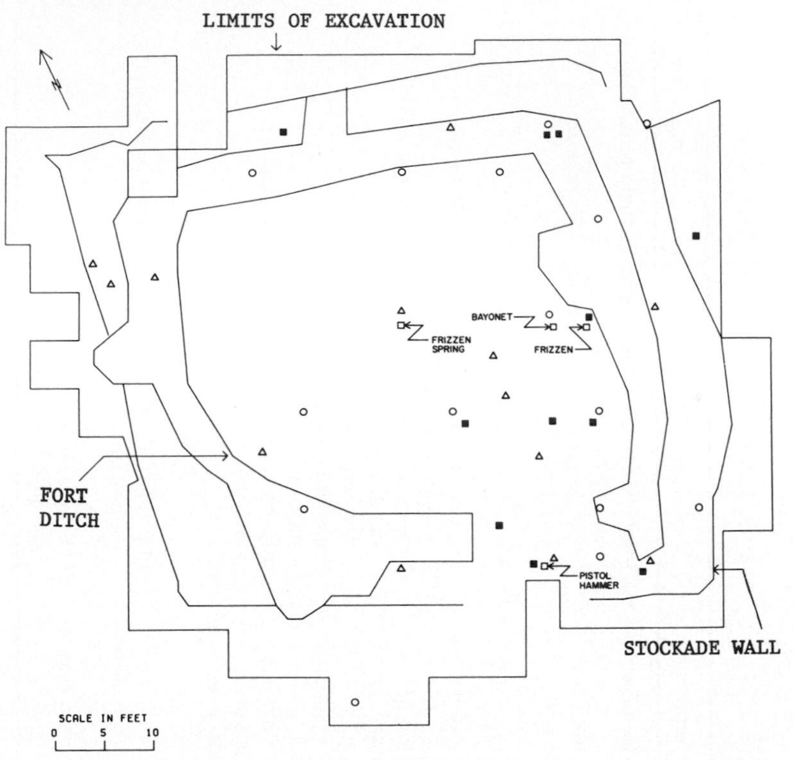

Figure 3.9. British ordnance, mound summit, Fort Watson (38 CR1). △ = gunflints; ○ = musket ball (undistorted); ■ = lead sprue; □ = other.

In his consideration of the processes leading to the formation of the archeological record, Schiffer (1975) has constructed a number of lawlike statements. For the process of loss, he suggests that the probability of loss will vary inversely with an object's mass, all other variables held constant. In addition to the undistorted musket balls on the mound summit, there were numerous other objects that were apparently lost (Figure 3.5). Most of these are small, incidental personal items such as buttons, buckles, a coin, etc., and most are about the size of a musket ball. Since these items are suspected to have been deposited in the archeological record by the process of loss just as the musket balls were, the possibility of their association with musket balls should be considered. Comparison (Figures 3.5, 3.9) reveals little probability of direct association. Musket balls are evenly distributed between the northeastern and southeastern quadrants, whereas incidental personal items cluster in the northeastern quadrant (Table 3.7). This lack of association of musket balls with incidental personal items is probably related to two factors. First, some of

TABLE 3.6

Comparison of Group III Lead Balls with All Other Ordnance

Area of stockade	Lead balls	Other ordnance	Total ordnance
Northern/southern halves of stockade (divided at N55)[a]			
Northern half	6	10	16
Southern half	7	8	15
Totals	13	18	31
Eastern/western halves of stockade (divided at E45)[b]			
Western half	4	10	14
Eastern half	7	10	17
Totals	11	10	31

[a] H_0: There is no significant difference between type of ordnance and area of stockade (N–S). By Fisher's exact probability test, $p = .2498$. Therefore H_0 cannot be rejected.

[b] H_0: There is no significant difference between type of ordnance and area of stockade (W–E). By Fisher's exact probability test, $p = .2498$. Therefore H_0 cannot be rejected.

TABLE 3.7

Comparison of All Ordnance with Incidental Personal Items[a]

Area of stockade	Ordnance	Personal items	Combined
Northern/southern halves of stockade (divided at N55)[b]			
Northern half	O = 16	O = 37	53
	E = 18.055	E = 34.945	
Southern half	O = 15	O = 23	38
	E = 12.945	E = 25.055	
Totals	31	60	91
Eastern/western halves of stockade (divided at E45)[c]			
Western half	O = 11	O = 18	29
	E = 9.879	E = 19.121	
Eastern half	O = 20	O = 42	62
	E = 21.121	E = 40.879	
Totals	31	60	91

[a] O = observed; E = expected.

[b] H_0: There is no association between type of artifact and area of stockade. $\chi^2 = .1856$, $df = 1$, $.707 > p > .50$. Therefore, H_0 cannot be rejected.

[c] H_0: There is no association between type of artifact and area of stockade. $\chi^2 = .055$, $df = 1$, $.90 > p > .80$. Therefore, H_0 cannot be rejected.

the items listed as "incidental personal" may have reached the archeological record by discard rather than by loss. For instance, as mentioned earlier, a good buckle might be discarded because the strap to which it is fastened has broken. Intentional discard of several items in a specific location might conflict with the general pattern of lost items. Second, and most important, lost items were probably deposited at different times while significantly different activities were underway. If, as suggested earlier, the mound summit was used prior to the battle as an officers' quarters, this 4-month period of activity would no doubt produce lost items in patterns possibly quite different from those patterns produced during the pressure of a siege. Thus, a weak relationship between lost musket balls and lost nonordnance artifacts is to be expected from the archeological record of the cultural events that took place on this site.

Results of the evaluation of the loss process inside the stockade lead to the conclusion that the British musket balls were quite probably lost during the battle and that the flash may indicate that balls were being manufactured on the site. Nevertheless, the balls may also have been lost in activities unrelated to the use of balls or to some unsuspected activity, and these should remain reasonable alternative interpretations.

The distorted balls found in the interior of the stockade have been postulated to have been deposited by significantly different means than those depositing the spherical .70 caliber balls. Apparently the Americans fired these balls into the fort during their attack. Evidence of rifling on some of the balls of Group I reinforces the American source since the historical documents mention rifles as part of the weaponry (Gibbes 1853:57; Lee 1812:52).

The deposition of these distorted balls in the stockade is considered to be the product of a significantly different process than the loss of the British balls. The British balls were lost unconsciously in usable condition. The distorted balls, on the other hand, were utilized and discarded at specific points inside the stockade. As such, these artifacts are examples of primary refuse that should relate directly to the activity being performed at the time of deposition, i.e., firing at British soldiers.

Examination of the distribution of the distorted balls (Figure 3.10) indicates that they are concentrated within the southeastern half of the stockade if it is divided along the diagonal. A few isolated balls were located adjacent to the northwestern walls; however, the major portion of the northwestern half of the fort was without distorted lead balls. This distribution of artifacts has direct implications for the placement of the American tower. We know from the documents that the tower was designed to fire into the stockade. Finding balls inside the wall on the southeastern side of the compound and only against the wall on the

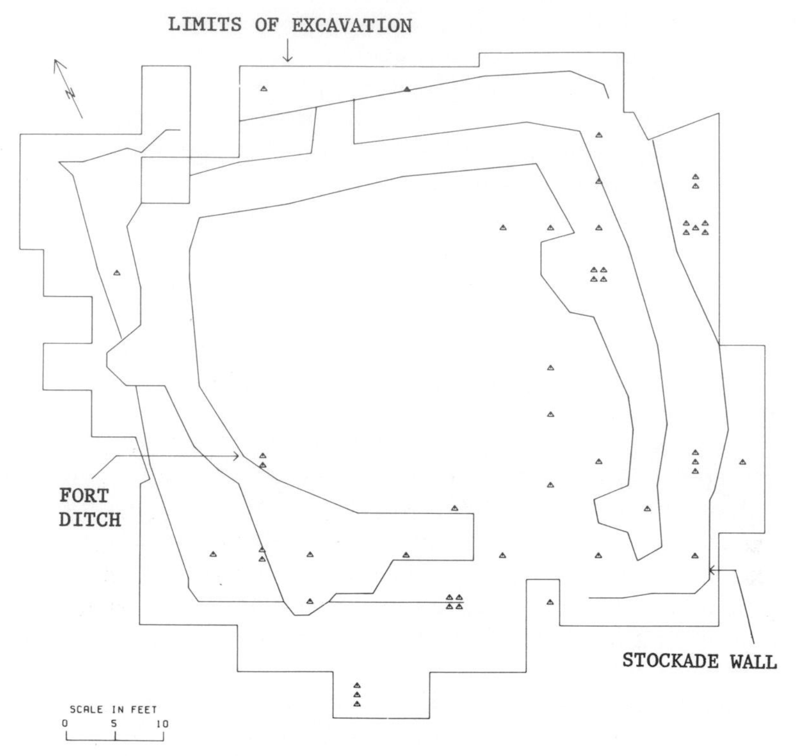

Figure 3.10. Distribution of flattened lead balls, mound summit Fort Watson (38 CR1). Δ= 1 ball.

northwestern side indicates that the American tower was located north or northwest of the mound.

The location of the tower to the north or northwest and associational and superpositional data (Ferguson 1975b) suggest that the two earthen platforms (Figure 3.1) were probably part of the traverse erected by Lieutenant McKay. Thus, from the spatial pattern of this primary refuse the locational details of the historically known assault from the tower and the British defense have been clarified.

The two caliber-groups of distorted balls indicate that there were at least two types of weapons firing from atop the tower into the stockade. However, the range of variation within the two groups of distorted balls is much larger than that of the group of undistorted balls. Perhaps this is to be expected of specimens that have been severely distorted and for which caliber must be computed from specific gravity. Nevertheless, the erratic pattern of caliber in Group I implies that perhaps more than one type of rifle fired these balls. The pattern of Group II is more clustered and may represent only one type of gun.

The caliber of the distorted balls poses an interesting question. Peterson (1968:40) states that the average caliber of rifles used by the Americans during the Revolution ranged from .55 to .60. Allowing for windage, a range of from .43 to .56 caliber for Group I specimens generally fits the American rifle category. On the other hand those specimens from Group II with a range from .60 to .66 caliber better fit the description of a .69 caliber French Charleville musket (Gluckman 1965:40–46; Peterson 1956: 172–173). With allowance for windage these muskets would have used a ball of about .63 (Peterson 1968:60) or .64 caliber (Gluckman 1965:45–48). Yet Lee (1812:52) referred to "riflemen" being positioned in the tower. He does not mention any other type weapon, and it seems logical that riflemen would have been used in this kind of situation.

The inconsistency of ball size and character for Groups I and II require careful consideration. The association of Group II balls with the tower does not seem completely reasonable according to the historical records or logic. Yet, examination of the distribution of Group II balls reveals that they clearly lie within the stockade with the balls of Group I. The conclusion of this consideration is that a musket, perhaps a Charleville musket or a musket styled after the Charleville, was also used in the attack from the tower.

The data concerning distorted lead balls have interesting implications about the relationship between historical and archeological evidence. Lee's statement reflects an obviously expected association between a type of weapon and the activity of firing from a location where the accuracy of a rifle would be highly desirable. Yet, the archeological data tell another story. In short, Lee's cognizant description of the situation is not supported by the empirical evidence. Weighing firsthand evidence against historical description, the weight of interpretation should favor the actual evidence rather than the description of a person who perhaps would not have mentioned a musket even if he had known it to have been used.

Regardless of the kind of gun firing from the top of the tower, the process of deposition is still discarding primary refuse as a result of a specific activity—firing from the top of the tower. Since this activity is completely different from the activity and type of deposition engaged in by the British when they lost the balls of Group III, and since there were different cultural formation processes at work in the deposition of these artifacts, then there should be little correlation of occurrence of these artifacts in small areas. Examination of Figures 3.9 and 3.10 reveals that although the balls of Group III were found all over the interior of the fort, distorted balls were recovered only from the southern and eastern halves of the fort and along the stockade wall. This difference reflects

Figure 3.11. The American attack on Fort Watson. Archeological evidence indicates a two-pronged attack from the northwest and the southeast.

the variable pattern created by loss as opposed to the discard of primary refuse.

THE BATTLE

Since the location of the tower has been generally specified by an examination of the archeological record, we can proceed with an analysis of the tactics used to force the garrison to surrender. It is known from the historical documents that there was a precedent for an original American attack from the south—an attack designed to cut the British off from their water supply. With the American tower to the north, a southern attack in the final assault would have been a logical tactic. From their vantage point in the tower American marksmen would have been able to cover the southern interior of the fort, making it practically impossible for the British to protect their southern exposure. With little opposition the Americans could then tear away the abatis and attack the gate of the fort (Figure 3.11). Under such conditions the British surrendered.

SUMMARY AND CONCLUSIONS

Exploratory excavation was begun at Fort Watson with two primary factors concerning the historical material in mind. A review of the historical documents indicated that the British occupation of Fort Watson was probably the only significant historic component and that the site had not been significantly disturbed since the embarrassingly abrupt abandonment by the British. The first step in excavation and analysis was to test these initial suggestions through archeology.

Excavation immediately indicated that the suggestion of a lack of disturbance was correct. In most cases British features were found at the base of the topsoil, and the only place the site had been significantly disturbed was along the shore of Lake Marion. Testing the purity of the eighteenth century component was the next step. This was done through an analysis of the type and temporal placement of artifacts found on the site. Ceramics as well as many other artifacts were important in this testing.

Ceramic analysis suggested that either the site was not a single component or that the compiled data used to evaluate the temporal position were wrong. One kind of pearlware popular on the site was given an initial occurrence date of 1790 on South's Mean Ceramic Date Formula chart. A reexamination of the information from the site indicated that this material was spatially associated with Revolutionary War period artifacts. This associational data, together with the documentation, was used to reevaluate the temporal position of this pearlware. On the basis of information from Fort Watson, the date for the initial appearance of this ceramic type (annular pearlware) in America can be pushed back from 1790 to 1780.

After the temporal and spatial characteristics of the artifacts were under control, the next step was to develop hypotheses that could be tested in order to increase understanding of the activities that took place at Fort Watson. One of the most interesting factors from the point of view of methodology is that South's Mean Ceramic Date Formula generated a hypothesis that has socioeconomic and/or functional implications. On the basis of the initial hypothesis, typological and formal distribution studies were performed. These examinations indicated significant differences in the distribution of the type and form of ceramics for the stockaded and nonstockaded proveniences as well as for proveniences within the stockade. These differences prompted a refinement of hypotheses concerning activities that will be tested through the use of recovered artifacts as well as further excavation.

In reviewing the analysis of ceramics from this site, we can say that so far they have contributed three primary units of information:

1. Studies have refined our knowledge of the temporal placement of annular pearlware.
2. Differences in the distribution have outlined different areas of activity on the site.
3. The ceramics together with historical information on value and

function have enabled us to make some hypotheses concerning the structure of activities within a field camp of the British army.

Analysis of the lead balls found during the excavation together with the accounts of the battle and ideas about the different processes of deposition of the balls have contributed to a better understanding of the battle. We can state, in conclusion, the following:

1. While occupying the fort the British soldiers dropped balls designed for use in the Brown Bess musket. The distribution of these balls is similar to the distribution of other forms of ordnance refuse left by the British. However, the distribution of these balls is not similar to that of nonordnance lost refuse.
2. Distorted lead balls fired into the fort by the Americans came from at least two types of weapons, a rifle and perhaps a musket. The latter weapon was not mentioned in the historical accounts.
3. The distorted lead balls are primary refuse representing discards from a particular activity. Through analysis of this refuse the location of the firing tower used by the Americans was determined.
4. Combining archeological data with historical information, we may conclude that the American ground assault was most probably directed toward the southern portion of the fort in the vicinity of the gate. The tactic was apparently for ground troops to attack from the south under cover from marksmen in the tower.

The success of this interpretation of a small fort and battle in South Carolina in the year 1781 may be measured in two important ways—one historical, the other methodological. If this interpretation survives criticism of the analysis as well as new information in the form of historical documents or subsequent archeological investigation, the success will be measured by the recovery of human activity that has been glossed over by the writers and rewriters of the historical record. The battle of Fort Watson is important in the traditional structure of history as an element in the recovery of South Carolina by the Americans. Yet, it is also important because human beings lived and died there. Archeological–historical analysis helps us retrieve the story of this activity from obscurity and place it into our knowledge of the past. Once known, this information may be considered singularly or it may be used in conjunction with other information to help us understand the patterns of human behavior.

At this stage of archeological development the methodological measure of success is perhaps as important as the historical success. This measure is important because it reflects the developing ability of archeology to take a group of "things" left over from an activity that occurred in the past and wrench information that includes, but extends beyond, the simple form and function of the artifact. The cultural formation processes defined by Schiffer and modified by South are models that explicitly define the timeless processes by which people deposit things in the archeological record. In the present analysis the explicit recognition of artifacts as primary, secondary, and de facto refuse suggested different kinds of consideration for the different artifacts. Through these means, statements concerning the British occupation as well as the American attack were made. Thus, the success of this interpretation shall measure the success of the models of cultural formation processes.

The application of the formation process models in archeological analysis together with subsequent reinforcement and/or their modification should significantly improve our ability to interpret past behavior from the pattern of discarded, lost, and abandoned material things. In the present analysis, the model and the modification seem to have proved their usefulness.

REFERENCES

Ferguson, Leland G.

1973 Exploratory archeology at the Scott's Lake site (38CR1) Santee Indian Mound—Fort Watson, Summer 1972. *Research Manuscript Series* No. **36**. Institute of Archeology and Anthropology, Univ. of South Carolina, Columbia.

1975a Analysis of ceramic materials from Fort Watson, December 1780–April 1781. *The Conference on Historic Site Archeology Papers 1973* **8**(1):2–28. Institute of Archeology and Anthropology, Univ. of South Carolina, Columbia.

1975b Archeology at Scott's Lake, exploratory research 1972, 1973. *Research Manuscript Series* **68**. Institute of Archeology and Anthropology, Univ. of South Carolina, Columbia.

Gibbes, R. W.

1853 *Documentary history of the American Revolution, 1781–1782.* Columbia: Banner Steam-Power Press. South Carolina.

Gluckman, Arcadi

1965 *Identifying old U.S. muskets, rifles, and carbines.* Harrisburg, Pennsylvania: Stackpole.

Godden, Geoffrey A.

1966 *Illustrated encyclopedia of British pottery and porcelain.* New York: Bonzana Books.

Greener, William

1858 *Gunnery in 1858.* London: Smith, Elder.

Johnson, William

1822 *Sketches of the life and correspondence of Nathanael Greene,* Vol. II. Charleston, South Carolina A. E. Miller.

Lee, Henry

1812 *Memoirs of the war in the Southern Department of the United States.* New York: Bradford and Inskeep.

McKay, James
n.d. The journal of the blockade at Scott's Lake, Lt. Colonel Balfour to Sir Henry Clinton, May 6, 1781. The British Headquarters Papers, the *Carleton Papers*. On file at the South Carolina Department of Archives and History.

Noël Hume, Ivor
1969 Pearlware: Forgotten milestone of English ceramic history. *Antiquities* **95**:390–397.
1970 *A guide to artifacts of Colonial America*. New York: Knopf.

Peterson, Harold L.
1956 *Arms and armor in Colonial America 1526–1783*. New York: Bramhall House.
1968 *The book of the Continential soldier*. Harrisburg, Pennsylvania: Stackpole Books.

Schiffer, Michael B.
1972 Archaeological context and systemic context. *American Antiquity* **37**(2) 156–165.
1975 Cultural formation processes of the archeological record: A general formulation. Paper presented at the Eighth Annual Meeting of the Society for Historical Archeology, Charleston, South Carolina.

Siegel, Sidney
1956 *Nonparametric statistics for the behavioral sciences*. New York: McGraw-Hill.

South Stanley
1971 A comment on alkaline glazed stoneware. *The Conference on Historic Site Archaeology Papers 1970* **5**(2):171–185.
1972 Evolution and horizon as revealed in ceramic analysis in historical archaeology. *The Conference on Historic Site Archaeology Papers 1971* **6**(2):71–116.
1974 Palmetto parapets. *Anthropological Studies* No. 1. Institute of Archeology and Anthropology, Univ. of South Carolina, Columbia.
1975 Deriving data on culture process: Evolution, chronology, and human behavior through historical archeology. Paper presented at the Eighth Annual Meeting of the Society of Historical Archaeology, Charleston.
1977 *Method and theory in historical archeology*. New York: Academic Press.

Watson, John W. T.
n.d. Letter to Sir Henry Clinton. On file at the W. L. Clements Library, Univ. of Michigan, Ann Arbor and the Institute of Archeology and Anthropology, Univ. of South Carolina, Columbia.

Archeological Variability—Sociocultural Variability

RICHARD F. CARRILLO

The Piedmont area of South Carolina was settled primarily by people of both British and German cultural traditions (Meriwether 1940). During 1974, excavations at the sites of two houses built and occupied by representatives of these two traditions (Wilkins *et al.* 1975; Carrillo 1976) were undertaken by the Institute of Archeology and Anthropology at the University of South Carolina.

The artifactual data used in this chapter were obtained during excavations undertaken at the two sites: the Bratton House (Figure 4.1), a log structure built ca. 1774–1780 by an individual whose cultural tradition was British; and the Howser House, a stone house built ca. 1803 by an individual of German cultural tradition (Figure 4.2). Although the archeology was undertaken to define architectural details for restoration of the structures, the excavations were seen as an opportunity to define pattern variation within the archeological data possibly reflecting sociocultural differences.

RESEARCH DESIGN

The objectives of this study can best be expressed in the form of the following hypotheses:

1. Systematically controlled excavations at the Bratton and Howser houses should reveal, through quantitative analysis, archeological variability reflecting specific behavioral activities.
2. General refuse disposal patterns in contrasting sociocultural systems (i.e., British colonial and German American) should be

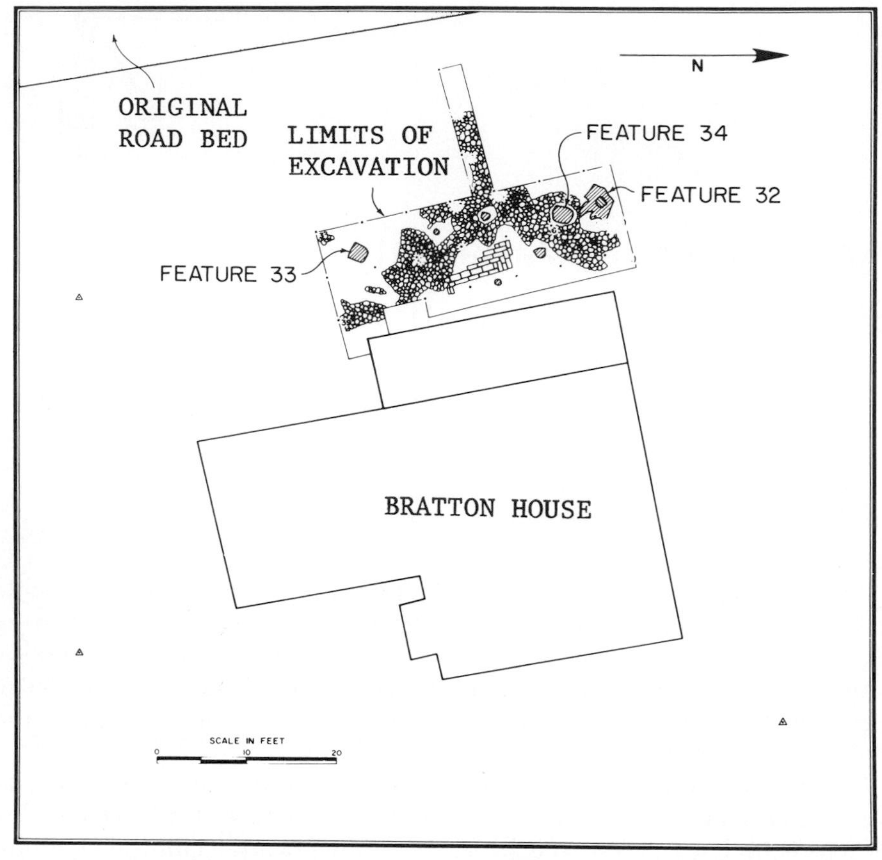

Figure 4.1. Brattonsville excavation map (38YK21). [stone pavement symbol] = stone pavement; [brick symbol] = brick.

revealed in contrasting artifact relationships at the Bratton and Hoswer houses.

3. Historical documentation and archeological evidence suggest that in the British colonial system refuse will be consistently discarded adjacent to the structure (Bratton House), whereas in the German American system (Howser House) there would be little if any systematic discard of refuse adjacent to the structure (Binford 1962:217–225; Fries 1922–1954; Glassie 1973:329; South 1967, 1972a, 1977). Therefore, a greater association among artifact classes is expected to occur at the Bratton House than at the Howser House as a result of sociocultural differences.

Archeologists (Reid *et al.* 1974; Schiffer 1972; Schiffer and Rathje 1973; Schiffer, this volume) have begun to urge the examination of the archeological record with the goal of determining the behavior responsible for producing that record. The archeological record represents a static—and seemingly ambiguous—directly observable by-product of a

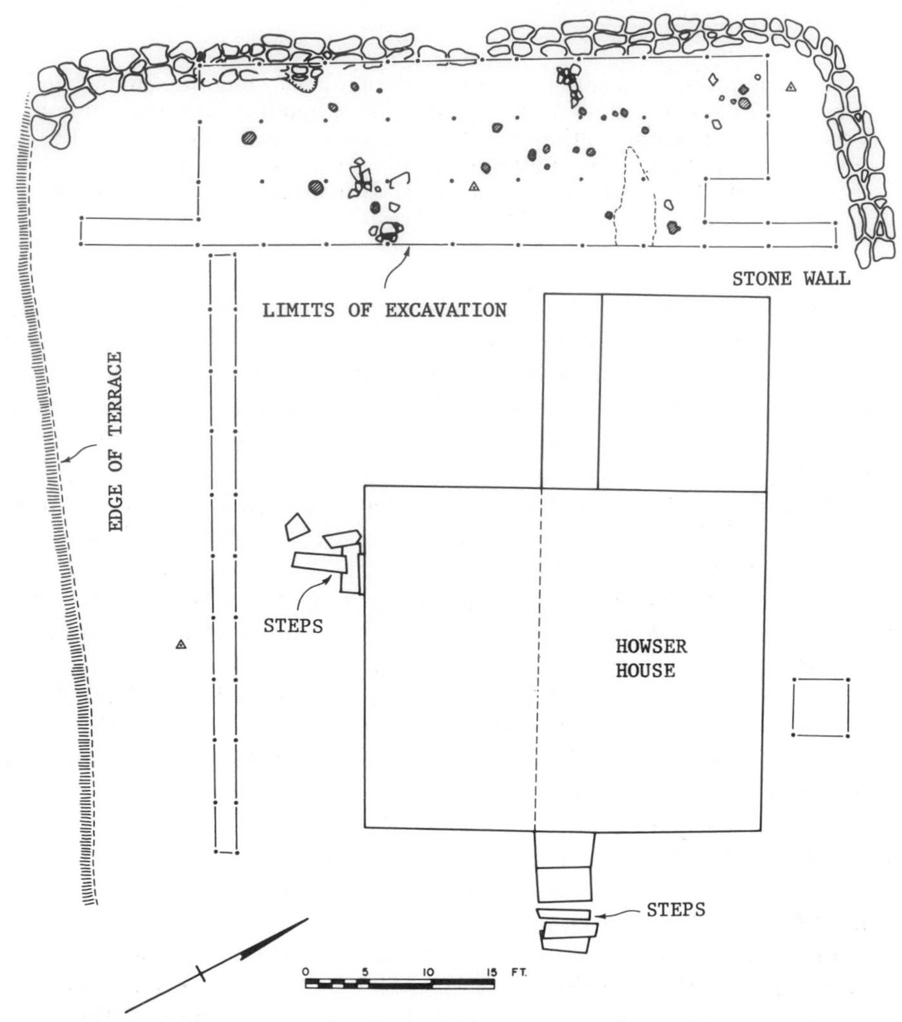

Figure 4.2. Howser House excavation map (38CK3) at King's Mountain National Military Park. ⬭ = stone; ⬬ = miscellaneous shallow depressions.

cultural system. Cultural and noncultural formation processes affecting this record must also be considered (Binford 1975:251; Fritz 1972:135–157; Reid *et al.* 1975:209–224).

In 1962, Lewis Binford stated that

> artifacts having their primary functional context in different operational sub-systems of the total cultural system will exhibit differences and similarities differently, in terms of the structure of the cultural system of which they were a part. Further . . . the temporal and spatial spans within and between broad functional categories will vary with the structure of the systematic relationships between socio-cultural systems [1962:218].

He went on to add,

> We cannot dig up a social system or ideology . . . , but we can and do excavate the material items which functioned together with these more behavioral elements within the appropriate cultural sub-systems. The formal structure of artifact assemblages together with the between element contextual relationships should and do present a systematic and understandable picture of *the total extinct* cultural system [1962:218–219].

Charles E. Cleland (1970:7–23) indicated that on the basis of obvious differences between the French and British occupants at Fort Michilimackinac in their technological, social, and ideological systems, it was quite logical to assume that the differences exhibited between these systems would have resulted in significant differences in the subsistence patterns.

Within the systems attributable to German American and Anglo-American traditions, obvious differences in architecture have been noted: "Base concepts composed of squares were used to generate . . . Anglo-American typological families, and German American architectural design commences with differently composed base concepts with inevitably distinct results [Glassie 1973:329]."

Archeological excavations conducted at the sites of Bethabara (South 1972a) and Brunswick (South 1977) in North Carolina, eighteenth century German colonial and British colonial towns respectively, revealed a difference in refuse disposal practices. At Brunswick, South found that the residents of structures dated ca. 1725–1776 discarded their refuse adjacent to their homes, at both front and back doors. He has named this phenomenon the *Brunswick Pattern* (South 1977). Excavations undertaken at the Paca House, an eighteenth century structure located in Annapolis, Maryland, also revealed a pattern similar to the Brunswick Pattern (South 1967). At the site of Bethabara, dated 1753–1772, only low densities of artifacts were recovered from areas adjacent to the structures (South 1972a).

The artifact data from the Bratton and Howser houses were examined in order to determine whether specific activities relative to each structure could be delineated, and whether archeological variability related to sociocultural variability could be discovered.

ARCHEOLOGICAL SYNOPSIS

The archeology at the Bratton House was done adjacent to the front porch. Two stratigraphic zones were delineated, surface and subsurface. The surface zone consisted of 2–3 inches of dark brown humus. The subsurface zone was a shallow brown clay soil approximately 3–5 inches in thickness. Artifacts were recovered from both zones. In addition, a feature (32) was found near the northwestern corner of the excavation in Unit 7.

At the Howser House, excavations were made at the back of the structure. Four stratigraphic zones were delineated, surface through Level D. Only Levels B and D will be included here, as they are representative of the earlier occupation, ca. 1803–1817. The house was occupied into the 1930s (Carrillo 1976). Level D consisted of the initial occupation period of the structure overlaying a yellow subsoil. Level C was fill brought in to level the back yard behind a retaining wall. Level B represents the humus that accumulated above the fill and was dated, using ceramics, at 1816.94 (South 1972b).

Artifact Analysis

Four classes of artifacts were used in this analysis: Ceramics, Bottle Glass, Window Glass, and Nails. All these artifacts were recovered in sufficient quantity to make them amenable to statistical examination.

Items in the four classes were assumed to have performed different functions in the systemic context. Ceramics and bottle glass functioned as subsistence-related items, whereas window glass and nails functioned as architecturally related items.

The strategy used was to analyze the spatial distribution and relationships of artifacts throughout the excavated area as follows:

1. Test for artifact class variability between the material recovered from the various zones, in order to determine whether the zones should be treated as homogeneous entities. This was accomplished using a chi-square (χ^2) test, which determines significant associations between two or more variables.
2. The Spearman's Rank Correlation Coefficient test (Seigel 1956:259–260), which indicates the degree to which variables are related (in this case artifact classes), was used to make determinations regarding variability.

Surface and Subsurface Comparison—Bratton House

The chi-square test was conducted to compare the cultural material recovered in the surface zone with that from the subsurface zone (Table 4.1).

In the section that follows, I shall discuss the artifact classes and sets for probable suggestions concerning the formation processes involved in their occurrence in the archeological record. These will be discussed in

TABLE 4.1
Artifact Frequencies from Various Proveniences[a]

Artifact class	Frequency	Percentage
	Surface zone	
Ceramics	1	.4
Bottle Glass	131	46.0
Nails	15	5.2
Window Glass	138	48.4
Totals	285	100.0
	Subsurface zone less Feature 32	
Ceramics	42	24.1
Bottle Glass	21	12.1
Nails	55	31.6
Window Glass	56	32.2
Totals	174	100.0
	Feature 32	
Ceramics	8	7.1
Bottle Glass	11	9.7
Nails	26	23.0
Window Glass	68	60.2
Totals	113	100.0

[a] A difference was indicated between the two zones (χ^2 = 161.54, $df = 3$, $p < .001$).

terms of two types of refuse deposits thought to be responsible for the formation of the archeological record as defined by Schiffer (1972:161). *Primary refuse* is defined as refuse discarded at its place of use; e.g., activities associated with blacksmithing. *Secondary refuse* consists of refuse discarded at a place apart from the location of use, e.g., subsistence items such as bottle fragments found in a dump.

SUBSISTENCE ITEMS

A single sherd of whiteware was found in the surface zone. The subsurface zone produced an assortment of 16 different styles of dinnerware, each represented by only a few sherds (Figure 4.3). The mean ceramic date for the ceramics was 1825.6. The contrast between the surface and subsurface zone for bottle glass was quite obvious (Figures 4.4 and 4.5). The bottle glass recovered in the surface zone consisted of twentieth century whiskey-bottle-glass fragments. The glass formed clusters created by the breakage of individual bottles. The excavations conducted at Brunswick (South 1977) evidenced a similar phenomenon. South stated that eighteenth century wine-bottle fragments were found in rubble superimposed above a burned layer inside a structure. He indi-

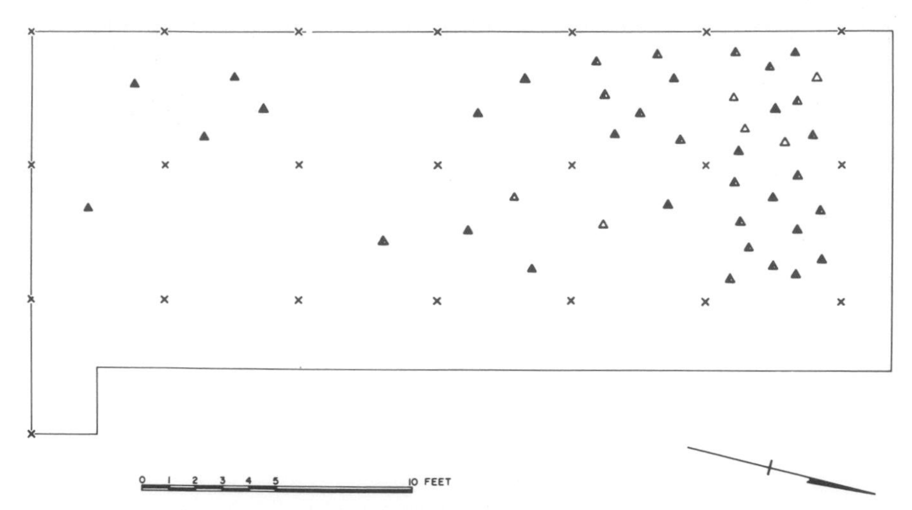

Figure 4.3. Brattonsville subsurface ceramic distribution map. △= creamware fragment; ▲= pearlware fragment.

cated that the ruin was used as a place for disposal of bottles after the structure's destruction. This particular behavior is not uncommon, as is usually found in yards of abandoned houses and in empty lots.

In the subsurface zone, a similar pattern as that encountered with ceramics was revealed. Both are believed to represent secondary depositions in contrast to the bottle glass in the surface zone, which represents primary deposition. Because of the virtual absence of ceramics no tests were conducted between ceramics and bottle glass in the surface zone. The Spearman's Rank Correlation Coefficient test between ceramics and

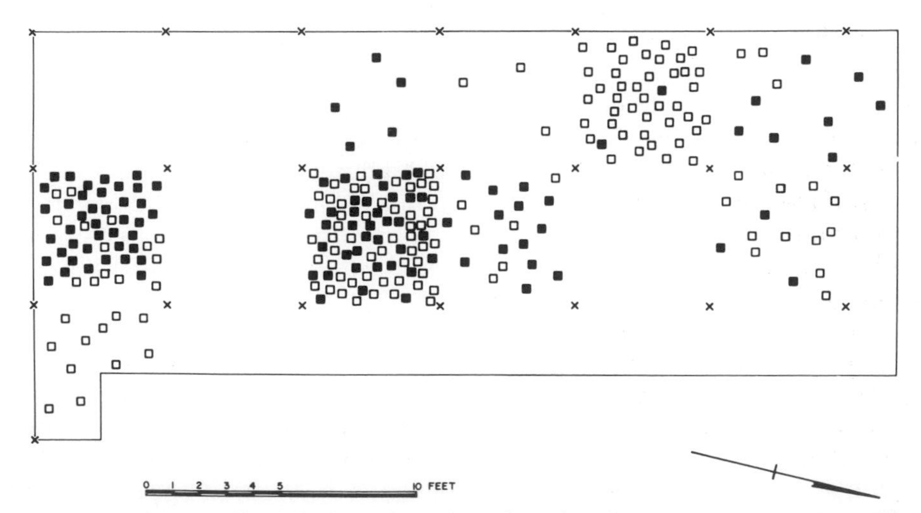

Figure 4.4. Brattonsville surface bottle and window glass distribution map (38YK21). ■= bottle fragment; □= window glass fragment.

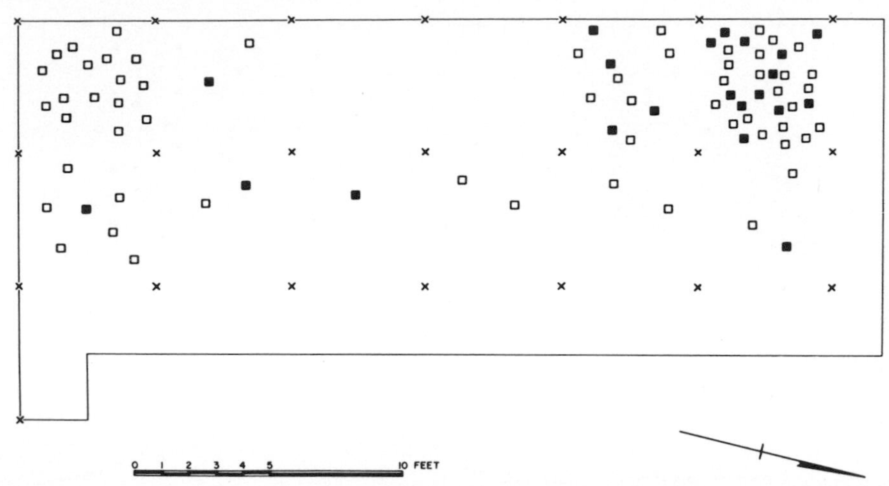

Figure 4.5. Brattonsville subsurface bottle and window glass distribution map (38YK21). ■ = bottle fragment; □= window glass fragment.

bottle glass retrieved from the subsurface zone revealed a positive correlation (r_s = .88, p < .01). This correlation indicates the probability that behaviorally these two classes were being used simultaneously within the systemic context and therefore were being expended accordingly.

ARCHITECTURAL ITEMS

A difference between the architecturally related artifacts was found between the surface and subsurface. In the surface zone window glass comprised 90.2% and nails 9.8%. The subsurface zone yielded 50.5% for window glass and 49.5% for nails (Figures 4.6 and 4.7). From the correlation obtained between these classes for the surface zone (r_s = .02, p > .05), it is possible to infer a difference in their disposal. In other words, the behavioral activity that resulted in the disposal of the window glass was different than that for the nails. The high quantity of window glass in the surface zone may have resulted from breakage of the windows after abandonment of the structure ca. 1955. In contrast, the window glass and nails from the subsurface zone revealed a positive correlation between these classes (r_s = .82, p < .01).

With the exception of two round and three wrought nails, 89% of the nails recovered from the subsurface zone were cut nails. Cut nails were initially introduced ca. 1790. The recovered nails were of the variety produced ca. 1820+ (Noël Hume 1970:253). The historical record indicates that a structure was built in this location between 1774 and 1780, and the entire occupation span encompassed a period of approximately 180 years ending in 1955 (Wilkins *et al.* 1975). Therefore the nails

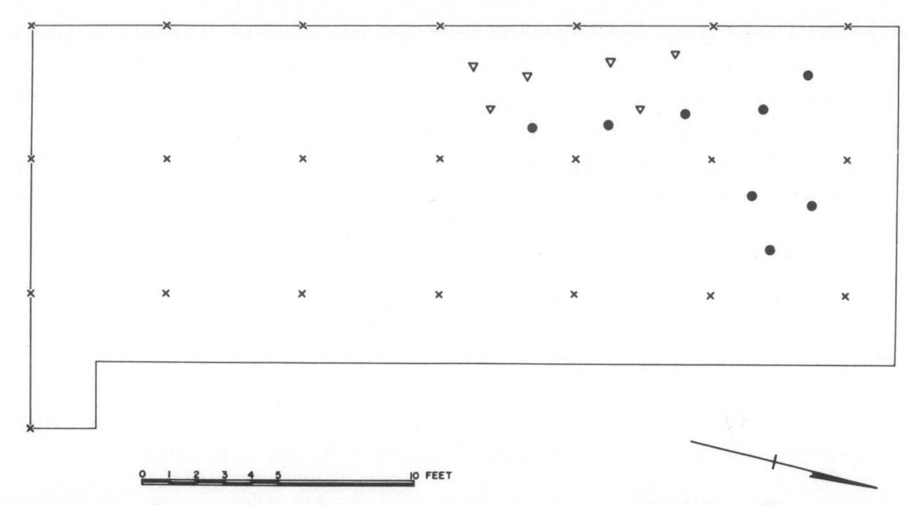

Figure 4.6. Brattonsville surface nail distribution map (38YK21). ▽ = wire nail; ● = cut nail.

recovered were not the type that would have been used in the initial construction. The historical record further indicates that the structure underwent two subsequent renovations between 1820 and 1876. A positive correlation was obtained between ceramics and nails ($r_s = .75$, $p < .01$). The mean ceramic date obtained for the ceramics was 1825.6. The mean ceramic date has been found to approximate closely the median occupation date of a site (South 1972b). The median date for the structure, in this case, was 1865. This date was approximately 40 years later

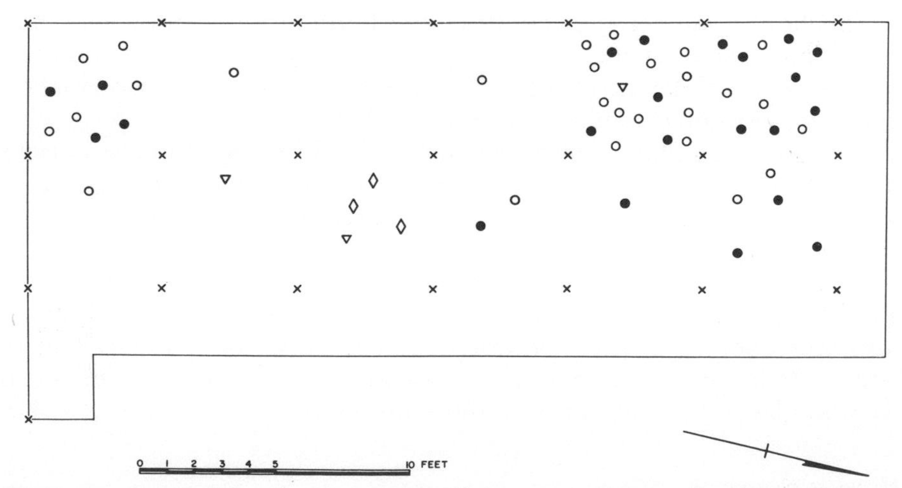

Figure 4.7. Brattonsville subsurface nail distribution map (38YK21). ◊ = wrought nail; ○ = cut nail; ▽ = wire nail.

than the mean date obtained for the ceramic sample. Therefore, using the cut nails dated ca. 1820+ and the mean ceramic date of 1825.6, in addition to the positive correlation obtained between these classes, and between window glass and nails, it appears that the dates reflect a period of intensive special activity, i.e., the renovation that is documented to have taken place between 1820 and 1876. Archeological data suggest, therefore, that the renovation probably took place during the early part of this period.

The renovation activity may also be reflected by the data from Feature 32, a tree-root mold that contained a higher frequency of architecturally related artifacts than subsistence artifacts (Figure 4.1). The chi-square test between the general subsurface material and that found in Feature 32 was $\chi^2 = 26.01$, $df = 3$, $p < .001$, indicative of variability. The following percentage relationships were established for the two samples:

Feature 32	*Subsurface*
Nails (26) 23%	Nails (55) 32%
Window Glass (68) 60%	Window Glass (56) 32%
Ceramics (8) 7%	Ceramics (42) 24%
Bottle Glass (11) 10%	Bottle Glass (21) 12%

The architecturally related artifacts comprised 83% of the sample. The entire subsurface sample also had a higher percentage of architecturally related artifacts (64%).

NONRELATED ARTIFACTS

Although strong associations were found between artifacts assumed to be functionally related (i.e., ceramics and bottle glass; window glass and nails), meaningful associations were not derived in tests conducted between these functional classes. The only exception was the association obtained between ceramics and nails.

The comparison between bottle glass and nails resulted in associations that were not significant (surface: $r_s = -.6$, $p > .05$; subsurface: $r_s = .57$, $p > .05$). Using these associations we can infer that their disposal was a result of separate behavioral processes.

Similar associations were noted in comparing bottle glass and window glass (surface: $r_s = .45$, $p > .05$; subsurface: $r_s = .38$, $p > .05$). Although tests were not conducted between ceramics and the other classes of artifacts found in the surface zone, the association between ceramics and window glass was again similar to those just mentioned ($r_s = .52$, $p > .05$).

Howser House

In contrast to the archeological patterning revealed at the Bratton House, the Howser House (Figure 4.2), constructed ca. 1803, revealed a different pattern. The builder and occupant of the house was a German American (Bearss and Adlerstein 1974). So that comparable samples may be used, the same area at both the Bratton House and the Howser House should, ideally, be excavated. However, erosion at the front of the Howser House made this impossible. Therefore, a different side of the house is used in each case. The problem, however, may not be as serious as it might at first appear. Stanley South (1977) has demonstrated at Brunswick Town, North Carolina, that cultural debris was found throughout the entire adjacent area of the excavated structures. At Bethabara, North Carolina South noted that few artifacts were recovered throughout the excavated adjacent areas (1972). He also demonstrated (1977) that the patterned relationship between artifact classes and groups for the entire area of a ruin sometimes held firm when different areas of the yard were involved, and tended to hold even at the level of the 10-foot square. Therefore, our assumption at the Bratton and Howser houses was that, although different areas in relation to the houses are involved, the artifact relationships would indeed reflect the general refuse disposal pattern at each structure.

The excavations at the Howser House revealed five zones, which were statistically verified (Carrillo 1976). Two of the zones were associated with the original occupants of the structure. In the initial zone, D, only 12 artifacts were recovered throughout the excavated area. Alterations were undertaken between ca. 1803 and 1817, at which time a retaining wall was constructed and the rear area filled and leveled. The cultural material recovered in the zone located above the fill is the subject of this study (Figure 4.8). This zone, designated Level B, was dated 1816.9 using the Mean Ceramic Date Formula (South 1972b). The zones above (surface and Level A) were apparently the result of different formation processes (Carrillo 1976).

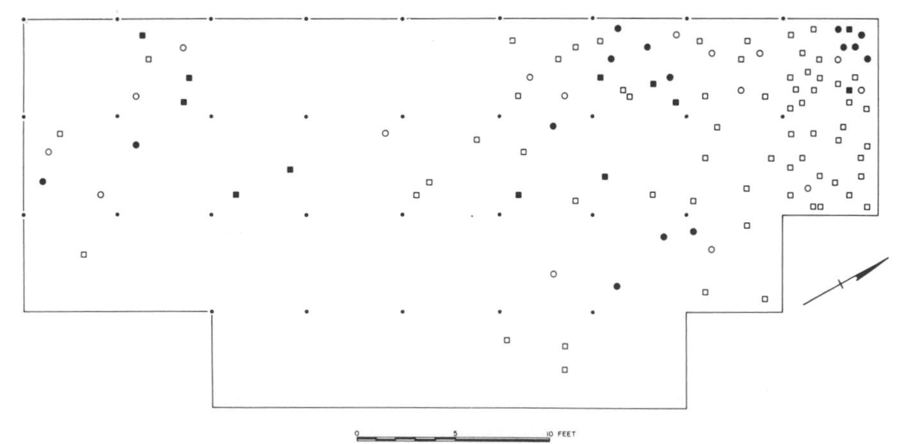

Figure 4.8. General artifact distributions—Howser House, Level B (38CK3). □ = ceramic fragment; ○ = bottle glass fragment; ■ = window glass fragment; ● = nail.

TABLE 4.2
Artifact Correlation Coefficients at the Howser House

Ceramics and Nails	$r_s = -.20, p > .05$
Ceramics and Bottle Glass	$r_s = .20, p > .05$
Ceramics and Window Glass	$r_s = -.18, p > .05$
Nails and Bottle Glass	$r_s = .17, p > .05$
Nails and Window Glass	$r_s = -.01, p > .05$
Bottle Glass and Window Glass	$r_s = .05, p > .05$

The Howser House artifacts were treated in a similar manner as those at the Bratton House. The same four classes were used. The results obtained using the Spearman's Rank Correlation Coefficient test are seen in Table 4.2. The associations between the classes were not significant, suggesting that the artifacts were disposed of in a different manner than at the Bratton House, and that their disposal may have been influenced by accidental loss as well as incidental discard through time resulting in a lack of association. This lack of association is certainly a contrast to the case at the Bratton House.

The artifact class with the highest frequency was ceramics (Table 4.3), a decided contrast with the Bratton House.

DISCUSSION

As stated in the section on research design, an attempt would be made to view artifact data as a system of relationships aimed at defining specific activities relative to the archeological record at the Bratton and Howser houses.

At the Bratton House, variability was demonstrated between the cultural material recovered from the surface and subsurface zones. Statistical tests allowed inferences to be made concerning the probable activity that resulted in their occurrence in the archeological record.

TABLE 4.3
Artifact Frequencies from Level B

Artifact class	Frequency	Percentage
Ceramics	73	62.4
Bottle Glass	17	14.5
Nails	15	12.8
Window Glass	12	10.3
Totals	117	100.0

In the surface zone, the associations between the artifact classes made it possible to infer that the disposal of these artifact classes was different as a result of differing behavior involved in their disposal.

With reference to the cultural material from the subsurface zone, the front area of the Bratton House received cultural debris reflecting a specialized pattern. The artifact frequencies and associations obtained between artifact classes appeared to indicate primarily architecturally related activities. This pattern was found to be particularly strong in Feature 32; architecturally related artifacts comprised 83% of the total sample. A similar pattern was evidenced with the overall subsurface material in that architecturally related artifacts made up 64% of the total sample. The combined total for these artifacts was 74%. Because of the association derived between ceramics and nails the architectural material is thought to represent the by-product of architectural activity resulting from a renovation documented to have taken place sometime between 1820 and 1876.

The fact that a high ratio of architecturally related artifacts was found at the Bratton House is interesting. This finding is in contrast to the high ratio of kitchen-related artifacts found by South (1977) to characterize his Carolina Pattern, a pattern he has derived from sites of the British colonial system. The high architecturally related artifact ratio at the Bratton House may well reflect, as I have suggested, the renovation known to have occurred after 1820. A high architecture-to-kitchen artifact ratio was found by South (1977) to be diagnostic of his Frontier Pattern, composed of military sites and a trading post of the eighteenth century. The explanation of the high ratio of architectural artifacts in the Frontier Pattern and at the Bratton House is uncertain.

At the Howser House the archeological patterning was different. In two defined zones representative of the initial stages of occupation of the structure, the association between similar classes of artifacts found at the Bratton House was not present. In the initial zone, D, only 12 artifacts were recovered. In Level B, tests conducted among the various classes revealed no significant associations.

Based on these results, it appears that the general behavioral activity that contributed to the archeological record at the Howser House was clearly different from that at the Bratton House. From the lack of association of artifact classes at the Howser House we can suggest that a *random disposal* through time is involved, as opposed to a *selective disposal* in areas adjacent to the Bratton House.

Although there was a more random disposal of refuse at the Howser House than at the Bratton House, there was also a far greater ratio of kitchen-related artifacts (ceramics and bottle glass) at the Howser House.

This suggests a closer relationship of the German American Howser House refuse data to the Carolina Pattern of the British colonial system than do the data from the Bratton House. The Bratton House artifact dispersion and associations suggest those found in the Brunswick Pattern (South 1977), whereas the high architecturally related artifact ratio is more compatible with the Frontier Pattern than it is with the Carolina Pattern.

Just what these seemingly contradictory data mean in relation to the data outlined by South (1977) is not certain. What is certain is that fewer artifacts were found at the Howser House, apparently the result of random disposal, than at the Bratton House, and this is in keeping with expectations. The high ratio of kitchen-related artifacts at the Howser House, however, was unexpected, and is, in this respect, more compatible with what is known of a British colonial system. What are needed are firmer data relating to occupations of German American and German colonial structures so that a better understanding of variables can be worked out.

In addition to the interpretations concerning the specific behaviors thought to have been responsible for the creation of the archeological records at the Bratton and Howser houses, a second hypothesis is addressed to the proposition of attempting to define general refuse disposal patterns consistent with specific sociocultural traditions.

Based on the evidence obtained as a result of theoretical postulates (Binford 1962), and archeological, architectural, and historical data (Fries 1922–1954; Glassie 1973; South 1967, 1972, 1977), it seems that the differences in the archeological record at the Bratton and Howser houses may well be attributable to different behavioral patterns in different sociocultural systems, as hypothesized. The activity of discarding refuse close to domiciles has been archeologically demonstrated in excavations of eighteenth century British colonial households (South 1967, 1977). A similar situation occurred at the Bratton House. On the other hand, at the Howser House, no significant associations were found among the artifacts recovered from zones associated with the initial occupants of the structure, and the refuse appeared to be the result of random disposal over a period of time. This in itself suggests that perhaps this is connected to a German American culture pattern of refuse disposal, the lack of artifact association being a strongly suggestive factor. However, there is a strong indication that the Howser House artifact ratios are similar to those of the Carolina Pattern of the British colonial system. The explanation for this might be that by the early nineteenth century in the area of South Carolina where the Howser House is located the influence of the British American system was so dominant as to prevent the recognition of a German American pattern without further control of variables than was possible in this study.

SUMMARY

The dispersion, density, and association of artifact classes within the archeological record were examined for the purpose of discovering the kinds of refuse disposal patterns involved in producing that record. A contrast between such behavioral patterns was found between layers at the Bratton House and those at the Howser House. A second goal was aimed at examining the archeological record in the form of small samples from the yards at two structures having contrasting sociocultural traditions to discover, if possible, resulting contrasts in the archeological record. Such contrast was indeed found in a positive association of artifact classes at the Bratton House and a lack of association at the Howser House. These data are certainly suggestive of sociocultural variability resulting from the different cultural traditions represented at these houses. More studies are needed explicitly defining archeological variability on sites for which there is some documented control over sociocultural variability in order to more firmly establish causal links. The approach I have demonstrated here is merely a first step toward explaining sociocultural variability derived from the variability in the archeological record.

ACKNOWLEDGMENTS

I wish to acknowledge the following individuals, from whom I have benefited greatly in terms of ideas and discussions: Stanley South, whose pioneering work in the field of historical archeology has served as an exemplary model, for his encouragement and criticism; Leland G. Ferguson, whose work at Scott's Lake (this volume) stimulated the idea for viewing the data in the manner presented; Albert C. Goodyear, for his encouragement and for providing statistical assistance; Kennth Lewis and John House, for their assistance in the form of discussions and criticisms from which I benefited greatly; and Robert L. Stephenson, for allowing an atmosphere conducive to conducting meaningful research.

The research project at King's Mountain National Military Park was conducted through a grant provided by the National Park Service, Southeastern Archeological Research Center, Tallahassee, Florida. The archeological project at Brattonsville was funded through a grant obtained through the office of Senator Samuel D. Mendenhall, York County, and the National Park Service, under the provisions of the National Historic Preservation Act, administered through the South Carolina Department of Archives and History. Both projects were carried out through the Institute of Archeology and Anthropology at the University of South Carolina.

REFERENCES

Bearss, Edwin C., and Michael Adlerstein

1974 *Historic structure report, Howser House, historical and architectural data, King's Mountain National Military Park.* Denver: Denver Service Center, National Park Service, U.S. Department of the Interior.

Binford, Lewis R.

1962 Archaeology as anthropology. *American Antiquity* **28**(2):217–225.

1975 Sampling, judgment, and the archaeological record. *Sampling in archaeology,* edited by James W. Mueller. Tucson: Univ. of Arizona Press. Pp. 251–257.

Carrillo, Richard F.

1975 Historical, architectural and archeological research at Battonsville (38YK21), York County, South Carolina. *Research Manuscript Series,* No. **76.** Institute of Archeology and Anthropology, Univ. of South Carolina, Columbia.

1976 The Howser House and the Chronicle grave and mass burial, King's Mountain National Military Park, South Carolina. *Institute of Archeology and Anthropology Research Manuscript Series* 102. Columbia.

Cleland, Charles E.

1970 Comparison of the faunal remains from French and British refuse pits at Fort Michilimackinac: A study in changing subsistence patterns. *Canadian Historic Sites: Occasional Papers in Archaeology and History* No. 3, Ottawa.

Fries, Adelaide L.

1922–1954 *Records of the Moravians in North Carolina.* Vols. 1–8. Raleigh: North Carolina Historical Commission.

Fritz, John M.

1972 Archaeological systems for indirect observation of the past. *Contemporary archaeology,* a guide to theory and contributions, edited by Mark P. Leone. Carbondale: Southern Illinois Press. Pp. 135–157.

Glassie, Henry

1973 Structure and function, folklore and artifact. *Semiotica* **11**(4):313–351.

Meriwether, Robert L.

1940 *The expansion of South Carolina, 1729–1765.* Kingsport, Tennessee: Southern Publishers.

Noël Hume, Ivor

1970 *A guide to artifacts of Colonial America.* New York: Knopf.

Reid, J. Jefferson, William L. Rathje, and Michael B. Schiffer

1974 Expanding archaeology. *American Antiquity* **39**(1):125–126.

Reid, J. Jefferson, Michael B. Schiffer, and Jeffrey M. Neff

1975 Archaeological considerations of intrasite sampling. *Sampling in archaeology,* edited by James Mueller. Tucson: Univ. of Arizona Press. P. 209–224.

Schiffer, Michael B.

1972 Archaeological context and systemic context. *American Antiquity* **37**(2):156–165.

Schiffer, Michael B., and William L. Rathje

1973 The efficient exploitation of the archaeological record: Penetrating problems. *Research and theory in current archaeology,* edited by Charles L. Redman. New York: Wiley. Pp. 169–179.

Seigel, Sidney

1956 *Nonparametric statistics for the behavioral sciences.* New York: McGraw-Hill.

South, Stanley A.

1967 The Paca House, Annapolis, Maryland. Contract Archeology, Inc. Copy on file at the Institute of Archeology and Anthropology, Univ. of South Carolina.

1972a Discovery in Wachovia. Unpublished manuscript on file at the Institute of Archeology and Anthropology, Univ. of South Carolina, Columbia.
1972b Evolution and horizon as revealed in ceramic analysis in historical archeology. *Conference on Historic Site Archaeology Papers, 1971* **6**(2):71–116.
1977 *Method and theory in historical archeology.* New York: Academic Press.
Wilkins, Joseph C., Howell C. Hunter and Richard F. Carrillo
1975 Historical, architectural, and archeological research at Brattonsville (38YK21), York County, South Carolina. *Institute of Archeology and Anthropology Research Manuscript Series* 76. Columbia.

Artifacts and Status Differences— A Comparison of Ceramics from Planter, Overseer, and Slave Sites on an Antebellum Plantation

JOHN SOLOMON OTTO

Although it may be possible to infer "the relative socioeconomic level of a population and define any major status differences which existed at a site by means of the distributional analysis of ceramics [Miller and Stone 1970:100]," this assumption has not yet been tested (Fontana 1968:180; South 1972:100). Stanley South believes that status differences may be reflected more easily in seventeenth century rather than in eighteenth century ceramic assemblages because of the "rapid distribution of ceramic types over a broad area" resulting from greater availability in the eighteenth century (South 1972:75–77, 100). Excavation of a variety of eighteenth century sites, all dating to the same period but occupied by people of differing status, reveals in each site a similar distribution of ceramic types. Yet, analysis by shape rather than by type may be a "more sensitive indicator of *function* and possible socioeconomic level [South 1972:99]." South did not consider nineteenth century sites, though the distribution of ceramic types at these sites may reveal status differences.

To predict status differences accurately from the differences in ceramic types or shapes, one would have to excavate a number of sites and demonstrate a pattern. Another approach, however, involves the use of documents to establish the status of site inhabitants before comparing the ceramics. If ceramics from sites that were occupied by "historically known affluent people at one point in time" can be compared with ceramics from sites occupied by "historically known non-affluent individuals at the *same period in time,*" the differences in ceramic types and shapes could be explained by differences in known status and access to material resources (South 1972:100).

In order to test whether ceramics at nineteenth century sites reflect status differences, one would require ceramics from sites that were occupied by people who differed in status during the same years of the nineteenth century. Such a situation existed on antebellum Southern plantations, whose inhabitants included not only black slaves, but also white planters and white or black overseers (Couper 1839–1854; Fogel and Engerman 1974:201). Most white overseers were the sons of middle class farmers (Scarborough 1966:5). Therefore, representatives of the three major Southern classes could often be found living on the same plantation site at the same time.

In our case, Cannon's Point Plantation, a long-staple cotton plantation on Saint Simon's Island, Georgia, was occupied by an upper-class planter family, middle-class white overseers, and black slaves (Couper 1839–1854; Otto 1975:44–46). I have used documents to identify the inhabitants, to establish their relative social position in the county—the basic Old South community (Arensberg 1959)—and to identify the dwellings they occupied (Figure 5.1).

At Cannon's Point, refuse concentrations associated with a slave cabin, an overseer's house, and the planter's kitchen were partially excavated (Figure 5.2). A refuse zone at the slave cabin (I) contained no artifacts whose beginning date of manufacture was later than 1860; the ceramics from the zone yielded a mean ceramic date of 1817. Two refuse zones at the overseer's house (II–III) contained no postbellum artifacts; the ceramics in these zones dated to 1821. Finally, three refuse zones (II–IV) at the planter's kitchen, which contained only antebellum artifacts, provided mean ceramic dates ca.1815, 1818, and 1824 (see Appendix A, this chapter; Otto 1975:Tables 1, 4–5).

The Mean Ceramic Date Formula, which yields mean dates for the time span of manufacture of ceramics found in site contexts, demonstrated the chronological similarities of the ceramics used in the comparison (see Appendix A). A comparison of contemporaneous ceramics would show that differences in ceramic type distribution could be explained by differences in status rather than by chronological change.

The Cannon's Point ceramics came from sites occupied by people who differed in racial, social, and legal status and access to material resources during the same period in time. The Couper family, who owned Cannon's Point Plantation from 1794 to 1866, monopolized the plantation surplus—the food crops, the livestock, and the cash-crop of long-staple cotton. Using credit on cash-crop sales, the Coupers purchased slaves,

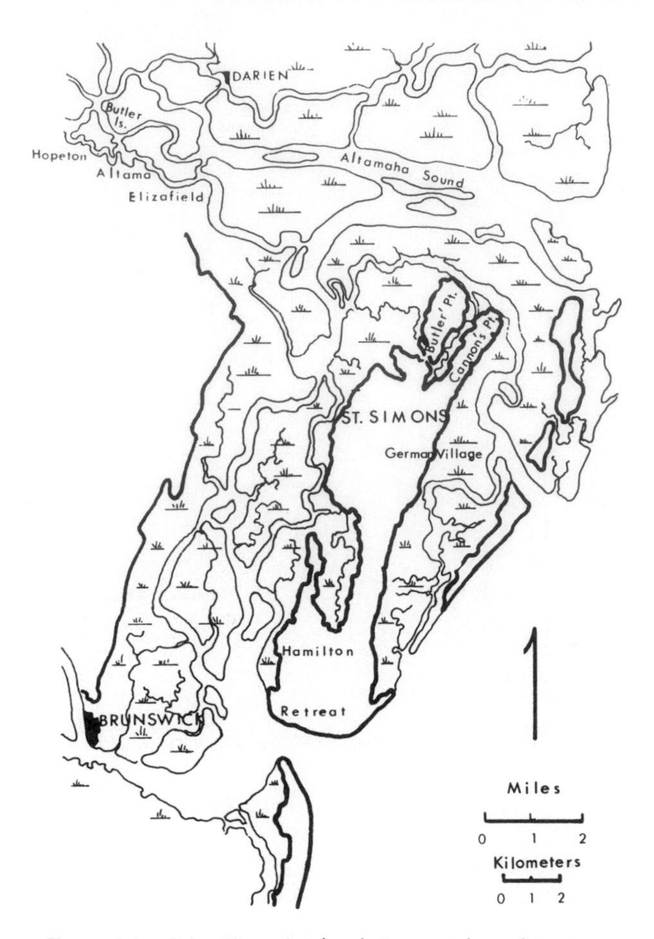

Figure 5.1. Saint Simon's Island, Brunswick, and Darien.

plantation supplies, luxuries, and household goods from their cotton agents or factors in Charleston, South Carolina (Couper 1839–1854). The Coupers also used a portion of the plantation surplus to provide their overseers with a house, a servant or two, and a modest yearly salary. And finally, the slaves received a portion of the plantation surplus in the form of standardized housing and food and clothing rations. From the sale of handicrafts, garden produce and the fowl and hogs they raised, the slaves also achieved a small cash income (Otto 1975:chaps. 1–2).

Although the Couper family obtained their household goods, including ceramics, from their Charleston factors, the slaves and overseers may have obtained their ceramics in three possible ways. First, the planter family, who provided the slaves and overseers with clothing, could also have provided the slaves and overseers with a special class of wares. Second, the planter family could have given their chipped, broken, and

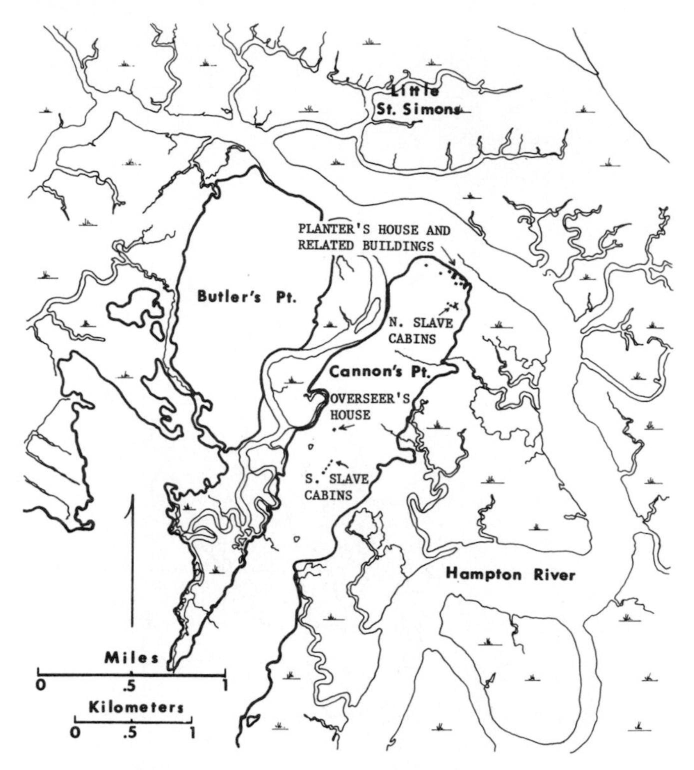

Figure 5.2. Cannon's Point Plantation.

discarded ceramic items to the slaves and overseers (Fairbanks 1974:79, 82). Third, the slaves and overseers could have purchased their own ceramics. The slaves and sell produce and handicraft items and may have purchased ceramics from shopkeepers in Brunswick or Darien. And the overseers, using credit on their yearly salaries, could have obtained ceramics from the planter's Charleston factors or from local shopkeepers.

So, there are three possible explanations for the appearance of ceramics at the slave and overseer sites. These hypotheses can be tested with the documentary and archeological evidence from the plantation.

CERAMICS—THE HYPOTHESES

Hypothesis 1

The planter family issued a special class of wares to the slaves and the overseers.

PROPOSITION 1A

If the planter family purchased ceramics for their slaves and overseers, the purchases should be listed in the Cannon's Point accounts, which were kept by James H. Couper from 1839 to 1854.

PROPOSITION 1B

Also, if the planter family issued a special class of wares to the slaves and overseers, there will be archeological evidence of this practice. The ceramic types at the planter's kitchen should differ significantly from the ceramic types at the slave and overseer sites. But there should be a similar number of ceramic types at the slave and overseer sites, and the percentages of ceramic types should be similar.

PROPOSITION 1C

If the planter family issued a special class of wares to the slaves and overseers, the ceramic shapes at the planter's kitchen should differ from the ceramic shapes at the slave and overseer sites. The elite planter family should have used a wider range of shapes than the slaves or overseers.

Hypothesis 2

The slaves and overseers used the ceramics that the planter family formerly used and then discarded.

PROPOSITION 2A

Since the planter family probably purchased large sets of tableware and teaware from their factors, items from these sets would then appear at the slave and overseer sites when the planter family gave discarded ceramics to slaves and overseers. Items from the same sets could then be identified from similarities in printed and painted decorations, though the flow of undecorated items would be difficult to trace.

PROPOSITION 2B

If the slaves and overseers used discarded ceramic items formerly owned by the planter, similar ceramic types should appear at all three sites. Although the quantities of sherds will differ at the three sites, the percentages of ceramic types should be similar.

PROPOSITION 2C

If the slaves and overseers used the planter's ceramic discards, there should be a similar range of ceramic shapes at all three sites.

Hypothesis 3

The slaves and overseers purchased their own ceramics.

PROPOSITION 3A

If slaves and overseers purchased their own ceramics and rarely used discards from the planter family, items from the same sets should rarely appear at all three sites.

PROPOSITION 3B

If slaves, overseers, and planters regularly purchased their own ceramics, the number of ceramic types and the percentages of the types will differ at all three sites.

PROPOSITION 3C

If slaves, overseers, and planters purchased their own ceramics, they would have used different ceramic shapes for different functions. A slave family would have had different ceramic needs than an unmarried overseer or an elite planter family. Consequently, different ceramic shapes should be expected at all three sites.

TESTING THE HYPOTHESES

Historical Data

The documentary evidence is inconclusive. The Cannon's Point accounts do not list the ceramic items that the overseers purchased; the ceramics are probably included in the "sundries" purchases in the overseer accounts, which are not itemized. In addition, there are no entries for ceramics in the lists of textiles, tools, and foods purchased for the Cannon's Point slaves; again, ceramics are probably included in "sundries" purchases (Couper 1826–1852; 1839–1854). No other documentary sources concerning the plantation describe how the overseers and slaves obtained their ceramics (Hall 1829: Kemble 1961; Lyell 1849; Van Doren 1929). Because of the inadequate documentary evidence,

Proposition 1A can neither be confirmed nor disconfirmed. The remaining propositions can be tested only with archeological evidence.

Archeological Data

USE OF CERAMIC DISCARDS

A test of Propositions 2A and 3A required a comparison of the surface decorations of the sherds recovered from all three of the plantation sites. Yet, the surface decorations of only five ceramic items from the slave cabin refuse matched the surface decorations of items from tableware and teaware sets found at the planter's kitchen. These items may have been purchased, used, and discarded by the planter family and then reused by the slaves. The examples of possible planter ceramic discards included elements of an underglaze blue hand-painted pearlware basket stand and four transfer-printed tableware items. One plate fragment came from a "G. PHILLIPS/PARK SCENERY" tableware set; and another plate fragment came from a tableware set marked "JOHN RIDGWAY AND CO./ ARCHIPELAGO PATTERN"; a third plate fragment came from a tableware set marked "ORIENTAL STONECHINA"; and a fourth plate fragment came from an unidentified transfer-printed tableware set. A plate from this set also appeared at the overseer's house site. Finally, the slaves may have used overseer discards, since saucer sherds from an unidentified transfer-printed teaware set were present at both the overseer's house and the slave cabin.

The archeological evidence for the use of planter ceramic discards confirmed Proposition 3A, because relatively few ceramic items at the slave cabin and at the overseer's house came from planter-owned sets. Only 5 of the 126 ceramic vessels at the slave cabin had counterparts in the tableware and teaware sets found at the planter's kitchen. Only 1 of the 135 ceramic vessels at the overseer's house may have been a planter discard. Conversely, the archeological evidence did not confirm Proposition 2A, for there was no evidence of the widespread use of planter ceramic discards by the slaves and overseers.

CERAMIC TYPES

A test of Propositions 1B, 2B, and 3B required a comparison of ceramic types from the antebellum refuse contexts at the slave cabin, the overseer's house, and the planter's kitchen (see Appendices B and C for site totals and totals for antebellum contexts). We found 23 types at the slave cabin, 24 types at the overseer's house, and 28 types at the planter's kitchen. Grouping the ceramic types by their surface decorations (see Fairbanks 1974:77) reveals the distribution shown in Table 5.1.

TABLE 5.1

Distribution of Ceramic Types Grouped by Surface Decorations (in percentage of sherds at each site) (Antebellum Refuse Contexts)

Type	Slave cabin	Overseer's house	Planter's kitchen
Total sherd count	*543*	*179*	*1242*
Banded	25	30	1
Blue and green edged	12	5	2
Underglaze hand-painted	5	5	4
Transfer-printed	21	14	77
Undecorated (creamware, pearlware, and white-ware	29	36	9
Others	7	10	7

The evidence presented in Table 5.1 and Appendix B confirms Proposition 1b. There is a similar number of ceramic types in slave and overseer samples. Also, there are similar percentages of banded, undecorated, and transfer-printed wares in the slave and overseer samples. Proposition 2B, however, was not confirmed. There was not a similar number of ceramic types at all three sites, and the percentages of ceramic types were dissimilar. Proposition 3B was not confirmed either. The numbers of ceramic types and the percentages of types were not substantially different at all three sites; rather, there were remarkable similarities in the number of types and the percentages of the types in slave and overseer samples.

In slave and overseer ceramic samples, banded (25% and 30% respectively) and undecorated (29% and 36% respectively) sherds are relatively common. Although some of the undecorated sherds may be the "plain parts of decorated specimens, largely the blue feather-edged [and shell

TABLE 5.2

Distribution of Ceramic Items Grouped by Shape and Function (in percentage of ceramic items at each site)

Ceramic item	Slave cabin	Overseer's house	Planter's kitchen
Total count	*126*	*135*	*309*
Tableware	64	58	52
Tea and coffeeware	21	31	27
Storage vessels (excluding bottles)	4	2	11
Dairy ware	0	1	1
Chamber ware	3	2	3
Others and unidentified	8	6	6

edged] [Fairbanks 1962:13]," other sherds come from undecorated hollowware and flatware items. In contrast, undecorated sherds comprise only 9%, and banded-ware sherds only 1%, of the planter's kitchen sample. Transfer-printed sherds, however, comprise 77% of the total kitchen sample; conversely, transfer-printed sherds constitute only 21% of the slave sample and 14% of the overseer sample. Finally, blue and green edged sherds occur more frequently in the slave sample than in the overseer and planter samples.

CERAMIC SHAPES

To test Propositions 1C, 2C, and 3C, I reconstructed ceramic items from the Cannon's Point sites. The shapes were identified by comparison with illustrations in Godden (1963, 1966), Whiter (1970), Coysh (1970), and various site reports. Detailed lists of the ceramic shapes and their probable function can be found in Otto (1975:Tables 19–21). See Table 5.2 for comparison.

There is a lower percentage of tableware and a higher percentage of storage vessels at the planter's kitchen than at either slave or overseer sites. More striking differences in ceramic shapes, however, appear in the tableware collections from the sites, as seen in Table 5.3.

The distribution of ceramic shapes presented in Tables 5.2 and 5.3 confirmed Proposition 1C. At the slave and overseer sites, there were similarities in the distribution of ceramic shapes. Serving bowls were rather common at both sites, and storage vessels were relatively rare. In contrast, serving bowls were relatively rare at the planter's kitchen, where serving flatware and storage vessels were more common. The evidence did not confirm Proposition 2C, for the range of ceramic shapes was not similar at the three sites. Also, Proposition 3C was not confirmed, since there were similarities in the ceramic shapes that slaves and overseers used.

TABLE 5.3

Distribution of Serving Bowls and Serving Flatware (in percentage of all tableware at each site)

	Slave cabin	Overseer's house	Planter's kitchen
Total tableware count	*80*	*78*	*161*
Serving bowls	44	24	8
Serving flatware (plates, platters, and soup-plates)	49	72	84
Other tableware shapes	7	4	8

Summary

A comparison of Cannon's Point ceramics confirmed Propositions 1B, 1C, and 3A:

Hypothesis 1

Proposition 1A	inconclusive
Proposition 1B	confirmed
Proposition 1C	confirmed

Hypothesis 2

Proposition 2A	not confirmed
Proposition 2B	not confirmed
Proposition 2C	not confirmed

Hypothesis 3

Proposition 3A	confirmed
Proposition 3B	not comfirmed
Proposition 3C	not comfirmed

Propositions 1B and 1C were confirmed; Hypothesis 1 may or may not be true, but it has not been disconfirmed. Apparently, the planter family purchased transfer-printed wares for their own use, and they purchased a special class of wares (banded, blue and green edged, and undecorated) to issue to the slaves and overseers (Table 5.1 and Appendix B). This practice explains the similarities in the distribution of ceramic types at the slave and overseer sites. Also, the planter family provided the slaves and overseers with special ceramic shapes such as serving bowls, whereas they purchased serving flatware for their own use (Table 5.3). Only occasionally did the slaves and overseers use the planter family's discarded ceramics.

There is still the problem, however, of explaining why the planter family provided the slaves and overseers with banded, edged, and undecorated wares instead of transfer-printed ware. Also, why did the planter family provide the slaves and overseers with serving bowls, which were rarely used by the planter family?

The most elementary explanation would be the relative cheapness of banded, edged, and undecorated wares and the relative costliness of transfer-printed wares. It would be difficult, however, to test this explanation. There are no detailed lists of ceramic purchases in the Cannon's Point accounts (Couper 1826–1852, 1839–1854), which would allow comparison of the ceramic types and their relative cost. Also, although the coastal newspapers carried advertisements listing the goods that merchants and factors offered, detailed descriptions of the ceramics are rare. The ceramics in the advertisements are never listed with their prices; rather, the advertisements contain such notations as "for sale on accommodating terms" or "sold low for cash" (*Brunswick Advocate* 1837–1839; *Darien Gazette* 1818–1828; *Savannah Georgian* 1832).

Another possibility is that there are correlations between ceramic types and ceramic shapes at the plantation sites. For example, the relative abundance of banded, hand-painted, and undecorated sherds at the slave and overseer sites may be related to the relative abundance of serving bowls at these sites. In turn, the relative abundance of transfer-printed sherds at the planter's kitchen may be related to the relative abundance of serving flatware at this site (see Tables 5.1, 5.3). Furthermore, the differences in ceramic types and shapes at the plantation sites may be related to differences in needs. Since serving bowls and serving flatware were used in food consumption, differences in their distribution may be related to dietary differences existing between the slaves and overseers and the planter family. This possible explanation can be restated as a hypothesis and tested with archeological, historical, and zooarcheological evidence.

DIET—THE HYPOTHESIS

Hypothesis 4

The slaves and overseers had different ceramic needs than the planter family, and this explains why certain ceramic types and shapes appear more often at the slave and overseer sites than at the planter's kitchen.

PROPOSITION 4A

Any, correlations between the ceramic types and shapes at the plantation sites should be revealed in the classification of ceramic shapes according to their surface decorations.

PROPOSITION 4B

Since there are similarities in the ceramic shapes at the slave and overseer sites, it will be necessary to demonstrate similarities in the food preparation and consumption habits of slaves and overseers to account for the similarities in ceramic shapes. Since the ceramic shapes at the planter's kitchen differ from those at the slave and overseer sites, it will be necessary to demonstrate differences between the dietary habits of the planter family and those of the slaves and overseers.

TESTING THE HYPOTHESIS

Archeological Data

Classifying the serving bowls from the plantation sites by their surface decorations reveals that banded bowls are most common. In fact, all the banded tableware items at the plantation sites were serving bowls—the "common bowl" shape with foot rings and carinated, flaring sides (see Godden 1966:173; Van Rensselaer 1966:341). This classification is seen in Table 5.4.

Classifying the serving flatware items (plates, platters, and soup-plates) by their surface decorations revealed that transfer-printed flatware constituted 74% of the total at the planter's kitchen. In contrast, transfer-printed tableware comprised less than 40% of the totals at the slave and overseer sites. But at these sites, blue and green edged, underglaze hand-painted, and undecorated flatware items comprised 59% of the total at the slave cabin and 54% of the total at the overseer's house. At the planter's kitchen, these wares composed less than 20% of the total (Table 5.5).

The correlations between ceramic types and tableware shapes become more apparent in Table 5.6. At the slave and overseer sites, banded serving bowls, blue and green edged flatware, and undecorated bowls and flatware are more common than at the planter's site. At the planter's site transfer-printed flatware makes up 62% of the total tableware, but transfer-printed flatware constitutes less than 30% of the totals at the slave and overseer sites.

The data presented in Tables 5.4–5.6 confirm Proposition 4A. Banded bowls were relatively more common at the slave and overseer sites, and transfer-printed flatware was relatively more common at the planter's kitchen. The differences in the distribution of ceramic types and shapes may be related to dietary differences existing between the slaves and overseers and the elite planter family.

TABLE 5.4

Distribution of Serving Bowls Grouped by Surface Decorations (in percentage of all serving bowls at each site)

Type	Slave cabin	Overseer's house	Planter's kitchen
Total serving bowls	*35*	*19*	*12*
Banded	66	68	75
Underglaze hand-painted	11	11	8
Undecorated	14	11	8
Other	9	11	8

TABLE 5.5
Distribution of Serving Flatware Grouped by Surface Decorations (in percentage of all serving flatware items at each site)

Type	Slave cabin	Overseer's house	Planter's kitchen
Total serving flatware items	*39*	*56*	*135*
Blue and green edged	31	20	10
Underglaze hand-painted	5	5	2
Transfer-printed	39	39	74
Undecorated	23	29	7
Others	2	7	7

Historical Data

On Cannon's Point Plantation, the slaves and overseers received or purchased rations of cornmeal, cracked rice, and rice flour. Also, they received or purchased cured meats, and they collected fish and game (Couper 1826–1852, 1839–1854; Otto 1975:Tables 36–38). Because they

TABLE 5.6
Distribution of Tableware Shapes Grouped by Surface Decorations (in percentage of all tableware items at each site)

Type	Slave cabin	Overseer's house	Planter's kitchen
Total tableware items	*80*	*78*	*161*
Banded			
Serving bowls[a]	29	17	6
Blue and green edge			
Serving flatware	15	14	8
Other[b]	0	1	0
Underglaze hand-painted			
Serving bowls	5	3	1
Serving flatware	3	4	1
Other	1	0	1
Transfer-printed			
Bowls[c]	1	1	0
Serving flatware	19	28	62
Tureens, etc.	4	1	8
Undecorated			
Serving bowls	6	3	1
Serving flatware	11	21	6
Tureens, etc.	3	1	1
Others (bowls, flatware, etc.)	3	6	5

[a] All banded tableware items were "common bowls."
[b] There was one blue edged tureen lid at the overseer's house.
[c] There were two transfer-printed bowls at the slave and overseer sites; these may have been tea or spill bowls.

possessed few cooking vessels, and they lacked the time needed for elaborate food preparation, the slaves and overseers probably cooked vegetables, grains, and any available meat in the same kettle (see Hilliard 1972:62). Pottages, meat and vegetable stews, and rice pilaus could be left simmering for hours, while slaves and overseers engaged in other tasks (see Booth 1971:17; Hilliard 1972:49; A Planter 1836:582–583). The slaves and overseers apparently ate the liquid-based stews from banded serving bowls and sopped up the pot liquor with bread made from cornmeal or rice flour (see Hilliard 1969:10, 1972:51). An ex-slave from South Carolina described such a stew: "The whole had been boiled . . . until the flesh had disappeared from the bones, which were broken in small pieces—a flitch of bacon, some green corn, squashes, tomatoes, and onions had been added [Ball 1859:139]."

In contrast, the planter family had the pick of the plantation livestock and garden produce; documents attest to the abundance of roast beef, pork, mutton, and steamed vegetables on the Couper's table. Also, slave fishermen supplied the ingredients for supplementary fish and terrapin soups (Lovell 1932; J. Couper 1828, 1832, n.d.; R. Couper n.d.). At the Couper's house, the roast meats were served on transfer-printed platters accompanied by tureens of steamed vegetables and seafood soups. The Couper family and the guests consumed these foods from transfer-printed plates and soup-plates (Tables 5.5–5.6).

Zooarcheological Data

The documentary evidence is corroborated by the zooarcheological evidence from the Cannon's Point sites. At the planter's kitchen, saw marks were present on the scapulae, ribs, and vertebrae of the cattle, hogs, and sheep, indicating that these animals were carefully butchered to produce roasts for the planter's table. But at the slave and overseer sites, no saw marks were present on the large domestic mammal bones; apparently, saws were not used to divide the carcasses into cuts and joints. Rather, the slaves and overseers cleaved open the bones with axes and cleavers and stewed them to obtain more nourishment from their limited meat (see Ball 1859:139; Chaplin 1971:14–15, 66; Otto 1975:357).

The documentary and zooarcheological evidence confirmed Proposition 4B. Slaves and overseers prepared their food in similar fashion, cooking different types of foods together in the same kinds of vessels and serving liquid-based food in banded and other bowls. Of course, they ate much of the food from flatware items, since these compose 49% and 72% of the total tableware at the slave and overseer sites (Table 5.3). Yet, the ceramic, documentary, and zooarcheological data suggest that stews, pilaus, and pottages were daily fare. At the planter's kitchen, however, the cooks generally prepared meats, vegetables, and seafoods separately and served them to the Coupers on transfer-printed tableware.

Summary

Propositions 4A and 4B were confirmed; the hypothesis may not be true, but has not been disconfirmed. There were correlations between the ceramic types and the tableware shapes at the sites. Moreover, the kinds of tableware shapes at the sites were related to the dietary habits of the site inhabitants. The slaves and overseers often consumed their foods from banded bowls, and the planter family ate their foods from transfer-printed flatware. Thus, differences in ceramic needs accounted for the distribution of tableware shapes and types at the plantation sites.

CERAMICS AND STATUS

The ceramic samples from Cannon's Point came from sites occupied by people who differed in known status during the same period in time. Therefore, status was held as a constant by means of historical controls, and differences in ceramics may be explained by differences in known status (see South 1972:100). In turn, the ceramic evidence from Cannon's Point may allow us to predict the status of site inhabitants at other early nineteenth century plantations by analyzing the distribution of ceramic types, shapes, and forms at these sites.

Ceramic Type

At Cannon's Point, there were differences in the frequencies of ceramic type sherds (see Table 5.1 and Appendix B). The significance of the differences was tested with the chi-square statistic (Appendix D, Test 1). The test revealed that the differences in type frequencies were statistically significant, and the classifications (status and ceramic types) were statistically associated. As a result, it should be possible to predict the status of site inhabitants at other early nineteenth century plantations by using the distribution of ceramic types.

The distribution of ceramic type sherds at Cannon's Point reflects the subordinate status of the slaves and hired overseers on the plantation. It appears that the planter family provided the slaves and overseers with a special class of wares perhaps judged more durable and suitable for laborers. This special class of wares included the banded, blue and green edged, and undecorated earthenware types, whose sherds are relatively abundant at the slave and overseer sites, composing almost 70% of the total sherds in the antebellum samples.

But, because of the similarities in the relative frequencies of banded, transfer-printed, and undecorated type sherds at the Cannon's Point slave and overseer sites (Table 5.1), these ceramic types may not be sensitive indicators of racial or social status. Rather, the distribution of ceramic types at the slave and overseer sites demonstrates only the subordinate status of the slaves and overseers in relation to the elite planter family. Blue and green edged sherds, however, are relatively more common at the slave site, composing 12% of the antebellum sample; thus, the relative frequency of blue and green edged sherds should be a sensitive marker of slave status.

Furthermore, the relative frequency of transfer-printed sherds should be a sensitive indicator of elite planter status. At the Cannon's Point planter's kitchen, transfer-printed sherds composed almost 80% of the total antebellum sample. In contrast, transfer-printed sherds composed less than 25% of the slave and overseer samples (Table 5.1).

Surprisingly, the relative frequency of porcelain sherds does not seem to be an indicator of status differences. Oriental and European porcelains represent only 2% of the slave antebellum refuse sample, 3% of the overseer sample, and 2% of the planter sample (Appendix B). Yet, the appearance of porcelains at eighteenth century sites or in inventories is generally believed to be a reliable indicator of status differences (Stone 1970; Teller 1968). Apparently, the relative frequencies of transfer-printed earthenwares and not ceramics are status indicators on early nineteenth century sites.

Ceramic Shape

At the Cannon's Point sites, there were differences in the frequencies of certain tableware shapes, such as serving bowls and serving flatware. The significance of the differences in shape frequencies was tested with the chi-square statistic (Appendix D, Test 2). The test revealed that the differences in shape frequencies were statistically significant, and the classifications (status and ceramic shape) were statistically associated. Thus, it should be possible to predict the status of site inhabitants at other plantations by using the distribution of the ceramic shapes.

The relative frequencies of certain ceramic shapes accurately reflects the known social status differences existing between the planter family, the overseers, and the slave laborers. Serving bowl shapes composed 44, 24, and 8% of the total tableware at the slave, overseer, and planter sites respectively. Conversely, serving flatware shapes composed 49, 72, and 84% of the tableware totals at the sites (see Table 5.3). Because of the differences in the relative frequencies of serving bowls and serving flatware, ceramic shape should be a more sensitive indicator of social status than ceramic type. The distribution of ceramic shapes from Cannon's

Point confirms the assumption that analysis "by shape would seem to be a more sensitive indicator of *function* and possible socioeconomic level" [South 1972:99] than analysis by ceramic type.

Ceramic Form

Ceramic form "is a generalized term which includes shape, as well as those other attributes from which types are defined [South 1972:71]." At Cannon's Point, there were differences in the frequencies of certain tableware forms such as banded bowls and transfer-printed serving flatware. The significance of the differences in tableware form frequencies was tested with the chi-square statistic (Appendix D, Test 3). The test revealed that the differences in ceramic form frequencies were statistically significant and the classifications (status and ceramic forms) were statistically associated. As a result, it should be possible to predict the status of site inhabitants at other early nineteenth century plantations by using the distribution of ceramic forms at these sites.

The relative frequencies of banded bowls and transfer-printed serving flatware at Cannon's Point reflect the known social status differences existing between the planter family, the hired overseers, and the slave laborers. Banded bowl forms composed 29, 17, and 6% of the total tableware at the slave, overseer, and planter sites respectively. In contrast, transfer-printed serving flatware composed 19, 28, and 62% of the tableware totals at the slave, overseer, and planter sites, respectively. (See Table 5.6.) Because of the differences in the relative frequencies of banded bowls and transfer-printed flatware, the distribution of these ceramic forms should be a sensitive indicator of social status. But at the slave and overseer sites, the percentages of blue and green edged flatware forms are remarkably similar, which makes it difficult to predict social status differences.

HYPOTHESES FOR FURTHER TESTING

The findings from the controlled comparison of slave, overseer, and planter ceramics can be restated as hypotheses for further testing at early nineteenth century plantations and other sites.

Hypothesis 5

On plantations where the planter family supplied the slaves and hired overseers with a special class of wares, banded, blue and green edged, and undecorated sherds should be relatively common at the slave and overseer sites. The percentages of these types should be similar at slave and overseer sites, comprising about 70% of the total sherds (Table 5.1). Since elite planter families purchased ceramics for their own use, transfer-printed sherds should be relatively abundant at sites occupied by planter families, comprising over 75% of the total sherds. In contrast, transfer-printed sherds should be relatively rare at sites occupied by slaves and overseers, composing less than 25% of the total sherds. Although the distribution of type sherds at slave and overseer sites should reflect their subordinate status, it may be difficult to predict social status or racial differences because of similar percentages of type sherds at these sites. Only blue and green edged sherd frequencies may be a reliable indicator of slave status.

Hypothesis 6

On plantations where the planter families furnished the slaves with ceramics, serving bowls should be relatively abundant, making up over 40% of the total tableware shapes. At sites occupied by middle-class overseers, serving bowls should be less abundant, constituting less than 25% of the total tableware shapes. At sites occupied by elite planter families, however, serving flatware shapes should be relatively abundant, comprising over 80% of the total tableware. Therefore, the distribution of serving bowl and serving flatware shapes at plantation sites should be sensitive indicators of social status differences on early nineteenth century plantations.

Hypothesis 7

On plantations where the planter family furnished slaves with ceramics, banded bowl forms should be relatively common, comprising about 30% of the tableware forms. In turn, on sites occupied by middle-class overseers, banded bowl forms will be less common, comprising less than 20% of the tableware forms. On both slave and overseer sites, blue and green edged serving flatware forms should comprise less than 20% of the total tableware. At sites occupied by elite planters, transfer-printed serving flatware forms should be relatively abundant, constituting over 60% of the total tableware forms. Consequently, the distribution of banded bowls and transfer-printed serving flatware should be sensitive indicators of social status differences on early nineteenth century plantations.

ACKNOWLEDGMENTS

I would like to thank Charles H. Fairbanks and Stanley South for reading and commenting on earlier versions of this chapter.

APPENDIX A

Applications of the Mean Ceramic Date Formula (South 1972)

Ceramic type number	Ceramic type name	Median date	Sherd count	Product
	Slave cabin site—refuse (*Zone I*)			
13	"Annular wares" pearlware	1805	97	175085
8	"Finger-painted" wares	1805	26	46930
19	Blue and green edged pearlware	1805	67	120935
17	Underglaze blue hand-painted pearlware	1800	19	34200
12	Underglaze polychrome pearlware	1805	7	12635
10	"Willow" transfer pattern on pearlware	1818	9	16362
11	Transfer-printed pearlware	1818	105	190890
20	Undecorated pearlware	1805	86	155230
2	Whiteware	1860	74[a]	137640
1	Brown stoneware bottle	1860	4	7440
5	Canton porcelain	1815	6	10890
			500	908237
		Mean ceramic date = 908237 ÷ 500 = 1816.5		
	Overseer's house site—refuse (*Zones II–III*)			
13	"Annular wares" pearlware	1805	18	32490
8	"Finger-painted" wares	1805	2	3610
6	Mocha	1843	13	23959
15	Lighter yellow creamware	1798	3	5394
19	Blue and green edged pearlware	1805	9	16245
12	Underglaze polychrome pearlware	1805	8	14440
10	"Willow" transfer pattern on pearlware	1818	3	5454
11	Transfer-printed pearlware	1818	16	29088
20	Undecorated pearlware	1805	52	93860
2	Whiteware	1860	36[b]	66960
3	Ironstone and granite china	1857	1	1857
1	Brown stoneware bottle	1860	1	1860
27	"Black basaltes" stoneware	1785	7	12495
5	Canton porcelain	1815	2	3630
			171	311342
		Mean ceramic date = 311342 ÷ 171 = 1820.7		
	Couper kitchen site—Zone II			
8	"Finger-painted" wares	1805	3	5415
15	Lighter yellow creamware	1798	11	19778
19	Blue and green edged pearlware	1805	2	3610
17	Underglaze blue hand-painted pearlware	1800	4	7200
10	"Willow" transfer pattern on pearlware	1818	10	18180
11	Transfer-printed pearlware	1818	141	256338
20	Undecorated pearlware	1805	2	3610
2	Whiteware	1860	38[c]	70680
3	Ironstone and granite china	1857	4	7428
5	Canton porcelain	1815	5	9075
			220	401314
		Mean ceramic date = 401314 ÷ 220 = 1824.2		
	Couper kitchen site—Zone III			
13	"Annular wares" pearlware	1805	3	5415
8	"Finger-painted" wares	1805	3	5415

APPENDIX A (continued)

Ceramic type number	Ceramic type name	Median date	Sherd count	Product
15	Lighter yellow creamware	1798	11	19778
19	Blue and green edged pearlware	1805	11	19855
17	Underglaze blue hand-painted pearlware	1800	15	27000
12	Underglaze polychrome pearlware	1805	8	14440
10	"Willow" transfer pattern on pearlware	1818	7	12726
11	Transfer-printed pearlware	1818	520	945360
20	Undecorated pearlware	1805	47	84835
2	Whiteware	1860	18[d]	33480
3	Ironstone and granite china	1857	6	11142
1	Brown stoneware bottle	1860	2	3720
5	Canton porcelain	1815	3	5445
			654	1188611
	Mean ceramic date = 1188611 ÷ 654 = 1817.5			
	Couper kitchen site—Zone IV			
15	Lighter yellow creamware	1798	6	10788
19	Blue and green edged pearlware	1805	13	23465
17	Underglaze blue hand-painted pearlware	1800	22	39600
12	Underglaze polychrome pearlware	1805	2	3610
10	"Willow" transfer pattern on pearlware	1818	3	5454
11	Transfer-printed pearlware	1818	239	434502
20	Undecorated pearlware	1805	12	21660
27	"Black basaltes" stoneware	1785	1	1785
5	Canton porcelain	1815	5	9075
			303	549939
	Mean ceramic date = 549939 ÷ 303 = 1815.0			
	Couper kitchen—refuse (*Zones II–IV*)			
13	"Annular wares" pearlware	1805	3	5415
8	"Finger-painted" wares	1805	6	10830
15	Lighter yellow creamware	1798	28	50344
19	Blue and green edged pearlware	1805	26	46930
17	Underglaze blue hand-painted pearlware	1800	41	73800
10	"Willow" transfer pattern on pearlware	1818	20	36360
11	Transfer-printed pearlware	1818	900	1636200
12	Underglaze polychrome pearlware	1805	10	18050
20	Undecorated pearlware	1805	61	110105
2	Whiteware	1860	56	104160
3	Ironstone and granite china	1857	10	18570
27	"Black basaltes" stoneware	1785	1	1785
1	Brown stoneware bottle	1860	2	3720
5	Canton porcelain	1815	13	23595
			1177	2139864
	Mean ceramic date = 2139864 ÷ 1177 = 1818.1			

[a] Includes 3 decorated whiteware sherds.
[b] Includes 27 decorated whiteware sherds.
[c] Includes 27 decorated whiteware sherds.
[d] Includes 10 decorated whiteware sherds.

APPENDIX B

Comparisons of Site Contexts (Type Frequencies and Percentages from Antebellum Refuse Contexts)[a]

Types	Slave cabin refuse		Overseer's house refuse (Zones II–III)		Couper kitchen (Zones II–IV, closed contexts)	
	Frequency	Percentage	Frequency	Percentage	Frequency	Percentage
Unglazed coarse earthenware	5	.9	1	<.6	4	.3
Glazed coarse earthenware	3	.6	1	<.6	16	1.3
Banded pearlware	97	17.9	18	10.1	3	.2
Banded whiteware	1	<.2	21	11.7	3	.2
Finger-painted pearlware	26	4.8	2	1.1	6	.5
Mocha whiteware			13	7.3		
Mocha drab yellow						
Banded drab yellow	14	2.6			1	<.1
"Orangeware"[b]					1	<.1
"Jackfield"-type ware					3	.2
Undecorated creamware			3	1.7	28	2.3
Blue and green edged pearlware	67	12.3	9	5.0	26	2.1
Underglaze blue hand-painted pearlware	19	3.5			41	3.3
Underglaze blue on bisque	1	<.2				
Underglaze polychrome pearlware	7	1.3	8	4.5	10	.8
Willow transfer-printed pearlware	9	1.7	3	1.7	20	1.6
Transfer-printed pearlware	105	19.3	16	8.9	900	72.5
Undecorated pearlware	86	15.8	52	29.1	61	4.9
Transfer-printed whiteware	2	.4	6	3.4	33	2.7

APPENDIX B (Continued)

Types	Slave cabin refuse		Overseer's house refuse (Zones II–III)		Couper kitchen (Zones II–IV, closed contexts)	
	Frequency	Percentage	Frequency	Percentage	Frequency	Percentage
Sponged whiteware					1	<.1
Undecorated whiteware	71	13.1	9	5.0	19	1.5
Ironstone and granite china			1	<.6	10	1.5
Brown stoneware bottles	4	.7	1	<.6	2	.2
Salt-glazed stoneware	2	.4	1	<.6	25	2.0
Lead-glazed stoneware	1	.2			3	.2
Alkaline-glazed stoneware					6	.5
Slip-coated stoneware	1	.2	1	<.6		
Unglazed stoneware	1	.2			1	<.1
Lead-glazed "black basaltes"			7	3.9	1	<.1
Lead-glazed red stoneware	13	2.4	1	<.6		
Undecorated European porcelain	2	.4	1	<.6	4	.3
Transfer-printed European porcelain					1	<.1
Sprigged European porcelain			1	<.6		
Canton porcelain	6	1.1	2	1.1	13	1.1
Gold overglaze Oriental porcelain			1	<.6		
Totals	543	100.0	179	100.0	1242	100.0

[a] Types based on South (1972); Noël Hume (1970).
[b] Charles Fairbanks, personal communication.

APPENDIX C

Site Total Comparisons (Type Frequencies and Percentages)

	Slave cabin site		Overseer's house site		Couper kitchen site	
Type	Frequency	Percentage	Frequency	Percentage	Frequency	Percentage
Unglazed coarse earthenware	7	1.0	1	<.2	4	.2
Glazed coarse earthenware	3	.4	1	<.2	33	1.6
Banded pearlware	103	15.2	24	4.5	8	.4
Banded whiteware	1	.2	23	4.4	5	.3
Finger-painted pearlware	27	4.0	4	.8	9	.4
Mocha whiteware			15	2.8		
Mocha drab yellow			14	2.7		
Banded drab yellow	15	2.2	9	1.7	1	<.1
"Orangeware"					4	.2
"Jackfield"-type ware					4	.2
Undecorated creamware			3	.6	62	3.1
Blue and green edged pearlware	82	12.1	29	5.5	39	1.9
Underglaze blue hand-painted pearlware	23	3.4	2	.4	63	3.1
Underglaze blue hand-painted on bisque	2	.3				
Underglaze polychrome pearlware	10	1.5	28	5.3	16	.8
Willow transfer pearlware	9	1.3	13	2.5	57	2.8
Transfer-printed pearlware	143	21.1	66	12.5	1346	66.3
Undecorated pearlware	105	15.5	158	29.9	84	4.1

APPENDIX C (Continued)

Type	Slave cabin site		Overseer's house site		Couper kitchen site	
	Frequency	Percentage	Frequency	Percentage	Frequency	Percentage
Transfer-printed whiteware	2	.3	15	2.8	117	5.8
Sponged whiteware	4	.6	1	<.2	2	.1
Undecorated whiteware	102	15.1	68	12.9	56	2.8
Ironstone and granite china			3	.6	19	.9
Brown stoneware bottles	4	.6	12	2.3	3	.2
Salt-glazed stoneware	5	.7	8	1.5	32	1.6
Lead-glazed stoneware	1	.2			11	.5
Alkaline-glazed stoneware					6	.3
Slip-coated stoneware	2	.3	2	.4	2	<.1
Unglazed stoneware	1	.2			1	<.1
Lead-glazed "black basaltes"			9	1.7	1	<.1
Lead-glazed red stoneware	14	2.1	4	.8		
Undecorated European porcelain	5	.7	8	1.5	11	.5
Transfer-printed European porcelain					3	.2
Sprigged European porcelain			1	<.2		
Canton porcelain	7	1.0	6	1.1	29	1.4
Gold overglaze Oriental porcelain			2	.4	1	<.1
Totals	677	100.0	529	100.0	2029	100.0

APPENDIX D

Test 1

Null hypothesis: The two classifications (status and ceramic type) are independent.

Alternative hypothesis: The two classifications are dependent.

Rejection region: Reject the null hypothesis if χ^2 exceeds the tabulated value of χ^2 for a = .05 and *df* = (rows − 1)(columns − 1) or df = (4)(2) = 8. The tabulated value of χ^2 is 15.5.

	Status			
Ceramic type	Slave	Overseer	Planter	Total
Banded	138(56.7)	54(18.7)	13(129.6)	205
Blue and green edged	67(28.2)	9(9.3)	26(64.5)	102
Transfer-printed	116(302.5)	25(99.7)	953(691.8)	1094
Undecorated	157(91.0)	64(30.0)	108(208.1)	329
Others	65(65.0)	27(21.3)	142(148.0)	234
Total sherds	543	179	1242	1964 (=n)

Since $\chi^2 = 770 > 15.5$, the null hypothesis is rejected and the two classifications (status and ceramic type) are assumed to be dependent.

The strength of this association can be tested with the contingency coefficient C:

$$C = \sqrt{\frac{\chi^2}{n + \chi^2}} = \sqrt{\frac{770}{1964 + 770}} = \sqrt{.2816} = .5307$$

$$C_{maximum} = \sqrt{\frac{r-1}{rows}} = \sqrt{\frac{4}{5}} = .8944$$

$$C_{adjusted} = \frac{C}{C_{max}} = \frac{.5307}{.8944} = .5934.$$

The value for C_{adj} suggests a strong association.

Test 2

Null hypothesis: The two classifications (status and ceramic shape) are independent.

Alternative hypothesis: The two classifications are dependent.

Rejection region: Reject the null hypothesis if χ^2 exceeds the tabulated value of χ^2 for a = .05 and *df* = (*r* − 1)(*c* − 1) = (2) (2) = 4. The tabulated value of χ^2 is 9.49.

	Status			
Ceramic shape	Slave	Overseer	Planter	Total
Serving bowls	35(16.6)	19(16.1)	12(33.3)	66
Serving flatware	39(57.7)	56(56.2)	135(116.1)	230
Other tableware shapes	6(5.8)	3(5.6)	14(11.6)	23
Total tableware shapes	80	78	161	319

Since $\chi^2 = 45.4$, and $45.4 > 9.49$, the null hypothesis is rejected and the two classifications (status and ceramic shape) are assumed to be dependent.

The strength of this association can be tested with the contingency coefficient:

$$C = \sqrt{\frac{\chi^2}{n+\chi^2}} = \sqrt{\frac{45.4}{319+45.4}} = \sqrt{.1246} = .3530$$

$$C_{max} = \sqrt{\frac{r-1}{r}} \quad \sqrt{\frac{2}{3}} \quad .8161$$

$$C_{adj} = \frac{C}{C_{max}} = \frac{3530}{.8161} = .4326$$

The value for C_{adj} suggests a rather strong association.

Test 3

Null hypothesis: The two classifications (status and ceramic form) are independent.

Alternative hypothesis: The two classifications are dependent.

Rejection region: Reject the null hypothesis if χ^2 exceeds the tabulated value of χ^2 for $a = .05$ and $df = (r-1)(c-1) = (2)(2) = 4$. The tabulated value of $\chi^2 = 9.49$

	Status			
Ceramic form	Slave	Overseer	Planter	Total
Banded ware bowls	23(11.3)	13(11.0)	9(22.7)	45
Transfer-printed serving flatware	15(34.4)	22(33.5)	100(69.1)	137
Other tableware forms	42(34.4)	43(33.5)	52(69.1)	137
Totals	80	78	161	319

Since $\chi^2 = 58.1$, and $58.1 > 9.49$, the null hypothesis is rejected and the two classifications are assumed to be dependent.

The strength of this association can be tested with the contingency coefficient:

$$C = \sqrt{\frac{\chi^2}{n+\chi^2}} = \sqrt{\frac{58.1}{319+58.1}} = \sqrt{.1541} = .3926$$

$$C_{max} = \sqrt{\frac{r-1}{r}} = \sqrt{\frac{2}{3}} = .8161$$

$$C_{adj} = \frac{C}{C_{max}} = \frac{.3926}{.8161} = .4811$$

The value for C_{adj} suggests a rather strong association.

REFERENCES

Arensberg, Conrad M.

1959 Summation and comments. In *Seminar on plantation systems of the new world, Social Science Monographs* 7. Research Institute for the Study of Man and the Pan American Union, Washington, D.C.

Ball, Charles

1859 *Fifty years in chains; or the life of an American slave.* New York: H. Dayton.

Booth, Sally S.

1971 *Hung, strung and potted: A history of eating in Colonial America.* New York: Clarkson N. Potter.

Brunswick Advocate

1837–1839 Newspaper on microfilm at the Univ. of Georgia Library at Athens.

Chaplin, Raymond E.

1971 *The study of animal bones from archaeological sites.* New York: Seminar Press.

Couper, James H.

1826–1852 Hopeton Plantation account book. James H. Couper Plantation Records (1826–1852) No. 185. Southern Historical Collection, Univ. of North Carolina Library at Chapel Hill.

1839–1854 Hopeton Plantation Journal. James H. Couper Plantation Records No. 185 Southern Historical Collection, Univ. of North Carolina Library at Chapel Hill.

Couper, John

1828 Manuscript M-186 (Letter to James Couper—May 24, 1828). Southern Historical Collection, Univ. of North Carolina Library at Chapel Hill.

1832 On the employment of oxen as substitutes for horses in agricultural operations. *Southern Agriculturist* **5:**286–290.

n.d. Manuscript. (*To salt meat in hot weather*). Folder 60. William A. Couper Papers No. 3987. Southern Historical Collection, Univ. of North Carolina Library at Chapel Hill.

Couper, Rebecca

n.d. Manuscript (*Catfish soup*). Fraser-Couper Family Papers (1850–1884). Georgia Historical Society Library. Savannah.

Coysh, A. W.

1970 *Blue and white transfer ware 1780–1840.* Newton Abbot, U.K.: David and Charles.

Darien Gazette

1818–1828 Newspaper on Microfilm. Univ. of Georgia Library at Athens.

Fairbanks, Charles H.

1962 European ceramics from the Cherokee capital of New Echota. *SEAC Newsletter, Papers Presented at the First and Second Conferences on Historic Site Archaeology* **9:**10–16.

1974 The Kingsley slave cabins in Duval County, Florida, 1968. *The Conference on Historic Site Archaeology Papers 1972* **7:**62–93.

Fogel, Robert W., and Stanley L. Engerman

1974 *Time on the cross: The economics of American Negro slavery.* Boston: Little, Brown.

Fontana, Bernard L.

1968 Bottles, buckets and horseshoes: The unrespectable in American archaeology. *Keystone Folklore Quarterly* **13:**171–184.

Godden, Geoffrey A.

1963 *British pottery and porcelains 1780–1850.* New York: A. S. Barnes.

1966 *An illustrated encyclopedia of British pottery and porcelain.* New York: Crown.

Hall, Basil

1829 *Travels in North America in the years 1827 and 1828.* Edinburgh: Cadell.

Hilliard, Sam B.

1969 Hog meat and cornpone: Food habits in the antebellum South. *Proceedings of the American Philosophical Society* **113:**1–13.

1972 *Hogmeat and hoecake: Food supply in the Old South 1840–1860.* Carbondale: Southern Illinois Univ. Press.

Kemble, Frances A.
1961 Journal of a residence on a Georgian plantation in 1838–1839 edited by John A. Scott. New York: Knopf.

Lovell, Caroline C.
1932 *The golden isles of Georgia.* Boston: Little, Brown.

Lyell, Charles
1849 *A second visit to the United States of North America.* New York: Harper.

Miller, J. Jefferson, and Lyle M. Stone
1970 Eighteenth-century ceramics from Fort Michilimackinac. *Smithsonian Studies in History and Technology* No. **4.** Washington, D.C.: Smithsonian Institution Press.

Noël Hume, Ivor
1970 *A guide to artifacts of Colonial America.* New York: Knopf.

Otto, John S.
1975 Status differences and the archeological record—A comparison of planter, overseer, and slave sites from Cannon's Point Plantation (1794-1861), St. Simon's Island, Georgia. PhD. dissertation, Department of Anthropology, Univ. of Florida, Gainesville, University Microfilms, Ann Arbor, Michigan.

A Planter
1836 Notions on the management of Negroes. *Southern Agriculturist* **9:**580–584, 625–627.

Savannah Georgian
1832 Newspapers on file at the Wimberley George de Renne Library, Univ. of Georgia at Athens.

Scarborough, William K.
1966 *The overseer: Plantation management in the Old South.* Baton Rouge: Louisiana State Univ. Press.

South, Stanley A.
1972 Evolution and horizon as revealed in ceramic analysis in historical archaeology. *The Conference on Historic Site Archaeology Papers 1971* **6:**71–106.

Stone, Garry Wheeler
1970 Ceramics in Suffolk County, Massachusetts, inventories 1680–1775—A preliminary study with diverse comments thereon, and sundry suggestions. *The Conference on Historic Site Archaeology Papers 1968* **3:** Part 2.

Teller, Barbara G.
1968 Ceramics in Providence 1750–1800. *Antiques* **94:**570–577.

Van Doren, Mark (editor)
1929 *Correspondence of Aaron Burr and his daughter Theodosia.* New York: Stratford Press.

Van Rensselaer, Susan
1966 Banded creamware. *Antiques* **90:**337–341.

Whiter, Leonard
1970 *Spode: A history of the family, factory, and wares from 1733–1833.* New York: Praeger.

A Subsurface Sampling Strategy for Archeological Reconnaissance

STANLEY SOUTH
RANDOLPH WIDMER

The study presented here is based on the analysis section of an archeological reconnaissance conducted at the request of the South Carolina Department of Wildlife and Marine Resources, and by the General Services Administration, Atlanta, Georgia. The reconnaissance was conducted during 9 days in January, in 1976, by four staff members of the Institute of Archeology and Anthropology at the University of South Carolina. The site was that of a proposed marine resources research center at Fort Johnson, South Carolina, on the south side of Charleston Harbor.

After an assessment was made of the archeological potential of the site, a research design was outlined based on the presence of both prehistoric Indian and historic nineteenth and twentieth century American occupation debris. Since the site consisted of sand ridges susceptible to erosion by wind and water, a subsurface sampling strategy was considered the best approach to discovery of the areas once occupied by man. Through such a strategy the density and dispersion of artifacts from occupation in prehistoric or historic times could be determined. The details of the study have been presented elsewhere (South and Widmer 1976). The purpose of this chapter is to present the basic outline of the sampling strategy used to achieve the goals of the reconnaissance, and the results emerging from it.

THEORETICAL BASE AND RESEARCH GOALS

The conceptual framework and research orientation under which the sampling carried out in this project was conducted is presented here. This base provides a summary of the problems, assumptions, hypotheses, postulates, and goals relevant to the data within the research frame of the project.

Although this presentation is divided for convenience into two sections on the basis of prehistoric Indian and historic American occupations, the theory, methods, and goals of the archeology are no different. Concepts and methods found valid for recovery and analysis of Indian-made lithics and pottery do not become invalid with the addition of historical documentation. The addition of the historical data base does not invalidate archeological analyses of lithics in the form of gunflints, and pottery in the form of creamware from the British colonial system. Thus the research strategy used in this project is an archeological approach to problem solving independent of the data-biased prejudice that suggests data from one cultural system to be somehow more "valid" than those from another. A major methodological goal of this study is the demonstration that data-biased prejudice has no place in a science of archeology.

Prehistoric Indian Occupation

The stone projectile points, fire-cracked rocks, lithic debitage and other cultural materials characteristic of the Archaic Period in the Piedmont area of South Carolina are not so often found in the coastal zone (South 1960). More characteristic of the coastal area is the concentration, on the high ground adjacent to the sounds and marshes, of middens containing oysters, clams, conchs, and mussels. These deposits of shell midden are seen as the result of the use of tidal marshes and streams by Indians during pottery-making times. Pottery is the attribute whereby the Archaic Period has been traditionally distinguished from the Woodland Period (Griffin 1952:352; Ritchie 1932). The basic hypothesis emerging from this patterning is that the subsistence base during the Archaic Period was hunting and gathering, nonshellfish exploitation of the natural environment, whereas the subsistence base during the Woodland Period was a combination of hunting and gathering with utilization of tidal resources. Very little is known about either of these periods in the coastal Carolina area. Such details as the length of time represented in shell midden deposits of varying depths and whether the deposits are the result of many seasonal visits or semipermanent occupations are only beginning to be explored. Biases are built into the archeologist by his attention being drawn to the areas where shell midden deposits are to be seen. These areas he calls "sites," as opposed to those areas where he does not see visible signs of shell midden on the surface. The archeologist knows little yet, however, of the functional and behavioral variables involved between those areas where shell deposits are located and those areas where they are not. Any study of an area of coastal Carolina, where this variability exists between shell deposits and areas of no shell, presents an ideal opportunity to examine the relevance of this patterning to the level of archeological theory now present; i.e., a period of subsistence based on nonshellfish exploitation of the natural environment, hunting and gathering (ca. 8000 B.C. to ca. 2500 B.C.), was followed by a period of hunting and gathering combined with shellfish exploitation (ca. 2500 B.C. to the eighteenth century) (Coe 1964; South 1960, 1973; Stoltman 1974).

The presence of prehistoric-occupation refuse on the ridge of site 38CH16 (Ridge 1, Figure 6.1), to the south of the sample frame, has resulted in an assumption that this ridge would be the major area of occupation by prehistoric Indian groups. The presence of a relatively heavy concentration of shell midden in the roadway across this ridge reinforced this assumption. The infrequency of surface evidence for shell midden deposition, and the absence of Indian ceramics or other cultural refuse in the area to the north of this ridge also contributed to a bias favoring this ridge as the likely site for major Indian occupation by those

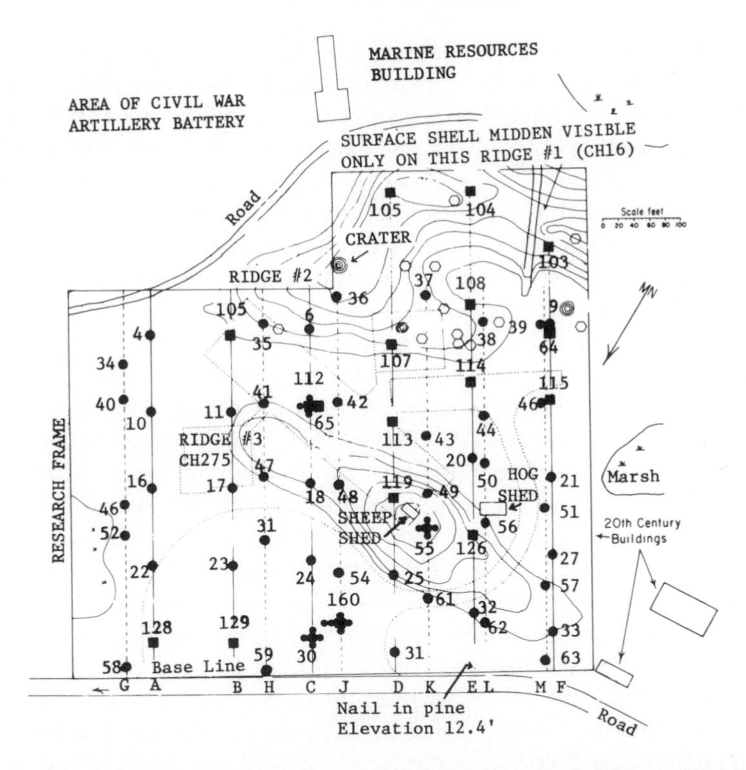

Figure 6.1. Provenience units within the research frame at Fort Johnson, South Carolina. ●23 = interval-aligned core sample #23 (lines A-F); ●46 = random-aligned core sample #46 (lines G-M); ■128 = 3′-square #128 at core sample #28; ✤30 = additional core samples 10′ from core sample #30; ····· = edge of proposed building area; ○ = Civil War brick rubble piles.

using the tidal resources of the marsh to the south of site 38CH16. The area of this visual bias based on shell concentration on the surface is seen in Figure 6.1.

However, a single test square into Ridge 3 (38CH275) revealed some oyster shell midden associated with prehistoric cultural material, suggesting that some occupation of Ridge 3 by Indians did take place. Based on this information, a major Indian occupation on Ridge 1 and a dispersed occupation on Ridge 3 were postulated. No evidence of Indian occupation was expected to be found in the very low ground area to the north of Ridge 3 and elsewhere in the area to be examined. Our hypothesis was this: If Indian occupation is revealed to have occurred in the low ground, we can no longer assume that the high ridges reflect the total area of Indian occupation in the area, an assumption frequently made in the past. As we will see, subsurface sampling revealed a different occupation density than that suggested by surface indications.

Historic American Occupation

Occupation of the area of the sample frame in the eighteenth, nineteenth, and twentieth centuries would be revealed by cultural materials known to have been used during this period of time (Noël Hume 1970; South 1972; 1977). The Charleston area was occupied in the seventeenth century by people participating in a British colonial system (Cheves 1897), so the area has been continuously occupied to the present. Occupation within the area of the sample frame during this period would result in cultural materials easily placed in chronological position through knowledge of manufacture periods of artifacts, particularly ceramics (Noël Hume 1970; South 1972). Frequency relationships of groups of artifact classes relating to behavior centered around the *Kitchen, Architecture, Furniture, Arms, Clothing, Personal, Tobacco Pipes,* and other activities should reflect those expected for sites of British colonial origin. The patterned range of expected redundancy and variability between artifact groups in sites of British colonial origin of the eighteenth century and two-thirds of the nineteenth century has been expressed in terms of a Carolina Pattern (South 1977). Sites of German American colonial origin, as well as Spanish American and French American origin, are expected to reveal highly contrasting patterns to that of the Carolina Pattern.

The explanation of pattern variability from sites representing different colonial expansionist systems lies in hypotheses directed at the system. German American colonial settlements would be expected to reflect a far greater reliance on self-sufficiency than would a contemporary British colonial town depending on a virtual line of ships to keep the occupants supplied with the latest goods from the mother country (South 1977).

Delineating pattern from the archeological record is the first step toward testing such hypotheses. Because of the distributive systems of nations during the period of American colonization, a far greater network is represented by the British colonial system, for instance, than is ever seen when material culture of the American Indian is involved. Therefore, artifacts from historic sites must be interpreted to a far more expansive system than artifacts from an Indian occupation. Before the sherds of ceramics and glass and the nails and bricks recovered on historic sites can be demonstrated to have relevance to broad nationalistic expansionist systems exploiting, developing, exploring, and settling America, the patterned relationships in the archeological record must be delineated. A control of great value in this process is historical documentation, which can allow for holding of one or more variables constant while examining the archeological patterning. It is this potential for controlling variables that holds the secret to the most effective use of historical documentation relating to historic sites.

Functional variability such as the position of the site on the colonial frontier also reveals pattern contrasting with the Carolina Pattern, which is based on domestic and military sites close to supply lines (South 1977). Functional variability within a site of British colonial origin is expected to be revealed through deviation of an artifact group's frequency ratio from expected margins; for example, a high *Clothing* group ratio reflects a tailor shop, whereas a high *Arms* group ratio reveals a military function for the sample (South 1977).

Late nineteenth century and twentieth century artifact patterns are not yet known, having yet to be delineated. Such data, however, can be placed in temporal context, and historical research can be used to examine the implications of function, status, and other cultural variables from such material remains of culture.

The present level of theory in historical archeology is oriented, as we have said, to testing ideas of chronology (South 1972), function (Ferguson 1975; South 1977), culture process (Dethlefsen and Deetz 1966), and status (Ferguson 1975; Otto 1975). Pattern in historical archeology is just beginning to be explored with a view of delineating nationalistic, ethnic, functional, status, and other variables on an intrasite and intersite basis (South 1977). Any recovery of cultural materials from the historic period within the sampling frame (Figure 6.1) would be expected to reveal patterning relevant to that already archeologically delineated, as well as to historical documentation. The goal of this pattern recognition is the testing and refinement of ideas about the behavioral processes that produced the static archeological record being examined.

The three-gun battery of the Civil War period located near the southwest corner of the survey frame reveals the use of the area during the mid-nineteenth century (Delafield 1865:War Department Map). The roadway cutting through the top of Ridge 1 on site 38CH16 reveals mid-nineteenth century bottle glass and ironstone–whiteware china (South 1974), as well as a friction primer for artillery (Ripley 1970:233), and South Carolina made alkaline-glazed stoneware (Greer 1971). In addition to this a number of piles of bricks scattered through the woods on Ridge 2, as well as a few on Ridge 1, suggest the ruins of Civil War period structures associated with the artillery battery (South 1959). These piles of bricks are characterized by several large conch shells among the rubble (Figure 6.1). Maps of the 1860s reveal several buildings in the area of Ridge 2 (National Archives 1860s). These surface indications suggest a military occupation of the area of Ridge 1 and 2 during the Civil War period. A sampling procedure designed to reflect occupation of various areas of the survey frame at different periods should reveal refuse resulting from this mid-nineteenth century occupation. Debris from such an occupation would be expected to take the form of refuse from domestic activities such as ceramics and bottles (kitchen artifacts), and bone and shell from meals, and architectural artifacts such as bricks, mortar, nails, and glass, as well as military-associated objects such as friction primers, percussion caps, musket balls, and military buttons. The area where such cultural items are expected to be revealed by a sampling procedure is shown in Figure 6.1 by the presence of brick rubble piles of the Civil War period.

At the northwest quadrant of the survey area two abandoned structures from recent use of the area can be seen. One of these, a sheep shed, is still usable. The other, a hog building, has been dismantled; only a concrete floor and a few standing wall timbers remain. These structures, and the area surrounding them, had been used by the Medical University of South Carolina to house animals used in disease-control research. A sampling procedure in the survey area should reveal some evidence of twentieth century debris here.

At the northwest corner of the survey area a Quonset hut and a guardhouse are still standing. These are being used by the South Carolina Marine Resources Division. Twentieth century debris is to be seen in this area also, and sampling in this corner of the sampling frame should reveal evidence of this occupation.

The present asphalt-paved King's Road to Fort Johnson extends along the northern side of the survey area. Debris associated with the construction of and use of this road might well be expected to be revealed in samples taken adjacent to this roadway.

Fences and power lines crossing the survey area are not expected to reflect their presence in the samples to be taken in their vicinity. The following hypotheses relate to these occupations within the sampling frame.

Hypotheses (Ideas Addressed to the Past Cultural System)

1. The contrast between the shell midden on the first ridge and the cultural data not associated with shell midden is hypothesized to represent the difference between a subsistence using *tidal resources* and one oriented more toward *hunting.*

2. It is expected that such a contrast would also reflect a *temporal difference,* with the *tidal-resource–subsistence pattern* being prevalent primarily during pottery-making times. Cultural material would represent *hunting* and accompanying food preparation activities dating primarily from the *Archaic Period.*

3. Ceramics in the area behind the first ridge not in association with oyster shell midden might suggest *dwellings* as opposed to *preparation and eating of foods* relating to tidal streams and marshes on the ridge *nearest these resources.*

4. If cultural data is recovered from the low ground around the higher ridges, then the surface evidence of oyster shell midden so often seen nearest the tidal marshes cannot be taken as reflecting the total *area of occupation on such sites.*

5. The occurrence of *postholes* in association with other cultural material suggests the presence of architectural features dependent on posts set below the surface of the ground. A concentration of such features suggests *architecturally related activity* as opposed to an area where no such features are present.

6. The occurrence of *pit features* in association with other cultural data suggests behavioral implications dependent on the form, content, and associations present. Such features suggest different behavioral activity from those areas where such features are not present; activity such as *food storage, cooking, and use of fire pits.*

7. The dispersion of functionally related artifact groups provides a means for the functional interpretation of behavioral variables. Building materials such as daub, burned wooden timbers, brick, mortar, and nails suggest *architecturally related activity* such as the building of dwellings, sheds, barracks, and lean-tos. The presence of ceramics and other containers, cooking utensils, hearths, and the like suggest *food preparation activities.* The association of artifacts related to *military activity* in higher than expected quantitative margins based on the *Carolina Pattern* would suggest military activity on the site.

8. The *dispersion of cultural materials from different temporal periods* provides the data necessary for interpreting the *culture history* of the site.

Postulates (Ideas Addressed to the Archeological Record)

Postulates addressed to the relationships within the archeological record are based on my studies in the Carolina area (South 1960, 1970, 1973, 1977).

1. The occurrence of oyster shell midden along the ridge paralleling the sounds and tidal marshes in the Carolinas associated with Indian pottery of the Wilmington and Cape Fear ware groups has been observed.
2. The thickest concentration of oyster shell midden on the ridge paralleling tidal marshes has been observed to be on the off-sound side of the ridge, not on top of the ridge itself.
3. The discovery in the coastal Carolina area of baked clay objects (man-made stone substitutes) not associated with shell middens indicates that such artifacts are not always found with such middens.
4. The Archaic Period on the coast of Carolina is not characterized by large quantities of lithic materials as is the case in Piedmont areas of the Carolinas.
5. The occurrence of cultural material not in association with shell middens on sites in coastal Carolina indicates that sites occur in areas where no shell midden exists.
6. Less shell midden concentration is expected in the area behind the first ridge paralleling the tidal marsh.
7. A higher percentage of cultural material not associated with shell middens would be expected to occur behind the first ridge paralleling the tidal marshland.
8. A higher percentage of nineteenth century cultural material would be expected along the southern two ridges in the sample frame, with twentieth century occupation debris dispersed in the area of twentieth century buildings and along the twentieth century road along the northern edge of the sample frame.

Assumptions (Ideas Linking the Archeological Record and Behavioral Processes)

Assumptions involving the relationship between the formation processes of the archeological record in relation to past behavioral processes are outlined as follows (Binford 1962, 1964; Schiffer 1972; Schiffer and Rathje 1973; South 1977).

1. The dispersion of cultural materials spatially and stratigraphically is considered to be the result of past behavioral processes and the formation processes of the archeological record.
2. The cultural data (such as oyster shell midden, ceramics, bone frag-

ments, and lithic materials) recovered within the sampling frame are considered primary refuse, deposited in the place of use and comprising in its patterning the potential for interpretations of causal behavioral processes.

3. The area of the sample frame is considered to be relatively undisturbed in regard to the mechanical removal of soil by man (cultural transformation processes).

4. The area of the sample frame is composed primarily of sand that is considered to have been blown by wind and transported by rainwater at varying rates depending on ground cover and other environmental variables, resulting in differential burying of cultural materials (natural transformation processes).

5. The quantitative variability and redundancy between artifact types, classes, and groups embodies the potential for interpretations of causal behavioral processes.

In order to apply these generalized assumptions to the specific case, methodological strategies directed at specific goals must be delineated (Asch 1975; Mueller 1975).

Methodological Goals (Specific Research Strategies Addressed to the Archeological Record)

Method-Testing Goals

1. Thirty random-aligned core samples will be compared with a set of 30 interval-aligned cores for the purpose of comparing:

a. the *time* involved to execute the procedures;

b. the *dispersion of cultural data* revealed by interpolation between sampling units illustrated with a computer mapping program (SYMAP);

c. the *combined interval-aligned samples with random-aligned samples* to discover the contrasts and similarities between the two smaller and the larger combined total of the core samples.

2. The dispersion of cultural data revealed by interpolations in the form of SYMAPS using data from *10 three-foot squares* will be compared with data from *80 core samples plus 20 others* (see page 129).

3. The dispersion of cultural data revealed by interpolations in the form of SYMAPS using data from all *17 three-foot squares* will be compared with that revealed by all *80 core samples.*

4. *Quantitative relationships* between the cultural materials from 3-foot squares and the adjacent core sample will be compared for determining the variability in the ratios between the smaller and larger samples to test the reliability of the core-sampling technique.

5. Areas of the sample frame containing *visible surface evidence* of

past occupation will be compared with SYMAP interpolations to determine the degree of fit.

Discovery Goals

1. Ten excavated squares stratified into 2 five-square sets on the basis of *high ground* and *low ground* will be compared as to the dispersion and density of artifact data revealed by SYMAP interpolations (synagraphic computer mapping program).

2. The *density and dispersion of cultural data* within the sample frame as revealed by SYMAP interpolations will be examined for determining the behavioral implications of this variability.

3. *Features* such as postholes and pits from *high-ground* and *low-ground* squares will be compared for determining behavioral implications from variability.

4. The dispersion of artifacts from *stratigraphic levels* in the core samples will be compared using SYMAP interpolations to identify cultural components from different *temporal periods* and different spatial areas within the sampling frame.

METHOD

The Core-Sampling Tool

A series of tests with various types of augers and a standard posthole digger was conducted. This comparison of tools clearly revealed the common two-handled, manual posthole digger to be the best tool for the purpose we had in mind. Subsurface sampling of archeological sites has been successfully carried out using this tool as early as 1947 (Stephenson 1970:63), and more recently by Wood (1975). Ferguson and Widmer (1976) and Percy (1976) have used power-driven augers with considerable success.

Most of the samples in the present sampling survey were taken to a depth of 4 feet. A few cores had soft, powdery sand at the 3-foot level; this sand could not be lifted out of the hole. As long as the sand was moist, the posthole digger would easily lift a column of soil.

The Core-Sampling Scheme—The Research Frame

We compared 30 random-aligned core samples with 30 interval-aligned samples in terms of time of execution and dispersion of samples within the research frame and found differences to be negligible. The primary argument for using a randomly chosen sample relates to the possibility of regularly spaced data; and whenever statistical comparison of the data is involved, random samples are preferred to help to avoid possible bias. (Mueller 1975). For adequate *coverage* of core-sample points within the research frame, however, sample cores taken along grid lines at intervals would be most effective, particularly when used in the discovery or reconnaissance phase of a research design.

The research frame within which the interval-aligned and random-aligned sets of core samples were taken measured 650 by 500 feet (Figure 6.1). Within this area, six lines (*A–F*) were cut through the undergrowth at 100-foot intervals perpendicular to a baseline paralleling King's Road to Fort Johnson. Six additional parallel lines (*G–M*) were cut after their position had been determined within 100-foot intervals for lines *A* through *F*, and randomly positioned for lines *G* through *M*. This resulted in 30 core-sample points for each set of six lines, a total of 60 core samples.

After the 60 core samples were obtained the area of those samples having Indian pottery present (Cores 12, 30, 55, and 60) was further examined by obtaining additional core samples in four directions at a distance of 10 feet from each original sample (Figure 6.1). We did this in order to pinpoint any concentrations of ceramics that may have been reflected by the pottery fragment from the original core sample. Only one of the additional 17 core samples taken with this goal in mind revealed pottery fragment. The 17 core samples were added to the original 60 samples for the purpose of illustrating artifact dispersion through SYMAP interpolation. The SYMAP (synagraphic computer mapping program) allows for the production of a map interpolating the density and dispersion of artifact classes within a research frame using core-sample data (Dudnik 1971).

Three additional core samples were taken from the top of Ridge 1 for comparison of this site 38CH16 with the area of site 38CH275, designated as Ridge 2, and Ridge 3. These three samples were combined with the other 77 samples, for a total of 80 core samples, resulting in the research frame seen in Figure 6.1.

A series of 17 three-foot squares was also excavated to provide some insight into the relationship between the subsurface core samples and the research universe as represented by three-foot squares.

Comparison of the Core Samples and the Test-Square Samples

The degree to which any sample can be seen to predict the archeological universe from which it is drawn can be determined only by totally excavating the universe and comparing these data with the sample. Since total excavation of the entire research frame is impossible, an insight into the degree to which the subsurface sample reflects the universe can be obtained by comparing the core sample with a 3-foot test square. The question still remains as to how much of the universe is reflected by a 3-foot-square sample. Nevertheless, simple ratio comparison between core samples and adjacent 3-foot squares might help us understand just what the core sample represents, at least in terms of a 3-foot-square area.

By computing the difference between a 3-foot test square (1296 square inches) and the 6-inch in diameter posthole digger core sample (28.3 square inches), the ratio is found to be 45.8 to 1. This ratio can be expressed as the *ideal expected ratio.* Since we are primarily concerned with examining our method, we are merely using this ratio as a base against which to project the empirical ratios of various artifact classes as they actually occur between 3-foot squares and core samples. This procedure can be seen in Table 6.1.

The shell class is the most frequently occurring object, and this has the ratio more closely approximating the ideal or expected ratio. Table 6.2 compares the frequencies of nineteenth century artifact classes from core samples and 3-foot squares.

We can see from the comparison in the table that the larger the quantity of artifacts present in a class, the closer the ratio is to the expected. Thus we can have far more confidence in the predictive character of a SYMAP interpolation of the dispersion of nails as reflecting a nineteenth century occupation area than we could have in one based on musket balls, for instance. Likewise, we could be more confident of the accuracy of a SYMAP interpolation based on 80 core samples of the dispersion of shell middens than one based on potsherds. This comparison, therefore, tells us which artifact classes are most suited for producing SYMAP interpolations from sample data. We are *not* attempting here to obtain a statistical statement of the predictive relationship between the sample and the universe. We are merely testing

TABLE 6.1
Comparison of Prehistoric Artifact Frequencies of Combined Test Squares and Corresponding Core Samples

Artifact	Artifact frequencies		
	Squares	Core samples	Ratios[a]
Shell	45575.5 grams	1612.4 grams	28.2:1
Bone	161.8 grams	11.4 grams	14.1:1
Lithics	5		
Charcoal	200.1 grams	22.5 grams	8.9:1
Potsherds	265	32	8.3:1
Clay Balls	17	5	3.4:1

[a] The expected ratio for each type of artifact was 45.8:1. Computed from the difference in the area of a 3-foot test square (1296 square inches) and that of a 6-inch-diameter core sample (28.3 square inches).

TABLE 6.2
Comparison of the Nineteenth Century Artifact Frequencies of Combined Test Squares and Corresponding Core Samples

Category	Artifact frequencies		
	Squares	Core samples	Ratios[a]
Ceramics	47	2	23.5 : 1
Bottle Glass	81	4	20.2 : 1
Total *Kitchen*	128	6	21.3 : 1
Window Glass	13	2	6.5 : 1
Nails	193	4	48.2 : 1
Construction Hardware	25		
Total *Architecture*	231	6	38.5 : 1
Balls, Sprue	6	5	1.2 : 1
Misc. Military	5		
Total Military (*Arms*)	11	5	2.2 : 1
Personal Items	1		
Tobacco Pipes	2		
Total all classes	373	17	21.9 : 1

[a] The expected ratio for each category was 45.8 : 1. Computed from the difference in the area of a 3-foot test square (1296 square inches) and that of a 6-inch diameter core sample (28.3 square inches).

the variability in the degree of confidence we can have in SYMAP interpolations of the various artifact classes we have recovered for the purpose of discovery. In doing so, we have found that shell middens and the *Architecture* and *Kitchen* artifact groups from the nineteenth century occupation are those in which we can have most confidence. With this information in hand we will use the SYMAP interpolations for these groups in the analysis to follow.

ANALYSIS

Classification of the Data

The artifacts and floral and faunal remains resulting from cultural activity recovered from the core-sampling procedure were classified into 14 groups for SYMAP analysis, as seen in Table 6.3.

SYMAP Ranking Schemes

In order to obtain a synagraphic computer map (Dudnik 1971) interpolating the dispersion and density of artifact classes and groups within the research frame from the 80 score samples, the data were quantified by weight or count. A ranking scheme was devised ranging from 0 through 4 for illustrating by means of SYMAP interpolations the relative density

TABLE 6.3
Core Sample Artifact Classification System for SYMAP Analysis

	Group	Class
1.	Shell	
2.	Bone	
3.	Lithics	
4.	Charcoal	
5.	Clay Balls	
6.	Total Potsherds	
7.	Plain Sherds	
8.	Deptford Series	
9.	Cape Fear Series	
10.	Wilmington/Hanover Series	
11.	19th Century *Architecture*	Nails
		Brick Fragments
		Mortar Fragments
		Window Glass
		Construction Hardware
12.	19th Century *Kitchen*	Bottle Glass
		Ceramics
		a. Stoneware
		b. Annular Ironstone–Whiteware
		c. Plain Ironstone–Whiteware
		Metal Flakes
13.	19th Century Military (*Arms*)	Balls, Shot, Sprue
		Percussion Caps
		Military Buttons
14.	20th Century Artifacts	Crushed Granite (Road Metal), Asphalt
		Quartz Pebbles (Sheep Shed)
		Misc. Items (Hog Shed)
		a. Hypodermic Needle
		b. Expanded Metal Lathing Fragments
		c. Copper Telephone Line Clip
		d. Other

of an artifact class. These ranking schemes were based on the clustering of the empirical data rather than by dividing the range into five equal parts (South and Widmer 1976). With these steps taken the SYMAP computer program was used for producing maps illustrating visually the interpolated dispersion and density of artifact classes. Over 230 such maps were evaluated, from which four drawings were made for use in the section to follow.

Dispersion of Twentieth Century Artifacts

One of the goals of the research design was to determine whether the core-sampling procedure would reveal twentieth century occupation in the areas of the research frame where visible evidence of such occupation can be seen. Within the research frame, two structures can still be seen, a sheep shed and hog shed, formerly used by the Medical University of South Carolina for disease control research (Figures 6.1–6.2). Along the northwest side of the research frame runs King's Road to Fort Johnson. The sampling design should also reveal evidence of this major twentieth century feature. The results of the SYMAP interpolation from the 80 core samples can be seen in Figure 6.2, where both the sheds are clearly indicated by the dispersion and density of twentieth century artifacts. The location of King's Road to Fort Johnson is revealed by three areas along the northwest side of the research frame, clearly identifying a twentieth century feature or features.

As the classification system reveals (Table 6.3), the data consist of granite metaling for the road, quartz pebbles for the sheep shed floor, and other twentieth century artifacts for the hog shed. Of particular interest was a hypodermic needle recovered in Core Sample 56, near the

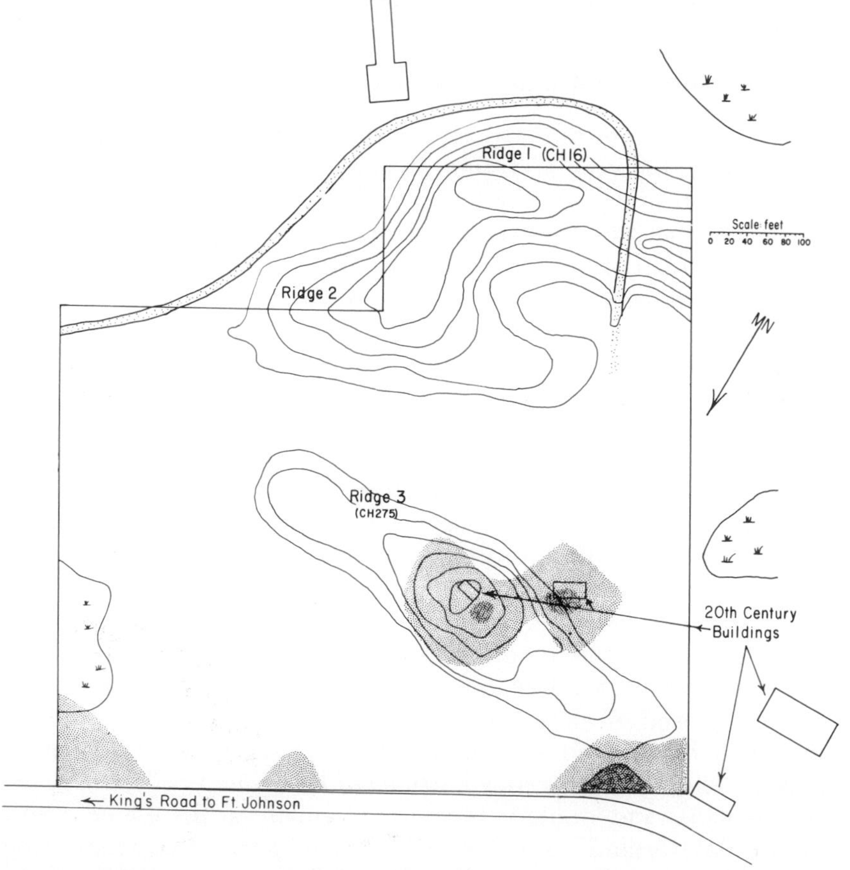

Figure 6.2. Dispersion of twentieth century artifacts interpolated from 80 core samples at Fort Johnson. ▩ = high density; ░ = low density.

hog shed, suggesting a medical function for occupation in this area. The expanded metal lathing fragments and copper telephone line clip, as well as other twentieth century artifacts, suggest functional relationships because of our knowledge of the use of these items. It is extremely encouraging to see that in a sampling design of this type we can not only pinpoint the occupation sites, the time period involved, but gain some insights into the function of the structures involved. The contemporary knowledge that these were medical facilities, with telephones, containing walls plastered on metal lathe, allows us to have a degree of confidence in interpretations to this effect based on the archeological sample. The major point here, however, is the fact that the sampling design revealed the twentieth century occupation known to have been within the research frame. As a discovery tool, therefore, this approach appears to have sensitivity enough to reveal such occupation. Specific functional and other problem solving would come in a later archeological phase designed to elicit such information after the sites are located by the procedure we have used here.

Dispersion of Nineteenth Century Artifacts

The closeness of the southern area of the research frame to a Civil War period artillery battery, and the presence of 13 brick rubble piles thought to represent chimney locations for military occupation of the site suggested that the core-sampling procedure should reveal artifacts of that period concentrated in this area. Also of interest was whether the sampling procedure would reveal the military function of the known mid-nineteenth century occupation. The only artifact specifically identifying the military function of the nineteenth century occupation on the site was a U.S. Army General Service button (38CH275-64A-11) of the type 263 used after 1854 by all enlisted men (Johnson 1948:65).

Cut nails, bottle glass, and other artifact fragments were of nineteenth century types, with the mid-manufacture date for ironstone being ca. 1857, and that for whiteware being ca. 1860 (South 1972). The evidence from the artifacts and historical documentation suggests a mid-nineteenth century time period for the occupation responsible for the debris found in the sampling survey.

The artifacts from the nineteenth century were classified into three groups, *Architecture, Kitchen,* and *Military* (Table 6.3). The *Architecture* group is composed of nails, brick fragments, mortar, window glass, etc., and the *Kitchen* group consists of bottle glass, ceramics, etc. The *military* group is made up of arms-related artifacts such as lead balls, shot, sprue, percussion caps, and military buttons. Normally arms-related artifacts cannot be interpreted as representing a military occupation unless specific military items such as bayonets, insignia, and military buttons are also present (South 1977). Since historical documentation and the presence of a military button both suggest a military occupation of the site during the Civil War period all arms-related artifacts recovered in this study were placed in the military *Arms* group.

The dispersion of *Architecture* and *Kitchen* group artifacts as revealed by SYMAP interpolation from the 80 core samples can be seen in Figure 6.3. The military (*Arms*) artifacts are shown by a star symbol as they were present in both the 80 core samples and the 17 test squares. There is clearly a concentration of nineteenth century artifacts related to architecture, food preparation (kitchen), and military (arms) activity in the area where the brick rubble chimney piles are located (Figure 6.3). This concentration is on Ridge 2, and along the west side of the research

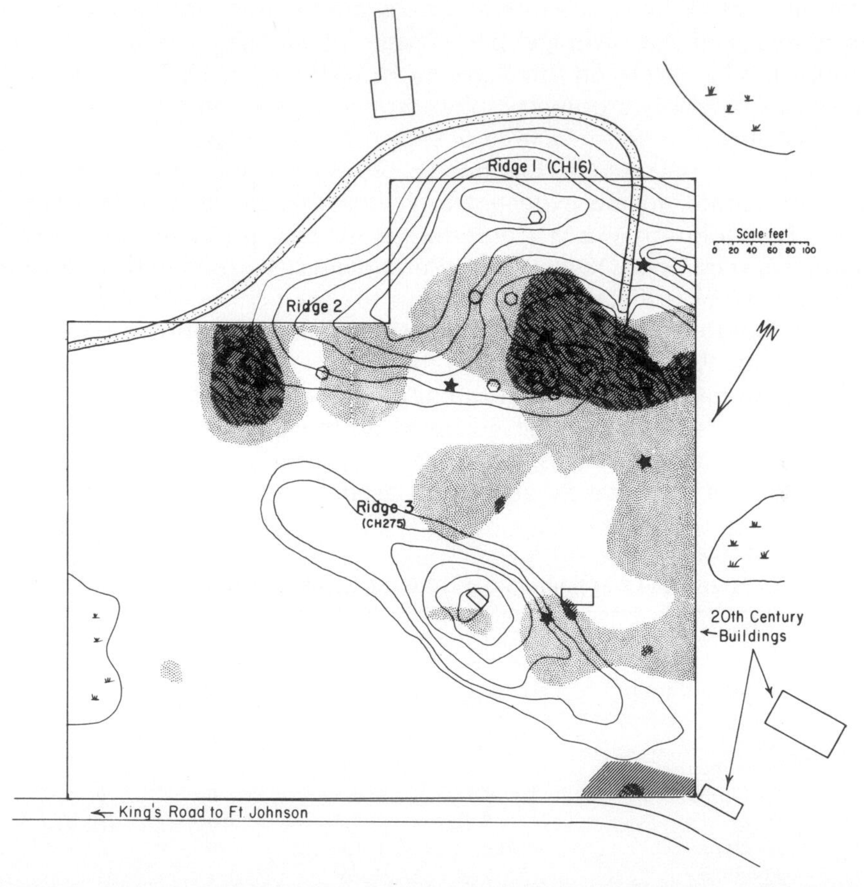

Figure 6.3. Dispersion of mid-nineteenth century artifacts interpolated from 80 core samples compared with the presence of military artifacts from 17 three-foot squares and 80 core samples. ░ = Architecture Group artifacts; ▨ = Kitchen Group artifacts, ★ = presence of Military Group artifacts; ○ = brick rubble piles from the Civil War period.

frame. The dispersion of nineteenth century occupation debris in the area predicted by the presence of architectural remains in the form of piles of brick rubble from chimneys reveals that the core-sampling procedure is an excellent discovery tool for pinpointing such occupation areas. This would have been so regardless of whether surviving piles of chimney rubble were to be seen on the site. Once such areas of occupation are pinpointed by a subsurface sampling scheme such as that used here, specific research designs for further problem solving can be constructed to focus on these areas.

Comparison of the Fort Johnson Data with the Frontier Pattern

Some sites of the eighteenth and early nineteenth centuries have been examined and the average percentage relationship between artifact groups has been termed the Carolina Pattern (South 1977). The Carolina Pattern is primarily a domestic phenomenon although some permanent military sites close to the source of supply are also expected to fall within its range. The percentage relationship between artifact groups from Fort Johnson would not be expected to match that of the Carolina Pattern since Fort Johnson was a Confederate military fort later captured by Federal forces (Scott 1880:4, 114). Percentages are obtained by dividing the total for all artifacts recovered into the total of each of eight artifact groups (South 1977). The percentages for Fort Johnson compared with the Carolina Pattern are shown in Table 6.4.

It should be noted here that the percentage for *Kitchen* and *Architecture* group artifacts are reversed between the Carolina Pattern and Fort Johnson, and that the *Arms* group for Fort Johnson is far greater than the upper limit of the *Arms* range in the Carolina Pattern. Clearly there is no

TABLE 6.4
Comparison of Fort Johnson Data with the Carolina Pattern

	Carolina Pattern		Fort Johnson	
Artifact group	Percentage	Range	Percentage	Count
Kitchen	63.1	51.8–69.2	33.6	142
Architecture	25.5	19.7–31.4	61.7	261
Furniture	.2	.1–.6	0	0
Arms	.5	.1–1.2	4.0	17
Clothing	3.0	.6–5.4	0	0
Personal	.2	.1–.5	.2	1
Tobacco Pipes	5.8	1.8–13.9	.5	2
Activities	1.7	.9–2.7	0	0
Totals	100.0		100.0	423

TABLE 6.5
Comparison of Fort Johnson with the Frontier Pattern

	Frontier Pattern		Fort Johnson	
Artifact group	Percentage	Range	Percentage	Count
Kitchen	27.6	22.7–34.5	33.6	142
Architecture	52.0	43.0–57.5	61.7	261
Furniture	.2	.1–.3	0	0
Arms	5.4	1.4–8.4	4.0	17
Clothing	1.7	.3–3.8	0	0
Personal	.2	.1–.4	.2	1
Tobacco Pipes	9.1	1.9–14.0	.5	2
Activities	3.7	.7–6.4	0	0
Totals	99.9		100.0	423

match of pattern here. This phenomenon of reversal of percentage relationship between *Kitchen* and *Architecture* group artifacts has been noted on frontier sites of the eighteenth century (South 1977). When we compare the percentages from Fort Johnson with the Frontier Pattern (Table 6.5), there is a far greater similarity. Here the Fort Johnson percentages for *Kitchen* and *Architecture* group artifacts are very close to the upper range of the Frontier Pattern, and the *Arms* group of artifacts falls in the middle of the range for the Frontier Pattern. The Frontier Pattern was based on data from Fort Ligonier, Pennsylvania; Fort Prince George, South Carolina; and a trading post at Spalding's Lower Store, in Florida (South 1977).

Intersite Comparison of the Fort Johnson Artifact Group Data

In order to illustrate the relationships between the Fort Johnson data and other sites, the domestic and military sites are presented for comparison in Table 6.6.

The Fort Johnson *Kitchen, Architecture,* and *Arms* ratio is certainly more in keeping with the military and trading post sites than with the domestic sites. The Fort Moultrie military refuse from both the British and American occupations is patterned with the domestic sites, and this phenomenon has been discussed elsewhere (South 1977). These data indicate that by comparing Fort Johnson quantitatively with other patterned data the identification as a military site could have been made from this comparison alone. The remarkable point to keep in mind here is that this interpretation has emerged from a miniscule sample of the Fort Johnson site drawn by using a core-sampling technique in combination with several test squares. When only the core-sampling data are

TABLE 6.6
Comparison of *Kitchen, Architecture,* and *Arms* Group Artifacts from Other Sites (in Percentage of All Artifacts at Site)

Site[a]	*Kitchen*	*Architecture*	*Arms*
Fort Ligonier, Pa. (1758–1766)	25.6	55.6	8.4
Fort Prince George, S.C. (1753–1769)	22.7	57.5	6.4
Fort Watson, S.C. (1781)	43.8	41.6	8.9
Fort Johnson, S.C. (1860s)	33.6	61.7	4.0
Fort Moultrie, S.C. (British) (1780–1782)	69.2	19.7	1.2
Fort Moultrie, S.C. (American) (1775–1794)	68.6	24.8	.6
Brunswick, N.C. (tailor shop) (1732–1776)	61.1	26.2	.1
Brunswick, N.C. (S10 dwelling) (1728–1776)	51.8	31.4	.3
Cambridge 96, S.C. (dwelling) (1800–1820)	64.6	25.2	.1
Camden, S.C., (town, 1.0% sample) (1758–1820)	71.4	22.0	.2
Spalding's Lower Store, Fla. (trading post) (1763–?)	34.5	43.0	1.4

[a] Dates given are for the approximate documented range of occupation.

used, the military function of the site is even more pronounced; 29.4% are military artifacts, in relation to kitchen (35.3%), and architecture (35.3%).

As demonstrated elsewhere (South 1977), the secondary-refuse pattern at the group level on a site tends to maintain considerable regularity regardless of whether one uses all artifacts from the entire site, or only those from the front yard, or those from the major midden deposit, or those from each excavated square. The sampling strategy at Fort Johnson produced a relatively small number of artifacts that, in spite of the smallness of the sample size, reflect the patterning seen on military sites from which large samples were recovered. This phenomenon certainly supports the previous observations regarding the cohesive and persistent nature of cultural pattern as seen in the archeological record. The pattern comparison seen in Table 6.6 is presented graphically in Figure 6.4.

Intersite Comparison of the Fort Johnson Artifact Ratios

The function of a site can also be examined through simple artifact ratios. Only two will be examined here, ceramics and arms. Table 6.7 illustrates this procedure using data from nine sites of the eighteenth and early nineteenth centuries (South 1977). Four domestic sites from the Carolinas are seen to have a ceramic ratio ranging from .44 to .79, whereas five military frontier sites of the eighteenth century have ceramic ratios ranging from .11 to .25. The ceramic ratio from all proveniences at Fort Johnson is found to be .13, a figure well into the lower range of the military frontier sites.

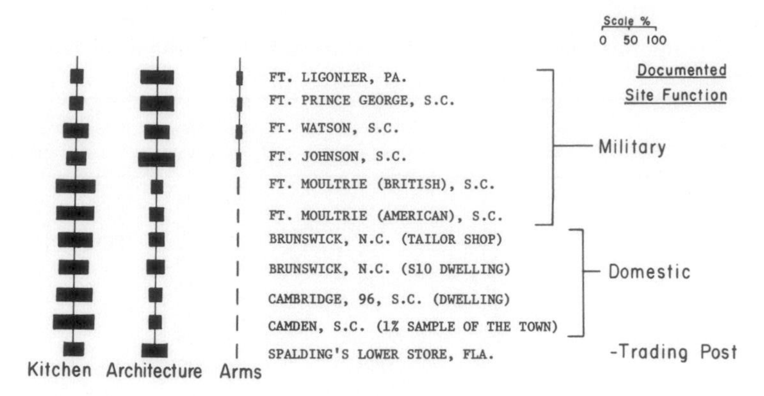

Figure 6.4. Intersite artifact group pattern at Fort Johnson.

Using the same procedure with the arms artifact classes for 10 eighteenth and early nineteenth century sites from the Carolinas, we can see a similar grouping of Fort Johnson with the military frontier sites. The domestic site pattern ranges from .0008 to .0034, whereas the military frontier sites have a range from .0056 to .0974. The Fort Johnson arms ratio of .0429 is clearly within the military frontier site grouping based on this means of comparison. This is illustrated in Table 6.8.

Comparison of ceramic and arms ratios from Fort Johnson with ratios from sites of known function has resulted in the identification of the Fort Johnson site as falling within the range of the military frontier sites of the eighteenth century. Whether this patterning will be found to hold true for other military sites of the mid-nineteenth century will have to await similar quantification analysis of data from such sites. These data do sug-

TABLE 6.7

Comparison of the Fort Johnson Nineteenth Century Ceramic Ratio with Ceramic Ratios from Other Sites

Site	Ceramics	÷	Artifact total less ceramics	=	Ceramic ratio[a]	Resulting site grouping
Brunswick S25	16288		20477		.79	Domestic sites
Brunswick S10	4618		8500		.54	
Brunswick S7	2521		5662		.44	
Cambridge 96	8751		11129		.79	
Fort Moultrie (American)	1217		4885		.25	18th century military frontier sites
Fort Moultrie (British)	269		1476		.18	
Fort Ligonier	3170		18608		.17	
Fort Prince George	764		6624		.11	
Spalding's Store	2796		13974		.20	
Fort Johnson	50		363		.13	

[a] Ceramic ratio is determined by dividing figure for ceramics by artifact total less ceramics.

TABLE 6.8

Comparison of the Fort Johnson Nineteenth Century Arms Ratio with Arms Ratios from Other Sites

Site	Arms	÷	Artifact total less arms	=	Arms ratio	Resulting site grouping
Brunswick S25	34		41235		.0008	Domestic sites
Brunswick S10	45		13073		.0034	
Brunswick S7	12		8171		.0014	
Cambridge 96	27		19853		.0013	
Fort Moultrie (American)	39		6924		.0056	18th century military frontier sites
Fort Moultrie (British)	20		2100		.0095	
Fort Ligonier	1820		19958		.0911	
Fort Prince George	471		6917		.0680	
Spalding's Store	227		16543		.0137	
Fort Watson	128		1314		.0974	
Fort Johnson	17		396		.0429	

gest, however, that similar cultural phenomena may well be involved in producing a patterned archeological record on French and Indian War sites, Revolutionary War sites, and trading post sites that is similar to that produced on military sites of the Civil War period.

We hypothesize that the explanation of this empirical patterning relates to the following variables: (1) the distance of military and frontier occupation from sources of supply; (2) the interruption by military duty of domestic patterns of acquisition and consumption of goods, and discard of the material by-products of behavior; (3) the utilization, in military units, of a single tin vessel and cup by enlisted men, with the few ceramic vessels being owned by officers (Francis Lord, personal communication), producing a dramatic drop in the consumption and breakage of ceramics and glassware, resulting in a high *Architecture*-to-*Kitchen* artifact ratio; (4) the "one firearm per family" pattern on domestic sites contrasted with the "one firearm per individual" pattern on military and frontier sites; (5) a frontier and military population dominated by adult males; (6) a functional and survival necessity for arms in frontier and military situations; and (7) the contrasting function between a permanent military garrison and a more mobile frontier outpost, with permanent garrisons having patterning more nearly approaching the domestic Carolina Pattern, because of the increased opportunity for replication of domestic lifeways. An explanation for the presently seen contrast between the Carolina Pattern and Frontier Pattern may well be that of sampling error, and this has been discussed elsewhere (South 1977).

Using the delineation of pattern from domestic, frontier, military, taverns, industrial, and other sites such as has been worked out with the

Fort Johnson data, we can begin to test hypotheses such as those listed here toward gaining a better understanding of cultural processes from the archeological record. In the presentation of data so far, we have been concerned with an ever-increasing specificity, moving from the level of broad redundancy represented by the Carolina and Frontier patterns to the examination of artifact groups such as *Kitchen, Architecture,* and *Arms,* and then to artifact classes such as the examination of ceramic ratios. In the section to follow we will examine the nineteenth century ceramic class of artifacts in more detail, dealing with functional form of the ceramic vessels.

A Functional Analysis of Nineteenth Century Ceramics from Fort Johnson

A total of 50 mid-nineteenth century ceramic fragments were recovered during the core sampling and test-square sampling of the Fort Johnson site. Plain and annular ironstone–whiteware (South 1974) made up 21 of these sherds, all of which were fragments of cups or bowls. The remaining 29 sherds were from stoneware jugs and jars or similar storage containers. These data suggest that ceramics at this site were limited to heavy stoneware vessels used for storage of liquids, and ironstone–whiteware cups and bowls used in the consumption of food. Note that plates were absent from the sample. This suggests that food was probably in a form more easily consumed from bowls than from plates, perhaps stew. These data are illustrated in Table 6.9.

The interpretation of these data relative to the consumption of stew-type dishes is entirely in keeping with what is known of the eating habits of Civil War period military personnel (Francis Lord, personal communication). The tin plate and cup were the basic equipment for food prepared in quantity in iron pots, a military tradition carried over from well

TABLE 6.9

A Functional Analysis of the Nineteenth Century Historic Ceramics from Fort Johnson

Ware group functional type	Stoneware[a]	Annular and plain ironstone–whiteware[b]	Totals	Ratio of stoneware to ironstone–whiteware
Cups and Bowls	0	21	21	
Plates	0	0	0	
Jugs and storage containers	29	0	29	
Totals	29	21	50	1.38 : 1

[a] 25 alkaline glazed, 1 feldspathic glazed, 3 unglazed.
[b] 2 plain, 11 annular, 7 presumed body sherds of annular vessels (plain), 1 red earthenware.

into the eighteenth century (South 1974). There would thus be little need for or access to ceramics by enlisted personnel. The officers, however, may well have used ceramic bowls and cups (South 1974). It is thought, therefore, that the bowls and cups of annular and plain ironstone–whiteware found at Fort Johnson are perhaps related to the officers present on the site as opposed to the enlisted personnel. The absence of plate fragments is certainly a pattern to be looked for on other military sites of the period.

There is evidence, however, to suggest that annular ware was a lower-class ceramic type in the nineteenth century. John Solomon Otto (1975, and this volume) has found that annular ware and edged ware were ceramic types found to occur at the overseer and slave quarters whereas transfer-printed ware was a predominant type at the planter's mansion. If the annular and plain ironstone–whiteware cups and bowls at Fort Johnson were the property of the officers as we have suggested, it would appear that they were availing themselves of cheaper ware in a military situation. We may find, therefore, that in a military system the ceramic wares used by upper-status officers are the same ones seen to be diagnostic of lower-class slaves and overseers in a plantation cultural system.

Another alternative we have not yet mentioned should be considered, and that is the possibility of occupation of the structures constructed on this site during the war by blacks after the war. On a map of the Fort Johnson area postdating the Civil War a notation is made to the fact that blacks were living here "under whose authority I know not [Willis Keith, personal communication]." If such was indeed the case, the ceramics we are dealing with may have been deposited by such an occupation. However, in such a situation we would not expect an exclusion of plates from the ceramic forms present. The greater use by slaves and overseers of bowls as opposed to flatware has been demonstrated by Otto (1975, and this volume). The *absence* of flatware plates, however, is considered to be suggestive of a military rather than a lower class civilian phenomenon in view of the evidence presently available.

Summary of the Analysis of Nineteenth Century Data

The sampling scheme has revealed a mid-nineteenth century military occupation concentrated on the second ridge within the research frame. The dispersion and density of nineteenth century artifact groups are the results of architectural (shelter), kitchen (subsistence), and military activity. Artifact percentages and ratios found at Fort Johnson fall within the predicted ranges for the Frontier Pattern (South 1977), based on eighteenth century military and frontier sites. This suggests that mid-nineteenth century military behavior patterns were similar enough to those of a century earlier that similarly patterned material remains were being produced to form the archeological record. The fact that modern armies in the field still travel with mess kits that are the equivalent of the tin cup and bowl, suggested as the behavioral explanation for the low ratio of ceramics on military sites, illustrates the tenacity of this behavioral pattern within a military system. If this patterned redundancy is verified in other studies, the challenge will then involve a search for specific variability allowing for more refined pattern recognition.

A functional analysis of nineteenth century ceramics recovered in this study has suggested that storage of liquids was a primary use for heavy stonewares, whereas annular and plain ironstone–whiteware cups and bowls were being used as substitutes for the usual military tin cup and plate, probably by the officers. The absence of fragments of plates supports the suggestion that the ceramic bowls of annular ware were being used to hold a somewhat liquid diet, probably stews, long associated with a military bill of fare.

Similar analyses of data from sites with known contrasting function will provide pattern in marked contrast with that seen reflected by the military occupation at Fort Johnson. Although the Fort Johnson data were the result of a sampling scheme designed to recover a miniscule fraction of the archeological record, the results as seen in this analysis are most encouraging, suggesting that similar research designs are destined to play a major role in future studies of data from sites for which there is the valuable addition of documentary control of some of the variables.

Dispersion of the Prehistoric Indian Artifacts

The sighting of shell midden on Ridge 1 (38CH16) at the south end of the research frame had focused attention on this site as the most obvious area of Indian occupation. However, the presence of mid-nineteenth century debris in this area also raised the possibility that this more recent occupation may have been responsible for at least some of the shell midden on this ridge nearest the tidal marsh. The subsurface sampling design was aimed at determining the extent of the prehistoric Indian occupation (as well as other occupation) by determining the dispersion of artifacts and related debris. The location of oyster shell midden was expected to reveal the area of occupation of those Indian groups using tidal resources concentrated on the forward Ridge 1, with preceramic remains from hunting activity expected in the area north of this forward ridge. The results of the SYMAP interpolation of the dispersion of Indian pottery and shell middens from the 80 core samples compared with the presence of pottery in the 17 three-foot squares are seen in Figure 6.5.

The dispersion of shell midden and artifacts illustrated in Figure 6.5 can be seen to form a triangle with the apex at the north central area of

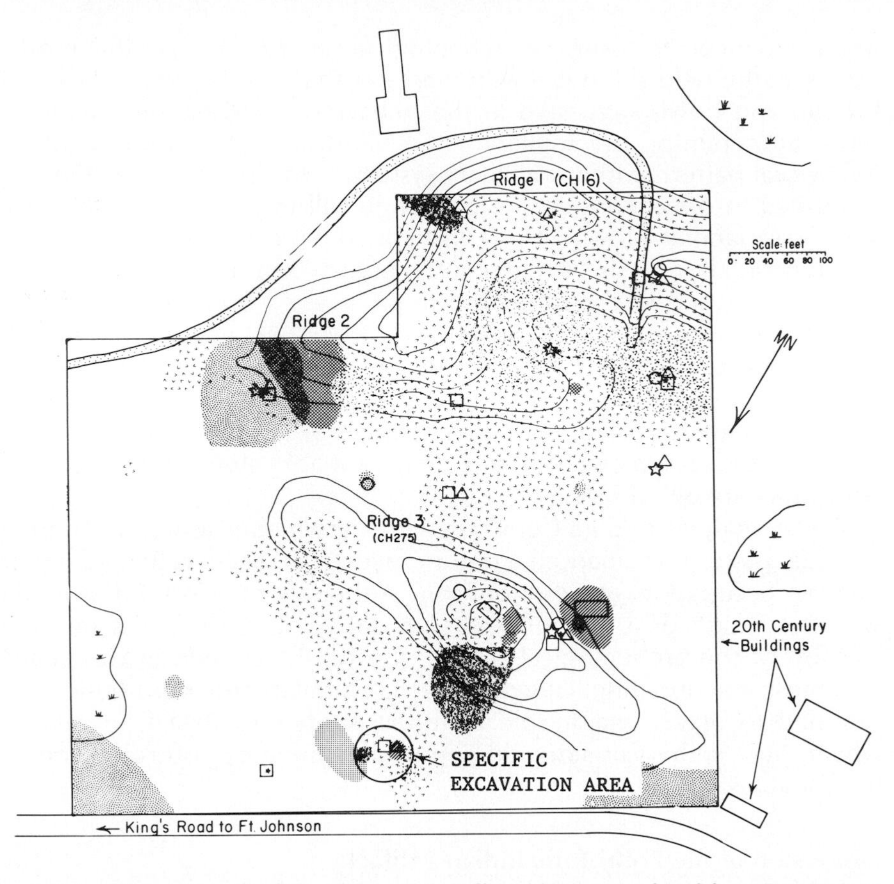

Figure 6.5. Dispersion of Indian pottery and shell midden interpolated from 80 core samples compared with the presence of pottery from 17 three-foot squares at Fort Johnson. Dispersion interpolated from core samples: ░ = Sand Tempered Plain, ▒ = Cape Fear Ware Group, ▦ = Wilmington Ware Group, ▓ = Deptford Ware Group, ⁘ = low density shell midden, ⁙ = high density shell midden, ▩ = baked clay objects. ●Presence of pottery in three-foot squares: ○ = Sand Tempered Plain, △ = Cape Fear Ware Group, □ = Wilmington Ware Group, ☆ = Deptford Ware Group, • = lithics.

the research frame and the base along the south side of the frame on Ridge 1. Note that this dispersion is centrally located between the marshes that border the research frame on the east and west. The greatest density is located not on the forward Ridge 1, but on Ridge 2, a lower elevation not directly exposed to the open expanse of tidal marsh. The dispersion of shell midden and its greatest density in relation to Ridge 2 is also seen to be to the north of the ridge away from the tidal marsh, not on the ridge itself. This phenomenon has been observed in many sites located on the mainland ridge paralleling the tidal marshes in southeastern North Carolina, where the greatest density of shell midden from Indian occupation is concentrated not on top of the ridges but on the off-sound side, just over the crest of the ridge (South 1960). It has been suggested that this location is a more sheltered one for consuming oysters in winter when cold winds blow from the tidal marshes. It should also be noted that the dispersion and density of charcoal and bone fragments also are located to the north of these ridges as is the shell midden (Figure 6.6).

The core samples were taken to a depth of over 4 feet with the post-hole diggers in order to reveal any deep-lying cultural components from the Archaic Period. In total, 16 lithic chips were recovered from the test squares; only two of these came from the light brown sand layer below the humus zone. Seventeen fragments of baked clay objects were found in four of the test squares, with 11 of these occurring below the humus zone. Twenty-four of the 265 potsherds from the test squares came from the light brown zone below the humus layer. This slight evidence for superposition on the site was not considered significant enough to warrant treating the artifacts stratigraphically for analysis purposes, so analysis focused on dispersion.

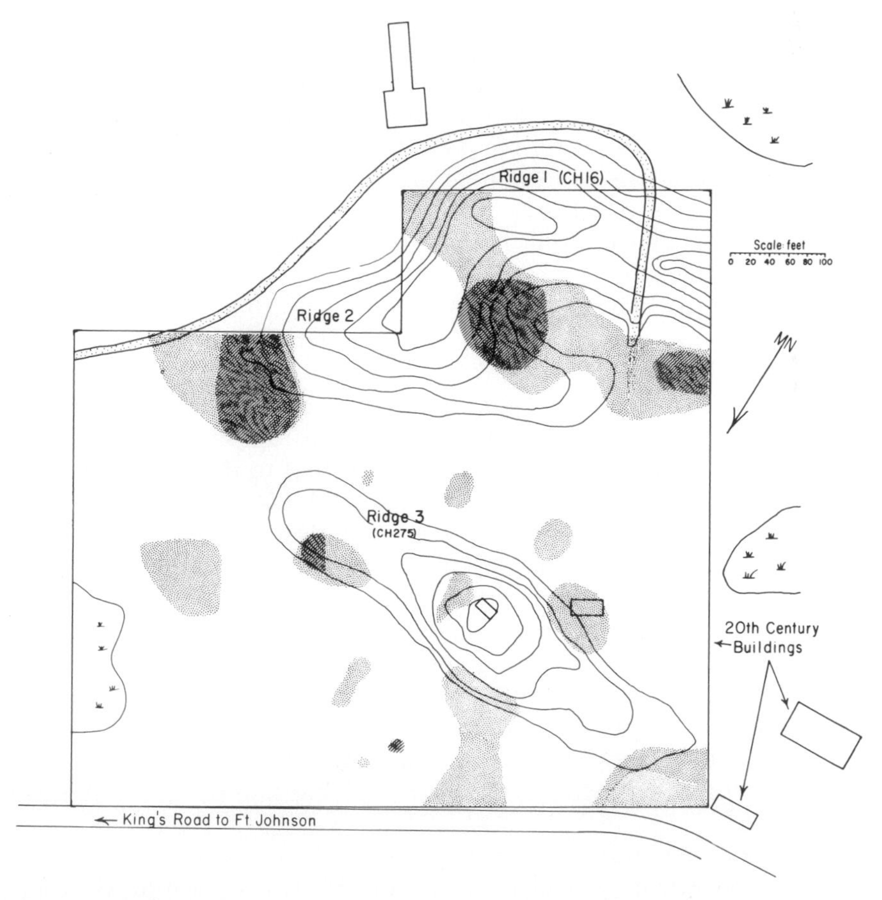

Figure 6.6. Dispersion of charcoal and bone interpolated from 80 core samples at Fort Johnson. ░ = charcoal, ▒ = bone.

Dispersion of Indian Pottery

From the dispersion of shell middens and pottery shown in Figure 6.5, a general correlation is seen. There are, however, areas where pottery was recovered but no shell midden was present. The pottery types present were fiber-tempered plain, sand-tempered plain, sherd-tempered plain, and temperless plain, as well as Deptford, Cape Fear, and Wilmington (Hanover) ware group types, covering a time span from ca. 1000 B.C. to ca. A.D. 1000 (South 1973). Fifteen of the 80 core samples contained a total of 47 pottery fragments, with 26 coming from core sample 12.

All but one of the test squares (128) contained pottery fragments. This dispersion of pottery in low-ground areas as well as on the higher ridges was a surprise, and is one of the major findings of the survey. Preconceptions based on the occurrence of shell midden on high ridges, on the lack of visible shell midden on ridges back of the midden-covered forward ridges adjacent to tidal marshes, or on assumptions about the lack of Indian occupation in low-ground areas, are seen as highly unwise as revealed by data from the present study.

Since 26 fragments of sand-tempered plain pottery came from Core 12, two test squares were excavated adjacent to this core (65 and 112). These revealed that a single pot of this ware was apparently involved, 88 more sherds of the same pot being recovered. This test revealed that scattered pottery concentrations representing a single broken vessel may well be found in the low-ground area off the main high-ground ridges. These may represent small campsites in these low-lying areas behind the higher ridges.

Contrary to expectations, the core sample with the greatest amount of shell midden was Core 60, located in a low, flat area at the north center of the research frame, an area where no shell at all was visible on the surface. Two sherds of Cape Fear Cordmarked pottery (South 1960) were also recovered from this core sample. The high density of shell midden in this unsuspected area, and the fact that 40 feet to the west, in Core 30, a Hanover Fabric Impressed sherd (South 1960) was found without associated shell, prompted a further examination of these sample areas. Four core samples were taken around each of these points at a distance of 10 feet, but none revealed additional pottery fragments. However, the Core-60 area revealed virtually no shell in three of the additional cores, but the westward one also contained a heavy concentration of shell. A fifth core sample was taken 10 feet further west, resulting in little shell being recovered (Figure 6.5). This procedure allowed the major dispersion of shell to be pinpointed to an area about 10 feet across, conjectured to represent a specific activity area, perhaps an oyster roast area or dwelling site.

The heavy concentration of shell in this small area was further sampled by placing Test Square 160 adjacent to Core 60. This square produced the heaviest concentration of shell discovered on the site, as well as 43 sherds of Hanover Fabric Impressed pottery (South 1960). This test suggested that the shell midden was a relatively contamination-free Hanover occupation area focused on use of tidal resources.

With the SYMAP interpolation of the core-sample data in hand (Figure 6.5), this area of variability, with Cape Fear pottery associated with a heavy concentration of shell, and Hanover pottery 40 feet away not associated with shell, became a prime area for conducting a specific excavation to determine, if possible, an explanation for this variability. The absence of early pottery suggested that perhaps here was a specific Cape Fear–Hanover activity area related to the consumption of tidal resources, oyster, clam, and conch.

The dispersion of Indian occupation refuse in a north–south area within the research frame rather than along the east–west axis of the forward ridge, as had been anticipated, suggested that the scattered occupation behind the ridges might represent individual campsites or habitation areas. The shell midden concentration in the area of Core 60 was thought to be such an area.

During the excavation of Test Square 64 a large quantity of shell midden was found in two pits, one of which had a Hanover sherd associated with the midden. These pit features are thought to be representative of many such features likely located on Ridge 2, where the major shell midden density is found (Figure 6.5). Because of the presence of all the ceramic types on Ridge 2, increasing the chance of intrusive mixing of behavioral by-products during various periods of occupation, excavation in this area of major shell midden density was considered less worthwhile than such an excavation conducted where there was a minimal chance for mixing of cultural components through sequential occupation. The area between Core 60 and Core 30 was therefore considered an ideal place to examine what might prove to be a single behavioral activity area. Such an area, if found to be associated only with Cape Fear–Hanover cord- and fabric-marked pottery might also provide shell or charcoal for dating the activity and the pottery associated with it, an important consideration since dating of these ceramic types is a present need for controlling chronology in the coastal Carolina area.

SUMMARY OF ANALYSIS AND EVALUATION OF THE RESULTS

Project Summary and Evaluation

The sampling survey of the research frame at Fort Johnson has revealed that a core-sampling design such as this is an excellent means for interpolating the dispersion of cultural materials. Not only was the subsoil sampling procedure effective in delineating occupation areas of the research frame, but it was also adequate in providing a sample from which quantitative pattern was sufficiently recognized that comparison with known patterns could be made using data from the nineteenth century occupation. Recognition of these quantitatively defined patterns has allowed functional interpretations regarding the military nature of the nineteenth century occupation. Analysis of the ceramic and arms artifact ratios has demonstrated a similar military function, with a consideration of ceramic form being used to derive interpretations regarding military status and suggestions as to the kind of food that was consumed.

The dispersion of nineteenth century and twentieth century cultural debris on the site was clearly revealed by the sampling scheme, and this dispersion was found to correlate remarkably well with the location of occupation activities within the research frame for which documented and visual evidence was available. The demonstration of the usefulness of this discovery tool for occupations of the historic period over which we have some control provides for a degree of confidence when prehistoric components are being analyzed by this strategy. The fact that a small amount of data from a core-sampling design can be seen to reveal such insights is certainly encouraging and suggests that such sampling may well become a major discovery tool for evaluating the archeological potential of a study area during a reconnaissance phase of research.

The dispersion of Indian occupation debris primarily on the second ridge rather than on the first ridge where visible surface evidence was present suggests that subsurface sampling is a far better means of making discovery of the occupation areas than is surface observation alone. The core sampling and testing strategy used here also revealed, through contrasting variability, an isolated area with potential for identification of a specific activity relating to the use of tidal resources. Testing of this postulate through more intensive excavation was called for, and such a project was carried out. A trench was excavated in the "specific excavation area" shown in Figure 6.5. This project was designed to test the hypothesis that this area represented a single component site resulting from the use of tidal resources, primarily oysters, by Indians using Hanover ceramics. This hypothesis was verified by the more intensive field study which located only Hanover ceramics in association with oyster shells from which two radiocarbon dates of 180 B.C. and 150 B.C. were obtained (South and Widmer 1976:71).

ACKNOWLEDGMENTS

We would like to thank our colleagues on this project, Susan Jackson, Leslie Beuschel, and David Ballenger, for their help with gathering the data. We also are indebted to Leland Ferguson and Robert Stephenson for reading the manuscript and offering their suggestions, and to Francis Lord and Willis Keith for their help with interpretive research.

REFERENCES

Asch, David L.

1975 On sample size problems and the uses of nonprobabilistic sampling. In *Sampling in archaeology,* edited by James W. Mueller. Tucson: Univ. of Arizona Press. Pp. 170–191.

Binford, Lewis R.

1962 Archaeology as anthropology. *American Antiquity* **28:**217–225.

1964 A consideration of archaeological research design. *American Antiquity* **29**(4):425–441.

Cheves, Langdon (editor)

1897 The Shaftesbury Papers and other records relating to Carolina and the first settlement on Ashley River prior to the year 1676. *Collections of the South Carolina Historical Society* V, Richmond.

Coe, Joffre L.

1964 The formative cultures of the Carolina Piedmont. *Transactions of the American Philosophical Society* **54**(5).

Delafield, R.

1865 Map of the defences of Charleston Harbor, South Carolina War Department. Surveyed between March 7 and May 20, 1865. South Carolina Library, Univ. of South Carolina, Columbia.

Dethlefsen, Edwin, and James Deetz

1966 Death's heads, cherubs, and willow trees: Experimental archaeology in colonial cemeteries. *American Antiquity* **31**(4):502–510.

Dudnick, Elliott E.

1971 *SYMAP user's reference manual for synagraphic computer mapping.* Department of Architecture, Univ. of Illinois at Chicago Circle, Chicago.

Ferguson, Leland G.

1975 Analysis of ceramic materials from Fort Watson, December 1780–April 1781. *The Conference on Historic Site Archaeology Papers* **8:**2–28. Institute of Archeology and Anthropology, University of South Carolina, Columbia.

Ferguson, Leland G., and Randolph J. Widmer

1976 Archeological examination of a transect through the Middle Savannah River Valley: The Bobby Jones Expressway, Richmond County, Georgia. *Research Manuscript Series* No. 89. Institute of Archeology and Anthropology, Univ. of South Carolina, Columbia.

Greer, Georgeanna H.

1971 Preliminary information on the use of the alkaline glaze for stoneware in the South 1800–1970. *The Conference on Historic Site Archaeology Papers* **5:**155–197.

Griffin, James B.

1952 *Archaeology of Eastern United States.* Chicago: Univ. of Chicago Press.

Johnson, David F.

1948 *Uniform buttons—American Armed Forces 1784–1948.* Watkins Glen, New York: Century House.

Mueller, James W. (editor)

1975 *Sampling in archaeology.* Tucson: Univ. of Arizona Press.

National Archives

1860s Maps of Fort Johnson, South Carolina. Record Group 77, HQ File I 17, Washington.

Noël Hume, Ivor

1970 *A guide to artifacts of Colonial America.* New York: Knopf.

Otto, John Solomon

1975 Status difference in the archaeological record—Of planter, overseer, and slave sites, Cannon's Point Plantation, St. Simon's Island, Georgia (1794–1861). Ph.D. dissertation, Department of Anthropology, Univ. of Florida, Gainesville.

Percy, George
1976 Use of a mechanical earth auger as a substitute for exploratory excavation at the Torreya site (8Li8), Liberty County, Florida. *The Florida Anthropologist* **29**(1):24–32. The Florida Anthropological Society, Gainesville.

Ripley, Warren
1970 *Artillery and ammunition of the Civil War.* New York: Van Nostrand Reinhold.

Ritchie, William A.
1932 The Lamoka Lake site: The type station of the Archaic Algonkin Period in New York. *Researches and Transactions of the New York State Archaeological Association* 7(4).

Schiffer, Michael B.
1972 Archaeological context and systemic context. *American Antiquity* **37:**156–165.

Schiffer, Michael B., and William L. Rathje
1973 Efficient exploitation of the archaeological record: Penetrating problems. In *Research and theory in current archeology,* edited by C. L. Redman. New York: Wiley. Pp. 169–179.

Scott, Robert N.
1880 *The war of the rebellion: A compiliation of the official records of the Union and Confederate armies.* Series I, (1). Washington, D.C.: U.S. Government Printing Office.

South, Stanley
1959 Fort Anderson Barracks (N18), excavation report. Brunswick Town State Historic Site. Raleigh, North Carolina: State Department of Archives and History.
1960 An archeological survey of Southeastern Coastal North Carolina. Brunswick Town State Historic Site, Wilmington. Manuscript on file at the Research Laboratories of Anthropology, Univ. of North Carolina, Chapel Hill.
1970 Baked clay objects from the site of the 1670 settlement at Charles Towne, South Carolina. *The Institute of Archeology and Anthropology Notebook* **2**(1):3–16. Univ. of South Carolina, Columbia.
1972 Evolution and horizon as revealed in ceramic analysis in historical archeology. *The Conference on Historic Site Archaeology Papers 1971* **6:**71–116. Institute of Archeology and Anthropology, Univ. of South Carolina, Columbia.
1973 Indian pottery taxonomy for the South Carolina Coast. In Leland G. Ferguson, A reviewer's note. *The Institute of Archeology and Anthropology Notebook* **5**(2):53–57. Univ. of South Carolina, Columbia.
1974 Palmetto Parapets. *Anthropological Studies* No. 1. Institute of Archeology and Anthropology, Univ. of South Carolina, Columbia.
1977 *Method and theory in historical archeology.* New York: Academic Press.

South, Stanley, and Randolph J. Widmer
1976 Archeological sampling at Fort Johnson, South Carolina. Institute of Archeology and Anthropology *Research Manuscript Series* No. 93. Univ. of South Carolina, Columbia.

Stephenson, Robert L.
1970 Archeological investigations in the Whitney Reservoir area, Central Texas. *Bulletin of the Texas Archeological Society* **41:**37–286.

Stoltman, James B.
1974 Groton Plantation, an archaeological study of a South Carolina locality. *Monographs of the Peabody Meseum* (1), Harvard Univ.

Wood, W. Dean
1975 A sampling scheme for subsurface archaeological survey. Paper presented at the 32nd Annual Meeting of the Southeastern Archaeological Conference, Gainesville, Florida. Department of Anthropology, Univ. of Georgia, Athens.

Sampling the Archeological Frontier: Regional Models and Component Analysis

KENNETH E. LEWIS

Anthropological archeology has been traditionally associated with the study of human behavior in its temporal aspect. It alone of the various fields of anthropology possesses a methodology able to investigate long periods of human history and retrieve data capable of answering questions regarding the evolutionary nature of sociocultural change. Archeology has the ability not only to recognize change but also to compare its formal and functional aspects cross-culturally to discern regularities that underlie general processes of change. Although the reconstruction of culture history is a necessary by-product of archeological research, the primary goal is the explanation of the observed phenomena.

With regard to the study of historical societies, archeology's potential role is particularly significant. Unlike the archeology of the prehistoric past, historical archeology deals with societies whose material remains are enhanced by direct analogy from documentary sources. This chapter will illustrate the manner in which archeology can be used to investigate sociocultural change in a historic situation. The type of change under consideration is a process of acculturation characteristic of frontier colonial societies. To deal with a phenomenon of this nature, it is first necessary to develop a research design employing a methodology capable of recognizing the characteristics of the "frontier model," which constitutes a formal statement of the process of frontier change. This research design will guide the collection and examination of data from sites occupied by a historic society that documentary research indicates is likely to have been affected by frontier change. The degree to which hypotheses for change specified by the frontier model are substantiated by the data will determine the adequacy of the design.

A primary concern in the construction of an adequate research design is the manner in which the recognition of certain types of sociocultural phenomena is related to the methodological foundations of the inquiry. An adequate methodology is crucial to the testing of hypotheses such as those generated by the frontier model because it must allow data to be gathered in a manner relevant to archeological test implications drawn from each hypothesis. It may, for instance, be necessary that the data be quantifiable to permit a distinction to be drawn between particular variables that otherwise would appear similar. Since the model of change to be presented here involves a process of change encompassing a substantial period of time and a relatively extensive geographical area, the methodology must be sensitive to both spatial and temporal aspects of change. Clearly the success of an inquiry into the operation of culture process depends on a methodology cognizant of those variables most critical to the change under investigation.

The advantages of conducting archeological research related to historically documented societies are obvious. If adequate, documents may yield inferences concerning both the interpretation of particular artifacts and the organizational and behavioral aspects of past sociocultural systems. Documentary evidence can corroborate archeological conclusions about human behavior; however, if used imprudently during the analysis of archeological data, such evidence can introduce information that may bias the outcome of the inquiry. For this reason, documentary data must be carefully admitted in the consideration of archeological evidence. They may, in the same manner as ethnographic information, be most profitably employed at what Gould (1971:175) has described as the "specific interpretation" level of archeological research. This level of interpretation entails using comparative information in the functional interpretation of archeological data within the context of an individual site. Documentary sources should not directly relate to the site under consideration. They may, however, refer to the sociocultural system of which it was a part to provide analogies useful in examining the archeological record. Thus, a pointed iron object with a triangular cross-section found in a site may be identified as a file, not because a document mentioned the presence of files at the site but rather because items of this description are known to have functioned as files in the larger sociocultural system of which the site was a part.

In summary, the primary consideration here is the development of a research design capable of discerning a particular process of past sociocultural change. The methodology employed must, of course, be sensitive to the nature of the process considered. Therefore, to develop a viable archeological research design it is necessary first to examine the frontier model outlining the nature of the change with which its methodology must cope.

THE FRONTIER MODEL

The historical development of North America from the time of the earliest European settlement has been characterized by a continuous and often rapid expansion and the occupation of new lands. Within the borders of what is now the United States this movement began in earnest in the eighteenth century and was virtually complete by the close of the nineteenth (Bartlett 1974:447). This period of American history may be viewed as one in which the colonization and incorporation of frontier lands into the social, economic, and political milieu of an expanding state system played a significant, if not a dominant, role. Frontier colonization, though hardly a phenomenon unique to America, definitely constitutes a process of change through which it is possible to interpret much of the United States history during its formative period.

The study of the frontier as a geographical phenomenon has occupied the minds of scholars in many fields (Allen 1959; Casagrande *et al.* 1964; Dawson 1934; Hallowell 1957; Kristof 1959; Leyburn 1935; Mikesell 1968; Prescott 1965; Thompson 1970, 1973; Turner 1893; Webb 1952; Wells 1973; Wyman and Kroeber 1957). Although their interpretations of the frontier itself vary considerably, several conclusions are shared by most. First, the frontier is the area in which the outer edge of an expanding society adapts to the conditions of attenuated contact with the homeland and the physical conditions of a new environment. Second, because of the nature of expansion, the frontier is both spatially and temporally impermanent. It is the zone of transition within which the "wilderness" is occupied and "civilized." Third, because the process of colonization is repetitive in nature, it is also evolutionary in the sense that the sequential pattern of change that once occurred in the center of a newly settled frontier region tends to be repeated along its periphery as settlement within the region expands. Because of the interrelationship between frontier change and the expansion of state systems by intentional colonization, the frontier may be seen as both the process of sociocultural change and the area within which it occurs.

The evolutionary nature of frontier change makes it necessary to consider particular events in relation to the larger process of which they were a part rather than as unique, isolated phenomena. With regard to the investigation of the archeological record, it is especially important to study a site as a part of the larger sociocultural entity within which it is related to its precedent and antecedent occupations as well as to those of contemporary sites. A site must be seen as a focus upon which a variety of social and natural variables converge differentially through time. It is a component within a sociocultural system constantly undergoing adaptive change as a result of expansion and migration. Although the process of frontier change reflects this adaptation by the system as a whole, components within the system may be seen to express aspects of it differentially. When placed in this perspective, individual sites take on a special significance in that they can selectively reveal facets of change on a regional basis.

A frontier may be defined as a region in which the dispersal of settlement into a new territory takes place. It is the zone that separates the unsettled and settled portions of a territory that lie within or under the effective control of a state (Kristof 1959:274; Weigert *et al.* 1957:115). Collectively it is referred to as the *area of colonization* (Casagrande *et al.* 1964:311). As a temporal phenomenon, the frontier arises with the first influx of permanent settlement[1] and ceases to exist only when an upper limit of growth is achieved, accompanied by a stabilization of the settlement pattern (Hudson 1969:367).

The area of colonization must remain tied to the metropolitan area[2] from which settlement originated, because it is largely dependent on the maintenance of a complex network of trade and communications linkages that serves as the route of movement for new immigrants and supplies as well as an outlet for colonial products. This network also provides the basis for the social, political, economic, and ideological integration of the newly settled territory.

Thus, the frontier may also be seen as a geographical expression of an exchange network designed to permit the incorporation of unsettled territory into a larger socioeconomic system. Frontier settlements function as nodes in this network and reflect the distribution of personnel and materials in the most efficient way to permit the integration of activities in a sparsely settled area. The limits of the exchange network at any given time effectively mark the boundaries of the area of colonization. These boundaries essentially delimit a "multifeature" region (Grigg 1967:492) characterized by the covariation of a number of cultural features relating primarily to the nature of the adaptation to the social and physical environment of the frontier. It is to the enumeration of these adaptive characteristics that the following model of sociocultural change is addressed (see Lewis 1975a).

The frontier model is characterized by the following five conditions. First, prolonged contact must be continually maintained between the colonists and their parent society. Second, as a result of its relative isola-

[1] It is necessary to point out that the nature of pioneer settlement discussed here may be best described as agricultural settlement characterized by relatively large tracts of land (Thompson 1973:11). This small-farm frontier stands in contrast to the "camp frontiers" of trappers, traders, and miners, as well as to the "exploitive plantation frontiers" (Leyburn 1935:5) in that the latter two do not necessarily constitute permanent settlement capable of becoming self-sustaining integral parts of the national culture of the metropolitan area.

[2] The term *metropolitan area* is used here in the sense of the mother state of the colony, not in the sense of a city and its satellite area (Casagrande *et al.* 1964:323).

tion and the attenuation of trade and communications linkages with the homeland the intrusive culture exhibits a sudden loss of complexity. Third, the settlement pattern in the area of colonization becomes more geographically dispersed than that of the homeland unless temporarily impeded by restrictive conditions. Fourth, the dispersed settlement pattern within the area of colonization is focused around central settlements called *frontier towns*. The frontier town serves as a nucleus of social, political, economic, and religious activities within a portion of the colony and as the terminus of the transportation network linking the area of colonization to the homeland through an entrepôt. Because it serves as the primary link to the national culture, the frontier town forms the nexus of the communications network within the colony (Casagrande *et al.* 1964:312). Finally, as the colony changes through time it also varies geographically. The pattern of temporal growth and change in a single community is replicated spatially, with those settlements closest to the moving frontier always representing the earliest stage of frontier development. As the colony expands with the influx of new settlers, areas of earliest settlement experience marked changes in population density and settlement pattern and become integrated at the national level (Steward 1955:48–49) with the sociocultural system of the homeland.

As the frontier expands, settlements grow and take on new roles as they pass through a "colonization gradient" (Casagrande *et al.* 1964:311). The functions of the original frontier towns become decentralized and those towns that no longer occupy strategic positions in the trade and communication network decline and may be completely abandoned.

In the following section of this chapter a research design will be developed to outline the method by which certain aspects of the frontier model may be investigated through an examination of the archeological record. This design is intended to apply to frontier situations in which two principal types of data exist—written documentation and the archeological record. These sources should not be viewed as conflicting or as qualitatively different, for they are comparable and complementary. Indeed, both may be seen as reflecting events of the same systemic context. Because we are concerned here chiefly with the analysis of archeological evidence, the aim of the research design will be to interpret the archeological data. Documentary evidence, or studies based upon it, plays two important roles in such a study—it provides for the development of background information on the particular colonization situation, and it is a means for independently testing conclusions derived from the archeological analysis.

The situation chosen for this investigation is the northern Piedmont region of the British North American colony of South Carolina. This region was occupied by English settlers as early as the second quarter of the eighteenth century and presumably functioned as a frontier area until several decades after the colony's political independence in 1783.

RESEARCH DESIGN FOR FRONTIER CHANGE

The ability of archeological methodology to deal with a phenomenon as complex as frontier change is grounded in several basic assumptions concerning the relationship between past behavior and the material remains that are its by-product.

The archeologist's ability to relate past behavior to material remains is based on the following set of assumptions, which are implicit in this report:

1. Culture may be viewed as those learned patterns of human behavior by which man adapts to his physical and social environment (Kottack 1974:4). Rather than a sum of traits, culture is a series of *interacting components* that are continually acting and reacting to one another, resulting in constant variation and change.
2. This interaction implies the existence of a *system* within which certain cultural mechanisms operate to regulate change or to maintain behavior within certain limits or boundaries (Rappaport 1968:4). In order to deal with a phenomenon as complex as human culture it is necessary to adopt an approach that stresses the interrelationship of all variables in the system rather than that between isolated characteristics of man and his environment (see Buckley 1967:41; Geertz 1963:9–10).
3. Just as human behavior may be seen as part of an interrelated system, separate activities not involving all parts of the system or all members of the society may be defined as *subsystems*. The number of subsystems increases with the level of complexity of the cultural system and, concomitantly, with the degree of specialization within it (Binford 1965:205).
4. Because behavior is not random, it is possible to observe patterns in human activities. A recognizable *structure* may be seen to appear in the systemic organization of technology, economics, religion, social organization, and other specialized activities. Changes in these patterns may be traced through time, and variation in systemic structure may be viewed as a historical phenomenon.
5. Of crucial importance is the assumption that the archeological record will exhibit particular *patterns* reflecting those patterns in the cultural system that produced them (Binford 1962) and will

indicate as well temporal changes occurring in those patterns and the system. In order to understand more clearly the relationship between a living behavioral system and the material record it leaves behind, recent studies have investigated those processes governing the transfer of artifacts from the former state of the latter (Schiffer 1972, 1975a).

6. It is also assumed that a comparative study of systemic culture change will permit the recognition of regularities in patterning that, in turn, may be seen to reflect processes of human behavior (Binford 1968:8; Steward 1949:2–3). A number of processes, such as the one discussed here, have been recognized by anthropologists dealing with ethnographic as well as archeological data. Because the latter have the capacity to yield information concerning sociocultural patterning through time, a study of the archeological remains of a past area of colonization should reveal the occurrence of the frontier process.

One of the most distinctive characteristics of the process of frontier colonization is its regional scope. A frontier system, though geographically extensive and culturally attenuated, remains socially and economically integrated by an extensive network of trade and communications linkages that also ties it to the metropolitan area. A research design capable of examining such a system must recognize this factor with regard to the specific questions it asks concerning the form, extent, and nature of the particular frontier under consideration.

The organization of research aimed at the examination of sociocultural change on a regional scale must necessarily involve a multistage approach that begins by defining broad, general aspects of the problem under study (see Binford 1964; Redman 1973). This chapter is concerned with the first phase of investigation. Its main goal is the recognition of a frontier in the archeological record. Because the spatial boundaries of an area of colonization are continually changing with the expansion of the frontier, it is best not to attempt to define the spatial boundaries of this phenomenon until its temporal limits are known. In order to establish the presence of a frontier so that its chronological scope may be ascertained, it is necessary first to identify its basic structural and organizational features. When such features are delimited in time, it should then be possible to proceed, in a subsequent stage of research, to a consideration of the frontier's geographical form and extent.

The recognition of a frontier as a sociocultural entity is dependent on the investigator's ability to identify the central economic features associated with a colonial area. These features are most readily discernible in the focal settlement of the area of colonization, the frontier town (Casagrande, *et al.* 1964:312). Because of the economic orientation of a colonial system, the primary mechanisms of integration on the frontier should be related to aspects of trade, redistribution, and communications. A frontier system is basically one of attenuated redistribution, involving the rapid outward movement of a large amount of goods through a frontier town in exchange for the collection of the product of the frontier, often in a raw or semiprocessed state. Settlement is spatially linked to this system and political organization is generally associated with the degree of concentration of frontier economic activity present. The frontier town, because of its pivotal position in the economic network, contains the mechanisms relating to the centralization of activities within the area of colonization. An examination of this key settlement should permit the observation of those activities that characterize a frontier.

Because of the evolutionary manner of frontier growth, the frontier town may also serve as a chronological scale for the development of the area it served. Beginning as a dispersed settlement with the earliest occupation of the region, a frontier town gradually expands as its geographical position relative to the area of colonization moves from the periphery to the center. Its location relative to a major route of trade and communications permits it to develop as a redistribution point for new settlement on the edge of the moving frontier. The frontier town not only defines the temporal limits of the frontier it serves but also reflects the form of the dispersed settlements in its early stages of development.

An examination of the frontier town with regard to the elucidation of its central economic activities forms the initial, and crucial, aspect of frontier research. The results of this inquiry must provide the groundwork upon which to base all subsequent research related to this settlement and the area it served. The investigation of a socioeconomic unit as multifaceted as a frontier town is a complex undertaking, especially when it is not possible to observe it directly as part of a functioning system. In order to identify and study an evolving frontier town through the analysis of its archeological remains, an approach must be taken that is designed to gather data relating to a wide variety of phenomena. Though not dealing in detail with any one aspect of the frontier town, it should recognize the settlement's major characteristics and thus identify its basic structural elements.

The archeological investigation of a frontier town may be organized in terms of four broad questions designed to provide a framework in which to formulate hypotheses aimed at identifying particular aspects of the settlement within the context of the specific example under consideration. The discovery phase of archeological research, in addition to ascertaining the general condition of the archeological remains at the site, attempts to elicit information concerning (1) the beginning and termination dates of the settlement's occupation, (2) the ethnic or cultural affiliation of the site's inhabitants as evidenced by their ties with the society of the metropolitan area, (3) the form and spatial extent of the past human occupations of the site, and (4) the nature of intrasite variability and the distribution of behaviorally significant archeological materials.

The archeological study of a suspected frontier town requires the use of a field research design capable of discerning variability throughout an entire settlement at once. The discovery phase of archeology may profitably employ a technique of investigation designed to gather a representative sample of the archeological materials distributed over a wide area. Because statistical treatment of the data obtained is desirable, the sample should be based on the random selection of units. Random selection offers the advantage of providing every such unit within the population (in this case the total area of the town) exactly the same change of being chosen (Dice 1952:28) and eliminates the potential bias inherent in a sample based on arbitrary measurements established by the investigator (Mueller 1974:3). Redman and Watson (1970:281–282) suggest that the stratified unaligned random sample provides the best method for examining artifact patterning because it prevents the clustering of sample units and ensures that no areas are left unsampled. It accomplishes this by dividing the site area into a series of large units based on the coordinates of the site grid.

Within each of these squares, one unit of a smaller size is randomly chosen. The relative sizes of the units involved will determine the percentage of the site sampled. Naturally, the greater the size of the sample, the more reliable will be the results; however, the difficulty of enlarging the magnitude of such a sample increases with the size of the site. For this reason, the proportionate size of the sample, in practice, usually becomes smaller as the area to be examined becomes larger. A reliable picture of the total population can be best obtained under these conditions by using the smallest size squares practical. This permits a maximum of area to be covered by a minimum of testing (Redman 1973:63). Archeologists have successfully used this technique to observe variation in the patterning of activities on sites of limited size (Redman and Watson 1970) and it is not unreasonable to expect that it will reveal the presence of those activities associated with a frontier town.

In summary, the research design employed here seeks to approach the study of an area of colonization through an analysis of its focal settlement, the frontier town. The discovery phase of research considered here will attempt to identify the basic organizational characteristics of the settlement as they relate to its role in a frontier system. Because the archeological investigation is of an exploratory nature aimed at uncovering evidence of broad patterns in the data, the excavations will involve the use of a sampling technique capable of examining extensive areas. The results of this analysis should not only confirm or deny the status of a particular settlement as a frontier town but also establish the chronological framework necessary to define the spatial extent of the area of colonization.

THE ARCHEOLOGICAL ANALYSIS OF THE SOUTH CAROLINA DATA

South Carolina in the Eighteenth Century: The Background of Colonization

In the previous section, four general questions were posed as the basis for the development of hypotheses regarding the expected nature of the archeological data if the latter represent the material remains of a frontier town. Before attempting to translate the questions into archeological hypotheses, it is necessary first to establish the existence of a potential frontier situation in the particular area under consideration and then to isolate the likely location of a frontier town within it.

The historical context in which a particular frontier situation is examined provides pertinent background information regarding the frontier. This information is discussed in terms of four conditions that are examined here in regard to the situation in the South Carolina Piedmont as it existed in the eighteenth century.

The first condition necessary to the development of a frontier is that an intrusive society must physically occupy an area on the periphery of or apart from its previously occupied territory. The presence of the English as an intrusive society in South Carolina began with the settlement of the coastal region in the late seventeenth century. By the early part of the eighteenth century Charleston had arisen as the major southern port town, providing a direct link to Great Britain and the other coastal American centers of trade and communication. Its location at the mouth of the Cooper River greatly facilitated the emergence of a plantation economy on the coastal plain in that it served as a collecting point for colonial export commodities and a distribution center for imported commercial goods and plantation slaves (Sellers 1934:5). Not only was Charleston the focus of the plantation economy but it was also the terminus of the British–Indian trade in the Southeast (Crane 1956:108). As the eighteenth century progressed the South Carolina colony expanded after a period of initial confinement due to the proximity of Spanish colonies and aboriginal resistance. The inefficient proprietary government was replaced by a Royal administration in 1719, integrating the colony more closely within the rapidly expanding and increasingly centralized politico-economic system of Great Britain (John 1962:371–372).

The expansion of the colony inland was given official sanction in the township plan of 1730, which projected a series of frontier settlements (Figure 7.1) to be settled by small farmers, stretching from the North Carolina border to the Savannah River. Each was laid out along one of the major rivers linking the frontier with the coast. Settlements in these locations would not only strengthen the frontier and increase production of raw export materials but help to counterbalance the rising slave population of the coastal plantations (Brown 1963:2).

One of the settlements proposed in this plan was Fredericksburg Township on the Wateree River. Like many of the other townships, it was not immediately occupied. Fredericksburg Township remained only a surveyed plat until the 1740s when small plantations were established on the Wateree near its confluence with Pine Tree Creek. Settlement tended to cluster along the "Catawba Path," a major land artery connecting the Piedmont with the coastal settlement of Charleston (Kirkland and Kennedy 1905:9–10). Because the vicinity of Fredericksburg Township was one of the earliest parts of the piedmont permanently

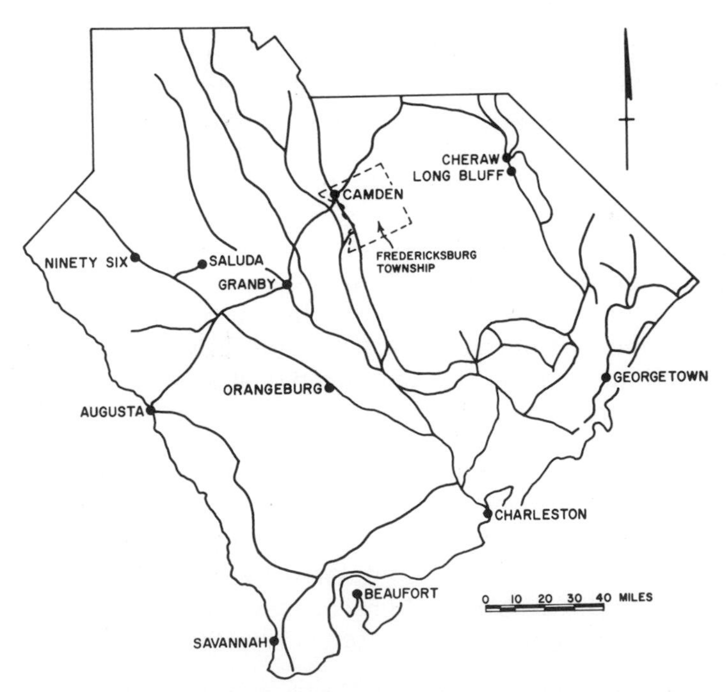

Figure 7.1. South Carolina in the eighteenth century, showing the locations of Camden and Fredericksburg Township relative to the road network of the period. Compiled from Drayton's, Stuart's, and Mouzon's maps (Schulz 1972:14, Figure 1).

occupied, it is here that the genesis of an area of colonization is most likely to have occurred.

The second condition states that the intrusive society must possess a level of sociocultural integration equivalent to that of a stratified society or state as defined by Fried (1967:187–190), for without the legitimization of force inherent at this level of organization the maintenance of the logistical base necessary to support a colony would be impossible. The state level of political organization is characterized not only by the presence of sharply defined social classes, but also by the development of markets as major distributive mechanisms and by the existence of more intensive patterns of economic and social differentiation (Sanders and Price 1968:44).

Eighteenth century Great Britain represents a highly developed European state, one that was expanding both its political and economic influence during this period. Wallerstein (1974:7) has suggested that it is impossible to examine the national histories of post-medieval European nations without recourse to the concept of a "world system" in which the cultures of all affected areas are tied in a web of mutual interdependence. He has chosen the term *world economy* to characterize this system because of the particular nature of its organization. Its self-contained development likens it to an empire but its capitalist economic mode, based on the fact that the economic factors operated within an arena larger than that which any political entity could completely control, prevented domination by a single nation. This situation gave capitalist entrepreneurs a structurally based freedom to maneuver and allowed a continual expansion of the world economy (Wallerstein 1974:348). The role of such commercial forces in the initiation of British colonial ventures in Scotland, Ireland, and America is well known. The flexibility of privately sponsored, economically oriented companies proved the key to the successful establishment of many early, sustained colonial settlements (Cheyney 1961; MacLeod 1928; Rowse 1957).

It is beyond the scope of this chapter to deal with the complex factors responsible for the world economy; however, it is necessary to cover one aspect of it that has particular relevance to the American frontier, that of the system's boundaries. Obviously an expanding world economy centered in Europe was not isolated and its very existence depended on exchange with areas outside its boundaries. This trade was of two types, that involving "external areas" dominated by other world systems and characterized by the exchange of preciosities, and that with areas inside the system's own periphery. The periphery is further defined as

> that geographical sector . . . wherein production is primarily of lower-ranking goods (that is, goods whose labor is less well rewarded) but which is an integral part of the overall system of the division of labor, because the commodities involved are essential for daily use [Wallerstein 1974:302].

Exchange between the periphery and the "core" states at the center of the system tends to be characterized by a "vertical specialization" involving the movement of raw materials from the former to the latter and the movement of manufactured goods and services in the opposite direction (Gould 1972:235–236). Such was the case in much of colonial North America, especially in the agricultural South (Sellers 1934:4).

Because the world economy of the eighteenth century was expanding, it was inevitable that its geographical structure would not remain intact indefinitely. A process integral to expansion is the formation of semiperipheral areas that function as collection points of vital skills and serve to deflect political pressures aimed at the core states from the frontiers of the periphery. Because they are still located outside of the political arena of the core states, however, semiperipheral areas are prevented from entering into political coalitions in the same manner as the core area states (Wallerstein 1974:350) and thus remain dependent on them. By the last half of the eighteenth century the British American colonies had attained a semiperipheral status, at least in certain coastal areas, with localized political and economic centers whose influence ranged into the interior.

The third condition that must exist in a frontier situation involves external sociocultural barriers to expansion. In order that the aboriginal inhabitants not pose such a barrier, their level of sociocultural organization must be less complex than that of the intrusive society. If this situation does not prevail, the latter cannot favorably compete for the resources of the frontier area.

Briefly, the peoples occupying the interior of South Carolina in the late seventeenth century may be characterized as societies organized at the chiefdom level of organization. Those in the north central Piedmont, who were eventually to become known as Catawbas, formed a regional element of the greater chiefdom of Cofitachique, an extensive sociopolitical entity that was in the process of disintegration as the result of European contact (Baker 1975:23).

The chiefdom level of integration (see Fried 1960; Sanders and Price 1968:42–44) involves organization based on the principle of ranked status with positions determined by closeness of relationship to the central status position, or chieftain. Authority in a chiefdom is linked to the role the chieftain plays in the redistribution of local product surpluses and is based in large part on the existence of sumptuary rules and ritual isolation. Unlike a state, however, the formal delimitation of power and coercive techniques of political control are absent. Thus the chiefdom is especially susceptible to organizational disruption resulting from outside economic competition for resources. Particularly erosive in South Carolina were the effects of the slave and deerskin trade in the seventeenth century. These brought about a marked increase in internecine warfare and introduced European diseases, resulting in the decimation and displacement of the aboriginal populations and the breakup of their sociopolitical structure (Baker 1975:43). By the time of the earliest permanent European inland colonization, the effects of previous contact had reduced the aboriginal societies to small, regional chiefdoms and remnant groups unable to compete with the intrusive society.

The fourth condition refers to the potential area of colonization itself. Essentially it requires that the physical environment of the area satisfy two conditions: it must be amenable to subsistence and commercial exploitation by the intrusive society and it must not contain natural barriers that would prevent access to all parts of the potential frontier. The last point is of particular significance in that the maintenance of trade and communications links are crucial to the survival of the colony.

The inland frontier in South Carolina was centered at the upper edge of the coastal plain. Here the fall line forms a zone of transition between the older igneous rocks of the Piedmont and the unconsolidated sediments of the coastal plain. Major rivers such as the Wateree are navigable up to this point. Much of the potential area of colonization lies in a physiographic region called the *sandhills,* a rolling, hilly belt about 30 miles wide and contiguous with the western edge of the coastal plain (Frothingham and Nelson 1944:5). The area is characterized by well-drained sandy soils generally suitable for cultivated crops. Poorly drained soils and swamps occur along stream floodplains (Craddock and Ellerbe 1966). In short, the Piedmont environment in the vicinity of Fredericksburg Township would have offered the potential for agricultural subsistence and, although stream navigation was limited, overland travel was largely unrestricted as witnessed by the presence of an elaborate system of trails developed for the Indian trade.

Clearly the historical situation in South Carolina during the first half of the eighteenth century satisfies the conditions necessary for the development of a frontier. The locations of foci of settlement within the Piedmont frontier, as in all colonial areas, are primarily dependent on access to the principal routes of trade and communications connecting the area of colonization with its entrepôt (see Rees 1975). In the second quarter of the eighteenth century, the major routes into the interior were those used by the Charleston traders to transport goods to and from the aboriginal peoples of the Southeast (Crane 1956:23). As the network of roads originated from Charleston, this settlement was ideally suited to become the entrepôt for all interior settlement in the colony.

The locations of interior settlements along these routes appear to have been governed largely by political factors. The 1730 Township Act, although orienting settlement locations to major rivers, also placed many adjacent to existing land routes. Fredericksburg Township on the Wateree River transected the Catawba Path. Along this route the settlement of Pine Tree Hill, later Camden, appeared in the 1750s to form the earliest inland settlement on the Santee River drainage (Kirkland and Kennedy 1905:9–10).

In order to investigate the archeological remains of this settlement with regard to its role as a frontier town, it is necessary to derive testable hypotheses within the framework of the four general questions to be considered in the discovery phase. First, however, the actual site of the settlement must be examined to establish its condition and spatial limits.

The stratified random sampling technique described earlier is capable of accomplishing both these tasks in addition to sampling the contents of the site. The determination of a site's extent would normally be accomplished by expanding the size of the sampled area until the limits of the occupied area become evident. At Camden, however, early exploratory excavations uncovered the remains of a Revolutionary War period palisade wall surrounding the settlement (Calmes 1968:21–22; Strickland 1971:60). Assuming that all structures within the contiguous settlement were contained within this wall, it was possible to confine archeological excavations to this area.[3]

Camden: The Sample Frame

The site of the old town of Camden lies in the southern part of the present city of the same name and is bounded by Bull Street on the north, Church Street on the west, Wateree Street on the south, and Market Street on the east. Broad Street (South Carolina Highway 521) bisects the site in a north–south direction and follows the assumed route of the Catawba Path (Figure 7.2). Most of the site is accessible to archeological investigation, except for the northeastern quadrant on which is constructed a complex of city athletic facilities. The accessible area of the site is quite large, however, totaling over 460,000 square feet. The discovery-phase excavations here used a stratified random sampling design (see Mueller 1974:32–34; Redman and Watson 1970) to examine 1% of the total site area. The sampling was achieved by surveying the site into 50 × 50 foot squares and excavating one 5 × 5 foot unit randomly selected within each. In all, 186 sample squares were completed.

The excavations revealed that the entire site of Camden has been under cultivation, resulting in the vertical mixing of the historic component. It is assumed, however, that this process has not greatly altered the horizontal distribution of the artifacts, and the patterns of their deposition should still be visible though many surface features may

[3] Documentary evidence confirmed that during the time the palisade was in use (1780–1781) all of the contiguous settlement lay within its circumference. Test excavations and survey of areas outside the wall revealed no evidence of extensive deposits of eighteenth century materials there.

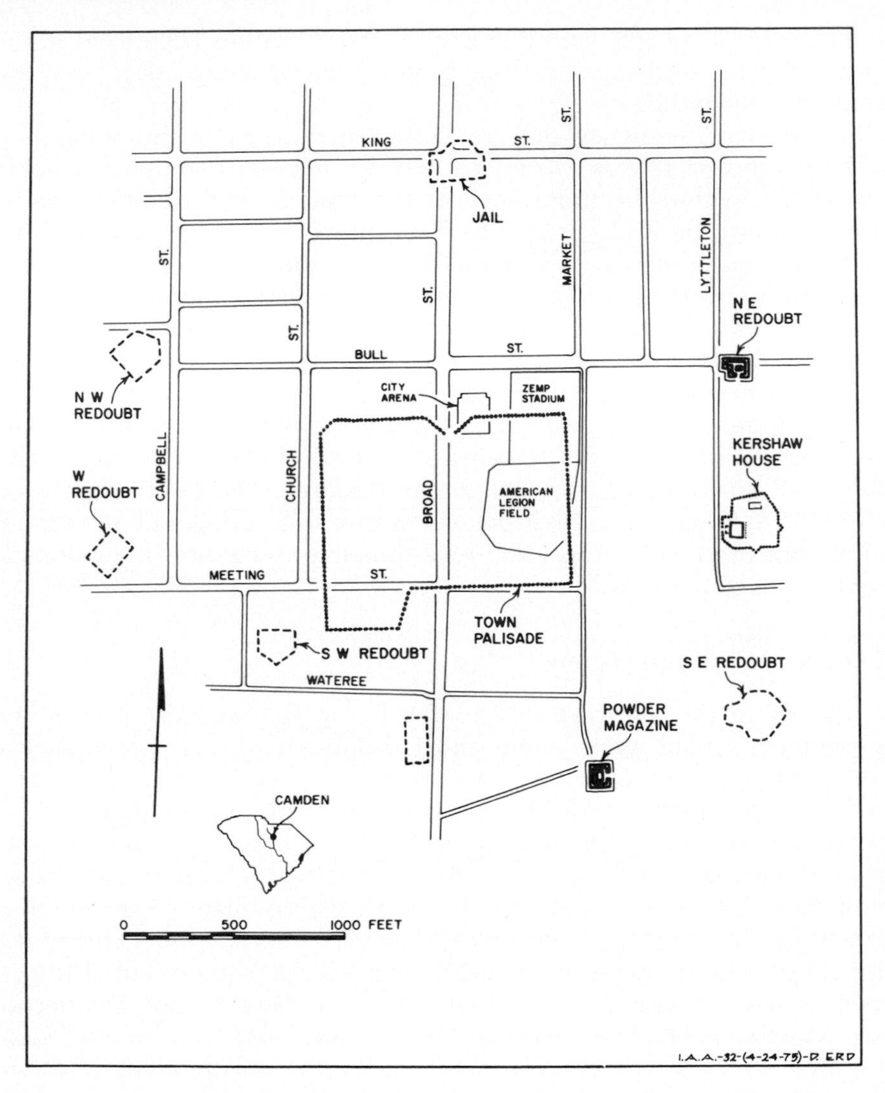

Figure 7.2. Camden (38KE1): plan of modern city with eighteenth century features superimposed. Documented structures that have not been located are shown in their approximate positions with dashed lines.

be unrecognizable. The virtual absence of post-eighteenth century material on the site suggests that the remains there represent a nearly uncontaminated occupation from the period that Camden is suspected to have served as a frontier town. Post-eighteenth century disturbance to the site does not appear to be extensive. The construction of Highway 521 has cut into the old land surface and a small portion of the site adjacent to the eastern edge of this road has been damaged by road-fill operations.

The settlement site itself lies on a gently southeastward sloping surface. In the southeastern quadrant of the site a deep gully was present in the past and is now filled in. In general the site consists of three layers: a gray loam lying directly below the surface, a pale brown sand underlying it, and a sterile red to red-yellow mottled sandy clay at the base of the profile. The historic component is confined to the gray loam except in those places where the pale brown sand is exposed at the surface and was disturbed by cultivation. In effect, the entire historic component used in the comparative analysis was recovered from a single zone throughout the site.

In order to analyze the results obtained in the discovery phase of excavations at Camden, it is necessary to set forth a number of hypotheses that postulate the form that the archeological data should take if they represent the remains of a frontier town in an eighteenth century British American colony. Because the discovery phase is designed to determine basic information about the site as both a formal and functional entity, the hypotheses must reflect these dual goals. The consideration of the hypotheses under the headings of the four general questions outlined in the previous section will serve to make statements relating to the site's form and function explicit.

ETHNICITY: THE QUESTION OF ORIGINS

The first general question refers to the ethnic or cultural affiliation of the site. As a frontier town on the periphery of a British world economic system, Camden would be expected to exhibit archeological evidence of its participation in this system. In order to determine the ethnic or national origin of a particular historic site, it is necessary to consider those archeological data that would vary in frequency of occurrence or in appearance according to the socioeconomic ties of the settlement. Perhaps the category of artifact that best meets these criteria is ceramics (Miller and Stone 1970:98), an artifact present in great quantity at Camden.

Documentary sources have identified the intrusive society as British, a fact that should be confirmed by the results of an examination of the archeological record. Three hypotheses are proposed to substantiate this statement. Each is based upon the expected form that the occurrence of these artifacts would assume if a colonial occupation by a state such as eighteenth century Great Britain were present. With regard to industrial development and innovation in ceramic technology, Britain was far ahead of her European neighbors and possessed an expanding system of overseas trade that dealt increasingly with the re-exportation of foreign commodities (Darby 1973:381; Lieberman 1972:80).

1. The first hypothesis states that British colonial sites, like sites of other competing European colonial states, should be characterized by a predominance of ceramics manufactured in the country of origin or its colonial possessions.
2. The rapid industrialization of the English ceramics industry and the accompanying proliferation of its product would be reflected in the presence of a greater variety of ceramic types on British sites than on those of its competitors in American colonization, France and Spain.
3. Finally, the commercial expansion of Britain in the eighteenth century brought an increase in the amount of foreign goods shipped through British ports. This process of re-exportation may be witnessed by the occurrence of such ceramic types as Oriental porcelains and Westerwald stonewares, both manufactured as export products (Noël Hume 1970:141,257). A comparison of the ceramic collections from the sites of eighteenth century British colonial American settlements suggests that the porcelains comprised from 7 to 30% of the total ceramics used, whereas Westerwald stonewares accounted for up to 5% (South 1972). Although Oriental porcelains are present in low quantities in both French and Spanish sites (Fairbanks 1973:170; Miller and Stone 1970:81), Westerwald stonewares appear to occur in French sites, and there in small numbers (Lunn 1973:185–187; Miller and Stone 1970:76).

An analysis of the ceramic assemblage at Camden substantiates the presence of a British occupation at this site. Of a total of 12,796 ceramic artifacts, 11,963 specimens, or 93% are of British or British colonial origin. Only 16 sherds represent the manufactured goods of competing European powers. The presence of Iberian storage jar fragments and Rouen faience may be explained by the use of the former as storage containers in many northern European countries (Watkins 1973:192–193) and the utilization by the English of the latter as a complement to British earthenwares following the removal of the embargo on such products in 1775 (Noël Hume 1970:142). In both cases these ceramics may be functionally grouped with re-exported wares transported through a British network of trade, and their presence does not indicate direct contact between the colony and either France or Spain nor the presence of an occupation representing either of these countries.

The variety of ceramic types predicted in the second hypothesis is verified by an examination of the archeological record. The presence of 32 types of British ceramics reflects the proliferation of English ceramic technology during this period and mirrors the diversity of types found in the archeological context of contemporary British colonial sites.

The presence of re-exported ceramics is witnessed by the appearance of the two most common foreign export wares, Westerwald stoneware and Oriental porcelain. An examination of the ceramic content of a representative sample of British North American sites (South 1972) indicates that the percentage occurrence of these ceramic types lies within predictable ranges (Lewis 1976). The Westerwald stoneware, comprising 1% of the ceramics at Camden, is within the range for this type; however, the low occurrence of porcelain, roughly 3% of the total, is well below the range for this artifact type and may be the result of a post–Revolutionary War disruption in the American trade with the Orient (Mudge 1962:18). The substantial occurrence of these ceramics reflects the regular appearance of re-exported wares in the transportation system that served the settlement of Camden, supporting the third hypothesis.

CHRONOLOGY: THE QUESTION OF TEMPORAL PERIOD

The second general question attempts to discern the temporal framework of the settlement. Documentary evidence suggests that the site of Camden was occupied as early as 1758 (Kirkland and Kennedy 1905:11). The settlement expanded in the subsequent period, reaching a peak of growth and prosperity in the 1790s. This was followed by a decline and the eventual abandonment of the old town site by 1820 (Schulz 1972:60). The median date of this historic occupation is 1788. In order to substantiate these dates archeologically, it is hypothesized that an examination of chronologically sensitive artifacts will reveal the period during which the deposition of the archeological record took place.[4]

A rough estimate of the time span of the past occupation is provided by a comparison of the use ranges of the ceramic artifacts. Because the site represents a temporally mixed context, it is possible to establish the beginning and termination dates of the occupation respectively by esti-

[4] In addition to the use of ceramics to determine the mean dates for British sites, two other techniques, utilizing English white clay pipes, have been developed by Binford (Maxwell and Binford 1961:108) and Heighton and Deagan (1972). These are based upon the use of straight line and exponential curve formulas respectively, and are designed to correlate periods of historical time with the rate of decreasing stem-hole diameter of the pipes. Unfortunately both these techniques break down in the last three decades of the eighteenth century and sites dating from this period contain increasingly greater numbers of specimens with larger hole diameters (Noël Hume 1963:23). For this reason these techniques would not appear to be applicable to a study of Camden due to its later occupation. Dates for the site using the pipe-stem formulas yield dates in the 1750s, well prior to the mean date of its occupation.

mating the closing date of the use range of the earliest type and the beginning date of the use range of the type commencing last. A comparison of these ranges suggests a *terminus post quem* no later than 1775, and a *terminus ante quem* no earlier than 1813.

The most accurate method of calculating a mean date for British colonial sites also involves the use of ceramic types. Stanley South (1972:83–84) has developed a technique by which to arrive at a mean date for the ceramics contained in an archeological deposit by first measuring the popularity curves of temporally definable ceramic types and calculating the median date for each. By then considering the frequency of occurrence of each type together with its median date, it is possible to ascertain the mean ceramic date. Based on a sample of 11,394 sherds, the mean ceramic date for Camden is calculated to be 1791, only 3 years removed from the median historic date.

Mean dates have also been calculated for each sample unit in which ceramics were present. All the units fall within the historic range and represent the period from 1763 to 1819. A frequency distribution of sample unit dates by year indicates a mode of 1791, indicating that the peak of the occupation with the greatest spatial dispersion occurred at this time. The tapering off of the popularity curve before and after this date presumably represents the expansion and contraction of Camden in the eighteenth and early nineteenth centuries (Schulz 1972:56). This cycle of Camden's growth, peak, and decline should be linked to a larger cycle of development in the frontier in general. Because of the central role the frontier town played in relation to the socioeconomic system of the area of colonization, the decline of such a settlement would be likely to signal a drastic change in this system such as that caused by the reintegration of the area at the national level at the close of the frontier period.

THE QUESTION OF FORM AND FUNCTION

Unlike the first two questions, which deal with the settlement as a whole, the third and fourth questions attempt to examine variation relating to form and function within the settlement. It is assumed that intrasite variability discernible in the archeological record will reveal patterns that reflect elements of the systemic structure of the society that produced this record. A central settlement within an area of colonization may be assumed to have performed a number of specific roles within the frontier system. Evidence of these roles should be present in the archeological record and should be reflected in the form of the settlement as well as in the spatial distribution of activities within it.

As a sociocultural entity on the British North American frontier,

Camden would have occupied a status comparable in many ways to certain other types of urban settlements in early industrial Europe. Its location on the periphery of the European world system, however, would have caused it to assume characteristics unlike those of settlements in the metropolitan area. Its role as a frontier town would require it to maintain certain functions while adapting to frontier conditions by restricting its socially integrating institutions and, consequently, aspects of its form as well.

When compared to the settlements in the urban hierarchy of eighteenth century Europe, the frontier town shares much in common with the "town," which is the lowest level of settlement in which exchange is conducted on an inter- rather than an intraregional basis. The town is also characterized by greater specialization in production, an increase in the variety of employment, and the marketing of a greater range of goods than are found in settlements further down on the urban scale (Blouet 1972:4). Grove (1972:560) also attributes political and social functions to the role of the town. He suggests that towns be assigned separate relative statuses in an urban hierarchy based upon the spatial extent of their influence (Grove 1972:561). Given the generally large area lying within the influence of a frontier town, it is possible to place such settlements relatively high in this hierarchy (see Ernst and Merrens 1973:559–560).

In terms of size and form, however, the frontier town differs strikingly from European settlements with comparable functions (see Flatres 1971:170), a feature that seems to have led many contemporary observers and even later historians (e.g., Sellers 1934:4) to overlook the actual urban functions of frontier town settlements in the colonial American South. The reasons for the insignificant appearance of these settlements are related to the nature of frontier expansion, specifically the rapid spread, and consequent widely dispersed settlement with a low population density, which prevailed in South Carolina throughout the colonial period (Potter 1965:661). Unlike the traditional process of European settlement evolution in which a settlement's relative status as a center for socioeconomic activity is tied to its population density and economic complexity so that settlement growth may be seen as a reflection of urban functions (Fox 1973:76), the frontier town comes into existence relatively rapidly. It does not arise solely to integrate settlements within a specified area economically on an intraregional basis, but also to tie such settlements into the network of a complex and often far-ranging interregional economic system. The frontier town is established as an economic center without first passing through a series of intermediate growth stages, and without taking on the roles and the forms of less complex settlement types. Consequently, the frontier town need not be as large as an English market town because it is not necessarily a population center that assumed urban functions, but rather a market center set up primarily to coordinate social, economic, and political activities.

THE FRONTIER TOWN AS A COMMUNITY—HYPOTHESES OF FORM AND FUNCTION

It may be best to view a frontier town as part of a larger, dispersed social entity. It serves as the site wherein are located the nexuses of the socially integrating institutions of the area of colonization it serves. The notion of "community" in an anthropological sense, defined as the "basic unit of organization and transmission within a society and its culture [Arensberg 1961:248]," appears to be useful in dealing with a settlement of this type. Arensberg's definition stresses function rather than form and sees the community in an organizational rather than in a spatial sense as, for example, Murdock does (1949:79). Thus, a community may include more than a single settlement and its form may even vary periodically according to the adaptive mode of the particular society (Trigger 1968:60–61). Camden, as a frontier town, seems to represent the focal point of a dispersed community, the limits of which are somewhat difficult to define, yet within which primary subsistence production and to a large extent residence lie outside the area of nucleated settlement.

Assuming that Camden, as a frontier town, was such a part-community, it is likely to have shared in, as well as differed from, patterns of settlement and activity distribution found in contemporary English market towns. The form of these patterns has been set forth in terms of three archeological hypotheses. They embody those characteristics that collectively should identify the frontier town as an entity and should distinguish diagnostic elements of its internal patterning.

1. The first hypothesis deals with the overall form of the frontier town. It is predicted that because most activities in a frontier town would tend to be associated with its function as a center of trade and communications on the frontier, one might expect to find evidence of its densest occupation along the major transportation routes connecting it with the outside world.
2. Because of the unique nature of settlement within the area of colonization, the large, permanent, localized supporting population normally associated with market towns in Europe should not be present in a frontier town. Consequently, the total number of structures is expected to be less in the latter. The abundance of land on the frontier and the absence of a need for consolidated defense or cooperative subsistence activities (see Page 1927:450) in the frontier town fail to provide the adaptive pressures that com-

monly resulted in the concentrated settlement pattern of European towns. It is likely that the settlement pattern of Camden, though compact in relation to that of the frontier as a whole, would not have been as compact or clustered as would those of Europe.

3. Because of the pivotal role played by the frontier town, the majority of the structures there should be associated with the centralizing functions of the settlement. These functions might involve activities relating to the transfer and storage of goods and commodities, small-scale manufacturing and maintenance, and political and social activities associated with the periodic gathering of persons for collective purposes such as trials, markets, or tavern socializing. Structures used solely as dwellings are not likely to have formed the majority of the structures at Camden. This situation would contrast markedly with its counterpart in the metropolitan area, where dwellings are usually the most numerous type of structure.

In summary, three hypotheses have been presented relating to aspects of the settlement's form and the distribution of past activities within it. In order to test the hypotheses with regard to the Camden data, archeological test implications must be set forth and examined. The degree to which the hypotheses are supported will determine the extent to which the settlement conforms to the model of the frontier town.

The Situation of the Town

The first hypothesis predicts that the densest part of the frontier town's occupation will be located adjacent to the primary route of trade and communications linking the settlement with the outside world. At Camden, this route would be the Catawba Path, and principal overland route to Charleston.

Documentary evidence provides some clues to the intended form of Camden but little information as to the actual distribution of settlement at the site. Surviving property records suggest that much of the land remained in large parcels throughout the eighteenth century and it is not possible to determine the locations of structures within them accurately (McCormick 1975). The earliest plat of the town, drawn in the early 1770s, shows a settlement arranged on a rectangular grid with a central square (Figure 7.3), a design employed in earlier English colonies in Ireland and later in North America (Reps 1972). A settlement built on such a pattern would have produced an arrangement similar to that of a European market town. A clue to the actual distribution of settlement is provided by a 1781 military map illustrating the town's fortifications (Figure 7.4). Though not drawn to scale, it indicates the relative positions

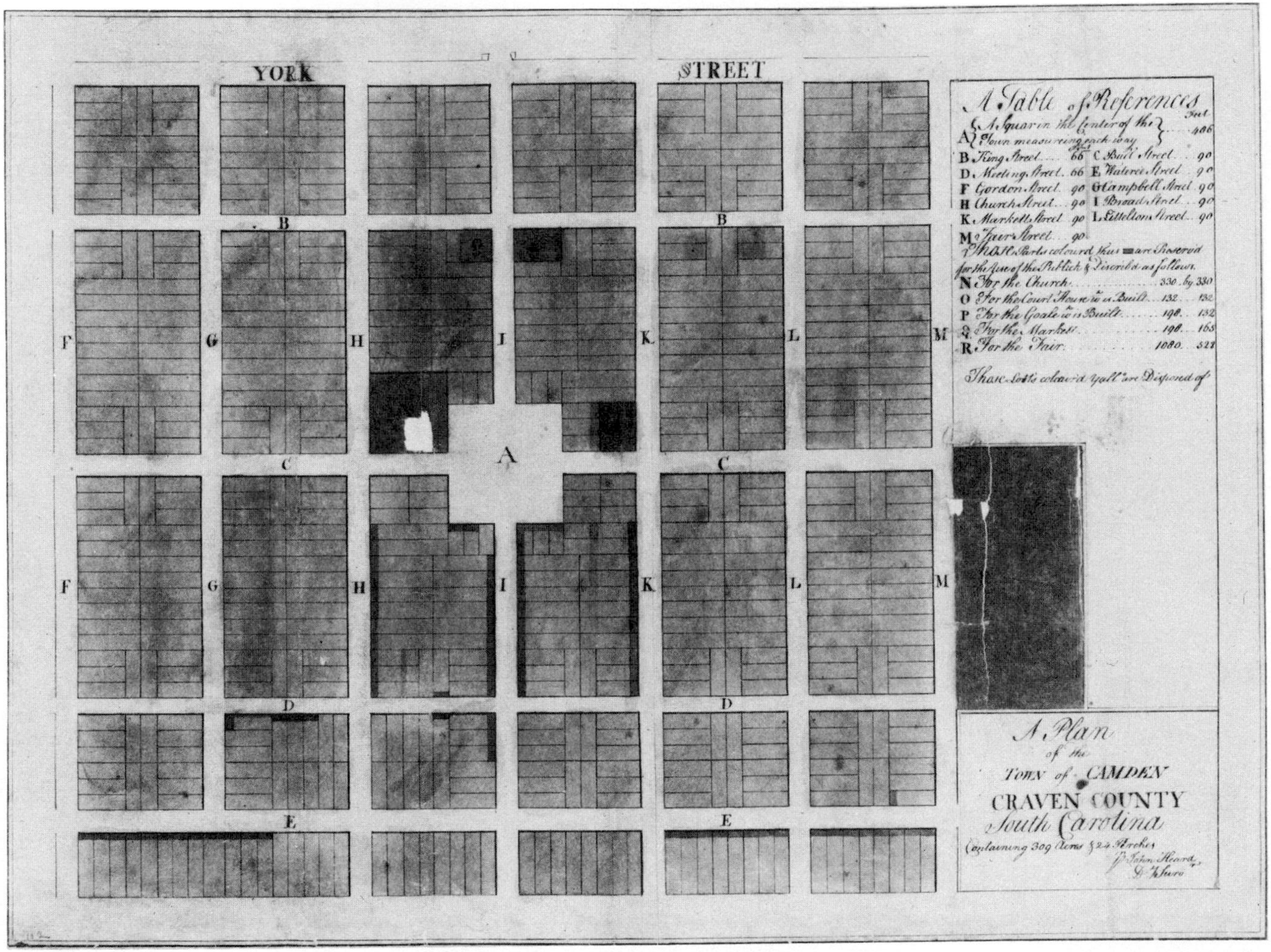

Figure 7.3. The Heard Plan of Camden, drawn in the early 1770s, showing the layout of the settlement as originally surveyed. From the South

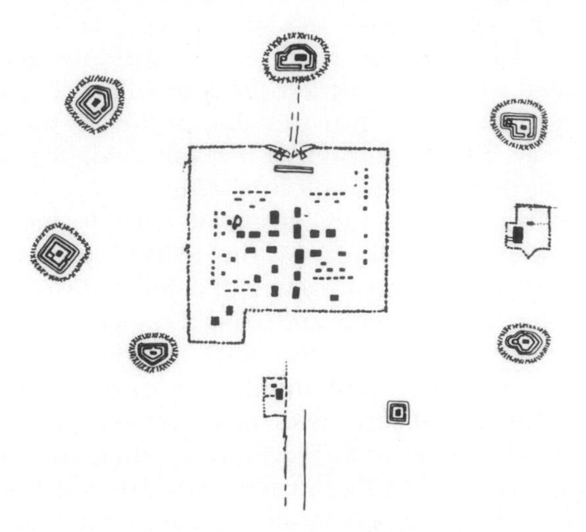

Figure 7.4. The Greene Map of Camden in 1781, illustrating the layout of the settlement and the military fortifications erected during the British occupation of the town, 1780–1781. From the Nathanael Greene Papers, May 12, 1781/155/II:161.

of what are assumed to be structures, and these tend to be situated along a central north–south road.

The structure arrangement suggested by the map is strikingly similar to that of the medieval "two row" settlements that were established along transportation routes to take advantage of trade (Page 1927:448). These linear settlements consist of structures with tofts[5] in back, facing each other across an open space, often no wider than a street (Roberts 1973:48). Cross streets occur in this type of settlement but, in general, structures on them do not extend far from the main street.

If it is assumed that colonial Camden represents a two-row settlement, then the distribution of artifacts in the archeological record should reveal a settlement pattern similar to that found in European villages of this type. Perhaps the most significant material element related to the overall pattern of settlement is the distribution of structures. Arche-

[5] The term *toft* is used here to refer to the immediate site of a dwelling or other principal structure and its outbuildings. It is both a spatial and functional unit in that it designates the area within which occur those activities that lie closest to and are most intimately concerned with the functions of the principal structure. As such, the toft is not confined to a specific size or form and may vary considerably according to the nature of the structure with which it is associated. In an urban settlement a toft might comprise an entire holding; however, in a rural settlement where holdings would include agricultural fields, the toft includes only that part of the holding in which activites immediately associated with the household are carried out.

ologically this should be evidenced by the differential occurrence of architecturally related materials across the site. This class of artifacts would include such items as brick, nails, window glass, and other artifacts associated with the construction of buildings. Even where extensive demolition of the actual structure has occurred, the distribution of these artifacts may be relied upon to provide evidence of its existence (see Carrillo *et al.* 1975:57; Lewis 1975b:67–70).

The distribution of architecturally related artifacts, including those in features at Camden as displayed by the SYMAP program, appears in Figure 7.5. It clearly shows the presence of at least 17 structures. Seven of these are arranged parallel with and roughly adjacent to Broad Street, five on the west side and two on the east. In addition to paralleling the main thoroughfare of the settlement, the distribution of structural remains implies the presence of two roads turning off Broad Street and running west at right angles to it. The more southerly of these is Meeting Street, off which are situated five structures to the north and one to the south. The other thoroughfare is an unnamed road or alley situated about three quarters of the way between Meeting Street and the north line of the palisade wall. Six structures occur adjacent to this road. The 1781 map (Figure 7.4) illustrates the alignment of five structures in approximately this position, suggesting that the northern cross-street existed as early as 1781. Its absence on the Heard map of the early 1770s as well as on other maps dating in the 1790s (Kirkland and Kennedy 1905:15,18), however, seems to indicate that it was not in use long before or after this time, though it may have persisted as an alley providing access to the rear of structures located along Broad Street.

The interpretation of structural remains on the east side of Broad Street is complicated by the limited extent of the archeological investigations there and the disturbed condition of this part of the site. Evidence of three structures is present here in the form of concentrations of architectural artifacts corresponding roughly to the positions of buildings indicated on the 1781 map. Two are located adjacent to Broad Street, and the third lies to the rear of them. Unfortunately the surface adjacent to the northeast corner of Broad and Meeting streets has been removed and it is impossible to search for evidence of the structure shown there. The remains of all other structures indicated on the 1781 map (Figure 7.4) lie beneath the public facilities.

In summary, the general form of the colonial occupation at Camden is basically that of an English two-row settlement, with a single main street and two cross-streets. This pattern of settlement appears to have evolved, in spite of the surveyed town plan's form, so as to maximize access to the primary route of transportation and communications connecting the frontier town of Camden with the entrepôt of Charleston on the one hand and the scattered interior settlements on the other.

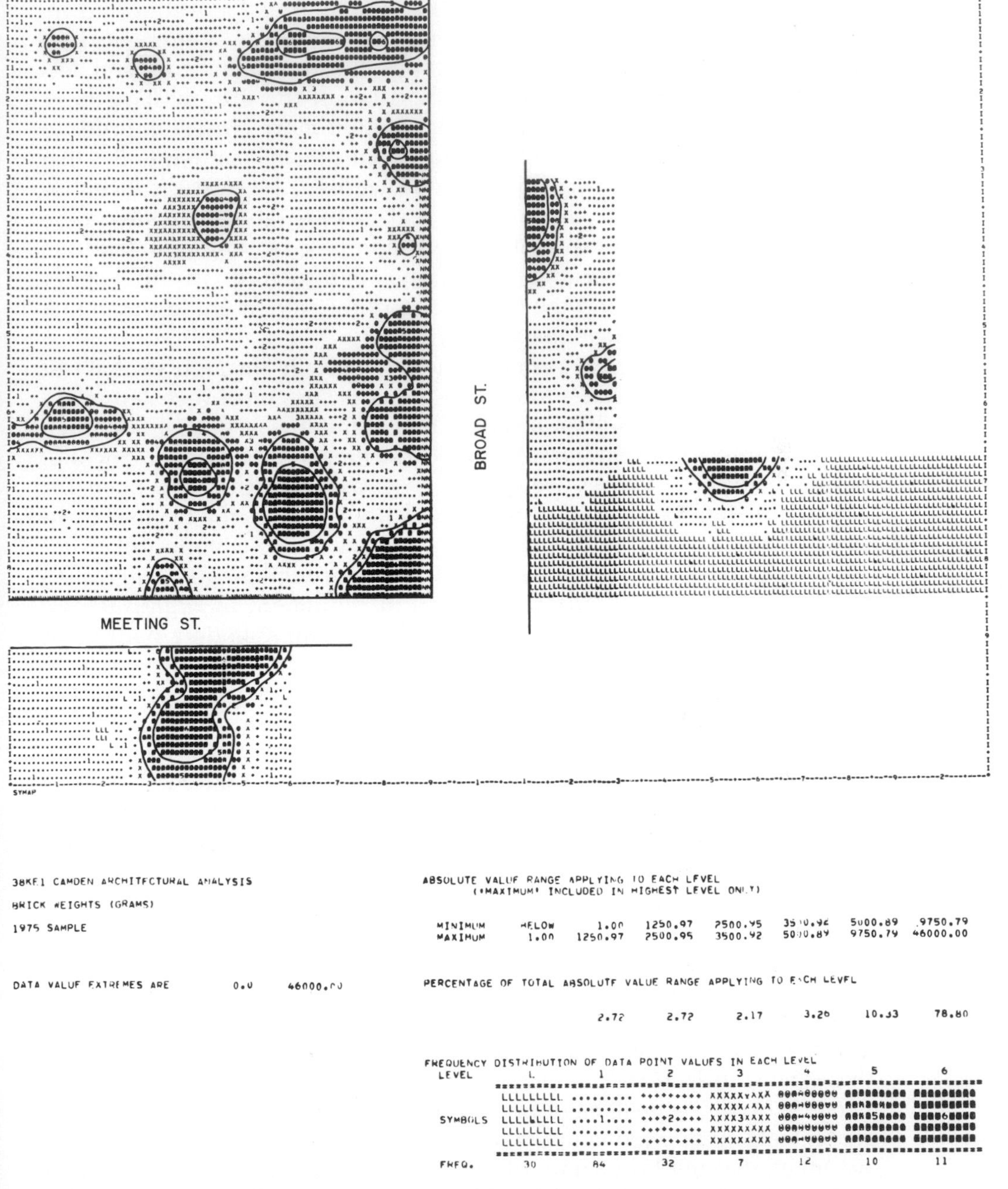

Figure 7.5. SYMAP illustrating the patterned spatial distribution of brick and architectural features.

The Settlement Pattern at Camden

The second hypothesis predicts that Camden, as a frontier town, should be distinguishable from contemporary European settlements having comparable socioeconomic functions by its smaller size and less compact settlement pattern. In the discussion of the present hypothesis it will be necessary to consider this distribution more closely in order to compare Camden to contemporary European settlements that performed similar roles. It is postulated that, because of the concentration of economic, political, and other socially integrating activities in the frontier town and the dispersal of the supporting farming population in the surrounding countryside, the number of structures in the frontier town would be fewer and the overall size of the settlement less than that of a comparable European market town.

This hypothesis may be examined archeologically through several test implications. The first states that the number of structures revealed in the archeological record will be less than that at the lowest end of the range of structures found in comparable settlements in England. Second, because fewer structures were built, it is assumed that the need for access to commercial street frontage was not as acute in a frontier town as in an English market town. For this reason, the distribution of structures should be more dispersed along the thoroughfares in contrast to the nearly contiguous clustered pattern of settlement in English towns. This dispersal should be especially noticeable in Camden because it would directly conflict with the surveyed pattern of long, narrow lots designed to allow a maximum number of property owners to share the commercially important street frontages (see Taylor 1974:64). Third, because of the more widespread spacing of structures, a variation in the size and shape of their accompanying tofts should be discernible. Rather than the long, narrow, rearward-facing tofts characteristic of English settlements, those in Camden should represent an adaptation to the more dispersed settlement pattern of the frontier.

With regard to the first test implication, comparative information on the size of eighteenth century market towns indicates that the settlements varied greatly in this respect. Populations varied from 60,000 persons in provincial centers like Bristol and Liverpool to less than 12,000 in regional centers such as Leicester and Exeter. Smaller centers with periodic markets supported populations ranging from 800 to several thousand (Patten 1973:129–130). Contemporary estimates, such as that by Eden (1973:32–33) in 1800, of houses per town indicate that the range of settlements mentioned would have contained from 116 to 12,000 houses. Assuming that the lower limit of this range is the approximate minimum size of a market town, it is logical to predict that a frontier town would contain a smaller number of structures. An examination of the archeological record at Camden should reveal that the structural remains will yield evidence of the presence of fewer structures than the 116 noted as the minimum for European market towns.

Archeological investigations at Camden uncovered evidence of 13 clusters of architectural material in the area west of Broad Street. If this figure is doubled to estimate the number of structures in the settlement, including that portion inaccessible to archeological investigation, a total of 26 structures are indicated. A comparison of this estimate to the number of structures shown on the 1781 map indicates a variation of only five, suggesting that the settlement portrayed on the map did not grow appreciably larger in the period after the American Revolution.

The discrepancy in the layout of structures predicted in the second test implication is confirmed by a comparison of the archeological structure layout and the plans of contemporary English market towns. Here typically the structures lay adjacent to the main roads, as at Camden, but they were constructed in a contiguous arrangement. This row pattern contrasts with the uneven dispersal of structures at Camden. The degree of variation from a clustered arrangement of the Camden structures may be expressed numerically by calculating a nearest neighbor statistic based on the distance between concentrations of architectural artifacts. The value R indicates the degree to which the distribution of a population, in this case structures, deviates from a random expectation (1.0) toward clustering (0) or even spacing (2.149) (Clark and Evans 1954:451). The value of R for Camden is 1.558, indicating a nearly random distribution of structures over the site with a deviation in the direction of even spacing.

Closely related to the settlement pattern is the distribution of tofts referred to in the third test implication. These areas lie adjacent to structures and should contain evidence of those activities associated with them. It should be possible to recognize tofts and define their limits based on the occurrence of certain types of features normally associated with toft activities. These activities may be broken down into two basic categories, disposal and maintenance–storage, each of which is generally associated with a different type of feature.

Studies of medieval and post-medieval living sites in England (Hurst 1971:116) and colonial living sites in British North America (South 1977) have shown that the toft was the general area for the disposal of refuse in pits or as scatter on the surface. The continual use of the toft for this purpose would eventually result in the development of one or more primary-refuse areas representing the discard from single or multiple activities carried out there. The extent of the area used for disposal should be reflected archeologically in the distribution pattern of pits. In Camden this pattern is expected to provide evidence of the expanded tofts characteristic of a frontier town.

The toft was also the location of intense activity related to the function of the structure. The toft usually contained outbuildings in which activities were conducted and tools and materials were stored. Such outbuildings might include privies, wells, workshops, storage buildings, barns, corncribs, and general purpose sheds (Hurst 1971:115; Noël Hume 1969; Sloane 1967). Because of the light construction used in many of these structures, often due to their temporary nature, they are likely to be characterized by the presence of postholes dug to secure their supporting members. In the case of certain types of structures subsurface features may also be present. If an outbuilding was of substantial construction, concentrations of architectural materials may also be present in the archeological record.

It is expected that a comparison of the spatial distribution of pit and posthole features at Camden with the archeological structural pattern will yield an approximation of the toft patterns associated with structures situated on the site. The results of this comparison are illustrated in Figure 7.6. It reveals a total of 12 areas of concentrated pit features and 14 areas containing postholes. These appear to cluster around the structural remains to form 10 distinct areas of localized activity, which may be tentatively identified as tofts for comparative purposes. These are designated Toft Areas 1–10 and are illustrated in Figure 7.7. Several of the toft areas contain evidence of more than a single structure and may reflect complexes of related buildings. The expected toft pattern is clearly revealed in the distribution of pit and posthole features at Camden. Tofts here seem to occur both to the rear and to the sides of structures; several buildings appear to have been totally surrounded by them. The expanded toft appears to be the universal form except in the case of the structure on the northwest corner of Broad and Meeting streets, where the toft is confined to a narrow strip behind the building.

Although defined only in an approximate manner, the toft pattern at Camden permits the site to be divided into smaller units for the purpose of analysis on the basis of assumed activity localization. It is probable that each of the units defined will yield information relating to the function of the cultural activities that once took place there.

In summary, the overall pattern of structures and tofts at Camden reveals a settlement much smaller and more dispersed than a contemporary English settlement with comparable urban functions. The large tofts at Camden contrast markedly with their narrow, confined counterparts and fall within the pattern characteristic of other English colonial settlements of the eighteenth century. These settlement characteristics clearly reflect a pattern adapted to an absence of a resident supporting population and, consequently, a reduced competition for commercial street frontages.

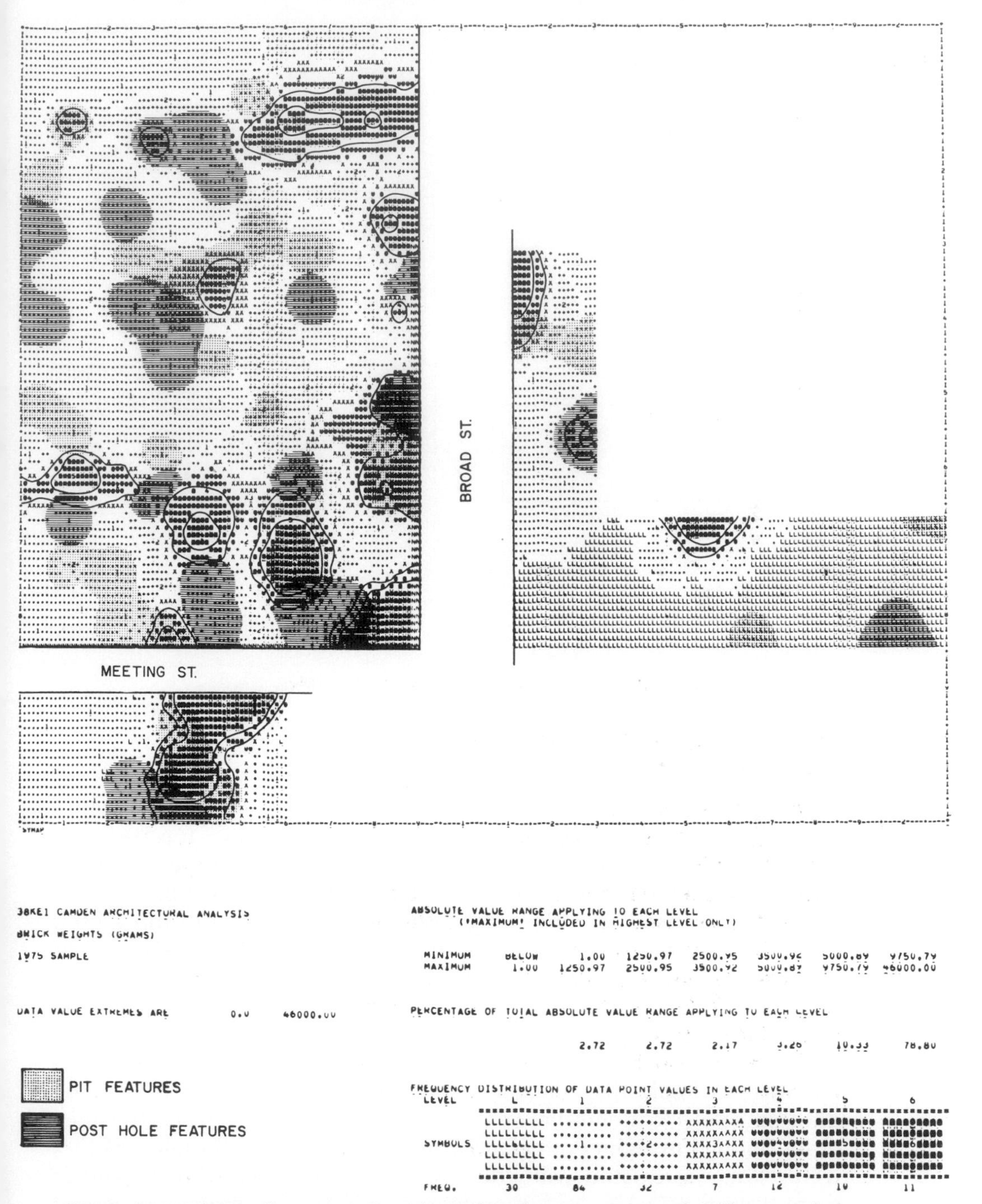

Figure 7.6. SYMAP illustrating the relationship between structural Evidence and the occurrence of pit and posthole features.

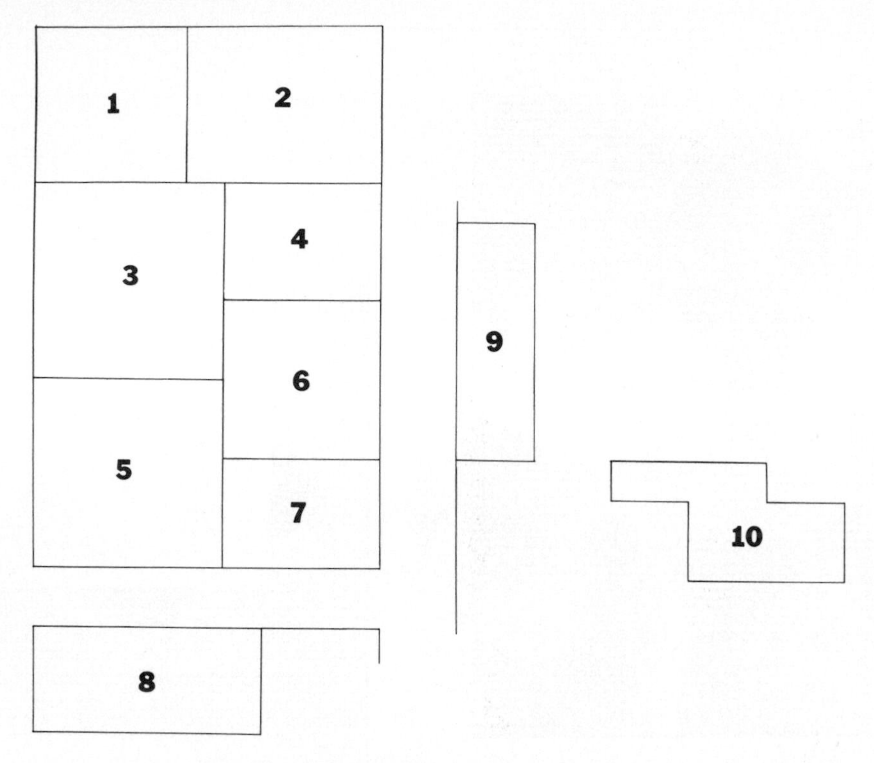

Figure 7.7. Plan of the toft areas at Camden.

The Distribution of Domestic versus Nondomestic Activity Areas

The last of the hypotheses deals with the primary role of the settlement as a center for socioeconomic activity on the frontier. It is based on the assumption that the emphasis in a past systemic context may be observed archeologically by considering the relative proportion of structure–toft units used for strictly domestic purposes to that of those used for other purposes. It predicts that a frontier town should be characterized by a greater proportion of nondomestic activity units and that the residue of this functional disparity will be discernible in the archeological record.

The distinction between domestic and nondomestic activities is not intended to imply that all structures of this period would have been devoted solely to domestic or nondomestic or other specialized purpose. During the eighteenth century most small-scale economic activities were closely associated with the living areas of those who worked at them (Patten 1973:136) and, therefore, it is likely that most units would contain at least some evidence of domestic activities. In order to test this hypothesis archeologically it is necessary to develop test implications that will predict the nature of the evidence capable of identifying strictly domestic occupations on the one hand and combined domestic and nondomestic occupations on the other.

Artifact Classes and Activity Sets. The first test implication predicts that it is possible to construct classes of artifacts that will vary with the degree to which domestic and nondomestic activities are represented in the archeological context. The artifact categories used here are designed to seek out functional differences in gross terms rather than to identify specific types of activities.

With regard to distinguishing data classes of historic material, only preliminary empirical studies have been conducted and the definition of functional data patterns has not been attempted. For this reason, it is necessary to use documentary and ethnographic analogy to develop data classes through which to examine functional variation at the site. In terms of recognizing the dichotomy of orientation in a frontier town, it is necessary to organize research in such a manner as to discern the archeological by-products of domestic and nondomestic activities.

The archeological record does not represent a total inventory of past activities but only the residue of such activities resulting from the operation of cultural formation processes. At Camden these processes would most likely include discard and loss (Schiffer 1975a:4–7, and this volume). Proceeding on the assumption that loss is related to artifact size and portability and discard is a function of the fragility of the artifact given normal use and the degree of lateral cycling and recycling that it may undergo during its normal use-life (Schiffer 1972:158–159), it should be possible to predict the general types of artifacts that would form the by-products of various past activities.

It has been noted that a domestic occupation in an eighteenth century British colonial site should be associated with a specific group of domestic-related activities involved with the production, preparation, consumption, and distribution of subsistence products. These activities comprise a subsistence activity set centered upon the principal structure and its toft. The archeological record of a domestic occupation may be expected to represent the by-products of this activity set. A commercial, industrial, or other nondomestic activity area would involve a technological activity set that would result in an output representing the manufacture, repair, modification, storage, and shipment of goods and commodities. The composition of nondomestic residue would differ from that of a domestic occupation because of the addition of new artifacts and the differential occurrence of those also found in domestic residue.

The latter is likely to reflect the use of similar artifacts in separate functional contexts. An example of such an artifact is ceramics, an imported item that played a prominent role in both subsistence and technological activity sets on the colonial frontier. As a domestic artifact it would have been brought to a living area and used there until broken. As there were few uses for broken ceramics, it would have been discarded in the toft to form part of a domestic rubbish deposit that accumulated throughout the duration of the area's occupation. Before finding its way into a domestic context, however, the same ceramic object would have passed through the hands of merchants, as did nearly all items imported into the colony. Although fragile artifacts, most ceramics would have left the commercial establishments where they were sold intact, leaving little evidence of their presence there. Thus, while the same object may be recovered from several archeological contexts, the nature of its occurrence in each, rather than its presence or absence alone, provides the key to the interpretation of the activities associated with each context.

The nondomestic commercial structure may be expected to contain evidence associated primarily with activities relating to the movement of goods and commodities rather than to these products themselves. Industrial structures likewise should not be characterized by the finished goods they produced, but by the presence of by-products of manufacturing processes and perhaps distinctive architectural form. It must be remembered that nondomestic structures, especially those situated within a nucleated settlement, are likely to have served as living quarters for those who worked there. Therefore, such a structure is apt to include some elements of both subsistence and technological activity sets and its by-product should reflect an occupation of this nature.

The archeological record may be viewed as the surviving by-product of the two activity sets. An examination of the archeological data by toft area should permit the observation of these sets in a number of locations at once. If the toft areas are treated as multiple independent refuse areas for the activity sets or combination of sets associated with each type of occupation (that is, each area and its contents are the result of deposition from either a domestic or nondomestic occupation), then it is logical to assume that the artifacts associated with each area will statistically reflect the functional difference in the occupations (Schiffer 1975b:64). It is expected that the proportional relationship between artifact classes will vary according to the nature of the activity that produced them. A comparison of the toft areas with regard to the relationship between artifact classes should reveal groups of areas characterized by the statistical similarity of their contents. These groups, in turn, form the basis for interpreting the distribution of domestic and nondomestic activities on the site. The distribution of activities determined here should establish whether or not the pattern of activity occurrence predicted in the hypothesis did exist in Camden.

The archeological by-product of a particular activity set is linked to the role the activity played within the larger sociocultural system. Thus, a subsistence activity set would be characterized by the occurrence of artifacts associated with the carrying out of subsistence-related activities. These might include the collection, processing, storage, and consumption of subsistence commodities as well as the storage and repair of tools and other articles associated with subsistence activities. Because the archeological record at Camden is assumed to be very largely the result of the cultural formation processes of discard and loss, the artifact classes expected to characterize a particular activity set would consist of items discarded or lost as the result of related activities. It is predicted that these classes will occur consistently in areas within which this activity set played a similar role. Because of the size of the representative sample obtained at Camden, it has been necessary to combine artifacts representing the by-products of several types of activities into classes large enough to yield statistically significant amounts of measurable data. Certain specialized artifacts are likely to occur in such low frequencies as not to be amenable to statistical analysis. Their occurrence, however, is significant in that it serves as a source for behavioral inferences that may be tested in subsequent stages of research.

The three classes of artifacts associated with a subsistence activity set are as follows:

Class 1: artifacts associated with the collection, processing, and storage of subsistence products. These items might include broken or worn-out farm tools or their parts, fishing equipment, and hunting equipment. All three of these subsistence strategies were employed on the Carolina frontier during the eighteenth century (Budd 1973:23; Lawson 1952; Woodmason 1953:245). Processing and storage artifacts could include remains of storage containers, food processing tools, and tools used in processing raw materials for purposes other than consumption, as in the making of cloth (Cripps 1973; Noël Hume 1970).

Class 2: artifacts associated with the consumption of subsistence products. This artifact class subsumes artifacts used in the preparation and consumption of foods. Cooking containers, cooking and eating utensils, drinking containers including case and wine bottles, serving equipment, and fireplace and other cooking hardware fall into this category (see Noël Hume 1970).

Class 3: faunal and floral remains of subsistence foods. The materials in this class consist of items that would form the residue of food preparation and consumption activities. Animal bone, eggshells, nuts, seeds, and pollen retrieved from sealed archeological contexts may be placed in this class.

Class 4: artifacts associated with solely technological activities, are included under a single class because of the likelihood of their low frequency of occurrence. These specialized items in this class are apt to be extremely varied according to the nature of the activity involved. Manufacturing activities such as pottery making, brick making, or smithing would be characterized by a substantial discard output (South 1963, 1967). Light industries producing a perishable by-product or activities concerned with the transfer, repackaging, storage, or exchange of goods or commodities, on the other hand, are not likely to have left behind a substantial residue in the form of discarded or lost material. In the case of all specialized nondomestic activities it is probable that all the tools and equipment used would have been valued more or less highly and therefore are not likely to have become part of a refuse deposit. For example, when his brewery in Camden ceased operations, John Kershaw "Sold ye Brewing Impliments . . . [Kirkland and Kennedy 1905:406]" rather than discarding them.

For these reasons it is likely that the distinguishing characteristics of a specialized technological activity might not consist solely of a high frequency of occurrence of specialized artifacts, but rather of the presence or absence of these items themselves. In a small sample, such as that examined at Camden, technological artifacts are likely to represent only a small portion of the total artifacts recovered unless high discard output activities were present. The probability of sampling error is high when the expected occurrence of a particular class of items is low. Therefore it seems best not to rely entirely on this class of data to identify the presence of a nondomestic occupation. Rather, it may be more fruitful to observe the technological activity class in combination with variation in the two artifact classes discussed next.

The remaining two classes of artifacts are unlike those just presented in that they represent the residue of activities that may have been part of either subsistence or technological activity sets, or of a combination of both.

Class 5: artifacts associated with the housing of persons and goods. This artifact class contains artifacts related to structures and their integral parts.[6] It is essentially an architectural class that includes such items as nails, spikes, building hardware, window glass, and locks. It might also subsume general household artifacts like furniture and their parts that would have been associated with structures of varied function.

Class 6: artifacts of a general nature associated with the presence of persons. The present class includes objects that would have been carried on the persons of individuals. As a consequence of their mobility, these

[6] Although an integral part of structures, bricks and brick fragments are not included in this artifact class because they constitute the principal datum upon which the toft areas here analyzed were defined. In that its presence in each area has been established, it would be inappropriate to use this same form of data to substantiate hypotheses predicting the nature of the data in the toft areas. To do so would constitute circular argument.

objects might have been lost or discarded in any or all places frequented by such individuals. This class includes clothing items such as buttons and buckles in addition to coins, tobacco pipes, and other "personables" like rings, bone brushes, watch fobs, spectacle lenses, watch keys, wig curlers, and many others (see South 1977).

The two artifact classes just outlined are of particular significance in the interpretation of the Camden sample data, not because they are indicative of the presence of a particular type of past activity but because the substantial quantity of material encompassed by them, when treated as a single category, may be used to measure the relative size of the subsistence artifact component at any part of the site. It is assumed that the architectural-personal artifact component of a toft area will remain consistent regardless of the nature of the activity performed at that area. Thus, the larger the relative size of the subsistence artifact category (composed of the first three artifact classes), the greater the likelihood that the subsistence activity set of which it represents the residue constituted the major activity in that particular toft area. A toft characterized by this activity set very likely contained a domestic occupation. Conversely, the smaller the relative size of the subsistence artifact category, the less likely the subsistence activity set is to have represented the principal activity there. As we are concerned with discovering the presence of a nondomestic occupation that is characterized chiefly by the absence of an archeological by-product, it is logical to expect that evidence of a technological activity set indicative of such an occupation will not be present in the archeological record. Instead, its presence would be evidenced by reduced size of the subsistence component.

Artifact Class Analysis. The numerical counts and percentages of the six artifact classes by toft area are shown in Table 7.1. In order to examine these classes with regard to area function, they have been combined into three activity categories as illustrated in Table 7.2. An examination of the percentage frequencies of the three categories reveals wide variation in the frequencies of the two larger categories, subsistence related and combined subsistence-technology related, together with a very low percentage in the technology-related category. When compared graphically (Figure 7.8) the percentages of the two major categories cluster into three groups.

The first group exhibits a high frequency of subsistence artifacts (79–81%) together with a lower frequency of subsistence-technological artifacts (18–20%). Technological artifacts total no more than 1% of the artifacts in any area. On the basis of this relationship it is possible to assign a domestic occupation to Toft Areas 2, 3, and 6.

The second group of tofts includes Toft Areas 1, 4, 7, 9, and 10. Here the percentage of subsistence artifacts is somewhat lower (71–74%)

TABLE 7.1
Comparison of Artifact Classes by Toft Area

Artifact class	Toft area 1	2	3	4	5	6	7	8	9	10	Totals
						Counts					
1. Collection, processing, storage	15	89	57	32	50	28	42	13	30	19	375
2. Consumption	768	3970	3400	1265	1509	2081	1558	965	1058	619	17193
3. Faunal	30	132	325	14	134	21	65	338	31	13	1103
4. Architecture	280	898	645	401	751	433	540	825	323	201	5297
5. Personal	37	190	229	60	74	45	72	16	69	23	818
6. Manufacturing debris	20	48	25	20	1	18	42	29	38	3	244
Totals	1150	5327	4681	1792	2519	2626	2319	2186	1549	878	25027
						Percentages					
1. Collection, processing, storage	1	2	1	2	2	1	2	1	2	2	1
2. Consumption	67	74	73	71	60	79	67	44	68	71	69
3. Faunal	3	2	7	1	5	1	3	15	2	1	4
4. Architecture	24	17	14	22	30	16	23	38	21	23	21
5. Personal	3	4	5	3	3	2	3	1	4	3	3
6. Manufacturing debris	2	1	1	1	0	1	2	1	2	0	1
Totals	100	100	101	100	100	100	100	100	99	100	99

TABLE 7.2
Comparison of Activity Categories by Toft Areas

Activity category	Toft area 1	2	3	4	5	6	7	8	9	10	Totals
						Counts					
1. Subsistence	813	4191	3782	1311	1693	2130	1665	1316	1119	651	18671
2. Subsistence–technological	317	1088	874	461	825	478	612	841	392	224	6112
3. Technological	20	48	25	20	1	18	42	29	38	3	244
Totals	1150	5327	4681	1792	2519	2626	2319	2186	1549	878	25027
						Percentages					
1. Subsistence	71	79	81	73	67	81	72	60	72	74	75
2. Subsistence–technological	28	20	19	26	33	18	26	38	25	26	24
3. Technological	2	1	1	1	0	1	2	1	2	0	1
Totals	101	100	101	100	100	100	100	99	99	100	100

whereas that of subsistence-technological artifacts is higher than in the previous group (25–28%). Technological artifacts range from less than 1 to 2% of the totals. Although the relative relationship of the two larger artifact categories is similar to that in the first group, the tofts in the second group form a distinct cluster apart from those in the first. No "intermediate" areas are present (Figure 7.8). For this reason it is possible to identify these areas tentatively as sites of less intense domestic occupations, perhaps representing combination residences and businesses.

The third toft group is composed of two toft areas (5 and 8) that contain a sizably lower percentage of subsistence artifacts (60 and 67%) and a much higher percentage of subsistence–technological artifacts (33 and 38%). Technological artifacts constitute no more than 1% of the totals. The marked difference between these areas and the other two groups is clearly discernible in Figure 7.8. The relative frequencies of the artifact categories in these areas suggests the presence of a greatly reduced domestic occupation as might be anticipated in an industrial area. The absence of manufacturing debris, however, seems to preclude the presence of an industry characterized by a nonperishable by-product. It is probable, then, that the two areas represent the remains of a nondomestic occupation of unknown type.

It is significant to recall here that the only known nondomestic activity

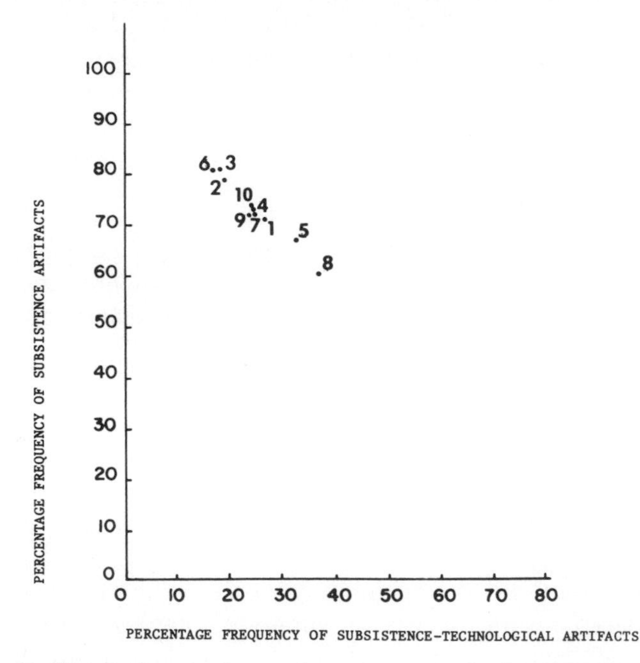

Figure 7.8. Graphic display of toft areas by occurrence of subsistence versus subsistence–technology artifacts.

center in eighteenth century Camden precisely located from documentary sources is Joseph Kershaw's brewhouse. It was the sole structure that occupied the block southwest of the intersection of Broad and Meeting streets during this period (Figure 7.2). The remains of this structure are situated in Toft Area 8, and the residue of the brewing activity appears to be evidenced by the low occurrence of the subsistence artifact component.

In summary, a comparison of the percentage frequencies of functionally significant artifact categories has resulted in the division of the 10 Camden toft areas into three groups. Although it is not possible to identify the precise nature of the activities represented by the archeological remains in each area, it is possible to distinguish a group that contains a high subsistence artifact component. This group presumably reflects the by-product of domestic occupation areas. The second group contains a relatively smaller amount of subsistence material and presumably represents a domestic occupation shared with that of another activity. This trend is taken further in the third group where it is likely that the domestic occupation comprised a still smaller portion of the total occupation in the areas falling within this group.

On the basis of this threefold division, it has been possible to demonstrate tentatively the distinction between domestic and nondomestic activity areas. It was predicted that because the frontier town represents a socioeconomic center in the area of colonization the ratio of nondomestic to domestic activity structures is likely to be high. In that Camden is presumed to have been an eighteenth century frontier town, it was anticipated that archeological evidence would reveal a significant number of nondomestic areas there. An examination of the data indicates that of 10 toft areas defined at the site, only three may be tentatively identified as having played a solely domestic role. The results obtained in this discovery phase of research are, of course, preliminary in regard to the precise identification of past activities; the functional definition of areas at the site must await more intensive investigation.

Intersite Comparison: The Carolina Pattern. The third test implication will treat the site as a single unit without regard to internal variability in order to compare it to sites of other settlements in colonial North America that are likely also to have functioned as frontier towns. This comparison should establish similarities in the patterning of the archeological record in settlements of this type in general. It will not aid in the comparison of intrasite activity patterns but should help determine whether or not the same general artifact pattern present at other comparable sites occurs at Camden. Stanley South (1977) has recently recognized several broad intersite artifact frequency patterns based upon the relationships of eight categories (groups) of artifact classes recovered from eighteenth century British colonial American sites. An examination of the sites at which each pattern was discernible reveals that the Frontier Pattern is generally associated with military and trading post sites on the periphery of or beyond the limits of the actual area of colonization. The Carolina Pattern, on the other hand, is associated with settlements inside the area of colonization. The differences observed in the two patterns have not been linked to specific functional differences in the types of sites in which they occur; however, South (1977) has suggested that the higher frequency of the *Kitchen* group artifacts in Carolina Pattern sites is closely related to the proximity of these sites to the supply network of the colony. The efficiency of the colonial trade and communications subsystem with regard to the distribution of imported manufactured goods is reflected by the consistency of this frequency in sites from several British American colonies. This test implication predicts that Camden, as a site situated within an area of colonization, will yield an inventory of artifacts that conforms to that of South's Carolina Pattern.

A comparison of the eight artifact category ranges and the frequencies of occurrence of these categories at Camden are illustrated in Table 7.3. It will be noted that, in general, the Camden data category frequencies agree with those of the Carolina Pattern. The frequencies of four of the low categories (*Furniture, Clothing, Personal,* and *Activities*) vary from the Carolina Pattern range by as much as .3% and presumably are the result of sampling error due to the smaller size of the sample. The deviation of *Kitchen* artifacts (2.2%) is greater in size and is very likely due to other factors. Perhaps the chief reason why the category of *Kitchen*

TABLE 7.3

Comparison of Carolina Pattern Observed Ranges and Camden Artifact Category Percentage Frequencies

Artifact group	Carolina Pattern frequency range[a]	Camden artifact category frequencies	Deviation	Artifact group totals
Kitchen	51.8–69.2	71.4	+2.2	17,134
Architecture	19.7–31.4	22.0	0	5,277
Furniture	.2–.6	.08	–.12	18
Arms	.1–1.2	.2	0	52
Clothing	.6–5.4	.3	–.3	60
Personal	.1–.5	.004	–.096	1
Tobacco Pipes	*1.8–13.9*	*3.1*	*0*	*750*
Activities	.9–2.7	2.8	0	683
Totals		99.884		23,975

[a] Data from South (1977).

artifacts is larger in the Camden sample is that the Camden data represent a sample of the site as a whole, including those parts peripheral to the areas of heaviest activity. The Carolina Pattern, on the other hand, is based on materials collected in intensive excavations of major site components, including structures, outbuildings, and recognizable middens. This work is not likely to have sampled the scattered deposits evidenced in the stratified random sample. The inclusion of these deposits in the archeological sample is likely to increase the frequency of occurrence of *Kitchen* artifacts because this category of artifacts presumably formed the greater part of scattered deposits than did *Architecture* artifacts, the other large category in the South scheme. This situation is the result of the operation of several cultural transformation processes acting differently upon the two categories of artifacts. *Kitchen* artifacts consist primarily of portable objects associated with the household. These would most likely have found their way into the archeological record through discard, a process that entailed their disposal and subsequent scattering in the toft. *Architecture* group artifacts would also have accumulated as the result of discard, especially during periods of construction, modification, and repair (Green 1961). The greatest amount of deposition of architectural artifacts would have been due to the destruction of a building by fire or its disintegration following abandonment, processes involving in-place deposition of materials near the site of their use.

The closeness of the artifact frequency pattern at Camden to the Carolina Pattern may be seen in a comparison of the former to the predicted range of the latter (South 1977). The limits of this range are based on a computation designed to predict the range within which there is a 95% chance that the next set of data may fall. The predicted range is substantially wider for each artifact category as may be seen in Table 7.4. The frequencies of all the Camden artifact categories fall within the limits of this range.

The Camden site as a whole may be seen to conform to the expectations of the Carolina Pattern. Adherence to this pattern does not, in itself, prescribe a specific function or set of functions to the settlement. It does, however, indicate a patterned similarity between Camden and other eighteenth century colonial sites of English origin in the Carolinas.

Summary of Artifact Analysis. In summary, preliminary archeological investigations at Camden have established the presence of certain conditions that identify the site as a frontier town. The employment of extensive sampling techniques has permitted the examination of the entire site, revealing significant functionally related patterns in the archeological record. These patterns have, in turn, formed the basis for the interpretation of the colonial settlement.

TABLE 7.4

Comparison of Carolina Pattern Predicted Ranges and Camden Artifact Category Percentage Frequencies

Artifact group	Carolina pattern predicted frequency range	Camden artifact category frequencies
Kitchen	47.5–78.0	71.4
Architecture	12.9–35.1	22.0
Furniture	0–.7	.08
Arms	0–1.5	.2
Clothing	0–8.5	.3
Personal	0–.6	.004
Tobacco Pipes	0–20.8	3.1
Activities	.1–3.7	2.8
Total		99.884

Clues to the ethnic affiliation of the settlement and the dates of the site's occupation have been ascertained through an examination of the ceramic artifacts recovered there. The Camden ceramic collection yielded specimens representative of an eighteenth century British colonial settlement. A mean ceramic date of 1791 was derived for the site as a whole; individual sample squares indicate a range of occupation from 1763 to 1819. The occupation of the greatest part of the site has a mean date of 1791. These dates conform closely to evidence obtained from documents indicating a range of occupation from 1758 to 1819, with a median date of 1788.

An estimation of the form and spatial extent of the settlement has been aided by the presence of the British palisade wall that delimited the bounds of the 1780 town. The actual distribution of the structures and activity areas was determined by plotting variation in the frequencies of occurrence of different classes of artifacts across the site. Patterns formed by the differential occurrence of artifacts served as the basis for the interpretation of functional variation within the site. Several significant conclusions have resulted from this aspect of the investigations.

As a frontier town, Camden was assumed to exhibit evidence of the functions carried out in a comparable market center in England. Because of the dispersed nature of settlement on the frontier, the large supporting population normally associated with a market settlement would not be present at Camden, resulting in a smaller settlement with a less clustered settlement pattern. An examination of the archeological data revealed a small settlement of less than 30 structures situated in a random pattern tending toward even spacing. Nondomestic activities, assumed to play a dominant role in a frontier town, appear to be associated with the majority of the structures and their toft areas. The nature of individual activities are difficult to identify, however, because of the absence of specialized by-products. It is assumed that most nondomestic activities at Camden were of a light industrial or commercial nature. Documents indicate the presence of such activities within the settlement.

Thus, the discovery phase of archeology has answered a number of broad questions about the form and nature of the colonial settlement of Camden. Its conclusions, though in many cases tentative, support the assumption that the settlement functioned as a frontier town as defined in the model. They also serve to demonstrate the utility of this archeological method in the investigation of culture processes in past societies.

CONCLUSIONS

The goal of this chapter has been to design and conduct archeological research capable of recognizing a particular process of past sociocultural change dealing with the adaptation of colonizing societies in frontier situations. In order to accomplish this, a multistage approach was initiated in which successive phases of archeological research would permit the identification of a frontier situation, its limits in time as revealed by an investigation of its focal settlement, and finally its spatial bounds as determined through the comparative study of other settlements.

In order to demonstrate the viability of archeological methodology in the investigation of frontier change, an attempt has been made to complete the first part of this research design. Because of the general nature of the research problem, the preliminary archeological examination employed the use of techniques capable of providing data relevant both to present questions and to the orientation of future research. This phase of research has been referred to as a *discovery* phase of archeology.

The present study has examined archeological data pertaining to the eighteenth century British colonial frontier in South Carolina. Discovery-phase excavations were employed to ascertain, in the absence of documentary or other sources, that a potential situation for frontier colonization did develop into a settlement frontier. The existence of a frontier is witnessed by the development of a frontier town, a settlement located so as to permit the establishment of trade and communications linkages between the older settled area and the newly occupied lands. The frontier town becomes the nexus of the transportation network of the area of colonization and its identification is crucial to the verification of frontier situation.

The archeological research design used in the discovery phase of excavations at Camden employed a stratified sampling technique to examine

1% of the total accessible area of the site. The results of this sample revealed evidence of the settlement's form and spatial patterning. This initial work has also provided clues to the differential occurrence of various broadly defined activities within the settlement. On the basis of this information it has been possible to identify Camden as having possessed several crucial features of a frontier town and as being likely to have served as a central settlement in the development of this area. The chronological span of the settlement's occupation also provides a useful gauge for the development of the frontier as a whole. Camden's beginning around 1760 suggests that the earliest settlement of the back-country took place at this time. Likewise, its decline as a frontier town in the second decade of the nineteenth century would suggest the expansion of the frontier and the assumption of its functions within the frontier system by other settlements.

With the location of the frontier town and the time of its occupation established, it is now possible to examine the frontier as a spatial entity and investigate sites dating from a comparable period with regard to their relationship to Camden and the frontier system for which it served as the focus.

The investigation of colonization in a particular area for which documentary data are available makes possible the controlled testing of conclusions reached through the analysis of the archeological record. It is important to realize, however, that the source of data used in the study of the past is not as significant as the larger framework in which it is examined. The analysis of the archeological record must not be seen as a means to tie particular observations to cultural phenomena but rather as a means to use archeological data as a potential source of information to test generalizations about culture process. Only in this manner will it be possible to approach the study of the past, be it prehistoric or historic, in terms of seeking explanations of phenomena rather than merely describing them.

ACKNOWLEDGMENTS

The author wishes to acknowledge the help of the following individuals and groups for their part in the completion of this chapter. Thanks go to the staff of the Institute of Archeology and Anthropology of the University of South Carolina for their support, and particularly to Stanley South and John H. House for their helpful criticism during the preparation of the manuscript and Jacqueline Carter for her assistance in the analysis and computerization of the archeological materials from Camden. The archeological investigations were sponsored by the Camden Historical Commission under grants from the Coastal Plains Regional Commission and the National American Bicentennial Committee.

REFERENCES

Allen, H. C.
1959 *Bush and backwoods: A comparison of the frontier in Australia and the United States.* East Lansing: Michigan State Univ. Press.

Arensberg, Conrad M.
1961 The community as object and sample. *American Anthropologist* **63:**241–264.

Baker, Steven G.
1975 The working draft of: The Catawba peoples: Exploratory perspectives in ethnohistory and archaeology. Report prepared for Duke Power Company and other sponsors of Institutional Grant J-100. Office of Research, Univ. of South Carolina, Columbia.

Barlett, Richard A.
1974 *The new country, a social history of the American frontier, 1776–1890.* New York: Oxford Univ. Press.

Binford, Lewis R.
1962 A new method of calculating dates from kaolin pipestem samples. *Southeastern Archaeological Conference, Newsletter* **9**(1):19–21.
1964 A consideration of archaeological research design. *American Antiquity* **29**(4):425–441.
1965 Archaeological systematics and the study of culture process. *American Antiquity* **3**(2):203–210.
1968 Archeological perspectives. In *New perspectives in archeology,* edited by Sally R. and Lewis R. Binford. Chicago: Aldine. Pp. 5–32.

Blouet, Brian W.
1972 Factors influencing the evolution of settlement patterns. In *Man, settlement and urbanism,* edited by Ruth Tringham and G. W. Dimbleby. London: Gerald Duckworth. Pp. 3–15.

Brown, Richard Maxwell
1963 *The South Carolina Regulators.* Cambridge, Massachusetts: Belknap Press of the Harvard Univ. Press.

Buckley, Walter
1967 *Sociology and modern systems theory.* Englewood Cliffs, New Jersey: Prentice-Hall.

Calmes, Alan
1968 Report of excavations at the Revolutionary War period fortifications at Camden, South Carolina. Camden District Heritage Foundation, offset.

Carrillo, Richard F., Joseph C. Wilkins, and Howell C. Hunter, Jr.
1975 Historical, architectural, and archeological research at Brattonsville (38YK21), York County, South Carolina. *Research Manuscript Series* No. 76. Institute of Archeology and Anthropology, Univ. of South Carolina.

Casagrande, Joseph B., Stephen I. Thompson, and Philip D. Young
1964 Colonization as a research frontier. In *Process and pattern in culture, essays in honor of Julian H. Steward,* edited by Robert A. Manners. Chicago: Aldine. Pp. 281–325.

Cheyney, Edward Potts
1961 *European background of American history: 1300–1600.* New York: Collier Books.

Clark, Philip J., and Francis C. Evans
1954 Distance to nearest neighbor as a measure of spatial relationships in populations. *Ecology* **35**(4):445–453.

Craddock, G. R., and C. M. Ellerbe
1966 *General soil map of Kershaw County, South Carolina.* United States Department of Argiculture, Soil Conservation Service, Fort Worth.

Crane, Verner W.
1956 *The southern frontier.* Ann Arbor: Univ. of Michigan Press.

Cripps, Ann
1973 *The countryman, rescuing the past.* Newton Abbot, Devon, U.K.: David & Charles.

Darby, H. C.
1973 The age of the improver: 1600–1800. In *A new historical geography of England,* edited by H. C. Darby. Cambridge, Massachusetts: Harvard Univ. Press. Pp. 302–388.

Dawson, C. A.
1934 The settlement of the Peace River Country, a study of a pioneer area. In *Canadian frontiers of settlement,* Vol. 6, edited by W. A. Mackintosh and W. L. G. Joerg. Toronto: MacMillan.

Dice, Lee R.
1952 *Natural communities.* Ann Arbor: Univ. of Michigan Press.

Eden, Sir Frederick Morton
1973 An estimate of the number of inhabitants in Great Britain and Ireland (1800). In *The population controversy,* edited by D. V. Glass. Farnborough, Hampshire, U.K.: Gregg International Publishers Limited.

Ernst, Joseph A., and H. Roy Merrens
1973 "Camden's turrets pierce the skies!": The urban process in the southern colonies. *William and Mary College Quarterly* Ser. 3, **30**(4):549–574.

Fairbanks, Charles H.
1973 The cultural significance of Spanish ceramics. In *Ceramics in America,* edited by Ian M. G. Quimby. Charlottesville: Univ. Press of Virginia. Pp. 141–174.

Flatres, P.
1971 Hamlet and village. In *Man and his habitat, essays presented to Emyr Estyn Evans,* edited by R. H. Buchanan, Emrys Jones, and Desmond McCourt. New York: Barnes and Noble. Pp. 165–185.

Fox, H. S. A.
1973 Going to town in thirteenth century England. In *Man made the land, essays in English historical geography,* edited by Alan H. R. Baker and J. B. Harley. Newton Abbot, Devon, U.K.: David & Charles. Pp. 69–78.

Fried, Morton H.
1960 On the evolution of social stratification and the state. In *Culture in history: Essays in honor of Paul Radin,* edited by Stanley Diamond. New York: Columbia Univ. Press. Pp. 713–731.
1967 *The evolution of political society, an essay in political anthropology.* New York: Random House.

Frothingham, E. H., and R. M. Nelson
1944 South Carolina forest resources and industries. *United States Department of Agriculture, Miscellaneous Publication* 552.

Geertz, Clifford
1963 *Agricultural involution: The process of ecological change in Indonesia.* Berkeley: Univ. of California Press.

Gould, J. D.
1972 *Economic growth in history, survey and analysis.* London: Methuen.

Gould, R. A.
1971 The archaeologist as ethnographer: A case from the Western Desert of Australia. *World Archaeology* **3**(2):143–177.

Green, H. J. M.
1961 An analysis of archaeological rubbish deposits. *Archaeological News Letter* **7**(3):51–54.

Grigg, David
1967 Regions, models, and classes. In *Models in geography,* edited by Richard J. Chorley and Peter Haggett. London: Methuen. Pp. 461–509.
Grove, David
1972 The function and future of urban centres. In *Man, settlement, and urbanism,* edited by Ruth Tringham and G. W. Dimbleby. London: Gerald Duckworth. Pp. 559–565.
Hallowell, A. Irving
1957 The impact of the American Indian on American culture. *American Anthropologist* **59**(2):201–216.
Heighton, Robert F., and Kathleen A. Deagan
1972 A new formula for dating kaolin clay pipestems. *Conference on Historic Site Archaeology, Papers* **6:**220–229.
Hudson, John C.
1969 A locational theory for rural settlement. *Annals of the Association of American Geographers* **59:**365–381.
Hurst, John G.
1971 A review of archaeological research. In *Deserted Medieval villages,* edited by Maurice Beresford and John G. Hurst. London: Lutterworth Press. Pp. 76–144.
John, A. H.
1962 Aspects of English economic growth in the first half of the eighteenth century. In *Essays in economic history,* Vol. 2, edited by E. M. Carus-Wilson. London: Edward Arnold. Pp. 360–373.
Kirkland, Thomas J., and Robert M. Kennedy
1905 *Historic Camden,* Vol. 1: *Colonial and revolutionary.* Columbia, South Carolina: State Printing Co.
Kottak, Conrad P.
1974 *Anthropology, the exploration of human diversity.* New York: Random House.
Kristof, Ladis K. D.
1959 The nature of frontiers and boundaries. *Annals of the Association of American Geographers* **49:**269–282.
Lawson, John
1952 *Lawson's history of North Carolina* (1714). Richmond, Virginia: Garrett and Massie.
Lewis, Kenneth E.
1975a *The Jamestown frontier: An archaeological view of colonization.* Ph.D. dissertation, Univ. of Oklahoma, University Microfilms, Ann Arbor, Michigan.
1975b The north parade ground structure. In Fort Washita from past to present, an archaeological report, edited by Kenneth E. Lewis. *Oklahoma Historical Society, Series in Anthropology* **1:**34–75.
1976 Camden: a frontier town in eighteenth century South Carolina. Institute of Archeology and Anthropology, University of South Carolina. *Anthropological Studies* 2.
Leyburn, James G.
1935 *Frontier folkways.* New Haven, Connecticut: Yale Univ. Press.
Lieberman, Sima (editor)
1972 *Europe and the industrial revolution.* Cambridge: Massachusetts. Schenkman Publishing.
Lunn, John
1973 Colonial Louisbourg and its developing ceramics collection. In *Ceramics in America,* edited by Ian M. G. Quimby. Charlottesville: Univ. Press of Virginia. Pp. 175–190.
Macleod, William Christie
1928 *The American Indian frontier.* New York: Knopf.

Maxwell, Moreau S., and Lewis Binford
1961 Excavations at Fort Michilimackinac, Mackinac City. Michigan, 1959 season. *Publications of the Museum, Michigan State Univ., Cultural Series* **1.**

McCormick, Jo Anne
1975 Preliminary report of documentary research on Camden, South Carolina. Camden District Heritage Foundation, typescript.

Mikesell, Marvin W.
1968 Comparative studies in frontier history. In *Turner and the sociology of the frontier,* edited by Richard Hofstadter and Seymour Martin Lipset. New York: Basic Books. Pp. 152–171.

Miller, J. Jefferson, and Lyle M. Stone
1970 Eighteenth century ceramics from Fort Michilimackinac, a study in historical archeology. *Smithsonian Studies in History and Technology* 4.

Mudge, Jean McClure
1962 *Chinese export porcelain for the American trade, 1785–1835.* New York: Univ. of Delaware Press.

Mueller, James W.
1974 The use of sampling in archaeological survey. *Society for American Archaeology, Memoir* **28.**

Murdock, George Peter
1949 *Social structure.* New York: MacMillan.

Nathanael Greene Papers
Papers of the Continental Congress. Washington, D.C.: Library of Congress. (available on microfilm).

Noël Hume, Audrey
1963 Clay tobacco pipe dating in the light of recent excavations. *Quarterly Bulletin of the Archaeological Society of Virginia* **18**(2):22–25.

Noël Hume, Ivor
1969 *Historical archaeology.* New York: Knopf.
1970 *A guide to artifacts of Colonial America.* New York: Knopf.

Page, William
1927 Notes on the types of English villages and their distribution. *Antiquity* **1**(4):447–468.

Patten, John
1973 Urban life before the industrial revolution. In *Man made the land, essays in English historical geography,* edited by Alan R. H. Baker and J. B. Harley. Newton Abbot, Devon, U.K.: David & Charles. Pp. 127–139.

Potter, J.
1965 The growth of population in America, 1700–1860. In *Population in history, essays in historical demography,* edited by D. V. Glass and D. E. C. Eversley. Chicago: Aldine. Pp. 631–679.

Prescott, J. R. V.
1965 *The geography of frontiers and boundaries.* Chicago: Aldine.

Rappaport, Roy A.
1968 *Pigs for the ancestors, ritual in the ecology of a New Guinea people.* New Haven, Connecticut: Yale Univ. Press.

Redman, Charles L.
1973 Multistage fieldwork and analytical techniques. *American Antiquity* **38**(1):61–79.

Redman, Charles L., and Patty Jo Watson
1970 Systematic intensive surface collection. *American Antiquity* **35**(3):279–291.

Rees, Peter W.
1975 Origins of colonial transportation in Mexico. *Geographical Review* **65:**323–334.

Reps, John W.
1972 *Tidewater towns, city planning in colonial Virginia and Maryland.* Williamsburg, Virginia: Colonial Williamsburg Foundation.

Roberts, Brian
1973 Planned villages from Medieval England. In *Man made the land, essays in English historical geography,* edited by Alan R. H. Baker and J. B. Harley. Newton Abbot, Devon, U.K.: David & Charles. Pp. 46–58.

Rowse, A. L.
1957 Tudor expansion: The transition from medieval to modern history. *William and Mary College quarterly* Series 3, **14**(3):309–316.

Sanders, William T., and Barbara J. Price
1968 *Mesoamerica, the evolution of a civilization.* New York: Random House.

Schiffer, Michael B.
1972 Archaeological context and systemic context. *American Antiquity* **37**(2):156–165.
1975a Cultural formation processes of the archaeological record: A general formulation. Paper presented at the 1975 meeting of the Society for Historical Archaeology, Charleston.
1975b Factors and "toolkits": Evaluating multivariate analyses in archaeology. *Plains Anthropologist* **20**–67:61–70.

Schulz, Judith J.
1972 The rise and decline of Camden as South Carolina's major inland trading center, 1751–1829: A historical geographic study. Unpublished M.A. thesis, Department of Geography, Univ. of South Carolina.

Sellers, Leila
1934 *Charleston business on the eve of the American Revolution.* Chapel Hill: Univ. of North Carolina Press.

Sloane, Eric
1967 *An age of barns.* New York: Balantine Books.

South Carolina Statutes
South Carolina Archives, Columbia, manuscript.

South, Stanley
1963 Exploratory excavation of a brick kiln at Town Creek, Brunswick County, N.C. North Carolina Department of Archives and History, typescript.
1967 The ceramic forms of the potter Gottfried Aust at Bethabara, North Carolina, 1755 to 1771. *The Conference on Historic Site Archaeology, Papers* **1**:33–52.
1972 Evolution and horizon as revealed in ceramic analysis in historical archaeology. *Conference on Historic Site Archaeology, Papers* **6**:71–116.
1977 *Method and theory in historical archeology.* New York: Academic Press.

Steward, Julian H.
1949 Cultural causality and law: A trial formulation of the development of early civilizations. *American Anthropologist* **51**(1):1–27.
1955 *Theory of culture change, the methodology of multilinear evolution.* Urbana: Univ. of Illinois Press.

Strickland, Robert N.
1971 Camden Revolutionary War fortifications (38KE1): The 1969–70 excavations. *Institute of Archeology and Anthropology, University of South Carolina, Notebook* **3**(3):55–71.

Taylor, Robert
1974 Town houses in Taunton 1500–1700. *Post-Medieval Archaeology* **8**:63–79.

Thompson, Stephen I.
1970 *San Juan Yapacani: A Japanese pioneer colony in eastern Bolivia.* Ph.D dissertation, Univ. of Illinois. University Microfilms, Ann Arbor, Michigan.

1973 Pioneer colonization, a cross-cultural view. *Addison-Wesley Modules in Anthropology* **33.**

Trigger, Bruce G.

1968 The determinants of settlement patterns. In *Settlement archaeology,* edited by K. C. Chang. Palo Alto, California: National Press Books. Pp. 53–78.

Turner, Frederick J.

1893 The significance of the frontier in American history. *Annual Report of the American Historical Association for the year 1893,* pp. 199–227.

Wallerstein, Immanuel

1974 *The modern world system, capitalist agriculture and the origins of the world-economy in the sixteenth century.* New York: Academic Press.

Watkins, C. Malcolm

1973 Ceramics used in America: Comparisons. In *Ceramics in America,* edited by Ian M. G. Quimby. Charlottesville: Univ. Press of Virginia. Pp. 191–198.

Webb, Walter Prescott

1952 *The great frontier.* Boston: Houghton Mifflin.

Weigert, Hans W., Henry Brodie, Edward W. Doherty, John R. Fernstrom, Eric Fischer, and Dudley Kirk

1957 *Principles of political geography.* New York: Appleton.

Wells, Robin

1973 Frontier systems as a sociocultural type. *Papers in Anthropology* **14**(1):6–15.

Woodmason, Charles

1953 *The Carolina backcountry on the eve of the Revolution* (1768), edited by Richard J. Hooker. Chapel Hill: Univ. of North Carolina Press.

Wyman, Walker D., and Clifton Kroeber (editors)

1957 *The frontier in perspective.* Madison: Univ. of Wisconsin Press.

The Historical and Ecological Position of Protohistoric Sites in the Slate Mountains, South Central Arizona

ALBERT C. GOODYEAR III

The question of historical relationships between the final prehistoric phases of southern Arizona and earliest known historic populations coresiding in the same area has been a longstanding problem for archeologists and ethnohistorians of the Southwest. In essence, this problem has revolved around the issue of whether or not the historically observed Pima and Papago were the direct descendants of the former prehistoric Desert- and River-related Hohokam societies. Like the question of Classic Hohokam and the early Pima of the Salt and Gila river regions (Winter 1973:67), in the Papagueria[1] an identical problem obtains in attempts to demonstrate a historical and cultural continuity between the Sells phase and the traditional Papago residents. The period between the prehistoric and historic period, about A.D. 1400–1700, has been referred to as the "dark age" since very little substantive archeological data have surfaced that would inform on this era (Haury 1950:18; Joseph *et al.* 1949:15).

Some of the conceptual difficulties archeologists have had with this so-called dark age have to do with the dearth of primary data known to relate to this transition period. Attempts have been made to excavate verified early historic sites such as Batki (see Haury 1950:18–21), but these efforts were blocked. In addition, there is the matter of what to look for in terms of material culture that might have been produced during that time (Haury 1950:19). Finally, on an explanatory level, there have been

[1] The ethnohistoric territory of the Papago that covered southwestern Arizona and the adjoining portion of Sonora, Mexico.

serious theoretical limitations in attempts to explain formal differences between the prehistoric Hohokam and the historic groups as well as to explain gaps in the culture history. There is no need to recapitulate the various historical reconstructions since they are presented in detail elsewhere (see Fontana *et al.,* 1962:84–93). All these arguments rely on such factors as immigration, abandonment, warfare, and other historically based events rather than systemic processes of a general nature. The primary units of analysis have been discrete traits, which are not necessarily useful or reliable for diachronic comparisons since their significance in behavioral terms has not been rigorously determined.

In the course of recent archeological investigations on the Hecla Mine property, located on the southern slopes of the Slate Mountains in the extreme northern section of the Papago Indian Reservation (Figure 8.1), a series of surface sites was encountered that produced a certain type of pottery not commonly recognized heretofore in the ceramic traditions of the area. An important exception to this statement would be Haury's (1950:345) comments regarding a late prehistoric, hard, thin, chocolate-colored brown ware from the upper levels of Ventana Cave, which is located approximately 20 miles (32 km) to the southwest of the Slate Mountains (Figure 8.1). As Haury (1950:345) perceptively noted, these ceramics are indeed unlike the red-on-buff pottery typically manufactured by the Riverine Hohokam or the well-known red-on-brown ceramics of the historic Papago Indians (see Fontana *et al.* 1962).

Because of its apparent similarity to some of the Yuman types of ceramics, this pottery was referred to as "Yuman" in the summary of archeological studies of the Hecla Mine (Goodyear 1975:28). The thin brown ware sherds,[2] some exhibiting marked wiping striae on the rims and shoulders, were thought to best match the descriptions of Tizon Brown ware as described by Dobyns and Euler (1958). All but one of the sherds from the Slate Mountain sites were examples of jars whose morphologies, based on rim and shoulder pieces, bore a strong resemblance to the jar forms of Cerbat Brown and Tizon Wiped minus the lugs on the latter (Dobyns and Euler 1958).

[2] Because of problems inherent with assigning names to ceramic "types" prematurely, I will merely refer to these sherds in the most distinctive and unambiguous terms as possible. The term *thin brown ware* will be used, for clearly these sherds are thinner and more brown than any ceramics observed throughout the prehistory and history of the study area. Haury's description of the ware is fairly complete: "In the non-micaceous class of pottery, about 1.5 per cent of the sherd sample is a thin, hard, and well smoothed ware of chocolate brown color. . . . Vessels were evidently exclusively jars. Wall thickness, the striking feature, ranges from 2.50 to 4 mm. . . . It was made by the coil paddle-and-anvil technique [1950:345]."

The sherds from the Hecla Mine study area range in color from a dark brown to a light grayish-brown and all are quite hard. Body sherds range in thickness from 2.5 to 6.5 mm with a mean thickness of 3.98 mm calculated from a random sample (n = 167). Temper

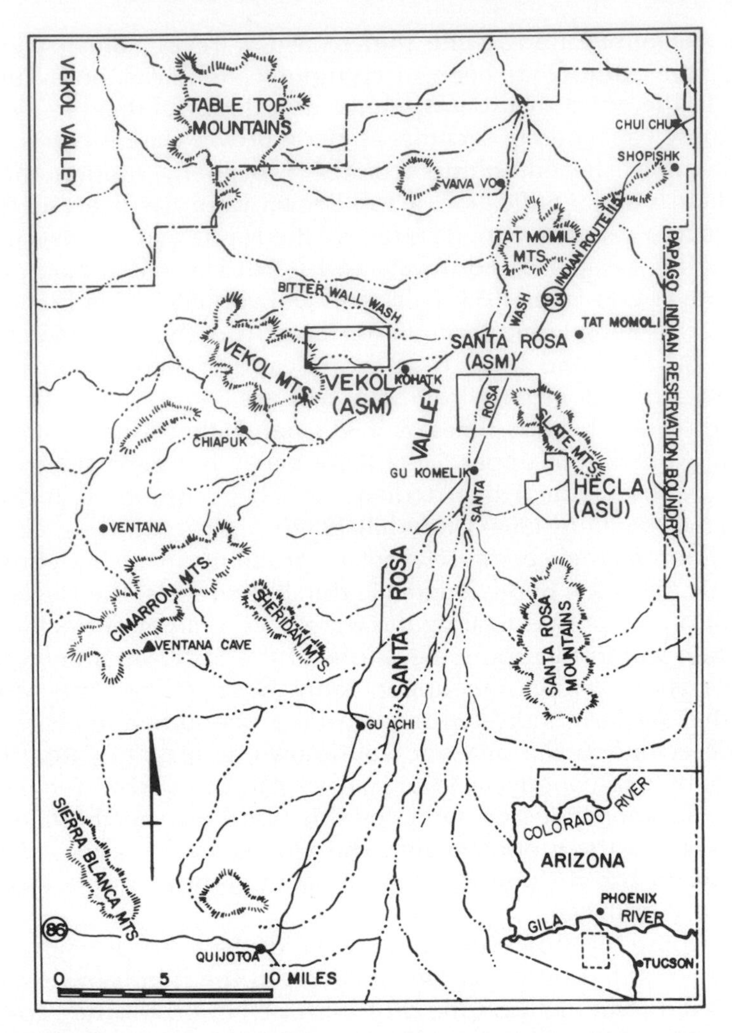

Figure 8.1. Position of the Hecla Mine study area and related projects within the Santa Rosa Valley region.

most often appears to be fine particles of feldspar, quartz, and schist. The paste is never micaceous, but occasional sherds exhibit infrequent flecks of gold mica, which probably relate to natural inclusions in the clay source. Some of the sherds also have fine chunks of soft white clay intentionally included which may represent ground-up potsherds. Vessel exteriors range from a distinct wiped condition about the rims and shoulders to a smoothed pebbly surface. Interiors are roughly wiped or smoothed and anvil dents are common. Vessel forms are consistently jars with deep expanding bodies, steep, almost straight-sided shoulders with slightly recurved rims and everted lips. Although difficult to determine from the small sherds, the mouths of the jars appear to be most often relatively closed as opposed to some of the wide-mouthed jars commonly made by the historic Papago. The rims are characteristically thin and sharp and constitute a comparatively small area of the total vessel. Vessel bottoms are always rounded or flat.

Since the publication of the thin brown ware as Yuman (Goodyear 1975:28), the author has been in communication with both Euler and Dobyns to the effect that it now seems most doubtful that the identification of these Papaguerian ceramics as Tizon Brown ware is correct.[3]

Neither does the ethnohistory of the Papagueria support the likelihood of such an identification. Tizon Brown ware has been successfully identified as a ceramic manufactured by the Havasupai, the Walapai, and probably the Yavapai of northwest and north central Arizona (Dobyns 1956; Dobyns and Euler 1958; Euler and Dobyns 1956). The homeland of such a ware is geographically quite removed from the Slate Mountains of southern Arizona and there is no historical evidence known from the 1700s onward that groups from the two areas ever had any contact. From the earliest historic times in 1698 when Father Kino contacted the village of Kohatk, the upper Santa Rosa Valley has been the traditional territory of the Upper Piman Indians, which in the desert include the Papagos (Hackenberg 1964; Underhill 1939).

In addition to their being relevant to problems involving chronology and ethnic affiliation of the enigmatic thin brown ware, the Hecla studies have indicated that sites bearing the ware have a rather distinctive spatial distribution within the upper elevations of the Slate Mountains. Surveys and excavations within the upper Santa Rosa Valley–Slate Mountain region thus far have indicated the ware is a phenomenon characteristic of the desert mountains and not well known, at least to date, from the valley floodplains (Goodyear 1975; Haury 1950; Raab 1974). Techno-functionally, the anomalous existence of this pottery is heightened by the fact that within the mountain sites the vessels are in nearly every case jars, a pattern also documented for the late thin brown ware at Ventana Cave (Haury 1950:345).

The purpose of this chapter is twofold—first, to attempt to help resolve the cultural-historical identification of the thin brown ware, and thereby shed some light on the protohistoric period for the Papagueria, and second, using relevant environmental and settlement-pattern data collected during the Hecla Mine projects (Goodyear 1973, 1975; Goodyear and Dittert 1973), to explicate culture-ecological relationships between populations using this characteristic ceramic and the biotic and abiotic resources native to the Slate Mountains. The latter effort is offered as a method of understanding past societies as functioning cultural systems and as a means of extending archeological analysis in the Papagueria beyond simple technological and "stylistic" studies.

[3] A representative collection of the thin brown ware sherds was sent to Robert C. Euler, one of the coauthors of the Tizon Brown ware typology, who replied that none of the sherds correspond to that classification (letter, 1975).

CHRONOLOGY AND CULTURAL IDENTIFICATION

The region of the upper Santa Rosa Valley witnessed a continuous occupational history, which extended back at least to A.D. 300, involving Hohokam-related aboriginal populations using pottery, growing cultigens, and residing in semisedentary or sedentary villages on the floodplain. In nearby Ventana Cave, located on the southwestern edge of the Santa Rosa Valley in the Castle Mountains, Haury (1950) has documented the outline of culture history for this part of the Papagueria, which began in the early Holocene and terminated with twentieth century Papago occupations. In recent years intensive archeological investigations have taken place in the Santa Rosa Wash (Canouts 1972; Raab 1974), in the adjacent Vekol Mountains (Stewart and Teague 1974), and in the Slate Mountains (Goodyear 1975; Goodyear and Dittert 1973; Raab 1974) (Figure 8.1). The latter studies have basically supported or amplified Haury's (1950) reconstruction.

It is important to note that the thin brown ware was not found surficially or stratigraphically associated with the prehistoric remains from either floodplain or mountain sites. Several late prehistoric Sells phase (see Haury 1950:6–8) villages were investigated by Raab (1974) on the floodplain, but produced no associations with the ware. The Sells phase is the last known prehistoric occupation of the area and probably declined or perhaps abandoned the region by the late fourteenth or early fifteenth centuries (Haury 1950:348–349). One sherd scatter containing the thin brown ware was encountered on the surface and adjacent to a large Sells phase village referred to as AZ AA:5:54 (ASM) (Raab 1974). This constitutes the only locus where the brown ware has been firmly identified on the Santa Rosa floodplain. The surveys and excavations of Raab (1974) on the floodplain adjacent to the Slate Mountains covered an extensive area approximately 9 square miles (23 km^2), and yielded over 40 discrete archeological manifestations. Almost without exception these sites were prehistoric in age. With the abovementioned exception near AA:5:54 (ASM), no examples of the thin brown ware were recognized.

The intensive and probability-based sampling surveys in the southern and western slopes of the Slate Mountains of both Raab (1974) and Goodyear (Goodyear 1975; Goodyear and Dittert 1973), covered a combined area in excess of 10-square miles (ca. 26 km^2), yielding literally hundreds of discrete archeological loci spanning the time of all ceramics-using peoples of the region. These loci were practically always surface scatters of artifactual debris lying unburied on a deflating colluvially derived desert pavement (see Goodyear 1975:Figure 3). The sites exhibiting the thin brown ware were in nearly every case, however, spatially unassociated with either prehistoric Desert Hohokam sites or those of the historic Papago (Bruder 1975; Goodyear 1975; Raab 1974). Several prehistoric and historic aboriginal extraction camps were recognized on the southern slopes of the Slates (Goodyear 1975); these were probably devoted to organ pipe, saguaro, and prickly pear cactus fruits and leguminous seeds, but characteristically yielded no examples of the thin brown ware. The latter phenomenon, beyond obvious chronological implications, is also of interest behaviorally since it suggests that the users of the thin brown ware were approaching resource procurement in different areas of the Slate Mountains or with different strategies (Goodyear 1975:28).

After the possible "abandonment" of the upper Santa Rosa Valley by the Sells phase people (ca. A.D. 1300–1400), or what archeologists recognize artifactually as a collapse of a sociotechnic system, there appears to be a hiatus in the occupational history of the area. The uncertainty of the hiatus is attributable to the fact no archeological studies have been performed on protohistoric sites such as nearby Kohatk (Figure 8.1), which may represent an indigenous early Papago village that evolved out of the extinct Sells phase system. Furthermore, the fact that sites bearing Tanque Verde Red-on-brown were no longer being created does not mean the people who painted such designs melted away into the dirt along with their decorative motifs. It may only mean the social or religious subsystem in which such decorated vessels operated became extinct or reorganized with other material culture systems.

In surveys immediately surrounding the Santa Rosa Wash in the Vekol Mountains (Stewart and Teague 1974) and in the Slate Mountains (Bruder 1975; Goodyear 1975; Goodyear and Dittert 1973; Raab 1974), numerous Papago sites were investigated, few of which definitely contained ceramics that would date to the early 1800s. The majority of historic Papago remains in these mountains date to the late 1800s and early 1900s. In no case was the thin brown ware recovered in a surface or subsurface association with known historic Papago remains; its distribution was nearly always in small, self-contained scatters spatially discrete from earlier and later remains.

The archeological data just reviewed clearly indicates that the thin brown ware dates to a period after the collapse of the Sells phase cultural system sometime during the period A.D. 1300–1400, and before the commencement of the late Papago utilization of the Slate Mountains during the late 1800s. Although not in itself definitive, most of the thin brown ware sherds are crisp and uneroded, a condition approximating that of the late historic Papago sherds. They are much less eroded than the Sells phase ceramics, which are often quite wind-abraded (Goodyear 1975:28). A temporal assignment of A.D. 1400–1850, although somewhat gross, would not be at variance with Haury's (1950:345) "late prehistoric" estimate suggested stratigraphically for the thin brown ware recovered at Ventana Cave.

Given these rough temporal parameters, the question of ethnic or cultural identification can be approached. The thin brown ware sherds are sufficiently different from both prehistoric and historic ceramic technologies to prompt hypotheses about non-Papaguerian origins. Haury (1950:244; Figure 8c–f) notes the occurrence of eight unusual incised jar fragments in the lot from Ventana Cave that Malcolm Rogers felt resembled Yuman pottery of the lower Colorado River area. Rogers identified one sherd as definitely Yuma II from the Lower Colorado, but the remaining 400-plus plainware sherds were described as "not typical" Yuman (Haury 1950:345). One hypothesis, therefore, relevant to cultural identification would be that the thin brown ware is related to contact with the western Yuman area (Haury 1950:345).

A second hypothesis is suggested on the basis of known early Papago history and the close proximity of the Papago village of Kohatk. The location of Kohatk has been established and lies about 8 miles (13 km) northwest of the Slate Mountains (Jones 1969; Stewart and Teague 1974:Figure 1). The existence of Kohatk was established as early as 1698 when Father Kino visited the village in his missionary travels.

Based on the previous information, there are at least two alternative hypotheses that can be formulated for the cultural identity of the anomalous brown ware. The available evidence for and against each of these will be presented.

Hypothesis 1

The thin brown ware assemblages of the Slate Mountains and Ventana Cave represent the archeological by-products of Lower Colorado Yuman groups making seasonal usage of wild plant resources native to the paloverde–saguaro communities.

In favor of such a hypothesis, although very minimal, would be the small number of incised sherds described by Haury and identified by Rogers as similar to Yuman (Haury 1950:345). Temporally, both the Ventana Cave assemblage and those from the Slate Mountains would roughly fit the time period when Lower Colorado Yuman peoples were coming up the Gila River on the northern periphery of the Papagueria. Henry Dobyns (personal communication) has communicated that after A.D. 1700 Yuman-speaking groups moved up the Gila River in the vicinity of Piman villages. These groups became intermingled with the Pima and ultimately became known as "Maricopa." Groups residing on the northern and northwestern boundary of the Papagueria may have seasonally foraged down into the botanically rich paloverde–saguaro communities of the desert mountains to the south and southeast. As

Dobyns (personal communication) has indicated, the closest of these groups would be lower Gila River Yuman-speakers who moved onto the periphery of the Papagueria in the 1700s and early 1800s. A terminal date of pre-1850 as suggested by Dobyns would not be at variance with the lack of association with the late historic (post-1860) Papago remains, which are not associated with the thin brown ware. In additional support of a seasonal usage by Yuman-related groups would be the fact that no floodplain agricultural villages have yet been found producing the brown ware, which would indicate year-round settlement in the Santa Rosa Valley.

Evidence against such a hypothesis is considerable. With the few exceptions stipulated by Haury (1950:345), the remaining thin brown ware sherds from Ventana Cave were not considered by Rogers to be typically Yuman. The few incised sherds that Rogers thought were good Yuman examples are interesting but hardly constitute firm evidence of the presence of Yuman-speaking people, especially since the 400-plus plainware sherds were not considered so. It is not uncommon to find decorated ceramics of obvious external origins in the Papagueria, such as Gila Polychrome (see Haury 1950:346; Raab 1974), but no one has seriously suggested the Salado "invaded" the Papagueria as well.

In this same vein, the thin brown sherds from both Ventana Cave and the Slate Mountains were not finished with a buff wash, the *sine qua non* of Lower Colorado Buff ware (Schroeder 1958). A representative collection of the thin brown ware was sent to Schroeder, who declared them to be unlike any of the Yuman types of the Colorado Buff ware with the exception of a single buff sherd, to be discussed. Furthermore, none of the associated decorated types as described by Schroeder (1958) were reported by Haury (1950:345) from Ventana Cave and none were observed either in the Santa Rosa Wash floodplain sites (Raab 1974) or on the southern and western slopes of the Slate Mountains (Goodyear 1975; Raab 1974).

A single isolated sherd of what is probably Colorado Buff ware was found on the southern slopes of the Slates [AZ AA:9:1, F53, L-1 (ASU) Goodyear 1975: 366] and constitutes the only evidence of such ceramics from the Hecla Mine study area. On the western slopes of the Slates, Raab (1974) found two sherd and lithic scatters that produced Colorado Buff ware (field No. 109 and 124). In the case of FN 109, Raab found what appeared to be fragments from a single jar in surface association with sherds of Wingfield Plain and 27 sherds of the thin brown ware. The probability of this being a spurious association due to accidental reutilization of the same activity space seems small. Raab only encountered four loci bearing the thin brown ware and only two of the suspected Colorado Buff ware, one of which surficially associated with the brown ware. The likelihood of false surface association is lessened by the fact these six sites were found in a survey area of about 2.5 square miles (6.47 km^2), which altogether yielded over 120 discrete loci or sites.

A total of three spatially discrete loci bearing Colorado Buff ware sherds were found on the south- and west-facing slopes of the Slates. All these sherds were typified by the distinctive pink, flesh-colored pastes with thin, yellow-tan washes on the vessel exterior that permitted the underlying paste to be observed (compare Rogers 1936:33). There is little chance of mistaking these sherds for the thin brown ware under discussion here.

In addition to being different from the distinctive buff wares, none of the thin brown sherds exhibited the characteristic stucco surface treatment. Schroeder (1958) has cited the application of a stucco to the exterior as a diagnostic attribute of lower Colorado Buff ware. Interestingly, stuccoing does commonly occur on the late historic Papago plainware jars in the Slate Mountains, with some sites producing such sherds dating to the early 1900s (Bruder 1975). This association implies that the greatest influence of Yuman ceramic technology on that of the local Papago has a rather late temporal position in the study area. Stuccoing is well correlated to the lower Colorado Yuman groups such as the Yuma, Maricopa, and Cocopa (see Rogers 1936:30–36) and it would appear likely that this surface technique was somehow introduced to the Papago potters of the Kohatk region during Kohatk–Maricopa contacts described for the late 1800s by Fontana *et al.* (1962:117–119).

Thus, based upon the preceding technological evidence, the probability is rather minimal that the thin brown ware occurs in the upper Santa Rosa Valley region as a result of seasonal usage by Lower Colorado Yuman-speaking groups. The attributes of the thin brown ware sherds in nearly every case are unlike those described for Yuman ceramics. The matter of not finding a floodplain village and thereby suggesting seasonal usage of mountain environments does not necessarily support the seasonal foraging hypothesis. The entire floodplain of the Santa Rosa Wash has not been surveyed, particularly the southern end, and the one known early Papago village of Kohatk has not been examined archeologically. The extensive floodplain surveys of Raab (1974) and the sites reported by Stewart and Teague (1974) lie to the north and west respectively of Kohatk.

Although substantial evidence is present for the invalidation of Hypothesis 1, it has seemed necessary to review the data relevant to a hypothesized Yuman-related occupation of the region intensively, since such an idea was at least suggested by Haury (1950:345) and more strongly advanced by Goodyear (1975:28). The latter case would now appear to be a clear example of misclassification.

Hypothesis 2

The assemblages of thin brown ware from Ventana Cave and the Slate Mountains represent the archeological by-products of indigenous protohistoric Papago groups making seasonal usage of wild plant resources native to the paloverde–saguaro communities.

Contrary to the Yuman situation, an indigenous floodplain village in the form of Kohatk exists immediately adjacent to the Slate Mountains on the Santa Rosa Wash (Figure 8.1). Although some structural changes probably took place in the early historic Papago settlement strategy compared to the late prehistoric Sells phase, it seems inconceivable that such a large village as Kohatk would not have utilized the abundant biotic and abiotic resources of the Slate Mountains. It is also difficult to believe that some material evidence would not be produced from subsistence-related activities.

The earliest known Papago were repeatedly observed by travelers to rely on wild plant and animal resources of the desert mountains. The Slate Mountains are the largest and perhaps most biologically productive of mountain groups in the vicinity of Kohatk. Quantitative vegetation studies performed for the Slate Mountains (Goodyear 1975; Raab 1974) and the Vekol Mountains (Sobelman 1973; Stewart and Teague 1974) indicate that there is generally a lesser density of economically useful wild plant species on the eastern slopes of the Vekols, which lie to the immediate west of present-day Kohatk (Figure 8.1). The ethnographer Jones (1969:194–195) has established that the early twentieth century Papagos from the villages of Kohatk and Tat Momoli preferred to gather on the slopes of the Slates as opposed to the more immediate Vekols. The Slate Mountains offer an extensive south-facing gradient, a condition known from studies in plant ecology to be the optimum habitat for the growth of heat-loving cacti and certain arboreals (Lowe 1964; Odum 1971; Shreve 1951). Stewart and Teague (1974:28) indicate that archeological sites are also less dense on the Vekol slopes as compared to the Slate Mountains suggesting a behavioral difference in exploitive preference as well.

Using floral, archeological, and ethnographic data, we can say that the Slate Mountains appear to be the best primary gathering area for upper-elevation plant species in the immediate Santa Rosa Valley region. Given the known importance of wild foods to all Sonoran Desert populations and the subsistence potential of the Slates, the existence of some types of gathering activities related to Kohatk or to contemporaneous villages seems highly probable.

In terms of ceramic technology, some of the sites producing the thin brown ware were also in surface association with a heavily schist-tempered plainware otherwise referred to as Wingfield Plain. Of the 27 loci consisting of two or more sherds of the thin brown ware, 12, or 44%, have sherds of Wingfield Plain included in the scatter. In the three sherd and lithic scatters encountered by Raab (1974) on the western slopes of the Slates, all three loci had Wingfield Plain present. Wingfield Plain is the dominant prehistoric plainware in the Santa Rosa Valley region, existing from the early Snaketown-related period (A.D. 300–500). It continued to dominate assemblages up through the late prehistoric Sells phase (Raab 1974). Schist temper in fact is the most common temper for the historic Papago plainware in the study area. Although some of the Wingfield Plain, or schist-tempered plainware, surficially associated with the thin brown ware could represent accidental reoccupation by the protohistoric groups over former prehistoric sherd scatters, most of this pottery is thinner and less eroded, and presents almost a smudged or burnished condition about the rims and lips. This latter condition, of course, may only be a result of its age since older sherds would have been wind-abraded for a longer period of time. Nevertheless, the fact that 50% of the scatters from both sides of the Slates have schist-tempered plainware associated seems unlikely to result from anything but a behaviorally significant relationship. Parenthetically, schist-tempered pottery is definitely not a technological attribute of the Lower Colorado Buff ware ceramics.

Furthermore, these sherd and lithic scatters in most cases appeared as spatially discrete entities suggesting a valid covariation. One such association is particularly noteworthy. AZ AA:9:1 F10 (ASU) (Goodyear 1975:160) consisted of a single spatially contained artifact scatter a few meters away from a cobble-rock ring. This scatter produced the characteristic thin brown ware spatially mixed with sherds from a small globular jar of Wingfield Plain; the latter displayed a small appliqüe strip or rim collar known to be an early Papago ceramic attribute Fontana *et al.* 1962; Haury 1950). This example of a rim collar was the only one observed from all sites in the Slate Mountains and was completely absent among Papago sherds recovered from later historic sites in the same study area.

Finally, a single houselike structure, AZ AA:5:4 F1 (ASU), was excavated within the Hecla Mine study area. This structure exhibited examples of the thin brown ware and a very thin schist-tempered plainware found on the floor and within hearths (Goodyear and Dittert 1973:61–65). This structure (Figure 8.2) was nearly square, judging from the postholes. One of the postholes still possessed a segment of what was probably ironwood, still intact, which was radiocarbon dated at A.D. 1370 or 580 ± 100 B.P. (Lab. No. RL-224) (Goodyear and Dittert 1973:62). The shape and apparent construction design of this structure, although similar in plan to twentieth century Papago cactus camp ramadas within the study area, is more substantial than the latter. Provision for a doorway was evident and there was a suggestion of a rill pattern in the

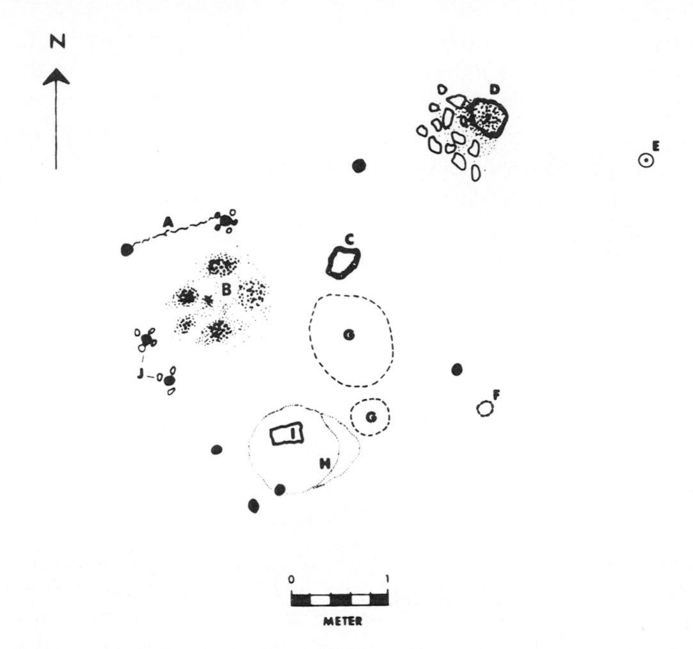

Figure 8.2. Excavated structure at AZ AA:5:4 (ASU), Feature 1. *A,* rill pattern; *B,* door hearth; *C,* pit; *D,* outside hearth; *E,* datum; *F,* possible postholes; *G,* faunal remains; *H,* basin hearth; *I,* stone anvil; *J,* doorposts.

soil where a wall would have been (Figure 8.2). Hrdlicka (1906:Plate IX, No. 3) published a photograph of a historic Pima house, which was square in outline, had a doorway about midway along one wall, and possessed straight walls made of saguaro ribs. According to Hrdlicka (1906:41), the Pima used this type of structure for storage and habitation. In terms of archeologically preserved features, such a house would resemble the structure excavated at AZ AA:5:4 (ASU).

Several amorphous hearths were discovered inside the structure, suggesting a winter occupation. One of the hearths (Figure 8.2, *H*) contained fragments of mammal bone, some of which may have been deer. Pollen analysis conducted on sediments taken from within features of the structure indicated no significant differences between the contemporary pollen rain and that presumably representative of the fourteenth or fifteenth centuries. No economic pollen types were observed that might inform on subsistence or seasonality (Gish 1975:267). Although no grinding paraphernalia were directly associated with the structure, numerous examples of broken manos and metates were found in adjacent trash scatters in surface association with the thin brown ware.

This structure with its habitation form of utilization is quite anomalous and completely unlike other archeological loci, both prehistorically and historically recorded on the western and southern slopes of the Slates.

The settlement implications of this structure will be discussed later. This site does decisively confirm the coassociation of the thin brown ware and the schist-tempered plainware in a recognizably closed context and helps partially date the brown ware in question to the late fourteenth century.

In summary of Hypothesis 2, the available evidence would argue in favor of a cultural relationship between the thin brown ware and an early indigenous protohistoric group in the area. The single radiocarbon date from the houselike structure, if valid, would indicate that the cultural system producing such ceramics was operative around the end of the fourteenth century. Such an early date suggests a close temporal and perhaps cultural relationship between groups producing the thin brown ware and the late prehistoric Sells phase, which is thought to have terminated at approximately this same time. If in fact the early Papago village of Kohatk was part of this same protohistoric complex, the thin brown ware may have been in production for a span of 300 years or so, since Kohatk was occupied by at least 1698. Given the large hunting–gathering basis of even late Papago groups in the desert, some utilization of nearby desert mountains by the residents of Kohatk is almost guaranteed. This probability is reinforced by the apparent high subsistence potential of the adjacent Slate Mountains. A common association with the thin brown ware was a schist-tempered plainware, previously referred to descriptively as Wingfield Plain. Schist-tempered pottery was the most common utility ware for all known prehistoric and historic ceramics-using peoples in this region. This also suggests that the makers of the thin brown ware somehow fit into this long-lived ceramic tradition of plainware. The three loci producing Colorado Buff ware are numerically minor. But one of these sites, as reported by Raab (1974), seems to have had the thin brown ware surficially associated. This further suggests, like the implied relationship with Kohatk, that some of the thin brown ware sites may date to the 1700s, since that was the time of earliest known movement of Yuman-speaking peoples up the Gila River.

The use of individual or aggregates of ceramic attributes or house forms can only be profitably used to a limited extent toward deriving cultural identifications and comparisons. These attributes, though potentially meaningful as technological and functional patterns, soon begin to suffer the same analytical limitations as traits; i.e., they are isolated phenomena not understood in their former systemic or behavioral contexts (Schiffer 1972). Additional components of the settlement–subsistence system need to be explicated, particularly the floodplain village of Kohatk, thereby allowing a more complete definition of the system, only part of which is now known from the mountain zones. Although not in a floodplain environment, this same thin brown ware is currently being found by archeologists from Arizona State University within the Sierra Estrella Mountains south of the confluence of the Salt and Gila rivers as well as near the Buckeye Hills area south of the Gila River (Weaver and Rodgers, personal communication). This indicates that the protohistoric ceramics in question are part of a larger area of interaction and are not restricted to the Santa Rosa Valley region.

Up to this point the thin brown ware has only been considered with regard to its historical and probable cultural affiliation. Even though the Slate Mountain remains probably represent only one aspect of the former settlement system, we might logically expect that the mountain activities were systematically linked with numerous other dimensions or subsystems of the society (Binford 1962). Given the manner in which these data were collected, they may also be examined from the viewpoint of human ecology using locational analysis. A trial formulation toward identifying the techno-environmental and subsistence contexts of the thin brown ware in the Slate Mountains will be offered next.

THE ECOLOGICAL POSITION OF PROTOHISTORIC BROWN WARE IN THE SLATE MOUNTAIN PALOVERDE–SAGUARO COMMUNITY

The Slate Mountains are typical of many small mountain groups in southern Arizona that trend north and south. Biogeographically, the Slate Mountains are part of the Lower Sonoran Desert life zone with biota typical of the Arizona Uplands (Hastings and Turner 1965:186, Figure 10; Lowe 1964:24; Shreve 1951:42). The Hecla Mining Company property, which encompasses the perimeter of the approximate 5-square-mile (13 km^2) study area, covers an extensive portion of the south-facing mountain slopes (Figure 8.3). The study area lies on an extended gradient, which ranges from an upper to a lower bajada, from 2200 to 1675 feet above sea level, about 3.5 miles (5.6 km) of which support a luxuriant paloverde–saguaro plant community.

Quantified vegetation studies were performed during the Hecla Mine archeological projects (see Goodyear 1975:52–56) in an effort to use the living and presumably stable environment as a functional attribute of archeological sites. A series of 12 floral species were selected for quantified mapping. Selection of these species was based upon their known economic importance to the Papago and Pima Indians. These species include *Lemaireocereus thurberi* (organ-pipe cactus), *Carnegia gigantea* (saguaro cactus), *Opuntia fulgida* (chain cholla), *Opuntia acanthocarpa* (buckhorn cholla), *Opuntia arbuscula* (pencil cholla), *Opuntia engelmannii* (prickly pear), Ferocactus (barrel cactus), *Prosopis juliflora* (mesquite), *Acacia constricta* (whitethorn acacia), *Olneya tesota* (ironwood), *Cercidium microphyllum* (paloverde), and *Fouqueria splendens* (ocotillo).

Figure 8.3. Southwestern slopes of the Slate Mountain study area and contemporary location of the Hecla Mine.

An in-depth description of floral and archeological sampling procedures is presented elsewhere (Goodyear 1975:37–57). Briefly, vegetation mapping was accomplished through the transect method and by recording numbers of relevant species found in randomized archeological sampling loci. Two transects that ran down the mountain slope through the middle of the study area were implemented. The transects consisted of linearly aligned contiguous quadrats each 30 × 50 m in size. Inside each quadrat the number and cover value (biomass estimate) of the 12 species were tabulated, and in the case of saguaro, the number of arms per plant was recorded. Only the data generated from Transect A (Goodyear 1975:54, Figure 16), which ran through the heart of the study area on the south slope, are used for statistical analysis in this chapter.

The plant ecologist Oosting (1956:51) has described the utility of transect studies where vegetation differences are apparent between two points or zones. The classic example would be moisture differences that occur on a gradient between an upland and a floodplain; transects are also useful for quantitatively measuring transitions between plant communities. Transect methods are particularly appropriate for vegetation studies in the Sonoran Desert mountains since their flora are characteristically structured by elevation (Halvorson 1970; Shreve 1951; Whittaker and Niering 1965). Although several ecological factors cause vertical zonation, one primary factor is that of substrate.

A major assumption in the use of contemporary vegetation patterns as an aid to archeological activity reconstructions is that the present floral conditions are approximately the same as those of the past 2000 years. Actually, the assumption is more basic. For contemporary vegetation patterns to be useful for archeological purposes, it must be assumed that the present spatial distributions of biomass maxima and minima have been stable through time and that those habitats supporting maximal biomass today were also the loci of maximum biomass in the past. It is not necessary to argue that the biomass values in those habitats have been the same through time, only that the spatial loci are the same.

Certain ecological and archeological data are available that support the assumption of zonal stability in mountain vegetation (Goodyear 1975:16–21). At the broadest level, that of the biome, it has been established that there have been no major changes in the basic climate and biota of southern Arizona since about 8000 B.C. (Martin 1963). Pollen analysis within the Hecla Mine study area of sediments that have been radiocarbon dated between A.D. 1200 and 1400 indicates no difference between paleo and present-day pollen rain (Gish 1975:267).

The phylogenetic adaptations of most Sonoran Desert plants also contribute to zonal stability. Such adaptations are so specialized that the concept of succession or climax is not meaningful; even when communities are destroyed the replacement plants are the offspring of former adult occupants (Shreve 1951:21). All the perennials are long-lived; many species live beyond 100 years, an indication of resistance to long-term environmental stress. Desert arboreals are phreatophytes, which obtain their moisture through deep root systems that tap the water table. The succulents, such as the cacti, obtain their water through soil moisture, which fluctuates according to the abundance of yearly rainfall. The cacti, however, adapt to short- and long-term moisture scarcity by storing water under tough waxy skins that prevent rapid evaporation.

The most specific determinant affecting spatial stability in mountain floral zones relates to the strong relationship between available moisture and substrate type. Substrate conditions relating to elevation, depth, slope aspect, and texture are the key variables governing the distribution of upland flora since these directly affect soil moisture (Hastings and Turner 1965; Lowe 1964; Shreve 1951). In studies of plant ecology, impressive correlations have been obtained between substrate and vegetation type and structure in the desert mountains (Halvorson 1970; Niering *et al.* 1963; Yang and Lowe 1956).

In summary, the evidence for a causal relationship between type and density of flora and the underlying substrate is abundant in the botanical literature. Regardless of the exact amount of living tissue existing in these habitats in the past, the argument can be made that various habitats will support varying quantities of biomass according to the relative quality of the substrate. The importance of such fixed habitats is this: "*Only radical climatic changes are capable of altering the desert mountain substrates and there is no paleoecological evidence from the last 10,000 years that would indicate such shifts occurred* [Goodyear 1975:20]."

Although somewhat circular, logically speaking, several specific examples of strong associations between maximum loci of economically useful species and predicted archeological tool sets were obtained in a previous study (Goodyear 1975). Archeological data are obviously not independent biological data, but such associations are exactly what would be expected if the major assumption of zonal stability were correct.

Archeological methods of sampling for the Hecla Mine study area have been detailed by Goodyear (1975). The upper portion of the study area, above the 1775-foot elevation, was sampled through an intensive survey attempting to map and collect all observed surface loci. Below this elevation, down to the 1675-foot elevation, about 13% of the area was sampled by a probability sampling method using a grid system for spatial dispersion. Actual sampling units consisted of circles with a diameter of approximately 267 feet (81.4 m). Inside the sample circles discrete clusters of artifacts and individual items were mapped as separate loci and given specific proveniences. This was done in an effort to collect archeological remains in a way most related to the artifactual deposits formerly associated with specific activities. Such loci most frequently consisted of isolated cobble and flake tools, debitage, pot breaks, and scatters of lithics and ceramics.

In order to use archeological data collected by the two different methods, a grid system identical to that used in the probability sample of the lower zone was overlaid on a map of the intensively sampled area and random sample circles were employed to select loci. This was necessary to standardize sampling conditions for the entire study area in order to make site density comparisons, which are critical to the following distributional analysis.

Using this method we chose 20 sites randomly out of a total sample of 32. These loci consist of sherd scatters, sherd and lithic scatters, and isolated brown ware sherds. All 32 loci are presented in Figure 8.4, with the loci chosen by the sampling method just described indicated by circles.

One apparent characteristic of the spatial distribution of these loci is their tendency to cluster in the middle portion of the mountain slope, an area typified by low foothills (see Figures 8.3 and 8.4). Accordingly, the hypothesis was formulated that the distribution of thin brown ware sites was nonrandom with respect to elevation on the south-facing slopes.

In order to test this hypothesis statistically, the area between 2000 and 1700 feet in elevation was divided into seven ranks, which followed contour intervals (Figure 8.4). Since different-sized areas are contained within each of the contour zones, and since varying numbers of random-sample circles occurred per zone, the total number of loci discovered by the number of circles was divided by the latter. Thus, the unit of measurement on the *y*-axis of Figure 8.5 is site density rather than simply frequency. According to the null statistical hypothesis of randomness, there should be no significant difference between the two distributions (Figure 8.5).

The hypothesis of randomness was tested by the one-sample Kolmogorov–Smirnov test as described by Siegel (1956:47–52). This test evaluates the degree of fit between an observed distribution of scores and a specified theoretical distribution from which the sample scores are hypothesized to have been drawn. The theoretical distribution in this case is randomness of site density by elevation, where each rank receives an equal value for the average site density. The theoretical cumulative frequency distribution under H_0 is expressed as $F_0(X)$, where each rank receives .5602. The observed sample distribution is written as $S_7(X)$, which is the cumulative distribution of the sample scores. The test focuses on the maximum difference in the two cumulative frequency distributions, or D (Figure 8.5). We are searching for any significant dif-

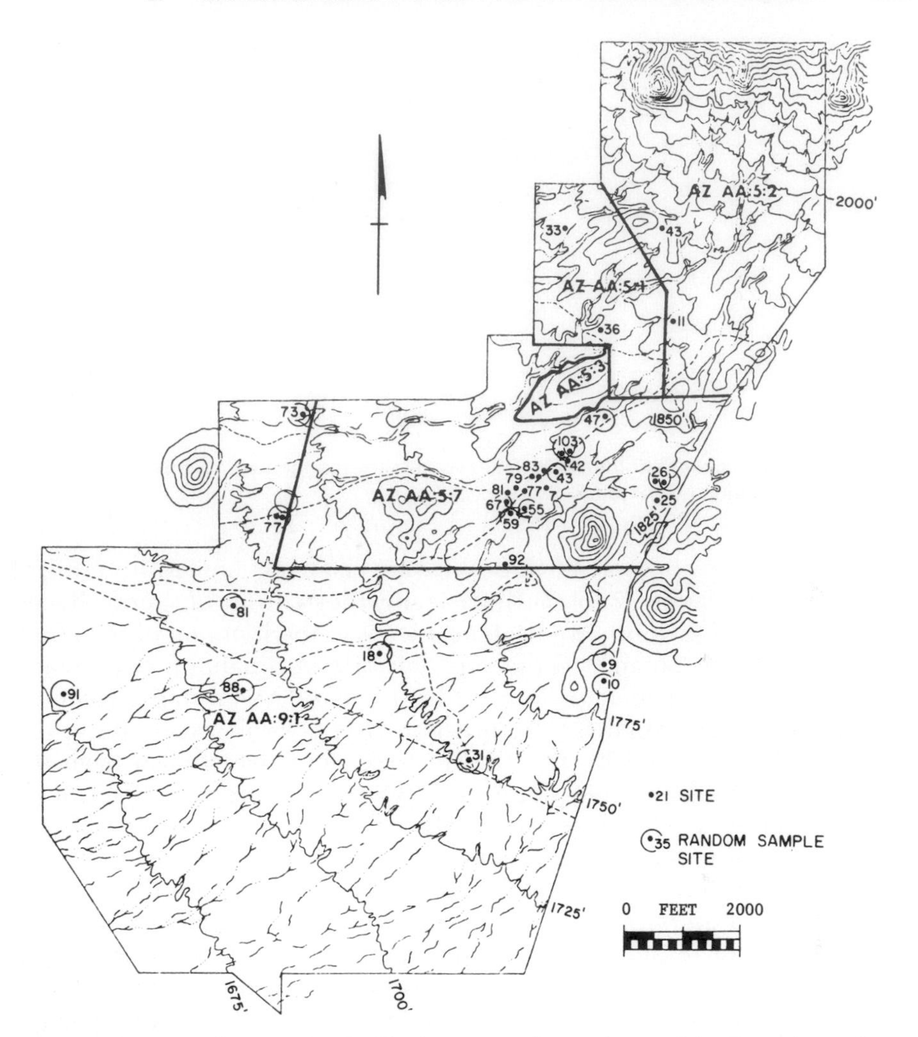

Figure 8.4. Protohistoric site distribution on southwest slopes of the Slate Mountains.

ference between the two distributions, or a two-tailed test, at alpha of .05 or less.

As can be observed from Figure 8.5, a maximum D value of .9520 was produced; this has an associated probability of less than .01 for n of 7 (Siegel 1956:Table E). It can be concluded that the density of thin brown ware sites is clearly nonrandom with respect to elevation on the south slopes of the Slates.

Given the rich array of biotic and abiotic resources natural to the Slate Mountains, particularly the economically useful flora, it should be possible to explain the existence and distribution of these sites based on their subsistence-related activities.

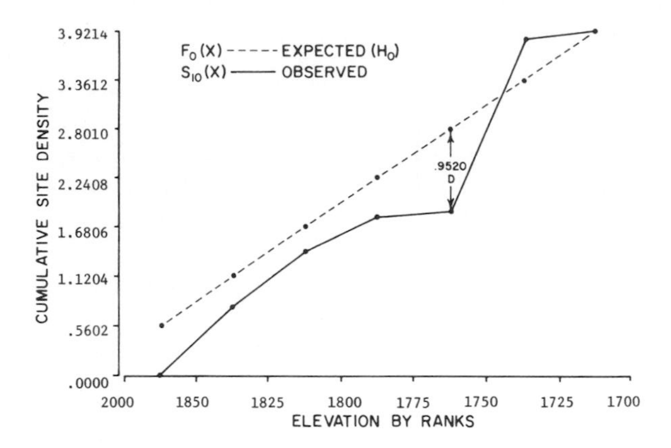

Figure 8.5. One-sample Kolmogorov–Smirnov test for randomness of empirical protohistoric site distribution by elevation.

The artifactual contents of these loci are relatively limited in terms of frequency and variety (Table 8.1). Basically, they consist of sherds, flaked stone, or both. Obviously we have no means at the moment of recognizing lithic loci attributable to the protohistoric occupations. No artifacts such as manos and metates, projectile points or nonportable facilities, such as hearths or structures, are present. One possible exception to this latter restriction could be the cobble-rock rings, which also have the greatest density in the mid slopes and which were frequently found in random sample circles that also produced the thin brown ware. These small artifact scatters, averaging only 6 m in diameter at the widest point of a locus (Table 8.1), suggest that perhaps only small groups of individuals were responsible for their deposition. No large clusters of sherds and lithics were found, nor were any examples of structures to suggest habitation sites. There are no natural water sources on the south slopes of the Slates and none were known to be used by the historic Papago (Goodyear 1975:9), a fact that would hinder year-round occupation of the mountain prehistorically under similar conditions. The small, dispersed, and technologically monotonous artifact scatters are strongly suggestive of simple extraction-and-procurement camps. If this is true it should be possible to explain their contents and spatial distributions in terms of local natural resources.

Many of the biotic and abiotic resources native to the Slate Mountains are well known and described (see Goodyear 1975:8–16). The frequency and distribution of practically all known economically useful plant species have been recorded and quantitatively mapped (Goodyear 1975:Appendix G). The periods of availability of flowers as well as buds and mature fruit and seed, are documented for these species in the botanical literature. Thus, the parameters surrounding species temporal

TABLE 8.1
Artifact Data from Protohistoric Thin Brown Ware Sites within Hecla Mine Study Area

Sites AZ AA:	Diameter of site (meters)	Thin brown ware	Wingfield Plain	Other	Flake tools	Cores	Debitage
5:1,F33,L-1	Unknown	18	0	0	0	0	0
5:1,F36,L-1	2	20	0	0	0	0	0
5:2,F11,L-1	10	20	1	0	3	8	6
5:2,F43,L-1	Unknown	15	7	0	1	0	0
5:7,F7,L-1	2	35	0	4[a]	0	0	0
5:7,F25,L-2	5	3	18	0	1	0	14
5:7,F26,L-2	10	35	25	0	2	0	4
5:7,F26,L-3	5	1	13	0	1	0	3
5:7,F42,L-1	5	17	0	0	2	3	23
5:7,F43,L-1	5	16	17	7[b]	1	0	2
5:7,F47,L-4	10	9	67	1[c]	7	3	27
5:7,F55,L-1	2	14	0	0	0	0	1
5:7,F59,L-1	10	1	13	0	0	0	1
5:7,F67,L-1	7	333	0	0	0	0	0
5:7,F77,L-2		1	0	0	0	0	0
5:7,F79,L-2	6	12	0	0	2	1	4
5:7,F81,L-1		1	0	0	0	0	0
5:7,F83,L-1	10	7	0	0	0	0	0
5:7,F83,L-3	10	1	0	0	1	0	2
5:7,F83,L-9		1	0	0	0	0	0
5:7,F92,L-2	10	12	0	0	1	0	5
5:7,F103,L-1	15	21	77	0	1	0	8
5:7,F103,L-3	8	20	0	0	0	0	0
9:1,F10,L-1	5	Present	Present	0	Unknown	Unknown	Unknown
9:1,F18,L-2	15	80	1	0	0	0	1
9:1,F31,L-7	2	4	0	0	0	0	0
9:1,F73,L-1	5	1	28	0	0	1	0
9:1,F77,L-2	3	123	0	0	0	0	0
9:1,F77,L-4	2	6	0	0	0	0	2
9:1,F88,L-3		3	0	0	0	0	0
9:1,F81,L-1		1	0	0	0	0	0
9:1,F91,L-3	7	160	0	0	0	0	2

[a] Unknown buff ware.
[b] Tanque Verde Red on brown.
[c] Wingfield Red.

and spatial variability have been recorded for the study area and are available for subsistence analysis.

The behavioral practices associated with the use and consumption of the economically useful plants as described ethnographically for the desert-dwelling Papago and Pima constitute a valuable source for archeological subsistence model building (see Goodyear 1975:58–234). Such sources as Russell (1908), Castetter and Bell (1937, 1942), Castetter and Underhill (1935), and Thackery and Leding (1929) provide numerous archeologically relevant descriptions of task-group size and composition, gathering strategies, and technologies associated with the extraction of floral foodstuffs.

By combining information derived from plant ecology and ethnography, we can formulate hypotheses about past subsistence systems, and we can test these hypotheses archeologically with techno-environmental predictions. The periods of availability for all 12 species have been presented in Goodyear (1975:Figure 46). Organ-pipe cactus and the seed-producing arboreals such as mesquite, paloverde, ironwood, and acacia need not be considered in this analysis since the maximal biomass densities for both types of resources occur above and below, respectively, the empirical range of protohistoric sites on the slopes of the Slate Mountains. Organ-pipe cactus occurs exclusively at elevations of 2000 feet or higher, an area well above the settlement pattern of the thin brown ware sites. The organ-pipe growth zone in the tops of the Slates produced a dense scatter of sherds and lithics exclusively referrable to the Sells phase. The dense arboreal biomass concentrations at the merging of the upper and lower bajada produced scatters of seed-processing implements such as shallow bowls and grinding tools attributable to a Santa Cruz–Sacaton occupation (Goodyear 1975:161–197).

The remaining species within the distribution of the protohistoric sites consist primarily of various *Opuntias* or chollas, which produce buds and flowers and some usable fruit, and the prolific fruit-producing cacti such as prickly pear and saguaro. There are no major scheduling conflicts among these species (Figure 8.6). This substantially reduces the complexity of gathering strategies and archeological locational analysis since the problem of two or more contemporaneously available species located in two or more zones would not occur.

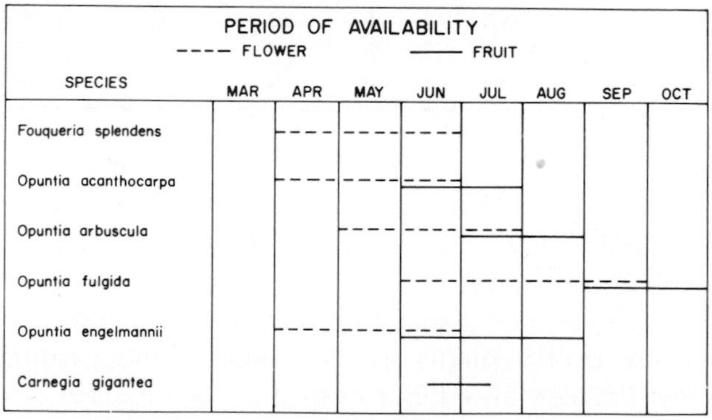

Figure 8.6. Periods of availability for buds, flowers, fruit, and seed of plant species growing within the settlement distribution of protohistoric sites.

Examining Figure 8.6, it is possible to isolate ecologically what can be termed a Bud–Flower subsystem (Goodyear 1975). This subsystem was botanically restricted to the spring months of April through June. The various cacti produce edible flowers and buds, which in ethnographic situations were eaten raw or baked in pits (Castetter and Bell 1942:59; Castetter and Underhill 1935:15; Thackery and Leding 1929:413–414). Castetter and Bell (1942:45) have described the importance of buds and flowers in the subsistence system of the early Papago. The end of winter was a lean period in the diet of desert people and the fresh green foods provided by the Bud–Flower subsystem formed a critical source of energy and nutrition, especially the latter (see Ross 1941:40).

In terms of Papago extraction and processing activities, few items of durable technology were associated with the exploitation of the Bud–Flower subsystem. Technologically, only picking tongs and baskets were required. The harvested buds were prepared by baking in pits. No roasting pits were found in the upper elevations, where the majority of these species grow, although two small roasting pits were excavated in the lower 1750–1725-foot contour zone. No significant quantities of subsistence-related pollen were recovered, however, such as those of the chollas (Gish 1975:Appendix A). One of these pits produced a radiocarbon date of A.D. 1220 (No. RL-358, 730 ± 110 R.C. years B.P.), which might be considered to be during the Sells phase (Goodyear 1975:72).

Although it is admittedly a limited index, currently the only means of archeologically identifying the presence of protohistoric sites within the study area is through the distinctive ceramics. Judging from the ethnographic accounts, however, there is little reason to expect pottery to be associated with the exploitation of the Bud–Flower subsystem. Baskets, obviously lighter in weight than ceramics, were used for picking and transporting the product, and pits, rather than pots, were used to cook the buds. The present-day maximum density of the bud-and-flower-producing cacti is not spatially isomorphic with other important fruit-producing species, which also prevents additional spurious spatial correlations. Thus, one would predict on technological and ecological grounds that the thin brown ware sites should not be associated with the denser distributions of the bud-and-flower-producing species.

Figure 8.7 illustrates the biomass density distribution of four species that produce buds and flowers. Of these four, *Opuntia acanthocarpa* (buckhorn cholla) is a type species often referred to by historic and ethnographic sources. *Opuntia engelmannii* (prickly pear) was an equally popular species but has been deleted from Figure 8.7 since pottery was utilized historically in the processing of its fruit. Prickly pear will be dealt with separately.

In order to test the prediction of "no association with the thin brown ware," chi-square tests were calculated for each species distribution by

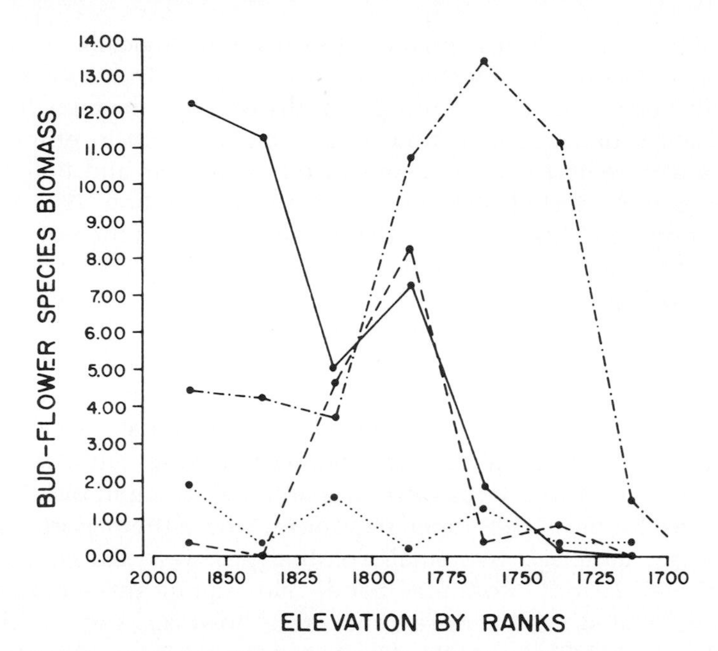

Figure 8.7. Biomass density distribution of Bud-Flower subsystem.—— = *Fouqueria splendens*; ---- = *O. arbuscla*; ····= *O. fulgida*; -·-· = *O. acanthocarpa.*

examining the ratios of sample circles to individual sherd-bearing loci as they occur within and external to the maximum densities of the species.

This method of testing can be illustrated using the distribution of *Opuntia acanthocarpa.* As can be observed from Figure 8.8, the maximum biomass density of buckhorn cholla occurs in three contiguous contour zones starting at an elevation of 1800 feet and continuing to the 1725-foot point. The primary site density for the protohistoric sites, however, would appear to be higher, ranging from 1850 to 1775 feet above sea level (Figure 8.9).

In order to test the suspected differences in distribution by elevation, a 2×2 chi-square problem was calculated (Table 8.2). The ratios are nearly identical for site density both under the maximum biomass area and away from it. This has resulted in a very low chi-square value that is not significant. The outcome of this test upholds the prediction of no association since the site distribution is random with respect to this species.

The three other species depicted in Figure 8.7 were also tested in the same manner using the chi-square test. The results were nearly identical with that for *Opuntia acanthocarpa,* with the exception of *Opuntia arbuscula* (pencil cholla). These outcomes were as follows: *Fouqueria splendens* (ocotillo), $\chi^2 = 2.93$, $df = 1$, $.10 > p > .05$; *Opuntia fulgida* (chain cholla), $\chi^2 = .22$, $df = 1$, $.70 > p > .50$. The significant chi-square of

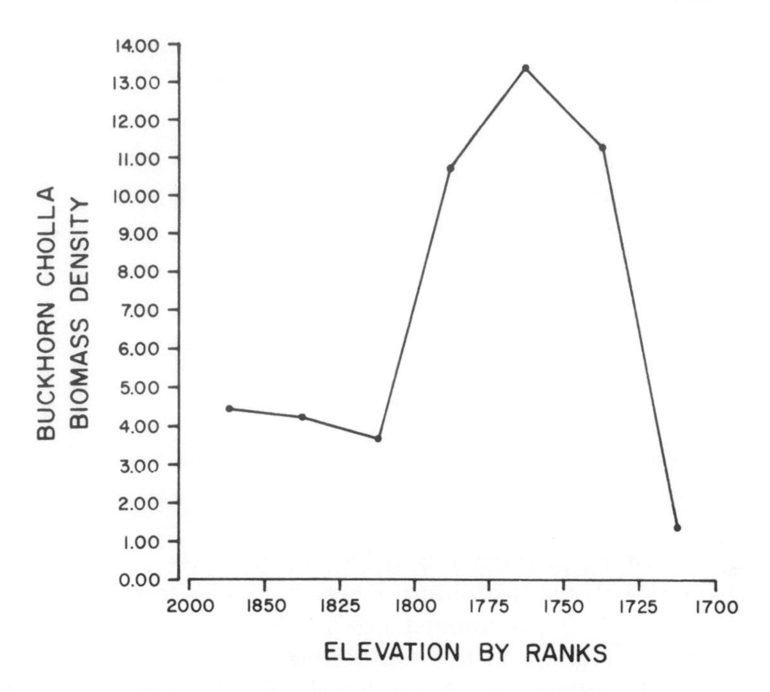

Figure 8.8. Biomass density distribution of *Opuntia acanthocarpa* (buckhorn cholla).

Opuntia arbuscula ($\chi^2 = 6.46$, $df = 1$, $p < .02$) can probably be explained in terms of a coincidental spatial association with prickly pear. This is the case since the contour zones where this species is maximum (Figure 8.7; 1825–1776 feet) is the identical area in which *Opuntia engelmanii* is also maximum. Recalling the ethnographic information, no mention is made of the Pima or Papago utilizing the rather small fruit of the pencil cholla with a ceramic extraction technology. The abundant fruit of the prickly pear, however, was quite commonly processed with clay jars.

TABLE 8.2

Chi-Square Test[a] for Significance Between Maximum Biomass Distribution of *Opuntia acanthocarpa* (Buckhorn Cholla) and the Maximum Density of Protohistoric Loci

	Sample circles	Loci produced	Totals
Under maximum mode (1800 to 1776 feet)	43 (42.57)	8(8.42)	51
Out of maximum mode (2000 to 1801 feet; 1725 to 1700 feet)	58(58.58)	12(11.57)	70
Totals	101	20	121

[a] $\chi^2 = .15$; $df = 1$; $.90 > p > .80$.

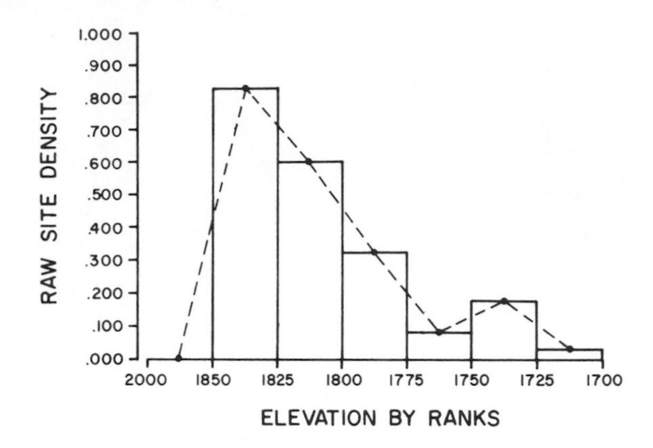

Figure 8.9. Density distribution of protohistoric sites on south slopes of Slate Mountains, Arizona.

In summary of the postulated Bud–Flower subsystem, the prediction of no associations with the protohistoric ceramic loci is found to be correct. This lack of association is understandable, because there was no functional need for ceramics in the exploitation of buds and flowers. With regard to the chi-square tests of the density distributions, a different outcome could have occurred with two different implications. If the test was positive in favor of association, it could have meant that protohistoric groups may have used pottery in processing these foodstuffs. Alternatively, it could have implied that the vertical boundaries of the various plant species had migrated up or down the slope thereby yielding a spurious association. The present outcome is consistent with the behavioral practices indicated ethnographically and with the assumption of spatial stability in the plant distributions of the Slate Mountains. Whether protohistoric groups actually used the buds and flowers is a moot question. Baking pits containing pollen from the chollas as well as radiocarbon dates will be required to answer this question.

As Figure 8.6 shows, one of the next temporally available resources would be the fruit of prickly pear. In the Slate Mountains the months of July and August seem to produce the greatest quantities of ripened fruit. In discussion with the Andrews family (native Papago citizens of nearby Gu Komelik), I was told that the period of mid- to late August was indicated as the optimal time for mature fruit harvesting (Goodyear 1975:120). There appear to be few scheduling conflicts with prickly pear and other species, since the Bud–Flower subsystem ceases early in the summer and the saguaro is known to be restricted to a 3- to 4-week span from late June to early July.

Historically, the Pima and Papago made prolific use of prickly pear fruit. The fruit was often eaten raw and processed into syrups and preserves for storage (Castetter and Bell 1942:60; Castetter and Underhill 1935:22–23; Russell 1908:75). The fruit was rendered into the various subproducts by boiling in plainware jars. None of the ethnographic accounts mention the usage of prickly pear seeds. Russell (1908:75) explicitly states that the Pima did not use them.

Now, if the protohistoric sherd and lithic loci represent primary-refuse outputs from prickly-pear-fruit processing, the following three predictions should be confirmed. First, there should be a predominance of jar forms in the ceramics since they were necessary for rendering and then transporting liquid products. Second, there should be no grinding paraphernalia associated with these loci since the prickly pear seeds were not ground or otherwise used. Finally, archeological loci exhibiting these two technological characteristics should be associated with the maximum density distribution of the species. This latter test implication is justified since no other nearby floral species are available simultaneously with prickly pear, thereby eliminating a mini–max or "ecotonal" strategy of camp location.

The first prediction is easily confirmed. As indicated previously, all vessel fragments observed in the study area that would indicate vessel morphology were consistently jars with the exception of a single bowl rim. Quantitatively, that would be 33 jar rims and one bowl rim. The probability of such a proportion occurring by chance is less than one in a thousand ($\chi^2 = 30.10$, $df = 1$, $p < .001$). In terms of discrete loci rather than sherds, eight sites produced only rim sherds of jars and one site had a rim sherd of a bowl.

The second expectation is also well met. There were no examples of seed-grinding equipment associated with or near these loci. This lack of grinding technology is characteristic of all areas between contour elevations of 1850 and 1700 feet (Goodyear 1975:143–145).

The final prediction is verified as well. Figure 8.10 presents the density of prickly pear by contour zones. Although the species is generally more dense at and above the 1775-foot contour, there is a distinct mode between 1825 feet and 1775 feet that has the highest density of all. A chi-square test was applied to the proportions of loci found by the sampling circles underneath these two maximum-density zones versus the ratio of sites to circles above and below them. Table 8.3 presents the outcome of this test.

As can be observed from Table 8.3, the number of protohistoric loci in the maximum zone of prickly pear growth is four times greater than in zones above and below it on the mountain slope. This distribution is statistically and behaviorally significant. Based upon the positive outcome of these three predictions, a rather good techno-environmental fit has been obtained between the known historic Papago and Pima subsistence patterns and the protohistoric thin brown ware sites.

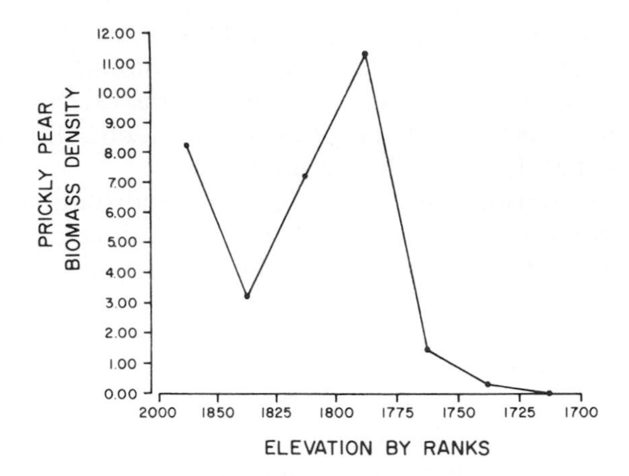

Figure 8.10. Biomass density distribution of *Opuntia engelmannii* (prickly pear), Prickly Pear Fruit subsystem.

The last floral resource contained within the distribution of the protohistoric sites is that of *Carnegia gigantea,* or saguaro cactus. Of all the cacti used by the Sonoran Desert Indians, the saguaro has been perhaps the mostly widely described and discussed. In terms of its accessibility, the fruit and seed have a highly restricted span of availability, occurring from the last 2 weeks of June through the first 2 weeks of July. The saguaro in this regard is extremely punctual and appears to bear fruit irrespective of previous droughts (Kearney and Peebles 1960:569; Thackery and Leding 1929:407).

Historically, the economic and socioreligious importance of saguaro fruit and its products is manifest. The sweet fruit is the first fresh floral food of the year high in calories as well as vegetable protein. If we consider only the fat-rich seeds, the saguaro has the highest caloric value per unit volume of any species in the paloverde–saguaro community

TABLE 8.3

Chi-Square Test for Significance[a] of Ratio of Sampling Circles to Thin Brown Ware Sites within the Maximum Prickly Pear Density Zones Versus the Other Zones

	Sample circles	Loci produced	Totals
Within maximum density (1825 to 1776 feet)	19(23.37)	9(4.62)	28
Out of maximum density (2000 to 1825 feet; 1775 to 1700 feet)	82(77.62)	11(15.37)	93
Totals	101	20	121

[a] $\chi^2 = 6.46$; $df = 1$, $p < .02$.

(Goodyear 1975:79; Ross 1941:42). The second-highest caloric content is contained in the fruit pulp. Extraction of foodstuffs centered largely around seasonal base camps where the collective efforts of one or more families were used to maximize the amount of energy procured and to minimize the restrictive period of availability (Goodyear 1975:100–101). Technologically, the primary means of extraction was by the use of jars for cooking and storing the fruit extract, and grinding tools for the processing of seeds. Although some "community pattern" or intrasite structure (see Binford *et al.* 1970) could also probably be expected, because of the variety of tasks performed and the multifamily camp personnel, the most distinctive artifactual characteristic of saguaro camps is the presence of grinding implements. Ethnographically, the saguaro was the only cactus commonly exploited for its seeds by means of a grinding technology.

The contemporary density distribution of saguaro biomass is illustrated in Figure 8.11. Basically, there is a bimodal distribution in the study area of the Slates (cf. Goodyear 1975:77–80). There is a trough of lesser density at about the 1800–1775-foot elevation, which probably reflects the topographic influence of a small valley between two hills. Both modes above and below this trough are extremely similar in biomass density (Figure 8.11). Under the conditions whereby gatherers focused only on saguaro,

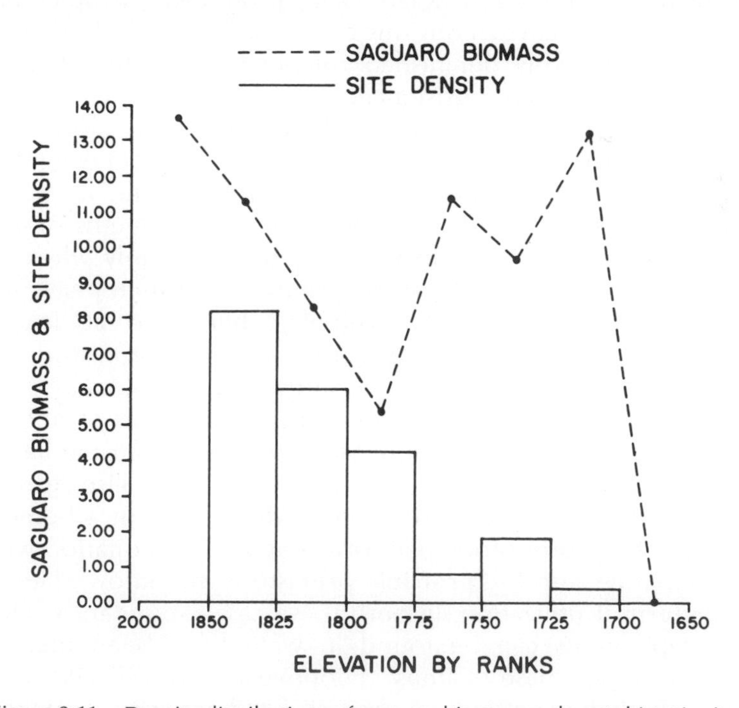

Figure 8.11. Density distributions of saguaro biomass and protohistoric sites.

a contingency that is ecologically feasible (see Figure 8.6), it could be predicted that processing camps would be located within the trough of lower density in order to facilitate gathering equally in all directions.

The protohistoric site distribution, as illustrated by the histogram overlaid in Figure 8.11, would indicate that such is not the case. It might be postulated that protohistoric groups were only procuring from the upper mode of Figure 8.11 as suggested by the general covariance of biomass and site density. This does not seem to be the case, however. Although the sites under the first biomass mode do have a predominance of jars, as demonstrated when testing the prickly pear extraction camp hypothesis, not one of the loci has any evidence of grinding implements. In other words, there is a better techno-environmental relationship with the prickly pear hypothesis.

The absence of grinding tools seriously weakens the inference of saguaro-processing camps for these sites. It would be extremely odd that no grinding industry was present if these loci represent saguaro camps. Strong evidence was found for both Hokokam-related and late prehistoric Sells phase saguaro camps at elevations above the protohistoric sites; all of the camps exhibited extensive evidence of grinding tools (Goodyear 1975:84–90). Furthermore, some of the historic Papago sites in the study area (Bruder 1975), as well as several Papago sites on the western slopes of the Slates (Raab 1974), produced examples of traditional manos and metates in obvious cactus camps, even though saguaro seed played a relatively diminished role in late nineteenth and early twentieth century Papago subsistence.

The lack of evidence for saguaro exploitation is made more enigmatic by the fact saguaro fruit has an average of 499 calories dry weight per 100 gm and prickly pear fruit has only 280 calories for the same measure (Goodyear 1975:Appendix H; Ross 1941:41). Thus, it seems strange that such a superior resource would be ignored, particularly when there is evidence that prehistoric and historic groups made such heavy use of it (compare Haury 1950:166). Accordingly, there are at least three hypotheses that may explain the apparent lack of protohistoric saguaro fruit and seed processing camps in the study area.

First, the sherd and lithic loci represent probable sites of both prickly pear and saguaro fruit processing where the seeds from the latter were either ignored along with prickly pear seeds or else ground up elsewhere. If the seeds were ground elsewhere, e.g., at a home floodplain village, the protohistoric pattern of saguaro exploitation would be at strong variance with the probable prehistoric and known late historic Papago pattern of utilization. In both these cases abundant evidence of grinding implements can be found in what have been identified as probable saguaro base camps (Goodyear 1975:77–119). Such a diachronically stable pattern of saguaro seed utilization suggests the existence of an optimal procedure for maximal saguaro exploitation passed down through the centuries. If the seeds were eschewed, the resource with the highest quantity of energy per unit volume would have been wasted, an average of 609 calories per 100 gm dry weight (Goodyear 1975:Appendix H-1). In terms of dietary requirements of an essentially subsistence-type economy, this seems highly unlikely.

The second hypothesis holds that the entire Saguaro Fruit–Seed subsistence subsystem was ignored altogether by protohistoric groups, in spite of the fact that the south-facing slopes of the Slate Mountains are and probably were an optimal location for saguaro procurement. Although this hypothesis is partially supported by the good techno-environmental correlation obtained for the hypothesized Prickly Pear subsystem, this hypothesis is weak, for reasons similar to those for the first hypothesis; it seems inconceivable that saguaro could be ignored under aboriginal conditions of subsistence.

Hypothesis 3 states that saguaro processing was done somewhere outside the transect-shaped study area of Figure 8.4. Although the three Hecla Mine projects covered a substantial area of the south slopes of the Slate Mountains, they by no means covered the entirety. This hypothesis, i.e., sampling error, seems the most probable of the three. As an example, the houselike structure excavated at AZ AA:5:4 (ASU) was located well within the heart of the cactus-bearing zones of the Slates at an elevation of about 1800 feet on the southwestern slopes. It lies, however, about a quarter of a mile to the west of the study area depicted in Figure 8.4. This site could represent, in part, a protohistoric cactus extraction camp. Quantities of mano and metate fragments, potsherds and flaked stone were present in immediately adjacent trash scatters, the density of which closely resemble those of the full prehistoric saguaro base camps in the study area. Taking the sherds and grinding stone fragments in conjunction with the established structure, there is a correspondence with nineteenth and twentieth century Papago cactus camps as well. The fact that the structure may have been occupied during the winter or spring, however, suggests that this site may not represent just a central extraction camp for this period.

It is significant to note, nonetheless, that evidence for protohistoric saguaro utilization was not found in the study area, possibly excepting AZ AA:5:4 (ASU), and that protohistoric groups were not reoccupying former prehistoric Sells phase or Hohokam cactus-processing camps. Furthermore, nineteenth and twentieth century Papago cactus camps did not occupy either prehistoric or protohistoric cactus camps, indicating yet other settlement pattern shifts. The lack of isomorphism among the three periods, particularly for the protohistoric period, is consistent with an overall pattern of settlement change observed both on the Santa Rosa floodplain and in the Slate Mountains. These shifts in settlement strategy, although currently unexplained, are perhaps the most interesting aspects of diachronic shifts in human ecology for the Santa Rosa–Slate Mountain region.

SUMMARY AND CONCLUSIONS

Recent archeological studies in the Santa Rosa–Slate Mountain region have revealed the existence and environmental distribution of protohistoric sites. Until recently little information in the form of primary archeological data has been available for the period between the close of the prehistoric Sells phase (A.D. 1250–1400) and the inception of the historic Papago as described ethnographically. At Ventana Cave, Haury (1950:345) appears to have recognized the thin brown ware that occurred late in the stratigraphic sequence. To date, the thin brown ware is best known from the desert mountains of this region as witnessed by Ventana Cave and the studies reported herein from the southern and western slopes of the Slate Mountains. New data recently gathered near the juncture of the Salt and Gila rivers indicate that the brown ware is not restricted to the Papagueria.

Two basic hypotheses relevant to cultural identification were offered for the thin brown ware sites. A Yuman-related affiliation was tested and found unlikely based on technological evidence of the ceramics. The indigenous Papago explanation was found more tenable based on an apparent surface and verified subsurface association of the thin brown ware with a schist-tempered plainware descriptively referred to as Wingfield Plain. One schist-tempered plain jar had a rim coil, which is known to be an attribute of early Papago ceramics. The thin brown ware and thin schist-tempered plainware were also recovered from a square structure, radiocarbon dated to the late fourteenth century, which bore a strong resemblance in terms of plan, probable wall type, and doorway position to a nineteenth century Piman house. Although not verified as yet by archeological means, the early Papago village of Kohatk is thought, on circumstantial grounds, to be related to the thin brown ware sites. Given the heavy emphasis on hunting and gathering in even late historic Papago subsistence, coupled with the high subsistence potential of the Slates, some archeological evidence of economic activities attributable to Kohatk should be present in the Slate Mountain. Since nearly all of Papago sites from the Slate Mountains are related to late nineteenth and early twentieth centuries, a relationship between late seventeenth and eighteenth century Kohatk and the thin brown ware is thereby implicated.

An attempt was made to determine what types of subsistence activities were performed in the Slate Mountains in association with the thin brown ware. Using data derived from plant ecology and ethnographic observations, but considering only those species found within the spatial and elevational range of the thin brown ware sites, three subsistence subsystems were postulated. Each of the three subsystems was tested separately, revealing the Prickly Pear subsystem to have the best techno-environmental fit. Modeling from historic Papago techno-behavioral characteristics, no ceramic remains were expected to be associated with species of the Bud–Flower subsystem. This prediction was well met and appears to uphold the assumption of vegetation stability in the Slate Mountains paloverde–saguaro community. No evidence for a subsistence relationship with saguaro was found, an inference based on the absence of grinding implements. Because of the saguaro's superior resource value, the lack of evidence for a Saguaro Fruit–Seed subsystem is considered particularly anomalous. Three alternative explanations were offered for this lack of association. Sampling error—i.e., that surveys on the south-facing slope failed to contact protohistoric saguaro fruit and seed processing camps—seems the most viable. The enigmatic existence of the houselike structure at AZ AA:5:4 (ASU) strongly suggests a locus of protohistoric saguaro fruit and seed processing because of the large numbers of ceramics and grinding tool fragments paralleling the prehistoric saguaro camps. If this site in fact represents protohistoric saguaro processing, it would complement other settlement strategy shifts that seem to characterize the protohistoric occupation of the Santa Rosa Valley–Slate Mountain region.

The fact that the distribution of protohistoric sites is not isomorphic with Sells phase sites in the Slate Mountains can be hypothesized to reflect major structural changes in the settlement strategy between two cultural systems. Within the Santa rose floodplain, Raab (1974) found numerous examples of Sells phase settlements of varying size including one large village with several extensive trash mounds. Raab's survey on the floodplain covered both the eastern and western sides of the Santa Rosa Wash over an area of approximately 7-square miles (18 km^2). Yet no protohistoric settlements were encountered; only a handful of sherds were found near AZ AA:5:54 (ASM). Clearly, within the spatial perimeter of the survey by Raab (Figure 8.1), there is a qualitative difference in floodplain settlement pattern. Although such negative evidence certainly does not prove or necessarily imply that there was no occupation of the Santa Rosa Wash by protohistoric groups, as in the case of the Slate Mountain extraction camp patterns, certainly some differences in settlement strategy are indicated. To reiterate, the contemporary village of Kohatk was not inside Raab's survey boundaries and it appears to be some 3 miles (4.8 km) to the west of his survey area (Figure 8.1).

The survey data generated by Raab (1974) on the floodplain and the historically established existence of Kohatk indicate that the change in settlement pattern on the floodplain may relate to the eventual concentration of houses or rancherias into a single large village. If the thin brown ware was produced by the early Kohatk groups, the lack of dispersed, individual settlements would be understandable in light of the agglutinated "defense" form of villages known to have been formed during early historic times (Hoover 1935).

The causes underlying shifts in settlement pattern from the late prehistoric to the early historic period have not been dealt with in this chapter. Several significant factors may have been at work, and these should at least be mentioned to guide future work. The collapse of the late prehistoric Sells phase may have been, at least in part, attributable to a deterioration in hydrological conditions of the Santa Rosa Wash. It has been argued elsewhere that the Classic Period Hohokam of the Gila and Salt drainages may have also been subject to environmental stress that disrupted agricultural systems (Weaver 1972). Some population reduction may have occurred because of a decrease in "carrying capacity" attributable to an increasingly xeric environment, as well as, perhaps, to diseases indirectly introduced from Mexico. During the 1600s and 1700s there apparently were population movements and dislocation by Yuman-speakers along the Gila River and by the Sobaipuri along the Santa Cruz Rivers. Just how any or all of these factors may have related to cultural change between the fourteenth and nineteenth centuries is unknown. These and other variables can be considered after processual reconstructions are made of settlement-subsistence systems. The small sites with the thin brown ware from the Slate Mountains, though admittedly representing only a fraction of the former cultural system, have given us a substantive basis with which to identify and continue to study what heretofore has been largely an ethnohistorical lacuna. Hopefully, this chapter has provided patterns and problems that will point to new directions for research in the Papagueria.

ACKNOWLEDGMENTS

This chapter would not have been possible without the aid of several individuals. The Papago Indian Tribe and the Hecla Mining Company of Casa Grande, Arizona, funded all three seasons of research on the Hecla Mine property. Alfred E. Dittert, Jr., Principal Investigator, aided in the analysis of ceramics. L. Mark Raab, assistant archeologist for the Hecla projects, kindly allowed me the use of his data from the Santa Rosa Wash survey. Don Weaver, Minnabell Laughlin, J. Simon Bruder, Robert C. Euler, and Henry F. Dobyns all offered useful comments.

REFERENCES

Binford, Lewis R.
1962 Archaeology as Anthropology. *American Antiquity* **28**:217–225.

Binford, Lewis R., Sally R. Binford, Robert Whallon, and Margaret Hardin
1970 Archaeology at Hatchery West. *Memoirs of the Society for American Archaeology* No. 24, **35**(4).

Bruder, J. Simon
1975 Historic Papago archaeology (Appendix B). In, Hecla II and III: An interpretive study of archeological remains from the Lakeshore Project, Papago Reservation, South Central Arizona, edited by A. C. Goodyear. *Arizona State University Anthropological Research Paper* No. **9,** Tempe, pp. 271–337.

Canouts, Veletta (assembler)
1972 An archaeological survey of the Santa Rosa Wash Project, A Corp of Engineers Project. Report on file Arizona State Museum, Univ. of Arizona, Tucson.

Castetter, Edward F., and Willis H. Bell
1937 The aboriginal utilization of the tall Cacti in the American Southwest. *University of New Mexico Bulletin* **307,** *Biological Series* 5 (1).
1942 *Pima and Papago agriculture.* Albuquerque: Univ. of New Mexico Press.

Castetter, Edward F., and Ruth M. Underhill
1935 The ethnobiology of the Papago Indians. *University of New Mexico Bulletin* **275,** *Biological Series* 4 (3).

Dobyns, Henry F.
1956 Prehistoric Indian occupation within the eastern area of the Yuman complex. Unpublished M.A. thesis, Univ. of Arizona.

Dobyns, Henry F., and Robert C. Euler
1958 Tizon brown ware: A descriptive revision. In *Museum of Northern Arizona, Ceramic Series* 3D, edited by Harold S. Colton. Museum of Northern Arizona.

Euler, Robert C., and Henry F. Dobyns
1956 Tentative correlations of Upland Arizona Yuman ceramics. Unpublished manuscript.

Fontana, Bernard L., William J. Robinson, Charles W. Cormack, and Ernest E. Leavitt, Jr.
1962 *Papago Indian pottery.* Seattle: Univ. of Washington Press.

Gish, Jannifer W.
1975 Preliminary report on pollen analysis from Hecla I, II, and III (Appendix B). In Hecla II and III: An Interpretive Study of Archeological Remains from the Lakeshore Project, Papago Reservation, South Central Arizona, edited by A. C. Goodyear. *Arizona State University Anthropological Research Paper* No. **9,** Tempe, pp. 254–270.

Goodyear, Albert C.
1973 Prehistoric settlement-subsistence systems in the Slate Mountains: A proposed study. Ms. on file, Department of Anthropology, Arizona State Univ. and Arizona State Museum, Univ. of Arizona.
1975 Hecla II and III: An interpretive study of archeological remains from the Lakeshore Project, Papago Reservation, South Central Arizona. *Arizona State University Anthropological Research Paper* No. **9.** Tempe.

Goodyear, Albert C., and Alfred E. Dittert, Jr.
1973 Hecla I: A preliminary report on the archaeological investigations at the Lakeshore Project, Papago Reservation, South Central Arizona. *Arizona State University, Anthropological Research Paper* **4.**

Hackenberg, Robert A.
1964 Aboriginal land use and occupancy of the Papago Indians. Ms. on file Arizona State Museum Library, Univ. of Arizona.
Halvorson, William L.
1970 Topographic influence on the pattern of plant communities, phenology, and water relations of a desert ecosystem. Unpublished Ph.D. dissertation, Arizona State Univ.
Hastings, James Rodney, and Raymond M. Turner
1965 *The changing mile: An ecological study of vegetation change with time in the lower mile of an arid and semi-arid region.* Tucson: Univ. of Arizona Press.
Haury, Emil W.
1950 *The stratigraphy and archaeology of Ventana Cave, Arizona.* Albuquerque: Univ. of New Mexico Press.
Hoover, J. W.
1935 Generic descent of the Papago Villages. *American Anthropologist* **37**(2):257–264.
Hrdlicka, Ales
1906 Notes on the Pima of Arizona. *American anthropologist* **8:**39–46.
Jones, Richard D.
1969 An analysis of Papago communities 1900–1920. Unpublished Ph.D. dissertation, Univ. of Arizona.
Joseph, Alice, Rosamund Spicer, and Jane Chesky
1949 *The desert people: A study of the Papago Indians.* Chicago: Univ. of Chicago Press.
Kearney, Thomas H., and Robert H. Peebles
1960 *Arizona flora.* Berkeley: Univ. of California Press.
Lowe, Charles H. (editor)
1964 *The vertebrates of Arizona.* Tucson: Univ. of Arizona Press.
Martin, Paul S.
1963 *The last 10,000 years: A fossil Pollen Record of the American Southwest.* Tucson: Univ. of Arizona Press.
Niering, W. H., R. H. Whittaker, and C. H. Lowe
1963 The Saguaro: A population in relation to environment. *Science* **142:**15–23.
Odum, Eugene P.
1971 *Fundamentals of ecology.* Philadelphia: Saunders.
Oosting, Henry J.
1956 *The study of plant communities.* (2nd ed.) San Francisco: Freeman.
Raab, L. Mark
1974 Archaeological investigations for the Santa Rosa Wash Project, Phase I Preliminary Report. Ms. on file Arizona State Museum, Univ. of Arizona.
Rogers, Malcolm J.
1936 Yuman pottery making. *San Diego Museum Papers* No. 2.
Ross, Winifred
1941 The present day dietary habits of the Papago Indians. Unpublished M.A. thesis, Univ. of Arizona.
Russell, Frank
1908 The Pima Indians. *Bureau of American Ethnology, Annual Report* **26:**3–390.
Schiffer, Michael B.
1972 Archaeological context and systemic context. *American Antiquity* **37:**156–165.
Schroeder, Albert H.
1958 Lower Colorado Buff ware—A descriptive revision. In *Museum of Northern Arizona, ceramic series* 3D, edited by Harold S. Colton. Museum of Northern Arizona.

Shreve, Forrest
1951 Vegetation of the Sonoran Desert, Vol. 1. *Carnegie Institute of Washington, Publication* **591.**
Siegel, Sidney
1956 *Nonparametric statistics for the behavioral sciences.* New York: McGraw-Hill.
Sobelman, Sandra
1973 Archaeological survey in the Vekol Mountains, Papago Reservation. Ms., Arizona State Museum, Univ. of Arizona, Tucson.
Stewart, Yvonne G., and Lynn S. Teague
1974 An ethnoarchaeological study of the Vekol copper mining project. Ms. on file Arizona State Museum, Univ. of Arizona.
Thackery, F. A., and A. R. Leding
1929 The giant cactus of Arizona: The uses of its fruit and other cactus fruits by the Indians. *Journal of Heredity* **20:**400–414.
Underhill, Ruth
1939 *Social organization of the Papago Indians.* New York: Columbia Univ. Press.
Weaver, Donald E., Jr.
1972 A cultural-ecological model for the classic Hohokam Period in the Lower Salt River Valley, Arizona. *The Kiva* **38**(1):43–52.
Whittaker, R. H., and W. A. Niering
1965 Vegetation of the Santa Catalina Mountains, Arizona: A Gradient Analysis of the South Slope. *Ecology* **46:**429–452.
Winter, Joseph
1973 Cultural modifications of the Gila Pima: A.D. 1697–1846. *Ethnohistory* **20**(1):65–77.
Yang, T. W., and C. H. Lowe
1956 Correlation of major vegetation climaxes with soil characteristics in Sonoran Desert. *Science* **123:**542.

Survey Data and Regional Models in Historical Archeology

JOHN H. HOUSE

Within prehistoric archeology in North America there has been an increasing emphasis on *regions* rather than individual *sites* as the major focus of research. This shift in emphasis is a result of two independent developments: first, a change within social science in our view of human behavior and the operation of cultural processes, and second, new environmental legislation that presents us, as archeologists, with the responsibility for cultural resource management in the face of massive land modification on an unprecedented scale (Gummerman 1973; King 1971; Lipe 1974; Schiffer 1975a). It will be argued here that these developments are also relevant to the archeological study of the *historic* past, and that regional models and research designs are increasingly appropriate to realizing the potential of historical archeology in North America.

Prehistoric archeology in North America has long been considered anthropology. Since the 1960s, however, most prehistoric archeologists have begun to view culture not simply as learned, shared behavior but as an adaptive behavioral system; they have begun to view the archeological record as having numerous dimensions of variability.

Stanley South (1977) has noted that historical archeology also seems to be undergoing a process of paradigm change. Some historical archeologists are beginning to see the archeological record of the historic past as relevant to a broad range of social science concerns, and historical archeology as sharing research goals with anthropology, social and economic history, and cultural geography (cf. Ascher 1974; Ascher and Fairbanks 1971; Binford 1972; Bowen 1975; Deetz 1971; Klein 1973; Smith and Davidson 1975).

An emphasis on regions in historical archeology is also developing as a response to the fact that the same massive land modification projects affecting prehistoric sites are affecting historic sites to a proportionate degree. Consideration of regional historical archeological data bases, regional research questions, and cultural resource management priorities are being forced on most of us, regardless of the particular social science paradigms we employ.

With regard to these issues, I shall attempt to explore in this chapter the relevance that archeological survey data of the kinds gathered in the course of prehistoric archeological research have to the investigation of human life in the historic past. This discussion will be illustrated with examples of archeological data generated by three recent environmental impact surveys in the central Mississippi valley area in northeast Arkansas and southeast Missouri. I shall also offer a few technical, methodological, and theoretical suggestions for putting into operation a regional research strategy in a multistage, nomothetically oriented, archeological investigation of the historic past.

ARE SURVEY DATA NECESSARY IN HISTORICAL ARCHEOLOGY?

The necessity of gathering survey data in prehistoric archeological research is obvious. It might be asked, however, to what extent the existence of maps, land patents, and other documentary records relied on by social historians and cultural geographers makes survey data on historic remains unnecessary and redundant. The answer to this question can be addressed both theoretically, by considering the processes by which the documentary record is formed and preserved, and empirically, by comparing comprehensive sets of corresponding documentary and archeological data.

As Schiffer (1975b) notes, documents are a result of transformation processes, just as the archeological record is. Valid use of documentary data, as any historian knows, entails consideration of the processes by which information about past events and conditions becomes recorded and preserved in documents. Documents, for instance, may be concerned with only specific things; they may be falsified; they become lost or destroyed. One classic review of the criticism of documents—in what may be termed a generalizing, nomothetic historical research strategy—is presented by Bloch (1953:79–138); another, under a somewhat less nomothetic paradigm, is presented by Collingwood (1946:249–281). Documents concerning early historic North America, particularly, may not contain all the information on human/land relationships of interest to the social scientist. Records from frontier situations may be especially incomplete. "Squatter" homesteads, for instance, are not recorded in land patents. Furthermore, as shall be demonstrated later, some ephemeral settlements and other activity loci, although economically important, may be very poorly documented even within the relatively recent past. Finally, it has been argued that confining historical archeology research to sites and phenomena documented in the historic record is an unwarranted limitation of the scope and potential scientific contributions of historical archeology (cf. South 1974, 1977).

This question—the relevance of survey data to historical archeology research—will be addressed empirically later in the chapter. The conditions of county records in several northeast Arkansas and southeast Missouri counties will be briefly reviewed, and fairly comprehensive sets of archeological survey data will be compared with available documentary data for certain areas in the Little Black River watershed in southeast Missouri.

REGIONAL QUESTIONS AND ARCHEOLOGICAL DATA REQUIREMENTS

One of the basic assumptions of modern multistage research in prehistoric archeology is that the behavioral repertoire of a society is participated in differentially by different social segments and that various activities take place at different times and at different loci. Accordingly, we would expect variability in the archeological record to stem not only from changing ideas in time and space but from numerous other processes as well. We expect the archeological record produced by a single society in the past to exhibit considerable variability within and between sites. The most appropriate research universe for investigating a past society, then, is not a single site but a *region,* the geographical area occupied by a past cultural system, society, or community. It is becoming obvious, to prehistoric and historical archeologists alike, that data from a single site, or even a few sites in a region, cannot form a basis for *typifying* the cultural behavior of a past society during a given interval in time (cf. Binford 1964; 1965; Struever 1971). The recognition and quantitative analysis of patterned variability in the historical archeological record on a regional scale has been begun by South (1977) in his definition of the Carolina and Frontier Artifact Patterns and the Brunswick Pattern of refuse disposal.

On a regional level, then, the archeological study of a past society requires reliable data on the totality of archeological sites formed by that society. Information on site *location* is relevant to inference of an array of past systemic variables that affect the location of static cultural phenomena about the landscape (cf. Haggett 1966; Johnson 1973;

Swedlund 1975)—but especially to inference of the specific natural resources central to the system's functioning. Information on site *variability* is relevant to inference of the total range of behavioral variability within the past society. And information on the *density* of various classes of archeological phenomena is a prerequisite for quantifying certain behavioral variables and statistically testing hypotheses about past cultural systems. The relevance of these three themes—*location, variability,* and *density*—to historical archeology will now be illustrated by concrete examples.

In the human geography of a past cultural system, as in many other aspects of such a system, historical archeologists are at a considerable advantage over prehistoric archeologists. They have available extensive documentary information pertinent to the society under consideration. It shall be demonstrated here, however, that documents cannot be considered *a priori* as a sufficient data base—or even the most appropriate data base—for investigation of all problems.

In the case of any regional data base, probabilistic sampling is a prerequisite for obtaining truly reliable information on all three parameters of the archeological record. Selecting the optimum sampling design for the investigation of a specific problem and determining the confidence intervals of the resultant parameter estimates remain major methodological problems in both prehistoric archeology (Mueller 1975) and human geography (Haggett 1966:191–210, 265–269).

OBSERVATION AND MEASUREMENT OF HISTORIC SITE LOCATION, VARIABILITY, AND DENSITY: EXAMPLES FROM THE CENTRAL MISSISSIPPI VALLEY AREA

Three Recent Surveys in the Central Mississippi Valley Area

The examples presented here are derived from three recent environmental impact surveys for land modification projects in northeast Arkansas and southeast Missouri. These land modification projects are as follows:

1. The Cache River–Bayou De View Channelization Project: a Corps of Engineers drainage project involving 230 miles of stream-channel enlargement and realignment in the 2000-square-mile Cache River basin in the Mississippi alluvial valley in northeast Arkansas (Schiffer and House 1975).
2. The Little Black River Watershed Project: a large-scale Soil Conservation Service flood-control project spanning the Ozark Highlands/

Mississippi Valley ecotone in southeast Missouri and northeast Arkansas. The impact zones surveyed consisted of 25 projected catchment basins or small reservoir sites in the uplands and approximately 16 miles of projected drainage ditch enlargement in the lowlands (Price *et al.* 1975).

3. The Poinsett Watershed Project: a relatively small-scale Soil Conservation Service flood-control project in northeast Arkansas on Crowley's Ridge, an upland remnant isolated within the Mississippi alluvial valley. The present survey (House 1975a) involved 12 small floodwater-retarding structure locations on the eastern slope of the ridge.

Only the Cache survey involved any kind of probabilistic regional sampling. The other two surveys were confined to specific zones in which direct impacts were projected. All three surveys, nonetheless, were the first intensive on-the-ground surveys of a number of dispersed, areally bounded survey units in their respective environmental zones. As such, they constitute a qualitative improvement over previous archeological surveys in the zones. The Little Black River survey yielded much more data on early historic sites than did the other two surveys.

All three surveys were operationalized as the potential first stage of a multistage research project involving both prehistoric and historic occupations. The Little Black River survey, in particular, was integrated with the long-term research design of the Southeast Missouri Archaeological Research Facility of "understanding man's changing utilization of the environment in a major ectone [Price *et al.* 1975:75]," a research theme encompassing both the prehistoric and historic portions of the archeological record.

The data generated by these surveys are not adequate for testing any hypotheses about early historic occupations in the regions involved. They do, however, suggest patterning in location, variability, and density of historic sites in the central Mississippi valley area.

Environment

The environment in the central Mississippi valley area has been summarized from an archeological viewpoint by Morse (1969:14–16), Fehon (1975), and Price *et al.* (1975:17–41). The Mississippi alluvial valley here varies from about 50 to about 80 miles in width (Figure 9.1). The valley is bounded on the west by the hilly, rocky Ozark Highlands. Crowley's Ridge, a hilly, insular area of dissected older alluvium and loess extending 200 miles from north to south, divides the valley into the eastern and western lowlands.

Land surfaces in the western lowlands consist primarily of flat, poorly drained relict braided stream terraces laid down by the late Pleistocene Mississippi River, but extensive areas of modern floodplain are present

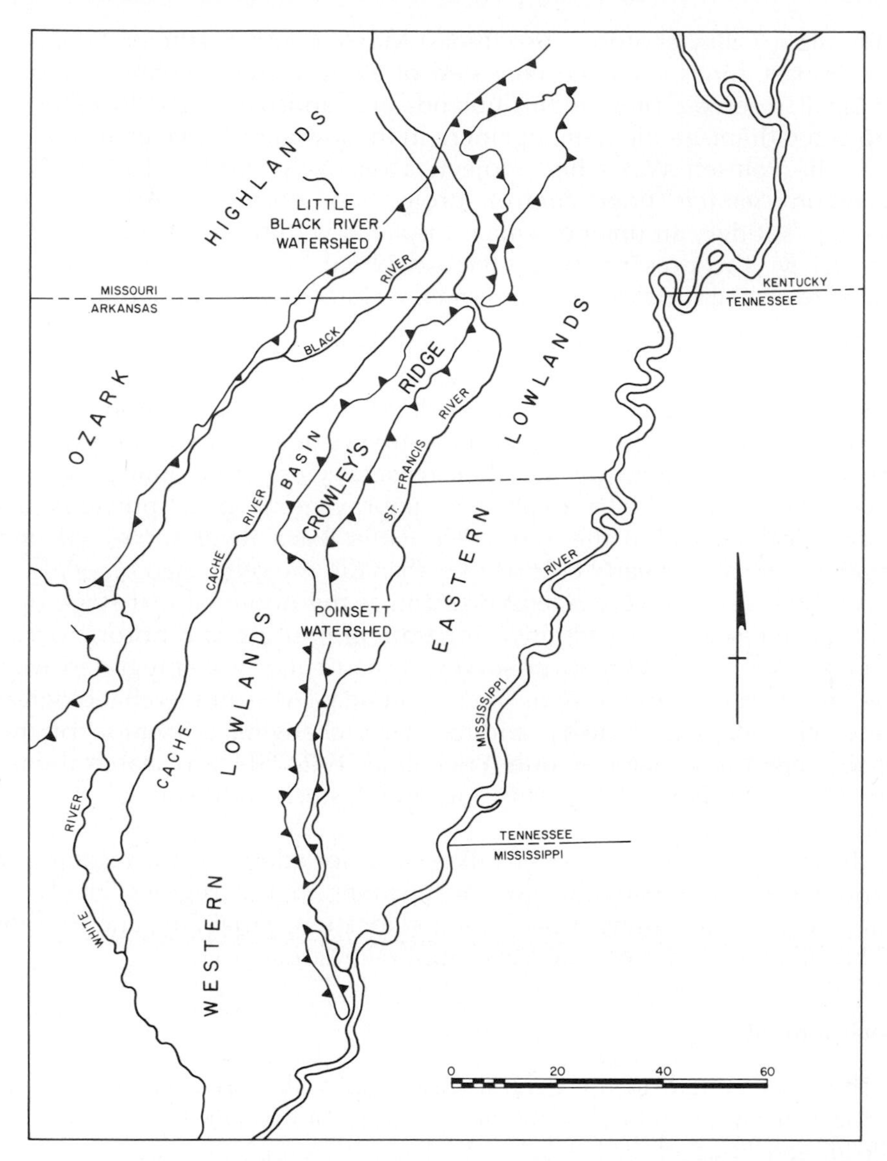

Figure 9.1. Central Mississippi valley area, showing the location of the Cache River basin, the Little Black River watershed, and the Poinsett watershed.

along major streams. The streams of the western lowlands include the White, Black, Current, and Little Black rivers, which rise in the Ozarks, and smaller streams such as the Cache and L'Anguille rivers and Bayou De View, which rise within the Mississippi alluvial valley.

In early historic times, most of the western lowlands were poorly drained and at least seasonally inundated. Cypress and tupelo swamp forest communities were present along major streams and in permanently ponded areas on the older terrace surfaces. The vast, seasonally flooded areas supported bottomland hardwood communities but oak–hickory forest was present on Crowley's Ridge and on higher, better-drained areas within the lowlands. The native vegetation in the eastern part of the Ozarks is primarily oak–hickory forest with some oak–pine and pure pine stands. Floodplain forest communities are, however, present along larger streams in the Ozarks.

Early History

The central Mississippi valley was crossed by the De Soto expedition in 1541. The earliest sustained European activity in the area, however, was of French hunters and traders traveling by river from Arkansas Post, St. Louis, St. Genevieve, Kaskaskia, and other early settlements of the Louisiana Colony in the eighteenth century (Ferguson and Atkinson 1966; Price *et al.* 1975). A land route known as the Natchitoches Path was established in the eighteenth century and continued to be a major trade and communications route in the early American period.

American traders, hunters, and squatters began to come into the area by the 1790s (Goodspeed Brothers Publishing Company 1889; Price *et al.* 1975; Schoolcraft 1853). In 1803, the transaction known as the Louisiana Purchase brought the area under the jurisdiction of the United States. American settlers in the Ozarks during the first decades of the nineteenth century seem to have been mostly highly mobile squatters, who moved west when the frontier moved west or when the land was patented by someone else. Lawrence County, which initially included most of northern Arkansas and part of southern Missouri, was established in 1815; its county seat was at Davidsonville on the Black River on a branch of the Natchitoches Path (Smith 1973; Smith and Davidson 1975). The earliest towns and villages in the Ozarks generally began after 1820. By the time of the Civil War, there were numerous farms, grist mills, and small villages in the upland portion of the Little Black River watershed and elsewhere in the Ozarks. The lumbering industry in the late nineteenth century brought an increase in settlement. Population probably reached its peak in the early twentieth century and declined after the exhaustion of the forests (Price *et al.* 1975).

The vast, mosquito-infested "bottoms" of the Mississippi Valley were apparently less appealing to the earlier settlers from Tennessee, Kentucky, the Carolinas, and elsewhere in the East, than were the Ozarks beyond. Early nineteenth century settlement in much of the Mississippi alluvial valley seems to have been confined to a few landings on major rivers (Holder 1966) and to Crowley's Ridge (Williams 1930). Many areas were logged during the late nineteenth and early twentieth centuries and scattered farms were established on higher, better-drained locations in the western lowlands. Settlement accelerated somewhat when the earliest drainage ditches were built in the early twentieth century, but extensive areas were cleared and cultivated for the first time only in the 1940s, 1950s, and 1960s.

Review and Evaluation of Some Documentary Sources for the Region

The condition of the country records in 17 northeast Arkansas countries is summarized by Smith and Davidson (1975:36–37). Because of such events as courthouse fires, the records of most of the counties are incomplete before the late nineteenth century. It is fortunate, however, that the records for Lawrence County, which originally included most of the 17-county area, and which date to 1815, are still intact. Duplicates of most county records were not filed elsewhere except for the individual's copy. General Land Office (GLO) survey plats are available, but for the most part they illustrate only major topographic features (Samuel D. Smith, personal communication).

The Missouri portion of the Little Black River watershed lies almost entirely within Ripley and Butler counties. The records in the Ripley County Courthouse in Doniphan and the Butler County Courthouse in Poplar Bluff have been intensively examined by Jim and Cynthia Price of the American Archaeology Division of the University of Missouri. A personal communication from Ms. Price forms the basis of the following discussion.

The county records in both courthouses are intact. Copies of General Land Office plats dating to various times between 1819 and 1855 are available among these records. These plats were prepared by different persons; some show only topographic features, whereas others show cabins, roads, fields, and other improvements. The surveyors were primarily interested in laying out section lines and archeological data suggest that the cultural information on GLO plats is more complete close to section lines.

Most land patents date from 1850 on, though a few patents in the Ozarks in Ripley County date from the 1830s. A number of problems with the use of land patents are evident: (1) squatters' homesteads are, by definition, not patented; (2) apparently not all patents are recorded in the patent books; and (3) a land patent does not necessarily indicate that settlement actually took place.

The deed books for the counties are extant but the earliest deeds date from the 1870s. Other county records are stored in these courthouses, but they are not readily available.

Both the GLO plats and the original surveyors' notebooks are available at the Missouri State Archives at Jefferson City. The notebooks sometimes record improvements or cabins not shown on the plats.

Intensive archeological reconnaissance in portions of the Little Black River watershed provides a preliminary basis for evaluating the completeness of the documents mentioned. These archeological data indicate that not only squatter cabins but also more permanent homesteads were often not recorded in the documents. A nonintensive survey of a township (36 square miles) in the lowlands located three ca. 1850–1870 homestead sites not recorded in land patents deed books, GLO plats, surveyors' notebooks, or any other sources examined by the Prices. By using early travelers' journals, the Prices succeeded in locating the site of the early nineteenth century Widow Harris cabin beside the Natchitoches Path in the upland portion of the watershed. This homestead is not recorded in any available county records. Ms. Price estimates, in summary, that probably only about one-half of the pre–Civil War settlements in the region are recorded in any country records.

Site Location

One of the major research designs used during the survey of the Little Black River Watershed Project was an investigation of the determinants of historic site location. In particular, some of the data gathered in the field and obtained from documentary sources were used to test some hypotheses about the location of nineteenth century homesteads in relation to such environmental variables as arable land, wild food resources for domestic animals, fresh water sources, and access to trade and communications routes.

In the Ozark Highlands portion of the watershed, present evidence suggests that through the mid-nineteenth century, American homesteads tended to be located on high terraces overlooking rivers and major creeks. The presence of perennial springs may also have been a determinant of settlement location. Three of the four habitation sites estimated to date from about 1850 were located on bluffs or terraces close to springs; the fourth site was located on a high terrace at the mouth of a hollow above the Little Black River. Documentary and archeological reconnaissance data suggest that the earliest settlement in the region was concentrated close to the Natchitoches Path. The only catchment basin of the proposed watershed project that was located on the Natchitoches Path was found to contain a standing ca. 1850 log cabin having an associated activity area perhaps representing a blacksmith shop (Price *et al.* 1975:104–111, 146–196).

When data on early historic site locations in the lowland portion of the watershed are compared with those on the location of thirteenth and fourteenth century A.D. prehistoric Indian occupations, a particularly interesting pattern emerges (Price *et al.* 1975:138). Both archeological reconnaissance data and information on GLO plats indicate that, like the prehistoric Indian sites, early nineteenth century homesteads were concentrated on high, sandy relict braided stream interfluves known locally as *sand ridges,* rather than on the intervening low-lying flats (Figure 9.2). Furthermore, the locations of the early historic homesteads correspond more closely with the Indian hamlet sites than with sites of larger villages. This suggests that in both past cultural systems, the prehistoric Mississippian Indian and the early nineteenth century frontier Anglo-American, the requirements of settlement location may have been similar. Both economies were based on maize agriculture; the need for arable land, a water source, and elevation above seasonal flooding probably operated in both cultural systems (cf. Lewis 1974:29–32). Interestingly, the majority of the initial homesteads in the lowland

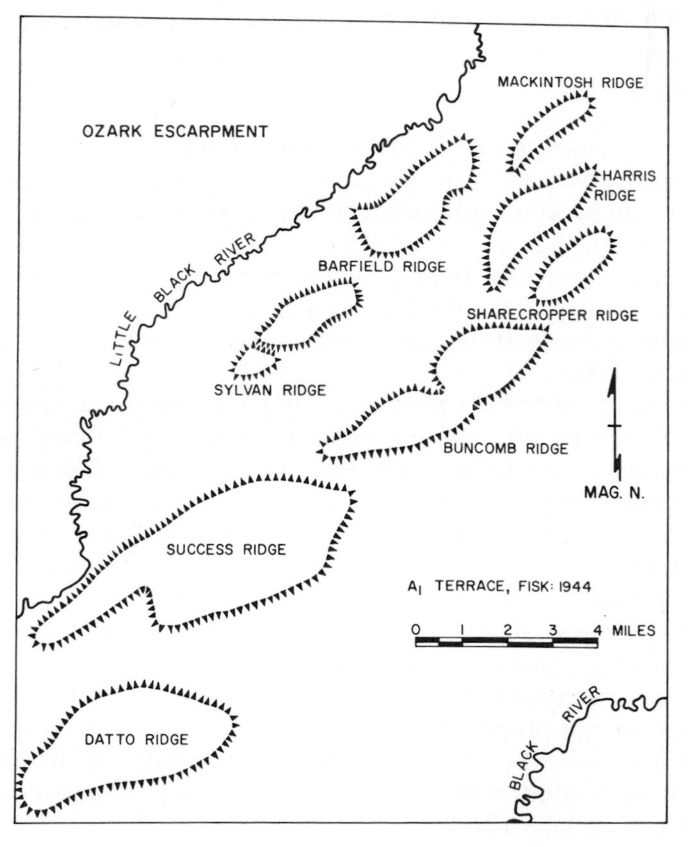

Figure 9.2. Sand ridge system of the lowland portion of the Little Black River watershed, Missouri and Arkansas.

portion of the watershed seem to have been abandoned by the time of the Civil War (Price *et al.* 1975:161).

Site Variability

Reliable data on variability among sites formed by a single past cultural system are prerequisite to making inferences about the behavioral variability within the system, and to understanding the articulation of that behavioral variability into a systemic whole. The survey of numerous proposed catchment basin sites and drainage channel routes throughout the Little Black River watershed brought many aspects of historic site variability in the watershed into sharper focus than was possible previously.

The most common type of historic site located during the survey was, as might be expected, the house site. One log cabin dating to the mid-nineteenth century was still standing, but nine other early to mid-nineteenth century house places located in the impact zones of the projects were completely in ruins, recognizable only by the observation of scattered foundation stones and the subsequent use of a metal detector to locate buried metal artifacts.

Other types of sites located in the impact zones included five late nineteenth to early twentieth century house places; two probable barn sites, including the mid-nineteenth century example illustrated in Figure 9.3; four stone spring boxes, presumably associated with unrecognized early house places outside the impact zones; three cemeteries not mapped on U.S. Geological Survey quadrangles; and a late nineteenth and early twentieth century school.

The logging industry in the Ozarks and the central Mississippi valley in the late nineteenth and early twentieth centuries had a major impact on the demography and environment of the region (Price *et al.* 1975:227–250). Evidence of logging activity was found in several of the projected catchment basis in the upland portion of the Little Black River watershed. This evidence includes segments of tram beds and sites of two temporary logging camps, and two ephemeral lumber mill towns.

We relocated the site of the mill town of King Bee, dating to the turn of the century, when we were guided to the spot by an elderly local resident. The site contained almost no standing structures but our informant indicated the position of numerous buildings he remembered from his childhood (Figure 9.4).

One quite important economic activity from the even more recent past is poorly documented—for obvious reasons. Sites of at least three moonshine stills, probably dating to the 1920s and 1930s, were found within the basins surveyed. The site illustrated in Figure 9.5 represents a particularly large operation; numerous mash barrels are indicated by the piles of barrel hoops and two cookers are represented by the two hearths.

Site Density

Testing models and hypotheses of past cultural behavior usually requires quantitative versus presence-or-absence, or "trait," data. On a regional level, these data may take the form of measurements of the density of archeological phenomena, though quantitative analysis of other aspects of the location of phenomena would be relevant to testing the implications of more complex models. Probabilistic sampling is especially crucial in the measurement of density. In the absence of probabilistic sampling, however, really marked differences in observed densities may nonetheless indicate underlying patterning. Such marked differences in density are apparent from comparison of data on early to

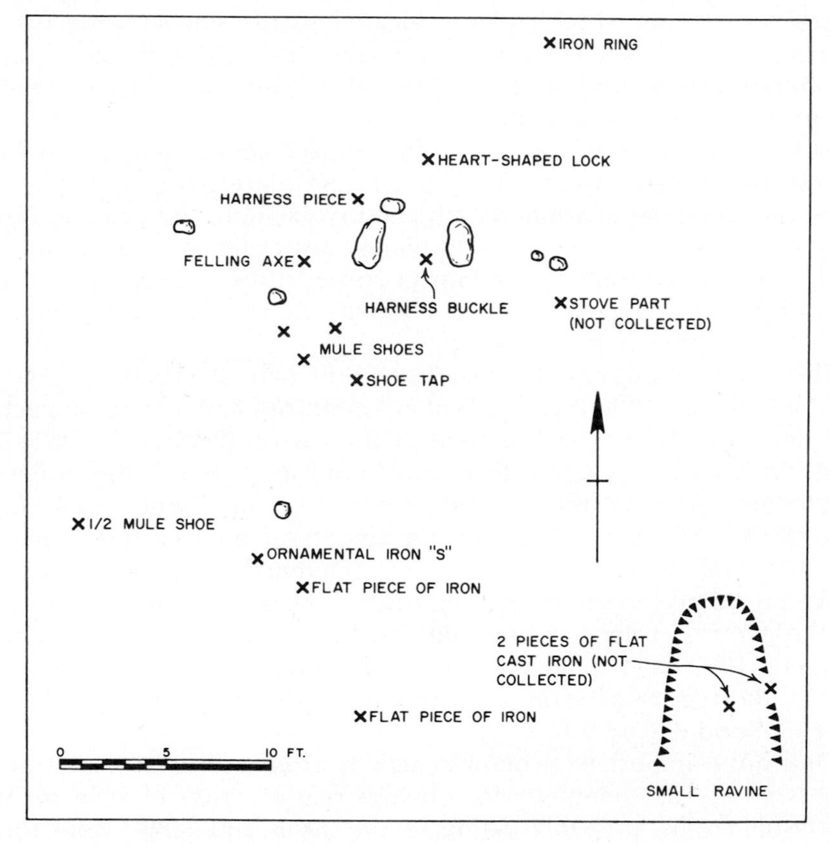

Figure 9.3. Sketch map of probable mid-nineteenth century barn site (23RI-H42), Little Black River watershed, Missouri.

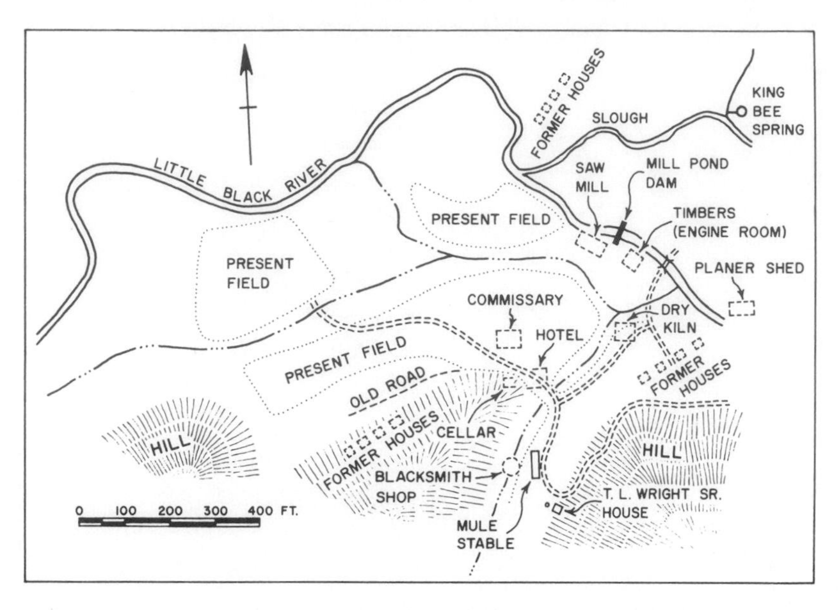

Figure 9.4. Sketch map of the King Bee lumber village site (23RI-H31) in the Little Black River watershed, Missouri.

mid-nineteenth century occupation generated by the Cache River Archeological Project and the Poinsett Watershed Project.

These two projects, as noted earlier, are located in two highly contrasting environmental zones in northeast Arkansas. The Cache River basin is predominantly a flat, low-lying, poorly drained area, which has relatively little land suitable for maize or cotton cultivation. It remained mostly wooded until around the 1940s. Crowley's Ridge, in contrast, is hilly and well drained. Historical sources (Goodspeed Brothers Publishing Company 1889; Williams 1930) make frequent references to pre-Civil War settlement on Crowley's Ridge but relatively few references to contemporary settlement in the surrounding lowlands.

Comparison of the archeological data gathered by the Cache River Project in 1973 and 1974, and the survey of the Poinsett Watershed Project in 1975 revealed differences in historic-site density quite consistent with the pattern of differential site density inferred from the historical sources. In the Cache River survey, a total of about 10-square miles throughout the basin was surveyed. Only two sites in this area produced probable evidence of early to mid-nineteenth century occupation (House 1975b:161). The Poinsett Watershed Project survey, on the other hand, covered a total of about 200 acres associated with 12 proposed floodwater-retarding structures. During the latter survey, three early to mid-nineteenth century homesteads were located within the area (House 1975a).

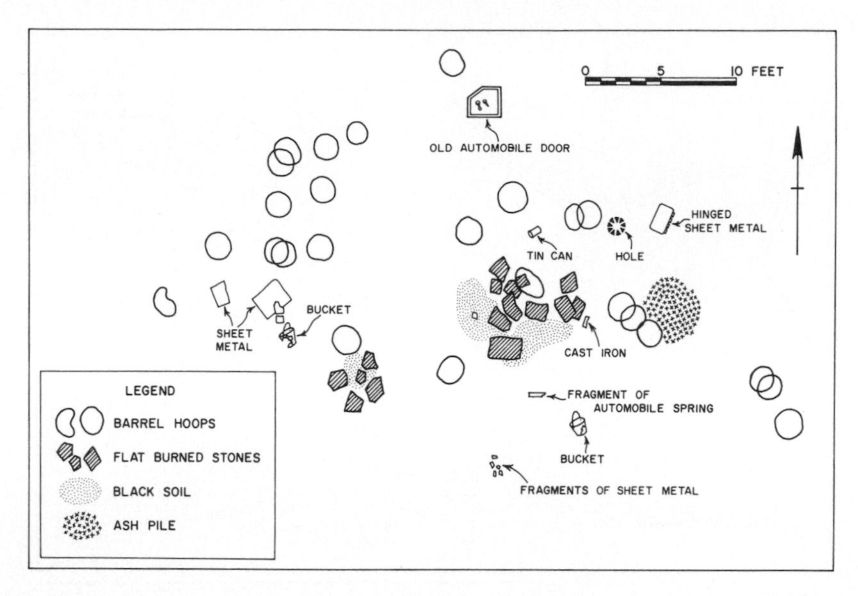

Figure 9.5. Sketch map of a moonshine-still site (23BU-H13) in the Little Black River watershed, Missouri.

CONSTRUCTING AND USING REGIONAL RESEARCH DESIGNS: AN ESSAY IN TECHNIQUE, METHOD, AND THEORY

The surveys discussed were carried out by persons whose primary research interests are in anthropology and North American prehistory. Though our prior familiarity with both history and historic artifacts varied widely, the research was a learning process and a challenge to all. We had to strive to learn to recognize early historic features and artifacts in the field and to integrate documentary and archeological data. We did, however, find our archeological survey skills and regional perspectives, developed in prehistoric research, to be quite useful and productive of insights into the cultural systems of the historic past as well.

We found that the use of a metal detector, however disreputable because of its employment by collectors and treasure hunters in search of the elusive minié ball, is a valuable remote sensing tool, particularly in woods and other areas of poor ground-surface visibility. Suspected site locations in the Little Black River watershed were often recognized by the presence of flat slabs of rock as possible foundation stones, ancient fruit trees, or the proximity of a stone spring box at the foot of a hill or terrace. Use of the metal detector served to confirm or disconfirm this suspicion quickly. Usually, collecting about six metal artifacts served to indicate the general time period of the occupation of the site. We considered it unwarranted to exploit the archeological record further during the initial survey phase by collecting more buried artifacts than necessary.

On both the Little Black River and Poinsett watershed surveys, "ethnographic" data from local residents proved important. The oral tradition is often a more complete source of information on specific events within roughly the last century than are any documentary sources. This is not to advocate the "ethnographic fallacy"—the oral tradition can be spectacularly erroneous—but to acknowledge that local informants can be a source of important leads and can provide many shortcuts to relevant archeological and documentary information (Vansina 1965).

In addition to the sticky problems of choosing the best regional sampling strategy, data collection was further complicated by the cultural resource management context of most archeological surveys. Though sampling is often incorporated at one level or another in environmental impact surveys and similar programs, one is usually constrained to gather data only within the direct—or, at most, the indirect—impact zones of land modification projects. These portions of space usually do not correspond to the ideal research universe for investigation of a given problem. The location of impact zones is usually biased in relation to environmental variables in a region. Albert Goodyear and Neal Ackerly (personal communication) are experimenting with techniques for measuring this bias. They are comparing values of specified environmental variables for the set of impact zones with a corresponding set of values for a randomized set of points in the same region. Thus the bias in nonprobabilistic sampling can be at least measured and perhaps compensated for in future surveys in the same region.

The process of identifying significant research problems in the historic past, constructing relevant models and hypotheses, and using these models and hypotheses in regional research designs has barely begun in the central Mississippi valley area. Smith (1973) and Smith and Davidson (1975) have cited the potential of the archeological sites of abandoned county seat towns in understanding the development of frontier society in northeast Arkansas. Morse (1975:194) has suggested the possibility that historic site data from the Cache River basin might prove useful in understanding the role of local environmental conditions and climatic change as early historic period settlement determinants. In various places in the Little Black River watershed survey report, Price *et al.* (1975) have suggested historical and anthropological problems for which survey data from the watershed might be relevant.

The development of regional models for use in the investigation of historic sites has also begun elsewhere in the Southeast. Smith (1975:10–11) has recommended the development of a community-study model for the Castalian Springs area in middle Tennessee, using archeological data both as a means of supplementing the written record and as an independent form of analysis. Smith sees the development of this model as a "long range objective based on the interpretation of numerous sites representing as many as possible of the activities peculiar to a given community [1975:10–11]." He hypothesizes that in the Tennessee central basin, the nineteenth century community is to be found at the level of the county. Smith has further observed (personal communication) that historical archeologists may have an advantage over prehistoric archeologists in that they need not necessarily define their research universe on purely archeological or environmental criteria.

Another regional model requiring both historical and archeological data in its testing is presented by Kenneth Lewis in another chapter of this volume. Lewis' archeological investigations in conjunction with the frontier model have so far been confined to the colonial frontier town of Camden, South Carolina. It will be noted that the implications of the model proposed by Lewis also require collection of data pertinent to the totality of contemporary sites in the surrounding region. Lewis' model of the colonial frontier in South Carolina is based in part on general models of stages in frontier development proposed by Dawson (1934), Casagrande *et al.* (1964), and others. These models would be particularly relevant to the formulation of archeologically testable hypotheses about the dynamics of frontier development in the central Mississippi valley area and elsewhere in North America.

The inferences and hypotheses presented in this discussion of the three archeological surveys obviously do not revolutionize our knowledge of the historic past in the central Mississippi valley area. I regard these inferences as part of a cumulative process: exploring the data base, recognizing meaningful patterns, and building testable models and hypotheses relevant to historical archeology in the regions involved. Hopefully, this process will continue and in the future we will work with better-formulated research questions and better definition of the methods and data classes—both archeological and documentary—pertinent to their solution.

CONCLUSION

Robert Ascher (1974:10–11) has predicted that a major change will take place in the restudy of America's past. Citing Lemisch's (1970:29) contention that the history of the powerless, inarticulate, and poor has yet to be written, Ascher suggests that historical archeology can become the "archeology of the inarticulate," a major source of information on the lives of those who left few or no written records of their experiences.

Realizing this goal, whether under a humanist paradigm, such as that advocated by Ascher, or a nomothetic, cultural evolutionary paradigm, such as that advocated by South (1977), will require viewing the archeological record, in a sense, independently of the historical record. The approach of confining archeological data collection and analysis to sites and phenomena named in the written record, relegating archeology to the role of an adjunct or "handmaiden" to historical research, has aptly been called "pseudo-history" by South (1977).

It is obvious that our increasing involvement with regional data bases is as much a response to the "crisis in American archeology" as to any paradigm change within the discipline. It is appropriate, nevertheless, that we view these regional data bases as including potentially significant undocumented historic sites, the archeological record of groups of people and kinds of behavior that are represented only very indirectly—or not at all—in the written record. It is yet too early to affirm the potential of such an approach. Perhaps it will only confirm what we already think we know about the historic past. But present indications are that these regional data will contribute to scientific explanations of events and processes in our historic past—and perhaps present us with some surprises as well.

ACKNOWLEDGMENTS

This chapter is an expanded and revised version of a paper entitled "Regional Data in Historical Archeology: Examples from Environmental Impact Surveys," presented at the symposium "The Methodological Frontier in Historical Archeology" at the Conference on Historic Site Archaeology, Gainesville, Florida, November 6, 1975. Three of my colleagues at the Institute of Archeology and Anthropology—Susan Jackson, Kenneth Lewis, and Stanley South—critiqued the present chapter and offered valuable suggestions. Darby Erd, the Institute artist, prepared the figures. Michael B. Schiffer also offered useful criticisms. I am especially grateful to James and Cynthia Price, without whose help this chapter could not have been written. Most of all, I want to thank Samuel D. Smith for his continued interest, advice, and help throughout the writing of this chapter and for his having first awakened me to the potential of historic site data for social science research when we were both doing archeology in northeast Arkansas in 1973–1974.

REFERENCES

Ascher, Robert
1974 Tin can archaeology. *Historical Archaeology* **8**:5–16.

Ascher, Robert, and Charles H. Fairbanks
1971 Excavation of a slave cabin: Georgia, U.S.A. *Historical Archaeology* **5**:3–17.
Binford, Lewis R.
1964 A consideration of archaeological research design. *American Antiquity* **29**:425–441.
1965 Archaeological systematics and the study of culture process. *American Antiquity* **31**:203–210.
1972 "Evolution and horizon as revealed in ceramic analysis in historical archaeology"—A step toward the development of archaeological science. *Conference on Historic Site Archaeology Papers* **6**:1–7, 126.
Bloch, Marc
1953 *The historian's craft.* New York: Knopf.
Bowen, Joanne
1975 Probate inventories: An evaluation from the perspective of zooarchaeology and agricultural history at the Mott Farm. *Historical Archaeology* **9**:11–25.
Casagrande, Joseph B., Stephen I. Thompson, and Philip D. Young
1964 Colonization as a research frontier. In *Process and pattern in culture, essays in honor of Julian H. Steward,* edited by Robert A. Manners. Chicago: Aldine. Pp. 281–353.
Collingwood, R. G.
1946 *The idea of history.* New York: Oxford Univ. Press.
Dawson, C. A.
1934 The settlement of the Peace River Country, a study of a pioneer area. In *Canadian frontiers of settlement* Vol. 6, edited by W. A. Mackintosh and W. L. G. Joerg. Toronto: MacMillan.
Deetz, James
1971 Late man in North America: Archaeology of European Americans. In *Man's imprint from the past: Readings in the methods of archeology,* edited by James Deetz. Boston: Little Brown.
Fehon, Jacqueline R.
1975 Environmental setting. In The Cache River Archeological Project: An experiment in contract archeology, assembled by Michael B. Schiffer and John H. House. *Arkansas Archeological Survey Research Series* **8**:17–28.
Ferguson, John L., and J. H. Atkinson
1966 *Historic Arkansas.* Little Rock: Arkansas History Commission.
Fisk, Harold N.
1944 Geological investigation of the alluvial valley of the Lower Mississippi River. *U.S. Army Corps of Engineers, Mississippi River Commission,* Vicksburg.
Goodspeed Brothers Publishing Co.
1889 *Biographical and historical memoirs of northeast Arkansas.* Chicago: Goodspeed Brothers.
Gumerman, George J.
1973 The reconciliation of theory and method in archaeology. In *Research and theory in current archaeology,* edited by Charles L. Redman. New York: Wiley. Pp. 289–299.
Haggett, Peter
1966 *Locational analysis in human geography.* New York: St. Martin's Press.
Holder, Virgil Howard
1966 Historical geography of the lower White River. Unpublished M.A. thesis, Univ. of Arkansas, Fayetteville.
House, John H.
1975a A preliminary archeological field study of twelve structure areas in the Soil Conservation Service Poinsett Watershed Project. Manuscript on deposit at the Arkansas Archeological Survey, Fayetteville.
1975b Summary of archeological knowledge updated with newly gathered survey data.

In The Cache River Archeological Project: An experiment in contract archeology, assembled by Michael B. Schiffer and John H. House. *Arkansas Archeological Survey Research Series* **8:**153–162.

Johnson, Gregory Alan
1973 Local exchange and early state development in southwestern Iran. *Anthropological Papers of the Museum of Anthropology, University of Michigan* **51.**

King, Thomas F.
1971 A conflict of values in American archaeology. *American Antiquity* **36:**255–262.

Klein, Joel I.
1973 Models and hypothesis testing in historical archaeology. *Historical Archaeology* **7:**68–77.

Lemisch, J.
1970 The American Revolution seen from the bottom up. In *Towards a new past: Dissenting essays in American History,* edited by B. J. Bernstein. London: Catto and Windus. Pp. 3–45.

Lewis, Barry R.
1974 Mississippian exploitative strategies, a southeast Missouri example. *Missouri Archaeological Society Research Series* **11.**

Lipe, William D.
1974 A conservation model for American archaeology. *The Kiva* **39:**213–245.

Morse, Dan F.
1969 Introducing northeastern Arkansas prehistory. *The Arkansas Archeologist* **10**(1–3):12–28.
1975 Research potential in terms of questions of regional prehistory. In The Cache River Archeological Project: An experiment in contract archeology, assembled by Michael B. Schiffer and John H. House. *Arkansas Archeological Survey Research Series* **8:**187–198.

Mueller, James W. (editor)
1975 *Sampling in archaeology.* Tucson: Univ. of Arizona Press.

Price, James E., Cynthia R. Price, John Cottier, Suzanne Harris, and John House
1975 An assessment of the cultural resources of the Little Black Watershed. Division of American Archaeology, Univ. of Missouri, Columbia.

Schiffer, Michael B.
1975a Archeological research and contract archeology. In The Cache River Archeological Project: An experiment in contract archeology, assembled by Michael B. Schiffer and John H. House. *Arkansas Archeological Survey Research Series* **8:**1–10.
1975b Cultural formation processes of the archaeological record: A general formulation. Paper presented at the Eighth Annual Meeting of the Society for Historical Archaeology, Charleston, South Carolina, January 7–11, 1975.

Schiffer, Michael B., and John H. House (assemblers)
1975 The Cache River Archeological Project: An experiment in contract archeology. *Arkansas Archeological Survey Research Series* **8.**

Schoolcraft, Henry Rowe
1853 *Scenes and adventures in the Semi-Alpine region of the Ozark Mountains of Missouri and Arkansas, which were first traversed by De Soto in 1541.* Philadelphia, Pennsylvania: Lippincott, Grambo and Company.

Smith, Samuel D.
1973 Prospectus for historic site archeology in northeast Arkansas. *Craighead County Historical Quarterly* **11**(2):7–17.
1975 Archaeological explorations at the Castalian Springs, Tennessee Historic Site. Report prepared for Tennessee Historical Commission and Tennessee Division of Archaeology.

Smith, Samuel D., and William V. Davidson

1975 County seat towns as archeological sites: Some Arkansas examples. *Conference on Historic Site Archaeology Papers* **8**:33–51.

South, Stanley

1974 Palmetto parapets: Exploratory archeology at Fort Moultrie, South Carolina, 38CH50. *Anthropological Studies* **1.** Institute of Archeology and Anthropology, Univ. of South Carolina, Columbia.

1977 *Method and theory in historical archaeology.* New York: Academic Press.

Struever, Stuart

1971 Comments on archaeological data requirements and research strategy. *American Antiquity* **36**:9–19.

Swedlund, Alan C.

1975 Population growth and settlement pattern in Franklin and Hampshire Counties, Massachusetts, 1650–1850. *Memoirs of the Society for American Archaeology* **30.**

Vansina, Jan

1965 *Oral tradition, a study in historical methodology.* Chicago: Aldine.

Williams, Harry Lee

1930 *History of Craighead County, Arkansas.* Little Rock: Parke-Harper.

Regularity and Variability in Contemporary Garbage

WILLIAM L. RATHJE
MICHAEL McCARTHY

GARBAGE ARCHEOLOGY

The Garbage Project of the University of Arizona was developed as "archeological ethnography," a new form of modern social science research. This aspect of the project has been described thoroughly elsewhere (Rathje 1974, in press a,b; Rathje and Hughes 1975). The project also has potential value to the traditional concerns of archeology—describing and analyzing patterns in the relationship between behavior and material culture in the past.

This potential is created by the fact that the Garbage Project is recording modern household refuse as it is generated in an ongoing cultural system. Archeologists in traditional arenas attempt to use material remains and their distributions to reconstruct many variables—sociodemographic characteristics, precise timing of actions, discard activities, and others—which the Garbage Project can measure more directly. Because so many different behavioral variables can be given reasonably accurate values, the Garbage Project has the potential to test and elaborate upon traditional methods of archeological interpretation.

Archeological interpretation is centered on analyzing patterns in material culture to reconstruct patterns in associated behaviors. The basis of such research is the assumption that specific patterns in behavior can be directly related to specific patterns in material culture. This assumption, which is intuitively obvious, has been tested many times and found useful (cf. Longacre and Ayres 1968, among others).

Archeological interpretation is also often based on the use of sociocultural characteristics. Such characteristics transcend simple discrete behaviors, such as patterns of purchasing detergent or canned foods. They are variables, such as family size, income, or ethnicity, that are usually seen as critical factors in producing patterns in lower level discrete behaviors. As sociocultural characteristics, family size and income can go far beyond specific numbers of people or specific rates of cash flow; they become the core of a number of behavior–material patterns, such as purchasing and consumption habits, associated with different family sizes and household incomes.

Sociocultural characteristics have been an important tool for archeologists. Their use is based on the assumption that material patterns, which can be directly documented in archeological remains, can become the key to sociocultural characteristics and from them to a number of behavior–material patterns not directly observable in the archeological record. Sociocultural characteristics are shortcuts to information on patterned behaviors. For example, archeologists have used the differential distribution of grave goods to identify degrees of social stratification. Once established, social stratification has often been employed to provide knowledge about a whole variety of behaviors—such as differential access to commodities, social status, and authority positions, as well as specific types of interpersonal behavior patterns—beyond those burial practices that have been documented archeologically.

The use of a few patterns in material remains to reconstruct sociocultural characteristics and implicitly associated behaviors raises important questions:

1. Are specific behavior–material patterns related systematically to general sociocultural characteristics such as family size, income level, and ethnic affiliation?
2. Are specific nondiscard behavior–material patterns that relate to general sociocultural characteristics still visible, after transformations, through discard practices and differential preservation, to archeological contexts?

A few preliminary answers can be formulated using Garbage Project data.

GARBAGE PROJECT DATA BASES

The Garbage Project is being conducted in the city of Tucson, an urban community of more than 360,000 inhabitants located in southern Arizona. Tucson is characterized by rapid population growth, a large proportion of Mexican American residents (27% in 1973), and a significant proportion of elderly residents (12% over age 65 in 1973).

Data Base 1 was designed as a long-term information record (cf. Rathje and Hughes 1975). Sampling procedures were based on grouping Tucson's 66 urban census tracts into seven clusters derived from 1970 federal census demographic and housing characteristics (Rathje and Gorman n.d.). Nineteen tracts were drawn to be representative of the seven census tract clusters. Within these tracts, raw data were picked up by Sanitation Division personnel from randomly selected residential units with clearly identifiable individual garbage containers. The refuse that these sample households put out for one (twice weekly) city garbage collection was the project's basic data observation unit.

Raw data were picked up within each sample census tract biweekly in 1973 from February through May and in November and December, weekly in 1974 from February through May, and weekly in 1975 from March through May and from October through December. Specific households were not followed over time; a new random selection of households was made each time refuse was collected. The total refuse studied includes garbage pickups from 223 households in 1973, 392 in 1974, 470 in 1975, and forms the basis for the project's Data Base 1.

Data Base 2 was the result of a combined interview–garbage collection project conducted by the Garbage Project and the University of Arizona Medical School (cf. Harrison n.d.). Three sample tracts were selected to represent variability in income and ethnic distribution: (1) Tract 11, a low-income Mexican American neighborhood; (2) Tract 38, a moderately low income mixed Mexican American and Anglo neighborhood; and (3) Tract 40.05, a middle-income Anglo neighborhood (Table 10.1). A set of 73 households was drawn to give approximately a 1.4% proportional representation of residential units in each tract. The households in the set were randomly selected from a list of all households in the tracts that had individual refuse collection. Between late 1974 and early 1975, garbage was picked up and analyzed from each of the 73 sample households for a period of 5 weeks.

TABLE 10.1
Income, Ethnicity, and Family Size Distributions, Data Base 2 Sample Households

Census tract number	Number of sample households	Ethnic background of head of household[a]			Number of households below $10,000 total income in the 12 months preceding study[a]	Average number of persons in sample households
		Anglo	Mexican American	Other		
11	16		16 (100%)		12 (75%)	4.3
38	25	7(29%)	17 (67%)	1 (4%)	15 (60%)	4.0
40.05	32	31 (97%)		1 (3%)	5 (15.6%)	3.6

[a] Percentages of all households in tract given in parentheses.

TABLE 10.2

Garbage Item Code List (F-75)

Item	Code	Item	Code	Item	Code
Meat—beef only*	001	Gelatin	062	Pipe, Chewing Tobacco, Loose Tobacco	127
Meat—other*	002	Instant Breakfast	063	Rolling Papers	128
Poultry—chicken only	003	Dips (for chips)	064	Household Cleaners (also laundry)*	131
Poultry—other	004	*Nondairy* Creamers + Whips	065	Household Cleaning *Tools* (not detergents)	132
Fish—(fresh, frozen, canned, dried)*	005	Health Foods*	066	Household Maint. Items (paint, wood, etc.)	133
Crustaceans + Mollusks (shrimp, clams, etc.)	006	Slop*	069	Cooking-Serving Aids	134
T.V.P. Type Foods*	007	Regular Coffee (instant or ground)*	070	Tissue Container	135
Cheese (including cottage cheese)	010	Decaf Coffee	071	Toilet Paper Container	136
Milk*	011	Exotic Coffee*	072	Napkin Container	137
Ice Cream (also ice milk, sherbet, popsicles)*	012	Tea*	073	Paper Towel Container	138
Other Dairy (*not* butter)	013	Chocolate Drink Mix or Topping	074	Plastic Wrap Container	139
Eggs (regular, powdered, liquid)*	014	Fruit (or veg.) Juice (canned or bottled)	075	Bags (paper or plastic)*	140
Beans (*not* green beans)*	015	Fruit Juice Concentrate	076	Bag Container	141
Nuts	016	Fruit Juice Powder (Tang, Kool-Aid)	077	Aluminum Foil Sheets	142
Peanut butter	017	Diet Soda	078	Aluminum Foil Package	143
Fats: Saturated*	018	Regular Soda	079	Wax Paper Package	144
Fats: Unsaturated*	019	Cocktail Mix (carbonated)	080	Mechanical Appliance (tools)	147
Corn (also corn meal and masa)*	022	Cocktail Mix (non-carb. liquid)	081	Electrical Appliance and Items	148
Flour (also pancake mix)*	023	Cocktail Mix (powdered)	082	Auto Supplies	149
Rice*	024	Premixed Cocktails (alcoholic)	083	Furniture	150
Other Grain (barley, wheat germ, etc.)	025	Spirits (booze)	084	Clothing: Child*	151
Noodles (pasta)	026	Wine (still + sparkling)	085	Clothing: Adult*	152
White Bread	027	Beer*	086	Clothing Care Items (shoe polish, thread)	153
Dark Bread	028	Baby Food + Juice*	087	Dry Cleaning (laundry also)	154
Tortillas*	029	Baby Cereal (pablum)	088	Pet Maintenance (litter)	155
		Baby Formula (liquid)*	089		
		Baby Formula (powdered)*	090		

Item	Code
Dry Cereals:	
Regular	030
High Sugar (first or second ingredient)	031
Cooked Cereals (instant or regular)	032
Crackers	033
Chips (also pretzels)	034
Fresh Vegetables▲	041
Canned Vegetables (dehydrated also)▲	042
Frozen Vegetables	043
Potato *Peel*▲	044
Fresh Fruit▲	045
Canned Fruit (dehydrated also)▲	046
Frozen Fruit▲	047
Fruit *Peel*▲	048
Condiments (relish, pickles, olives, vinegar, etc.)	049
Syrup, Honey, Jellies, Molasses	051
Pastries (cookies, cakes and mix, pies etc.)*	052
Sugar*	053
Artificial Sweetners	054
Candy*	055
Salt*	056
Spices (solid or powdered)	057
Baking Additives (yeast, baking powder, etc.)	058
Pudding	061

Item	Code
Pet Food (dry)	091
Pet Food (canned or moist)	092
TV Dinners (also pot pies)	094
Take Out Meals	095
Soups*	096
Sauces*	097
Prepared Meals (canned or packaged)*	098
Vitamin Pills and Supplements (commercial)*	100
Prescribed Drugs (prescribed vitamins)	101
Commercial Drugs:	
Aspirin (also acetaminophen)	102
Stimulants and Depressants*	103
Remedies (physical)*	104
Illicit Drugs*	105
Commercial Drug Paraphernalia	106
Illict Drug Paraphernalia	107
Contraceptives:	
Male	108
Female	109
Baby Supplies (diapers etc.)*	111
Injury Oriented (iodine, bandages etc.)	112
Personal Sanitation*	113
Cosmetics*	114
Cigarettes (pack)*	124
Cigarettes (carton)*	125
Cigars	126

Item	Code
Pet Toys	156
Gate Receipts (tickets)	157
Hobby Related Items	158
Photo Supplies	159
Holiday Value (nonfood)*	160
Decorations (non-holiday)	161
Plant and Yard Maint.	162
Stationery Supplies	163
Jewelry	164
Child School Related Papers*	171
Child Educ. Books (non-fiction)	172
Child Educ. Games (toys)	173
Child Amusement Reading	174
Child Amusement Toys (games)	175
Adult Books (non-fiction)	176
Adult Books (fiction)	177
Adult Amusement Games	178
Local Newspapers*	181
Newspapers (other city, national)*	182
Organizational Newspapers or Magazines (also religion)*	183
General Interest Magazines*	184
Special Interest Magazine or Newspaper*	185
Entertainment Guide (TV guide etc.)	186
Miscellaneous Items (specify on back of sheet)*	190

* See special notes (Rathje and Hughes 1975).
▲ See Fruit and Vegetable (Rathje and Hughes 1975).

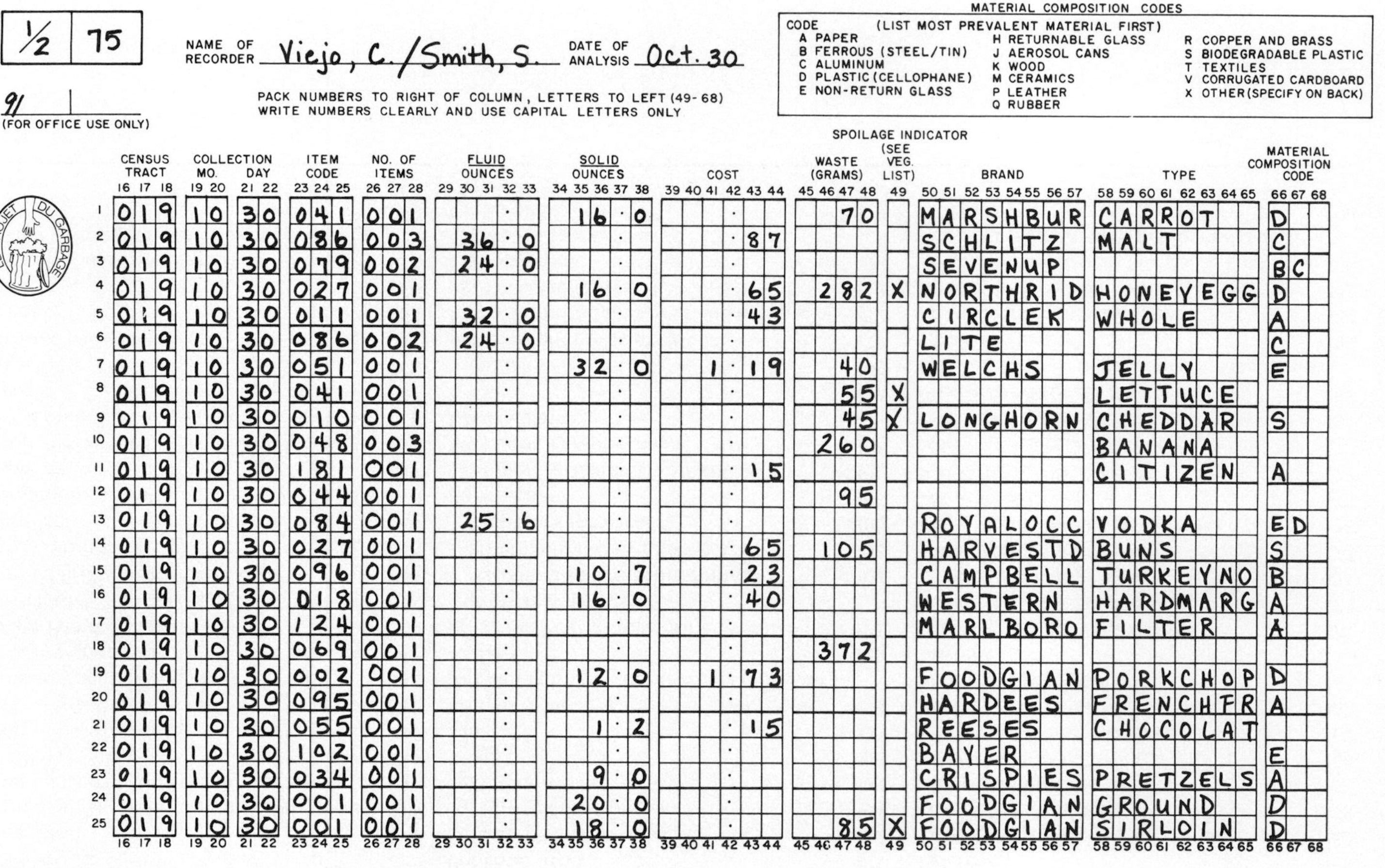

1/2	75

91 |
(FOR OFFICE USE ONLY)

NAME OF RECORDER Viejo, C./Smith, S. DATE OF ANALYSIS Oct. 30

PACK NUMBERS TO RIGHT OF COLUMN, LETTERS TO LEFT (49-68)
WRITE NUMBERS CLEARLY AND USE CAPITAL LETTERS ONLY

MATERIAL COMPOSITION CODES

CODE (LIST MOST PREVALENT MATERIAL FIRST)

A PAPER	H RETURNABLE GLASS	R COPPER AND BRASS
B FERROUS (STEEL/TIN)	J AEROSOL CANS	S BIODEGRADABLE PLASTIC
C ALUMINUM	K WOOD	T TEXTILES
D PLASTIC (CELLOPHANE)	M CERAMICS	V CORRUGATED CARDBOARD
E NON-RETURN GLASS	P LEATHER	X OTHER (SPECIFY ON BACK)
	Q RUBBER	

	CENSUS TRACT 16 17 18	COLLECTION MO. 19 20	DAY 21 22	ITEM CODE 23 24 25	NO. OF ITEMS 26 27 28	FLUID OUNCES 29 30 31 32 33	SOLID OUNCES 34 35 36 37 38	COST 39 40 41 42 43 44	WASTE (GRAMS) 45 46 47 48	SPOILAGE INDICATOR (SEE VEG. LIST) 49	BRAND 50–57	TYPE 58–65	MATERIAL COMPOSITION CODE 66 67 68
1	019	10	30	041	001		16.0		70		MARSHBUR	CARROT	D
2	019	10	30	086	003	36.0		.87			SCHLITZ	MALT	C
3	019	10	30	079	002	24.0					SEVENUP		BC
4	019	10	30	027	001		16.0	.65	282	X	NORTHRID	HONEYEGG	D
5	019	10	30	011	001	32.0		.43			CIRCLEK	WHOLE	A
6	019	10	30	086	002	24.0					LITE		C
7	019	10	30	051	001		32.0	1.19	40		WELCHS	JELLY	E
8	019	10	30	041	001				55	X		LETTUCE	
9	019	10	30	010	001				45	X	LONGHORN	CHEDDAR	S
10	019	10	30	048	003				260			BANANA	
11	019	10	30	181	001			.15				CITIZEN	A
12	019	10	30	044	001				95				
13	019	10	30	084	001	25.6					ROYALOCC	VODKA	ED
14	019	10	30	027	001			.65	105		HARVESTD	BUNS	S
15	019	10	30	096	001		10.7	.23			CAMPBELL	TURKEYNO	B
16	019	10	30	018	001		16.0	.40			WESTERN	HARDMARG	A
17	019	10	30	124	001						MARLBORO	FILTER	A
18	019	10	30	069	001				372				
19	019	10	30	002	001		12.0	1.73			FOODGIAN	PORKCHOP	D
20	019	10	30	095	001						HARDEES	FRENCHFR	A
21	019	10	30	055	001		1.2	.15			REESES	CHOCOLAT	
22	019	10	30	102	001						BAYER		E
23	019	10	30	034	001		9.0				CRISPIES	PRETZELS	A
24	019	10	30	001	001		20.0				FOODGIAN	GROUND	D
25	019	10	30	001	001		18.0		85	X	FOODGIAN	SIRLOIN	D

Figure 10.1 Garbage Project data recording form.

An interview took place during the last 3 weeks of the refuse collection period. Its purpose was to identify specific demographic, socioeconomic, behavioral and attitudinal characteristics associated with variability in the remnants of specific household-resource-management strategies. The interview schedule was standardized in both English and Spanish, and the single interviewer utilized was bilingual.

To make sure that no bias affected household discard patterns, households were not informed that their garbage was being analyzed. To ensure household anonymity, stringent safeguards were developed with the University of Arizona's Human Subjects Committee and the Tucson Sanitation Division. The information contained in detailed interviews and 551 garbage pickups from the 73 sample households is Data Base 2.

Since 1973 more than 300 student volunteers sorted, coded, and recorded all the items contained in the household garbage samples from both data bases. After sorting and recording, all items in the refuse were returned to the Sanitation Division for deposit in a sanitary landfill. Addresses and other personal information were not recorded in order to protect the privacy and anonymity of sample households. Student workers were provided with lab coats, surgical masks, and gloves and were given appropriate immunizations.

Items found in the refuse were sorted into more than 150 initial categories representing food, drugs, personal and household sanitation products, amusement and education items, communications media, and pet-related materials (Table 10.2). For each item the following information was recorded on precoded forms: (1) item identification category, (2) subcategory or type (for example, ground chuck as a type of beef), (3) original weight or volume (derived from package labeling), (4) cost, (5) brand, (6) material composition of containers, and (7) weight of any discarded once-edible food in grams (Figure 10.1). This detailed description of individual samples collected over a 3-year period forms the Garbage Project's Data Base 1 and Data Base 2.

TESTING A BEHAVIOR–MATERIAL CULTURE ASSUMPTION

The basic assumption that patterns in specific types of behavior have clear sociocultural correlates can be evaluated in a preliminary way with garbage data bases. A beginning is provided by 1973 Data Base 1 records and interview-survey data collected independently (by Project ECHO, Pima County Health Department) in the same sample areas. A comparison of these data tentatively identified a consistent relationship across census tracts between material culture and verbal behavior, specifically between interview elicitations about beer consumption and discarded beer containers (cf. Rathje in press a). The relationship was not a direct correspondence, but it was highly patterned. Garbage records of quantifiable containers showed significantly heavier beer consumption, in the form of more drinkers and higher rates of drinking, than was reported to interviewers. Thus, specific patterns in verbal behavior were found to be systematically related to specific patterns in material culture.

A second analysis, using Data Base 2 records, both interview and garbage, was able to go one step further and relate the patterning in material culture and verbal behavior to sociocultural characteristics. In the 73-household sample, all middle-income Anglo respondents provided reasonably accurate information on whether or not they consumed beer. This was not the case, however, in the lower-income tracts. In 22 households, respondents reported that they never purchased beer; however, over a 5-week period, the refuse of 18 households (or 82%) included discarded containers representing quantities that ranged from a low of five 12-oz cans to a high of 3½ cases (cf. Rathje in press b).

From these data, it was proposed that low-income Mexican American household respondents, in contrast to middle-income Anglo respondents, tend to distort their beer purchase–consumption behavior significantly by reporting no consumption at all, rather than by misrepresenting quantities involved. Material culture, behavior, and sociocultural characteristics are tied together by this proposition. If it holds true, sociocultural variables can be reasonably predicted for households in Tucson from the type of distortion identified between verbal behaviors and the material culture related to beer purchase and consumption.

Although relevant to theoretical considerations, this example is of limited practical value to archeologists because it requires reconstruction of verbal behavior. An example using purchases of household detergents may be more useful.

Example 1: Detergents

Data Base 2 household discard records over a 5-week period show clear patterns in the type and size of laundry detergent packages discarded in different census tracts. This patterning is assumed to relate directly to consumer purchasing behavior—but do patterns in material items also relate systematically to variability in sociocultural characteristics (such as family size and income) beyond specific purchase behaviors? The answer in this case is affirmative, but with a twist.

An archeologist examining detergent-packaging data to attempt to reconstruct behaviors beyond simple purchasing might well assume two "logical" sociocultural correlates:

TABLE 10.3
Household Size and Powdered Laundry Detergent Box Sizes, Data Base 2

Box size (ounces)	Number of discards	Average number of people per discarding household
20	22	4.45
49	28	4.25
84	11	4.18
171	13	4.08

1. Box sizes would correlate directly with the number of constituents in a household—the larger the box, the more people.
2. The cost per ounce of purchased detergent would correlate with the income level of the household—the higher the cost, the larger the income—based on the need of low-income families to conserve money.

These two assumptions form a neat picture. Large, low-income families would buy large boxes of relatively cheap (not name brand) detergents; small, middle-income families would buy relatively more expensive detergents in smaller boxes. The actual data, however, are the inverse:

1. The smallest families generally bought the largest box sizes of detergent, and the largest families generally bought the smallest box sizes (Table 10.3).
2. The highest costs per ounce generally occur in the households with the lowest incomes (Table 10.4). Extrapolating to a yearly figure, we find that low-income households in Tract 11 would pay approximately $18 a year for 780 oz of laundry detergent. Middle-income households in Tract 40.05 would pay approximately $4 less for the same amount.

TABLE 10.4
Cost of Powdered Detergent by Census Tract, Data Base 2

Census tract	Percentage of households in tract below $10,000 per year income	Total detergent (ounces)	Total cost ($)	Estimated yearly consumption per household (ounces)	Estimated yearly cost per household ($)
11	75	887	21.22	780	17.94
38	60	886	19.85	1165	26.10
40.05	15.6	1025	19.25	1130	21.24

Modern social scientists have a neat explanation that resolves both these apparent ironies. Being poor is economically inefficient. This statement is based on a simple dictum: the smaller the deal the worse the terms (Gladwin 1967). Many books and articles describe the dilemma of the poor.

> Having at any one time at most only a small amount of money, and never being sure that in the immediate future enough will be available to cover even minimum needs, the poor person is forced to spend whatever he has on the most urgent demands which arise each day. . . . The size and adequacy of the purchase . . . depends on how much money can be scraped together that particular day [Gladwin 1967].

Although modern social scientists might have known what to expect in detergent-purchase data, they have not successfully quantified the costs of the actual purchasing behaviors of the poor. Interview surveys in homes and price-inventory surveys in stores have, of course, been conducted, but the data are equivocal. Because prices vary over short periods of time, from store to store and from brand to brand, price inventories document store behavior, but not the behavior of specific consumers. The validity of interview surveys depends, to a large extent, on the description of "usual" or "average" behaviors, but the variety of options involved in shopping and the external effects of price fluctuations make it difficult for informants to describe their actual behavior accurately in those terms.

None of this variability, however, affects the accuracy of garbage analysis. The data in the galvanized garbage can are unequivocal in regard to the package sizes and costs of laundry detergents actually purchased by specific households. In this example, material culture analysis seems to be a reliable method, compared to other available techniques, of reconstructing actual purchasing behavior. In addition, this behavior seems to relate to specific sociocultural characteristics of purchasing households in a patterned, though somewhat illogical, manner. It is also significant that, although general sociocultural information may be known and correlated to general patterns in behavior, the real costs and effects of patterns in actual behaviors for specific populations are best obtained from material culture analyses.

The first example of behavior–material patterning illustrated a neat correlation with sociocultural characteristics. But this is not always the case. Some behavior–material patterns do not seem to correlate with sociocultural variability. There are a number of obvious examples—when food prices went up rapidly between 1973 and 1975, food intake and edible food discards at the household level decreased for all income, ethnic, and demographic groups. There are also many less obvious behavior–material patterns that crosscut various population segments.

When prices rapidly increase on a commodity, waste of that commodity increases (cf. Rathje in press a). Data the Garbage Project collected during the 1973 beef shortage and during the dramatic price increases on sugar products in 1975 led to this proposition. They also led to a hypothesized food "waste" equation. The equation simply proposes that there is a patterned relation between food waste and variability in household food inputs (cf. Rathje in press b). Bread data provide a good example. Standard, consistent consumption items are associated with low waste rates. In the case of 16-oz and 24-oz loaves, edible discards represent less than 5% of original input volume. Irregular items, those consumed with less consistency, are wasted at higher rates. Specialty breads, such as hamburger buns, frankfurter rolls, muffins, and rolls, are wasted at a rate of 10% of their original input volume (Rathje in press b). These patterns hold regardless of census tract characteristics and can be related to more general patterns of behavior. Another example, however, is even more interesting and more unusual.

Example 2: Mobility and Shopping Patterns

Tracts 11, 38, and 40.05 are significantly different in many respects: ethnicity, income, family size, and other sociocultural characteristics (Table 10.1). This differentiation applies to material culture as well: cost of houses, brands and costs of foods, other commodity attributes, and types and locations of local stores. The tracts are also clearly separated on the basis of the ownership of cars. In Tracts 11 and 38 more than 15% of the households have no cars, compared to only 3% in Tract 40.05. In fact, well over 50% of the households in Tract 40.05 have two or more cars, whereas fewer than 30% have more than one car in Tracts 11 and 38. This difference is extremely significant in Tucson, which is spread over a 90-square-mile area and has only a vestigial mass-transit system.

When differences in potential shopper mobility are combined with all the other differences between tracts, it would seem extremely logical to expect significant differences in actual shopping behavior—middle-income car owners would shop in a variety of locations around the city, whereas lower-income, less mobile shoppers would ply local stores.

This view was tested by means of a study of 565 store receipts found in Data Base 2 household refuse from Tracts 11, 38, and 40.05. After all possible receipts were tracked to their stores of origin and the stores' locations plotted on maps, 90.3% of all sales slips (144) from Tract 11 households had been traced to local stores (located within a 3-mile radius of the center of the tract). For Tract 38, the local receipts represented a similar 87.1% of the total slips (170). Tract 40.05 produced a surprise: 218 of 251 receipts, or 86.9%, were from local stores (Deal n.d.). This variability between tracts, less than 4%, is insignificant compared to the substantial differences in most sociocultural and material attributes.

Data like these are important beyond the conclusion that not all patterns in behavior are systematically related to standard measures of population differences. Such information can be useful in understanding regularities in social systems and, in this specific case, for implementing changes in food costs for low-income households, as well as for developing marketing strategies for retailers.

Other case studies of patterned interactions are easy to find in Garbage Project files, but to most archeologists they must seem simple. Garbage case studies become much more complex when the effect of discard behaviors on nondiscard behavior–material patterning is likely to be significant and must be evaluated.

DESCRIBING THE EFFECT OF DISCARD BEHAVIORS

The archeological recognition of specific behaviors, such as procurement or production of commodities, is usually not a simple job because discard behaviors intervene. As a result, archeologists must analyze discard behaviors in order to determine if they are patterned and if their effect on nondiscard behaviors can be taken into account and nullified. Garbage Project research is relevant to this concern.

During the 1975 sampling period for Data Base 1, edible food discard ("waste") in all census tracts added up to about 12% of the volume of food input at the household level (calculated from package labeling). Without information on garbage disposal behaviors, the tracts look similar in regard to food waste behavior—but are they?

Example 3: Garbage Disposals

Even with the direct access to data that the Tucson Sanitation Division has provided to the Garbage Project, it is clear that different households dispose of food waste in different ways, based on the use of garbage disposals, fireplaces, compost piles, and gardens, and the feeding of table scraps to pets. The utility and accuracy of modern garbage analysis of food waste depend on identifying patterns in the effect of specific behaviors and material artifacts on discard.

The Garbage Project recognized this requirement early and set out to quantify patterning in the behavior–material interactions that affect the discard of edible food, especially those involving garbage disposals. As a result, one of the principal research goals of Data Base 2, the garbage–

interview program, was to record the presence of disposals and to quantify their effect on garbage data (Harrison n.d.).

The attempt to define correction values for edible food ground down disposals began with a comparison of aggregate refuse variables from households with and without garbage disposals in Tract 40.05 (Table 10.5). The comparison was limited to this tract largely because only two sample households outside this tract reported having disposals; but also because the relative homogeneity in Tract 40.05 households of a variety of material and nonmaterial attributes minimizes the chance that other behaviors affected the amount of food waste found in refuse.

There were no statistically significant differences, based on a student's *t* statistic, between the two groups of households in any of the discard categories, although there was a clear trend for discards to exhibit lower means for households with disposals than for those without. Since the trend was consistent and in the expected direction, these data were thought to be appropriate to provide a preliminary correction factor for the effect of garbage disposals on edible food waste in household garbage.

Overall, the refuse of households with disposals contains about half the estimated percentage of food input discarded in the refuse of households without disposals (Table 10.5). Different types of food are clearly affected differentially by the presence of disposals. About one quarter of "plate scrapings" are apparently consumed by garbage disposals, as are close to half of the discards of animal protein foods, fats,

TABLE 10.5
Edible Food Discard in the Refuse of Households with and without Garbage Disposals, Tract 40.05, Data Base 2

	Percentage of estimated input discarded in refuse		
Type of food	(A) Households without disposals ($n = 10$)	(B) Households with disposals ($n = 22$)	(B)/(A) as percentage
Total solid food	5.87	2.86	49.0
Selected protein foods	3.63	2.14	59.0
Grain	5.45	3.37	61.8
Fruit	3.64	2.14	58.8
Vegetables	7.49	4.03	53.8
Packaged foods	3.26	3.18	97.6
Sugar and sweets	6.84	1.52	22.2
Fats	8.90	4.03	45.3
Plate scrapings (as a percentage of solid food discard)	21.0	16.0	76.0

fruits, vegetables, and grain products and more than three quarters of sugars and sweets. There is virtually no difference in amount of trash-can evidence of waste of certain packaged foods (soups, stews, sauces) between households with and without disposals, perhaps because of a relatively low rate of discard of these products by all households and because a larger proportion of the discard of these items may go down the drain even in households without disposals.

Although it is recognized that the present sample is extremely small, a correction factor of approximately 50%, given available data, seems appropriate to use on edible food discard records at the census tract level, given information on the proportion of households in the tract with disposals. This is a critical correction factor because garbage disposals are differentially distributed within census tracts in Tucson. For example, in Tract 19, 50% of the households have working garbage disposals; in Tract 3, only 15% are so equipped. Using the hypothesized correction factor, the percentage of food input discarded as waste is no longer similar for the population segments in these two tracts. Waste in Tract 19 becomes about 16% of input by volume; waste in Tract 3 changes to just less than 13%.

Other behaviors also affect food waste in garbage cans. The maintenance of vegetable gardens and compost piles is associated with significantly lower trash-can discard of edible food. Vegetable gardens were found to correlate with a lower discard of vegetables, compost piles with a lower discard of plate scrapings (Harrison n.d.).

Obviously, disposal behaviors can mask and exaggerate differences in nondisposal behaviors; but in the cases of garbage disposals, compost piles, and vegetable gardens, they do seem to be patterned in a logical manner, each differentially minimizing certain food discards. These overall patterns can be corrected so that nondiscard behavior–material patterns can be identified. An important future problem for the Garbage Project is to identify such specific behaviors and the need to apply a specific correction factor from material correlates, independent of census and other nonmaterial information.

PRESERVATION AND PATTERNING IN THE ARCHEOLOGICAL CONTEXT

The effect of disposal behavior on artifact patterning has been considered; but what happens to the patterning that remains after items are deposited in their archeological context? If we assume that the refuse from different census tracts is deposited in different locations in the Tucson area, would useful patterning survive the process of environmental degradation?

The first step toward an answer is to estimate what effect landfill soils would have on the deposited materials. The archeological context would probably only yield metals, glass, and heavy-milled plastics. Paper products, most organic materials, and light plastics would most probably degrade within a few decades. This transformation would represent a significant loss of information. By number of items discarded, virtually 90% of all household refuse would disappear; by weight, 70 to 80% of deposited residuals would be lost (Table 10.6). The remaining residuals would still hold information—but information passed through a strong filter.

One of the most interesting effects of this filter relates to the problem of typology. It is clear that counting objects and weighing objects give totally different results. For example, compare two different census tracts: Tract 11 and Tract 40.05. Using raw data counts of objects, the refuse from the two tracts looks similar. The only major difference is the larger number of heavy-milled plastics in Tract 40.05 (Table 10.6). In addition, there seems to be a trend toward higher rates of discard in Tract 40.05 than in Tract 11. When weights are used to record objects, the picture is entirely reversed (Table 10.6). The discard rate for Tract 11 is significantly greater than the rate for Tract 40.05; heavy-milled plastics are discarded by weight at five times the rate for Tract 40.05. The specific problem that is to be studied obviously affects which measure is used; however, there is an added difficulty to be taken into consideration when using weights. Because of variability in the composition of residential wastes in different tracts, preservation affects the two tracts differentially: 30% of the refuse by weight is left for Tract 11, but only 20% for Tract 40.05.

TABLE 10.6

Composition of Average Household Refuse Pickups, Census Tracts 11 and 40.05, Data Base 1[a]

	Average number of items per household per 3½ days		Average weight (pounds) per household per 3½ days	
	Tract 11 (n = 47)	Tract 40.05 (n = 36)	Tract 11 (n = 16)	Tract 40.05 (n = 20)
Total refuse	167.57	174.05	16.23	10.09
Metal items	11.96 (7.1%)[b]	12.96 (7.4%)	1.83 (11.3%)	1.05 (10.4%)
Glass items	3.66 (2.2%)	3.90 (2.2%)	2.88 (17.7%)	1.04 (10.3%)
Heavy-milled plastics	1.22 (.7%)	2.68 (1.5%)	.41 (2.5%)	.08 (.1%)
Total Nonbiodegradable refuse	16.84 (10.0%)	19.54 (11.2%)	5.17 (31.5%)	2.17 (21.8%)

[a] Fewer household refuse samples were weighed than counted. Counts are based on all sample households from spring 1973 through spring 1975. Weights were taken on a sample of households during fall 1974.

[b] Percentage of all items.

With these and other problems in mind, is it possible to retrace a relationship from material culture to behavior and finally back to sociocultural characteristics? The answer seems, once again, to be affirmative, but with another twist.

Example 4: Household Size and Food Can Sizes

A likely interpretive base for reconstructing family size can be derived from assumptions about food purchasing, preparation, and consumption behaviors. One way to define a household family unit is by the number of individuals who regularly eat meals together. Solid foods in cans do not keep well once the can is opened. Therefore, it seems reasonable that can sizes will directly reflect the number of household constituents who usually participate in meals. One obvious expectation derived from accepting these suppositions is that a greater percentage of large cans would be discarded by large family households than by small family households.

Data Base 1 records from two census tracts with large family sizes [Tracts 10 and 11, average household size of 3.8 (ECHO 1973)] and from two tracts with small families [Tracts 17 and 19, average household size of 2.0 (ECHO 1973)] were combined for a comparison. A graph contrasting the 1973 distribution of can sizes recorded by percentage of occurrence within large-family and small-family tracts suggests that the can size–family size assumption is plausible and might have general applicability (Figure 10.2). There are differences between the tracts in every size category, but the most striking is in the large-size cans. Thus, in 1973, tracts with large family households bought a significantly greater percentage of large solid-food containers than tracts with a smaller average family size.

The only difficulty with accepting this measure of relative family size is that through time the expected can size percentages steadily reverse themselves until the only difference between the two tract sets is that the small-family tracts discard a greater percentage of large cans than the large-family tracts. Thus, a reconstruction of family size based on the size of metal food-containers would be reversed and inaccurate.

One possible explanation for this pattern reversal seems to come from economic changes and the economic characteristics of households. No households in Tracts 17 and 19 were below the poverty level in 1973; more than 50% of the households in Tracts 10 and 11 were below the poverty level in 1973 (ECHO 1973). As prices rose by more than 15% between 1973 and 1975, the two population segments responded differentially, perhaps based on differences in their respective resource bases. Tract 17 and Tract 19 households seem to have responded to economic stress by buying larger cans of food, which are more expensive by the can but less expensive by the ounce; in Tracts 10 and 11, where

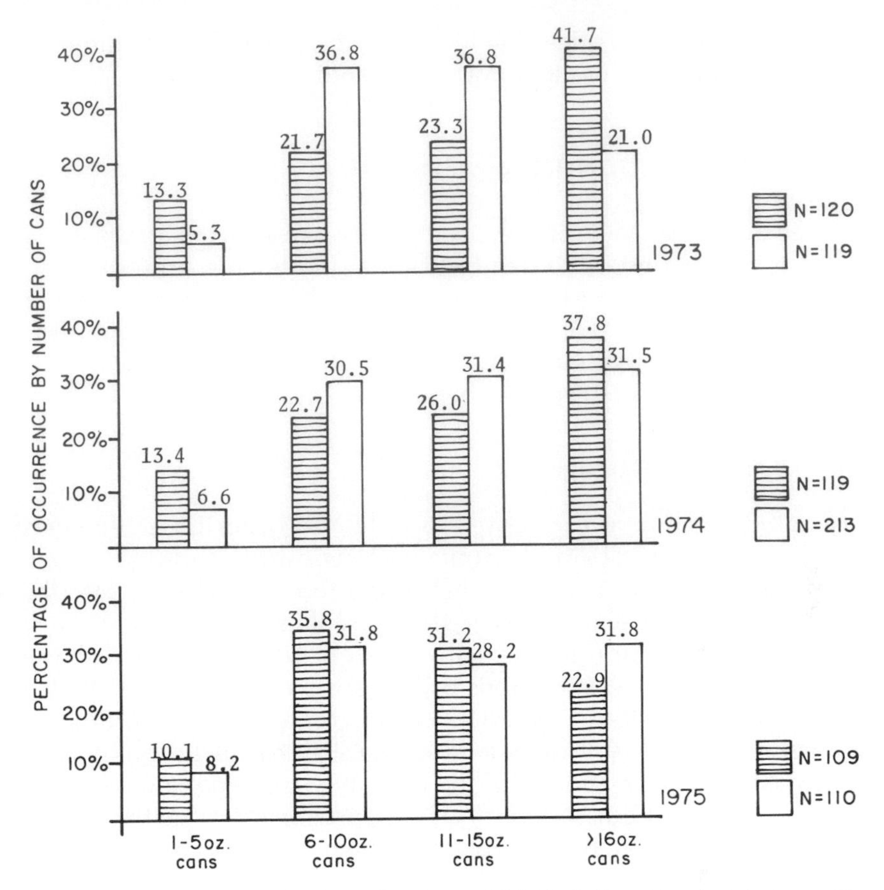

Figure 10.2. Discard of solid volume food cans 1973–1975, Data Base 1 ▤ = tracts 10 and 11. □ = tracts 17 and 19.

money was far more scarce, the response led to the purchase of smaller container sizes, which are cheaper by the can but more expensive by the ounce (see under Example 1: Detergents).

In this case (Example 4) patterned relationships are clear, but changes in general economic systems seem to have affected the forms of behavior–material patterning associated with general sociocultural characteristics. The behavior strategies associated with various sociocultural characteristics obviously change in response to different environmental situations. This factor calls into question the ability of archeologists to extrapolate specific behaviors from general sociocultural characteristics, especially if a long time-frame is involved, or for archeologists to use specific behavior sets to identify separate sociocultural characteristics at different times in a long cultural sequence. Specific behavior–material patterns are clear in archeological data; general sociocultural characteristics that consistently interrelate a number of specific behaviors may not be so easy to identify.

NEW PATTERN-RECOGNITION METHODS

It is all too easy to produce "cautionary tales" from garbage data. Therefore, it is important to demonstrate a potential to go beyond such comments and make a direct contribution to the recognition of patterns in the past. Garbage Project data can do this by providing a testing ground for new methods of archeological interpretation, which emphasize recognition of specific behavior–material patterns.

Example 5: Tin-Can Garbage

Crumpled, rusting tin cans pose a problem to historical archeologists. Some of these cans obviously contained foodstuffs; however, by the time the archeologist arrives, both the contents and labels describing them are gone. Usually the archeologist shakes his head and merely counts the cans, ignoring the subsistence-related function of these artifacts. Yet, for some time, foods in tin cans have constituted a significant portion of all foods consumed in the United States; therefore, for any inference on the subsistence base of a site that includes tin cans to be tested, the nutritive content of the cans must be approximated.

A method for producing reasonable approximations of the nutritive content once held in now empty tin cans has now been proposed (McCarthy n.d.). The method is based on repeated Monte Carlo simulations using the sizes of cans excavated from specific sites and can-content probabilities calculated from records of the national distribution of foodstuffs in standard can sizes. The end result of the Monte Carlo simulations is a range of nutritive values for the probable contents of the cans. This range represents the probable deviation of nutritive values for a local tin-can population that may be expected from the distribution of foods in standard can sizes. The data required for such estimates are relatively accessible.

Since 1904, the Census of Manufacturers and the National Canners Association Pack Statistics have published lists of how many cans of a specified foodstuff were produced in each standard can size during specified time spans. A separate matrix of the percentage of occurrence of different contents can be calculated for each standard can size at different time periods by using these national statistics.

Nutritive values for the various subclasses of standard can sizes can be calculated by relating the average weight of each foodstuff per standard can size [available from the Census of Manufacturers (Dept. of Commerce 1919) and Creuss (1948)] to the protein and caloric values of each foodstuff (cf. Bridges 1935; Creuss 1948; Locke 1911).

The actual number of cans collected from a site and placed into specific standard can sizes gives the parameters of the population whose distribution is to be simulated [for these sizes see Bridges (1935), Creuss (1948), Cameron (1950), and both the Census of Manufacturers (Dept. of Commerce 1919) and the National Canners Association Pack Statistics (1971)].

Utilizing the matrices for national frequencies of foods in cans and archeological data on the distribution of standard can sizes, a Monte Carlo simulation of the unknown distribution of foods inside a known number of standard-size cans is produced. Summary nutritive values are then calculated from the raw protein and caloric values obtained in a simulation. These values are then divided by the minimum daily requirement for calories (3000) and protein (70 gm) (National Research Council 1943). The final nutritive values represent the maximum number of days a man could subsist using only the foods contained in the tin cans.

Multiple Monte Carlo runs of the local population are conducted until a representative sample of all simulation nutritive values possible is achieved. This sample is determined when the curve produced by plotting coefficients of variation, computed for each run and preceding runs, levels off (cf. Szulc 1965:220). The end product is a range of nutritive values that reflects the variability probable when the distribution of a local population of tin cans is simulated from statistics on the national distribution of foods (McCarthy n.d.).

The assumption that national figures can accurately reflect local distributions and that therefore a reasonably close approximation of the nutritive values once held in discarded cans can be generated is central to the use of this technique. To strengthen this assertion, a test was constructed using cans of known content obtained by the Garbage Project. Nineteen units, each representing the cans recorded in Data Base 1 for a specific census tract from 1973 to 1975, formed the analysis units for the test.

Certain problems forced the use of only a portion of the canned food data. The first problem is that data recorded by Garbage Project personnel were derived directly from labels on cans. Exact content information was assured; however, this procedure made it difficult to assign standard sizes to cans, as only weight, not size of can, was recorded. The National Canners Association (1950) gives the average weight for various foodstuffs in standard can sizes. Four standard can sizes (Nos. 8z, 300, 2, and 2½) are readily discernible by weight of their contents, and the test was conducted using only these containers.

The second problem was that, after 1958, information was no longer available on the contents of soups in standard can sizes. Only cans of the

TABLE 10.7
Monte Carlo Matrix No. 1 (1968–1971)[a,b]

	Standard can sizes			
Food content	8z	2	300	2½
Vegetables	1–53	1–36	1–75	1–37
Fruit	54–99	37–62	76–100	38–100
Juice	100	63–100		

[a] Data from National Canners Association (1971).
[b] Sequentially numbered values assigned for percentage of occurrence of contents by standard can size. Thus, for the 8z can size, 53% contain vegetables, 46% contain fruit, and 1% contain juice.

four selected sizes that contained fruits, vegetables, or juices were used in the test of the simulation method.

The most recent statistics on the national distribution of canned food (1968–1970—cf. National Canners Association Pack Statistics 1971) were used to construct the Monte Carlo matrices (Tables 10.7–10.10). Totals for beans in the matrix were obtained from the specialties section of the bulletin. Protein and calorie man-day totals for known can sizes were computed by using the nutritive values calculated for each can type (Tables 10.11 and 10.12). These contents were multiplied by the occurrence of known types of food cans to form actual census tract totals;

TABLE 10.8
Monte Carlo Matrix No. 2—Vegetables (1968–1970)[a]

	Standard can sizes			
Food content	8z	2	300	2½
Asparagus	1–2	1	1–2	
Green beans	3–14		3–18	1–4
Wax beans	15–16		19–20	
Lima beans	17–18		21	
Beets	19–24		22–25	
Carrots	25–32		26–27	
Sweet corn	33–50		28–46	
Mixed vegetables	51–54		47–49	5
Peas	55–72		50–63	
Potatoes	73–74		64–66	6–11
Pumpkins			67	12–16
Sauerkraut	75–79		68–69	17–26
Spinach	80–81		70–71	27–30
Tomatoes	82–84	2–3	72–82	31–67
Beans	85–100	4–100	83–100	68–100

[a] Data from National Canners Association (1971).

TABLE 10.9
Monte Carlo Matrix No. 3—Fruit (1968–1970)[a]

	Standard can sizes			
Food content	8z	2	300	2½
Applesauce	1–54		1–20	
Apricots	55–58		21–24	1–4
Red cherries			25–26	
Cranberries	59–62		27–38	
Figs			39	
Fruit cocktail	63–74		40–64	5–17
Mixed fruit	75		65	18
Grapefruit	76		66–72	
Peaches	77–88		73–89	19–80
Pears	89–95		90–98	81–92
Pineapples	96–99	1–100		93–98
Plums			99	99–100
Sweet cherries	100		100	

[a] Data from National Canners Association (1971).

these totals were compared to totals obtained in 10 independent runs of the simulation using just food-can-size data (Tables 10.13 and 10.14).

A chi-square test [(observed − expected)^2/expected] was used to determine whether there was a significant deviation between the known population and each simulated population (Mostellar and Rourke 1973:160). In this application, the expected values were the nutritive values calculated from the known contents of the cans, whereas the observed values were the values produced by the simulation of those can sizes. Because the size of calorie man-day values was too small for the test, calorie man-day totals for all tracts had to be lumped together by simulation run to test for statistical significance. Protein man-day totals for 14 of the 19 tracts were large enough for the tests to be conducted.

TABLE 10.10
Monte Carlo Matrix No. 4—Juice (1968–1970)[a]

	Standard can sizes	
Food content	8z	2
Grapefruit		1–29
Grape and orange		30–32
Orange		33–54
Pineapple	1–100	55–72
Tomato		73–100

[a] Data from National Canners Association (1971).

TABLE 10.11

Protein (in grams) and Calories (kilocalories) for Standard Can Sizes—Vegetables

	8		2		300		2½	
	Calories	Protein	Calories	Protein	Calories	Protein	Calories	Protein
Asparagus	42	3	127	9	77	6	145	11
Green beans	46	3	139	10	84	6	158	11
Wax beans	194	12	583	38	355	23	663	43
Lima beans	194	12	583	38	355	23	663	43
Beets	60	1	181	1	110	1	205	2
Carrots	77	2	231	6	141	4	263	7
Corn	241	8	723	23	439	14	822	26
Mixed vegetables	146	8	438	23	292	14	547	26
Peas	138	6	412	18	250	11	469	21
Potatoes	265	4	795	11	483	7	904	12
Pumpkin	79		238	1	145		271	1
Sauerkraut	51	2	152	7	92	4	173	8
Spinach	54	13	159	38	97	23	181	43
Tomatoes	54	6	163	17	99	11	185	20
Beans	318	17	954	51	580	31	1085	58

The chi-square results of the calorie man-day totals indicate an accurate simulation of the known nutritive values of the Garbage Project data. All 10 calorie man-day simulations estimated the known contents of the cans within the .40 level of significance. The protein man-day simulated values, however, appeared to be somewhat suspect. Altogether, 128 of 140 simulated protein man-day values were close to actual values; only 12 values were significantly deviant from the actual values of the known samples at the .05 level (Table 10.14). Do the "successful" simula-

TABLE 10.12

Protein (in grams) and Calories (in kilocalories) for Standard Can Sizes—Fruits

	8		2		300		2½	
	Calories	Protein	Calories	Protein	Calories	Protein	Calories	Protein
Applesauce	241	1			439	1	822	2
Apricots	251	2			458	3	855	6
Cherries	198	1			362	2	677	4
Cranberries	434				791	1	1480	1
Fruit cocktail	101	1			184	2	345	3
Grapefruit	82	1			149	3	280	5
Peaches	248	2			453	3	847	6
Pears	201	1			366	2	685	4
Pineapples	265	1	624	3	483	3	904	5
Plums	253	1			424	2	793	4

TABLE 10.13
Calories Man-Days (Garbage Data 1973–1975, Data Base 1)

Actual man-days	Simulation run number	Simulated man-days	Chi-square values
87.0	1	84.7	0.06
	2	82.0	0.29
	3	85.1	0.04
	4	80.0	0.56
	5	81.6	0.33
	6	77.9	0.95
	7	81.2	0.39
	8	81.2	0.39
	9	82.4	0.24
	10	81.6	0.34

tions constitute a large enough number that confidence may be placed in the results of the protein man-day simulation? An application of the sign test will answer this question.

The sign test, a nonparametric test based on a binomial distribution, is used to determine the significance level of the distribution of a population composed of two classes of individuals. The population of results from the protein chi-square test may be divided into two classes: suc-

TABLE 10.14
Protein Man-Days (Garbage Data 1973–1975, Data Base 1)[a]

Tract	Actual man-days	Simulation run number 1	2	3	4	5	6	7	8	9	10	Runs deviant at .05 level (χ^2 test)
1	9.8	7.1	6.6	4.9	6.9	5.7	6.3	6.7	9.0	6.6	7.4	0
2	9.7	7.3	7.8	9.2	8.2	7.6	9.2	8.8	7.8	7.7	8.6	0
3	17.2	8.4	7.7	7.7	7.8	7.9	8.6	7.6	8.0	5.9	9.0	10
4	7.2	6.3	6.0	6.6	6.1	6.5	5.9	6.4	4.5	6.0	6.1	0
6	7.5	4.6	6.4	7.3	6.3	7.6	7.4	6.4	8.7	5.7	6.0	0
8	7.8	8.3	5.9	4.6	7.2	9.7	6.9	8.2	5.9	7.3	5.9	0
10	11.2	7.2	6.2	4.4	7.7	4.5	8.5	5.8	6.9	5.9	5.4	2
11	7.4	4.6	5.8	6.5	4.4	5.3	6.5	4.4	4.7	5.9	5.4	0
18	9.0	6.5	7.1	6.3	6.9	7.7	8.1	6.8	5.3	6.3	7.2	0
19	8.7	4.0	7.2	4.7	5.2	4.9	8.4	5.3	6.1	3.4	5.5	0
20	13.1	8.5	9.9	8.1	6.2	8.3	6.9	6.4	7.3	7.4	8.1	0
16	9.5	6.5	5.7	4.8	4.5	6.8	5.5	4.4	4.1	4.9	6.3	0
24	6.7	7.3	3.7	5.2	4.2	3.6	5.4	4.6	4.6	4.6	4.8	0
23	9.6	5.3	7.4	6.1	6.2	6.3	5.3	6.0	5.4	6.3	6.3	0
												12 total

[a] Tracts 7, 14, 17, 38, and 40.05 have been excluded because of inadequate man-day totals.

cessful results and deviant results. For confidence to be placed in the successes, each value should exceed the critical value set by the .05 level of significance. In distributions whose population numbers exceed 90, approximate critical values for the sign test may be found by taking the nearest integer less than that calculated by the formula: $(n - 1)/2 - k \sqrt{n + 1}$, where k equals 1.2879 for the 1% value (Beyer 1968:398). At the .01 level of significance for a population of 140 this value is 86. Since the observed number of successful chi-square values is much higher than this (128), it is relatively safe to use the approximations of protein content provided by the simulation.

Although less confidence can be placed in the protein man-day values than in the caloric man-day values, reasonable approximations of actual nutritive values can probably be achieved by using the Monte Carlo technique. The assumption that local nutritive values are significantly correlated with national nutritive values seems more reasonable.

CONCLUSIONS

These Garbage Project examples suggest answers to the two questions posed at the outset of this chapter:

1. Specific nondiscard behaviors that relate to general sociocultural characteristics are often still visible after disposal and differential preservation transformations to the archeological record.
2. Specific behavior–material patterns are often, but not always, related systematically to general sociocultural characteristics—family size, income level, and others. Where these relationships hold, however, they may be counterintuitive. In other cases, the relationship may vary radically as separate sociocultural characteristics affect behavior–material patterns in ways that mask or distort other relationships. In addition, some significant behavior–material patterns do not seem to be related to easily identified sociocultural characteristics. Only specific behavior–material patterns seem to remain relatively immutable.

In the brief examples presented in this chapter, it is as important to contrast population segments by the consumption of beer, by the costs of purchases of detergents, by edible food discard, and by differential responses in the purchase of canned foods to inflation as it is to describe the specifics of their family size, ethnicity, or income. All these data are discrete but interconnected pieces of information—basic behavior units—and should be treated as such. General "glosses," loaded with implicit behaviors, miss the variety in basic strategies that is the essence of "adaptation" in cultural systems. Useful generalizations about strategies of cultural adaptation can be built from the basic sets of data, such as empty tin cans, that archeologists excavate; they do not need to be assumed from a limited view of the potential of the archeological record.

The current goal of the Garbage Project, both as a new form of social science research in contemporary societies and as a method of refining traditional archeological interpretation, is to build models of strategies of adaptation employed by populations in different areas of Tucson from sets of discrete behavior–material patterns. These multidimensional models of adaptive behavior cannot be handed down from general sociocultural characteristics identified at the population level; they must be built from the ground up. Hopefully, Garbage Project studies will make a contribution toward supplanting the role of general sociocultural glosses within archeological interpretation with quantitative models of adaptive strategies, pieced together from the garbage of both past and present.

ACKNOWLEDGMENTS

Major portions of this research were supported by Grant AEN716371 from the RANN (Research Applied to National Needs) Division of the National Science Foundation, by the University of Arizona College of Medicine and by Biomedical Sciences Support Grant RR07002 from the National Institutes of Health. Work is continuing through grants from the Frito Lay Company and the Chevron Oil Company.

Appreciation is due to Tom Price, Director of Operations, City of Tucson; Carlos Valencia, Director of Sanitation, City of Tucson; the personnel of the Sanitation Division; the dedicated student volunteers who have made the Garbage Project possible; Dileep G. Bal, Deputy Director of the Pima County Health Department; Judy O'Hora of the Arizona Regional Medical Program; Wilson Hughes, Field Director of the Garbage Project; Gail Harrison, Nutritionist of the Garbage Project; Sherry Jernigan, Research Director of the Garbage Project; and Marvin "Swede" Johnson, A. Richard Kassander, Jr., and Raymond H. Thompson of the University of Arizona for administrative support.

REFERENCES

Beyer, William H.
1968 *CRC handbook of tables for probability and statistics.* Cleveland: Chemical Rubber Co.

Bridges, Milton A.
1935 *Food and beverage analysis.* Philadelphia: Lea and Febige.

Cameron, F. S.
1950 *Canned foods in human nutrition.* Greenwich: American Can Company.

Cruess, William V.
1948 *Commercial fruit and vegetable producers.* New York: McGraw-Hill.

Deal, Krista Chere
n.d. *Mobility and patterns of shopping in Tucson.* Ms., Arizona State Museum Library, Univ. of Arizona, Tucson.
Department of Commerce, Bureau of the Census
1919 *Census of manufacturers 1911,* Vol. II: Reports for selected industries and detail statistics for industries by states. Washington, D.C.: U.S. Government Printing Office.
E.C.H.O. (Evidence of Community Health Organization)
1973 *Pima County ECHO report: October, 1972–June, 1973.* Pima County Health Department, Tucson, Arizona.
Gladwin, Thomas
1967 *Poverty U.S.A.* New York: Little, Brown.
Harrison, Gail G.
n.d. Socio-cultural correlates of food utilization and waste in a sample of urban households. Unpublished Ph.D. dissertation, Arizona State Museum Library, Univ. of Arizona, Tucson, Arizona.
Locke, Edwin Allen
1911 *Food values: Practical tables for use in private practice and public institutions.* New York: Appleton.
Longacre, William A., and James E. Ayres
1968 Archaeological lessons from an Apache wickiup. *In New perspectives in archaeology,* edited by S. R. Binford and L. R. Binford. Chicago: Aldine. Pp. 151–159.
McCarthy, Michael
n.d. It's in the can. Ms., Arizona State Museum Library, Univ. of Arizona, Tucson.
Mosteller, Frederick, and Robert E. K. Rourke
1973 Sturdy statistics: Nonparametric and order statistics. Reading, Massachusetts: Addison-Wesley.
National Canners Association, Research Laboratories
1950 *Canned foods in human nutrition.* Washington: National Canners Association.
National Canners Association, Division of Statistics
1971 Canned food pack statistics. Washington: National Canners Association.
National Research Council
1943 Reprints and circular series, number 115. Washington, D.C.: U.S. Government Printing Office.
Rathje, William L.
1974 The Garbage Project: A new way of looking at the problems of archaeology. *Archaeology* **27**(4):236–241.
in press a In praise of archaeology: Le Projet du Garbage. In Historical Archaeology and the Importance of Material Things. *Society for Historical Archaeology, Special Publication Series* 2 (ms. 1976).
in press b Archaeological ethnography. In *Ethnoarchaeology: Tasmania to Tucson,* edited by R. A. Gould. Albuquerque: Univ. of New Mexico Press.
Rathje, William L., and Frederick J. E. Gorman
n.d. The Garbage Project: Report no. 1. Ms., Arizona State Museum Library, Univ. of Arizona, Tucson.
Rathje, William L., and Wilson W. Hughes
1975 The Garbage Project as a nonreactive approach. In *Perspectives on attitude assessment: Surveys and their alternatives,* edited by H. W. Sinaiko and L. A. Broedling. Manpower Research and Advisory Services, Smithsonian Institution, Technical Report No. 2. Washington, D.C. Pp. 151–167.
Szulc, S.
1965 *Statistical methods,* translated by C. D. T. Forrester. Oxford: Pergamon Press.

Idiosyncratic Behavior in the Manufacture of Handwrought Nails

RONALD C. CARLISLE
JOEL GUNN

This chapter has experienced a reasonably lengthy period of gestation, and the lines of inquiry channeled into it are numerous. Foremost in the minds of the authors are archeological concerns, particularly the possible discernment of idiosyncratic trait clusters within archeological assemblages. One of us (Carlisle) has chosen historical archeology as a field of primary concern for his professional training; the other has been active in the development of computer applications in the field of archeology. The prime impetus for the present study represents an amalgamation of these interests to which are appended an admiration for the craft of blacksmithing and an anthropological concern with the idiosyncratic patterns the practitioners of that art display. Gunn (1975) previously developed a methodology designed to differentiate the lithic products of individual flint knappers based upon highly personalized or idiosyncratic patterns of flake production. The process has the potential of enabling decisions to be made about the number of knappers at work within a given archeological lithic assemblage. Adovasio and Gunn (1974) have likewise searched for idiosyncratic traits discernible in coiled basketry. The present study attempts to apply a similar set of criteria to a commonly recovered artifact of historical archeological excavations, the handwrought nail.

THE MANUFACTURE OF HANDWROUGHT NAILS

Prior to the introduction of the cut nail, nails were necessarily the products of individual manufacture. The steps employed in this process varied then, as today, from blacksmith to blacksmith, but certain basic procedures can be isolated. The stock from which the nail is made is selected and heated in a forge. It is then quickly removed, placed on the flat of an anvil and struck with a hammer. By this means the shank is tapered into an elongated quadrilateral pyramid. In this process, the "point," or distal end of the nail, also achieves its distinctive morphological configuration.

The shank of a nail produced in this manner tapers on all four sides, thereby providing one of the major technological distinctions between wrought and cut nails (Nelson 1963). When the desired shape, length, and thickness are thus achieved, the nail stock is either reinserted into the forge for reheating, or the nail is separated from the nail stock by cutting on a *hardie,* a chisel-like implement the shank of which can be inserted into an aperture in the anvil appropriately termed the *hardie hole* (Jernberg 1927:11).

Upon the separation of the developing nail from the nail stock, the nail is reheated in the forge, withdrawn with tongs, and inserted into a *header* (illustrated in Schwartzkopf 1916:44). The header is a device used in the production of the head of a handwrought nail. Headers vary in complexity. Some are nothing more than holes drilled or punched through suitable lengths of iron or steel. Others may have a handle, whereas yet others may be designed to be inserted into a vise. The heated but headless nail is dropped, tip first, into the header, which itself is placed over either the hardie or the *pritchel hole* (Schwartzkopf 1916:18), the second of two apertures usually found at the rear of an anvil. If the pritchel hole is used for this purpose, the hardie can be left in place for the cutting of the next nail. The overall effect of this step is the conservation of time since the hardie need not be removed during the production of every nail. Having inserted the heated nail into the header positioned over the pritchel hole or the hardie hole, the smith flattens the proximal end of the nail by smartly striking it around its circumference. Often, if the shank of the nail is too thin, it is necessary to bend the proximal half-inch or so slightly, so the nail will not slip through the header. In this manner, a flat to slightly domed head is formed on the nail. After a few seconds, often by the time the heading process itself is completed, the nail has sufficiently cooled and contracted to enable the smith to turn the header over and tap the just-completed nail out of the heading device. Quenching in oil or water follows, and the nail is ready for use.

As is apparent from the foregoing description, the efficient production of handwrought nails is time-consuming in comparison to the mechanical production of cut or wire nails. The completion of the steps in the process results in a finished product characterized by a series of nominal and continuous attributes. It seemed likely that such attributes could be systematically measured and compared with the ultimate goal of distinguishing the work of a particular blacksmith. That this can frequently be done on a nominal basis alone seems certain. Blacksmiths themselves are often able to select their own work from among a group of objects. Such ability, however, is mercurial and runs counter to the objective verification demanded by modern scientific inquiry.

A number of questions were therefore put forth, and the following experiment was designed to investigate them. Specifically, we wished to know the following:

1. Whether the nails produced by one blacksmith are readily discernible from those produced by other blacksmiths on the basis of a number of identifiable attributes of a continuous type;
2. the nature of these attributes;
3. whether there is a critical number of attributes that enables an investigator to identify the work of one man;
4. whether the work of experienced blacksmiths varies internally more or less than that of neophyte smiths.

The last item is perhaps the most important, since it directly approaches the relationship between one's facility with a craft and one's temporal experience in it. An assumption here is that craft workers, particularly those emphasizing repetitious output of similar products, are essentially technologically conservative; once an acceptable format has been devised, efficiency in production demands a minimum of alteration in the technological steps employed. The adoption of such an approach should render to the experienced artisan's work a more compact, less statistically variable range of attribute characteristics. In the particular case at hand, the more experienced blacksmiths should produce nails of greater internal similarity than should less practiced craftsmen.

METHODOLOGY

In order to answer the questions raised, an experiment was devised in which each of five blacksmiths[1] (see also Appendix A) was shown a

[1] Finding "blacksmiths" is not as difficult as one might think. The Pittsburgh metropolitan area *Yellow Pages* retains the craft title as a separate heading with no less than six names given. The term, however, has apparently come to denote something more than the typical village smithy. Of the six listings, only one could be considered a blacksmith pure and simple. The others ran the gamut from tool steel redressers to ornamental-iron mongers employing a wide range of machines that transcend the range of tools historically employed by smiths. One such "blacksmith" offered to make our 30 nails by altering the heads of cut nails with an automatic hammer. His offer, needless to say, was refused. The best single source of blacksmiths in the traditional sense remains the craft fair or exhibition. It does not appear that many blacksmiths are anxious to lend to their craft a corporate or formally associative nature; we failed to locate any regional guild, club, or group that promoted the dissemination of blacksmithing knowledge.

"model" nail, i.e., an ideal type, which they were then asked to duplicate as closely as possible using only those techniques that might be used in a nonexperimental situation. Specifically, no external objective scales of length, width, etc., were permitted to be used. Rather, each blacksmith was requested to "eyeball" his product. Each of the five participants was asked to produce 30 nails, from a suitable stock. No control was enforced on the type of stock material employed and no time limit was placed on the production of the nails. Each smith was requested simply to duplicate the model nail to the best of his natural ability. Smiths were not permitted to reexamine the model once they had studied it; the only template for it was the mental image formed during the inspection period. The use of a model nail was considered an essential step in the project, as it ensured that each smith was not working simply with the idea of producing *a* nail but with an eye toward the production of a particular *kind* of nail. Furthermore, the model provided a standard reference point with which the work of all the smiths could be compared.

One complication in the experiment was obvious from the outset. When initially approached about the project, most of the blacksmiths seemed curious as to why we should want handwrought nails when cut nails could be purchased commercially. This necessitated a brief but factual explanation of the purpose of the project. Consequently, each blacksmith *was* aware that his products would be compared with the work of others and with the nail model. The extent to which such knowledge may have prompted each smith to attempt the achievement of an unusual degree of uniformity within his nail group is therefore difficult to assess. However, each participant was assured at the outset that we wished him to make the nails with no greater or less concern and attention than he would expend on a more pragmatic undertaking.

An additional complication involved the degree of familiarity possessed by each smith with the process of hand producing nails. Roberts[2] has written of the "conservation of technological information and skills [1971:207]" evident in many crafts. He writes,

> Expressive activities can contribute to the preservation of outmoded or obsolete technology which may still under some circumstances have "stand by" utility. It is equally clear that ordinarily this selection is not determined by some "rational" estimate of the storage needs of the cul-

[2] The authors would like to express their debt of gratitude to Professor John M. Roberts of the Anthropology Department of the University of Pittsburgh whose work on the expressive aspects of technology provided one of the motivations to undertake the present study. Although the immediate concern lies with the products of expressive behavior, ultimately it is the blacksmith himself about whom we wish to learn. Dr. Roberts' own work and his frequent conversations have gone a long way in helping to deal with this aspect of technology from an anthropological viewpoint.

> ture. Some skills and artifacts are preserved expressively, but others are not. Bowmen have been mentioned, but where are the amateur wheat cradlers [Roberts 1971:209]?

Rhetorically, one might just as easily ask, "Where are the amateur nail makers?" It is evident from our work with blacksmiths that not only may certain crafts be preserved, or lost, *in toto,* but certain segments of crafts may likewise be differentially preserved, lost, or stored in the limbo of standby utility. Nail making among the blacksmiths involved in this project definitely had only such standby utility. Only one of the blacksmiths interviewed included nail making as a regular part of his repertoire, though all were conversant with the process by which such nails had been produced historically. As a consequence, differences in years of experience among the blacksmiths must be construed to reflect differences in blacksmithing experience in general and not differences of experience in the production of nails alone. When each nail had sufficiently cooled to permit handling it was tagged with a sequential number from 1 to 30 and deposited in a paper bag labeled with the name of the blacksmith. Usually the completion of the production of a nail preceded the tagging of its immediate predecessor. Consequently, each smith was able to contrast his latest product visually with what had gone immediately before. Detailed comparisons, however, were not permitted. Information pertinent to each blacksmith, including the length of time he had practiced the craft, from whom he had studied, and whether he had made nails prior to the time of the experiment, was ascertained.

Following the completion of each set of nails, individual nails within a given set were measured, using Helios needle-nosed dial calipers. All relevant measurements and nominal evaluations were coded on a standard computer coding form.

In order to assess their idiosyncratic predictive value, 17 selected continuous attributes were submitted to stepwise discriminant function analysis and canonical analysis (Dixon 1974). For the purposes of this discussion, nomimal attributes were not considered in the statistical treatment of the data. The internal attribute consistency of each smith's work was subsequently assessed by computing the coefficient of variation demonstrated by the two most discriminatory variables obtained via stepwise discriminant function analysis.

The ultimate application of the technique discussed in this chapter must center on its reliability in discerning idiosyncratic patterns in an *artifactual* data base. To help determine this reliability, a hypothetical archeological situation was established in which the set of 150 nails was treated as though it were a provenienced set of artifacts recovered from an archeological site. A factor analysis was run on those variables dis-

Buildings

Blacksmiths	A	B	C	D	E
1	X				
2		X	X		
3				X	
4					X
5					X

Figure 11.1. Assignment schedule of blacksmiths' nails to a hypothetical five-building compound.

criminant function analysis showed to be highly idiosyncratically predictive. Factor scores for those two factors accounting for the greatest variance were then calculated and plotted. As part of the simulation, it was assumed that the entire set of nails had been collected from a site composed of a compound of five buildings. Prior to running the factor analysis described, the five smiths were arbitrarily assigned to the five buildings as though they had participated in their construction in the manner shown in Figure 11.1. Note that Blacksmith 2 was assigned to two buildings and that Building E was constructed using the nails of two blacksmiths. In this way various distributional possibilities in the factor analysis could be tested. The factor plot of the 150 nails was subsequently studied in order to ascertain its accuracy in unraveling the building-to-blacksmith assignments experimentally imposed.

Experimental Results

Stepwise discriminant function analyses are designed to augment the discriminant power of variables by multiplying each variable by a coefficient and adding a constant. The results of these calculations are displayed in Table 11.1, in which the discriminatory power of a given attribute varies directly with its *F*-value. The 10 most discriminatory variables of the 17 selected for analysis are presented in descending order of their predictive potency.

From Table 11.1 it can be seen that the number of head facets present on a nail and the length of the header wear pattern along the shank of the nail are the two most discriminatory traits isolated in the study.

Figure 11.2 presents an *F*-matrix array of the 10 most discriminatory variables entered for each of the five blacksmiths in the study. This provides an analysis of the significance level at which one smith's work

TABLE 11.1

The Ten Most Discriminatory Attributes for Assessing Idiosyncratic Patterns in Handwrought Nails.

	Attribute		
Rank	Number	Name	F-value[a]
1	12	Head facets	115.6
2	17	Header wear length	68.5
3	2	Maximum proximal width	23.2
4	24	Head thickness	15.3
5	7	Miminum head width	15.2
6	18	Number of head fissures	7.2
7	1	Overall length	4.7
8	20	Number of head sprues	4.5
9	22	Shank taper	3.1
10	4	Minimum proximal width	2.8

[a] High *F*-values corresponding to a high discriminatory capacity and are results of stepwise discriminant function analysis.

differs from that of the other four. Values in the table exceeding 2.56 are significant at the .01 level of confidence.

From Figure 11.2 it can be seen that Blacksmiths 1 and 2 are the least discriminated pair in the study. Nevertheless, their work can be discriminated at a very acceptable level of confidence and the program was able to classify all but 12 nails out of the total of 150 into the appropriate group. Figure 11.3 presents a diagramatic display of the discrimination discerned among the five blacksmiths in the study and is based only upon the two most important canonical variables listed in Table 11.1. The area encompassed by each of the circles is proportional to the range of variation demonstrated internally by each of the smiths; intersecting circles indicate areas of attribute-range overlap.

Internal attribute consistency within the production of a smith was assessed by computing the mean, standard deviation, and coefficient of

Blacksmith Number	One	Two	Three	Four
Two	11.6			
Three	86.7	70.1		
Four	31.7	18.8	34.2	
Five	14.1	36.1	67.1	35.4

Blacksmith Number

Figure 11.2. *F*-Matrix with first 10 variables entered. Critical value = 2.56; $p < .01$; $df = 10 \times 137$.

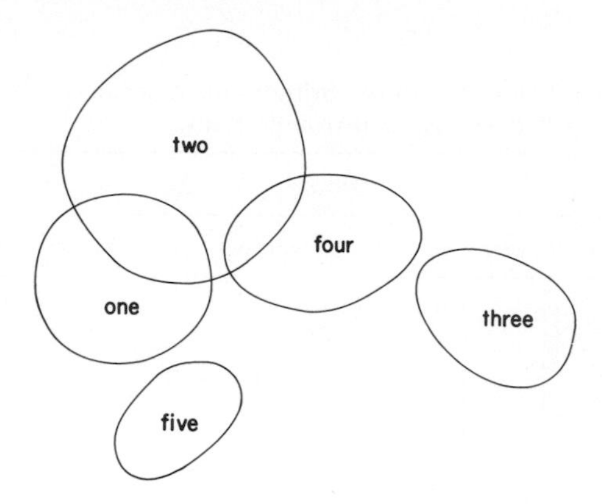

Figure 11.3. Range of variation and range of overlap of the work of five blacksmiths.

variation for the number of head facets and the maximum proximal shank width of each nail in the sample. The number of head facets was selected because of its high discriminatory capacity; maximum proximal shank width demonstrated the greatest discriminatory capacity of the simple linear measurements obtained. Table 11.2 shows the internal attribute consistency ordering obtained from this procedure.

Note that Blacksmith 5 is the most internally consistent in both attribute categories and that Blacksmith 1 is the second most consistent. Blacksmiths 2, 3, and 4 show differential degrees of internal consistency in the two attribute categories. Summing the consistency ratings for

TABLE 11.2

Internal Attribute Consistency Ordering of Blacksmiths Based on Coefficient of Variation Calculations for Number of Head Facets and Maximum Proximal Shank Width

Blacksmith	Arithmetic mean	Population standard deviation	Coefficient of variation	Consistency rating
		Number of head facets		
1	19.5	5.2	.27	2
2	14.3	4.8	.34	3
3	2.0	1.2	.60	4
4	5.6	3.4	.61	5
5	18.8	3.9	.21	1
		Maximum proximal shank width		
1	6.0	.47	.08	2
2	6.0	.59	.10	4
3	3.9	.74	.19	5
4	5.4	.49	.09	3
5	5.6	.17	.03	1

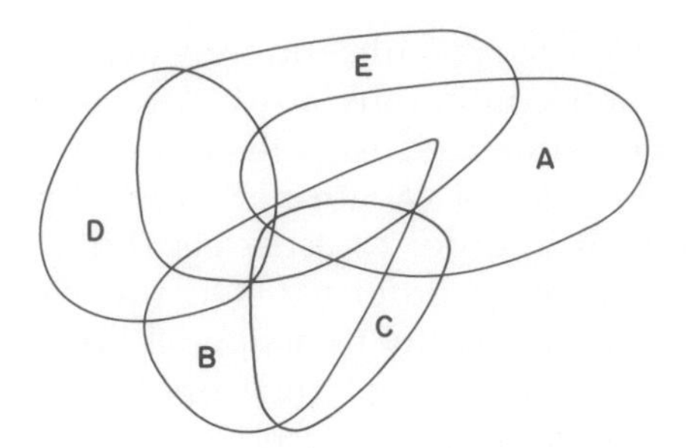

Figure 11.4. Factor analysis plots of the two most discriminatory variables in the study. Extreme outliers not encompassed.

these three men, however, shows that Blacksmith 3 is the least internally consistent.

Figure 11.4 shows the results obtained from plotting factor scores of the first two factors, which account for most of the variance within the data. Initially the plot appears to be somewhat confusing; closer inspection, however, clearly shows certain recognizable patterns. Hypothetical Buildings A and D occupy discrete sections of the distribution, a fact that could be interpreted as the result of employing the products of entirely different blacksmiths. Additionally, Buildings B and C show significant distributional overlap. This could be interpreted as reflecting a situation in which the products of one smith were used in separate buildings. A check of Figure 11.1 shows that in both these cases the factor analysis has successfully "diagnosed" the simulated construction schedule.

A much different picture emerges in the case of Building E, however. It shows considerable overlap with Buildings A (Blacksmith 1) and D (Blacksmith 3) and to a somewhat lesser extent with Buildings B and C (Blacksmith 2). A correct assessment of the blacksmith-to-building relationship in the case of Building E based on factor analysis *alone* would consequently be problematical, since the most likely conclusion would be that the structure had been built by Blacksmiths 1 and 3 with some assistance from Blacksmith 2, a conclusion known in this case to be erroneous.

SUMMARY

This study has attempted to develop a methodology for the extraction of culturally relevant data from a little-studied artifact of many historical period sites, the handwrought nail. To this end, an experimental project was undertaken in which each of five blacksmiths was asked to produce a series of 30 handwrought nails to the approximate specifications embodied in a type nail that each smith was permitted to study. The resultant sample of 150 nails was subsequently evaluated on the basis of a total of 26 nominal and continuous attributes. Seventeen of these (all continuous) were then subjected to statistical tests to assess both their internal and external ranges of variation. Stepwise discriminant function analysis was first applied in order to ascertain those attributes possessed of the highest discriminatory potential. On the basis of these results, further work resulted in the ability to assign all but 12 of the 150 nails to their manufacturer. Computation of the coefficient of variation of two key attributes makes it possible to assess the relative standing of one blacksmith to another in terms of internal attribute consistency. Finally, a simulated archeological situation was established and tested with the object of linking a building construction schedule to a blacksmith schedule by means of predictions based on assessed idiosyncratic variables. In regard to the last, it should be noted that in two of the three cases tested, experimental predictions yielded results that enabled correct conclusions regarding blacksmith-to-building schedules to be drawn. In the third case, no direct relationship could be accurately discerned solely on the basis of observed idiosyncratic patterns.

In regard to the four specific questions put forth at the beginning of this chapter, it appears that idiosyncratic patterns *are* discernible experimentally in handwrought nails and that idiosyncratic patterns may be assessed by an examination of a series of continuous attributes. Further, it appears that accurate idiosyncratic patterns can be determined by canonical variables among which the number of head facets displays a commanding discriminatory power. In this regard, the number of head facets on a handwrought nail stands in an analogous situation to the number of chipping facets present on chipped lithic artifacts (Gunn 1975). The visual variation in the nail heads from the five blacksmiths can be seen in Figure 11.5.

It also appears that there is a direct correlation between attribute regularity and the length of time a blacksmith has practiced the art of handwrought nail manufacture. An examination of Figure 11.3 is revealing in this regard. Blacksmith 2 displays the greatest range of attribute variation, whereas Blacksmith 5 displays the least. This observation is fully consistent with the fact that they are respectively the least experienced and the most experienced of the five blacksmiths involved in the project. It should also be noted that Blacksmith 3, an experienced metal redresser but one not thoroughly accustomed to nail making, demonstrated a small range of attribute variation even though from Figure 11.3 it is apparent that at least in regard to the two highly discriminatory variables considered he is the least consistent of the five smiths. The extent to which Blacksmith 3's departure from "normal" nail making procedures as outlined in Appendix B may help to account for this dichotomy.

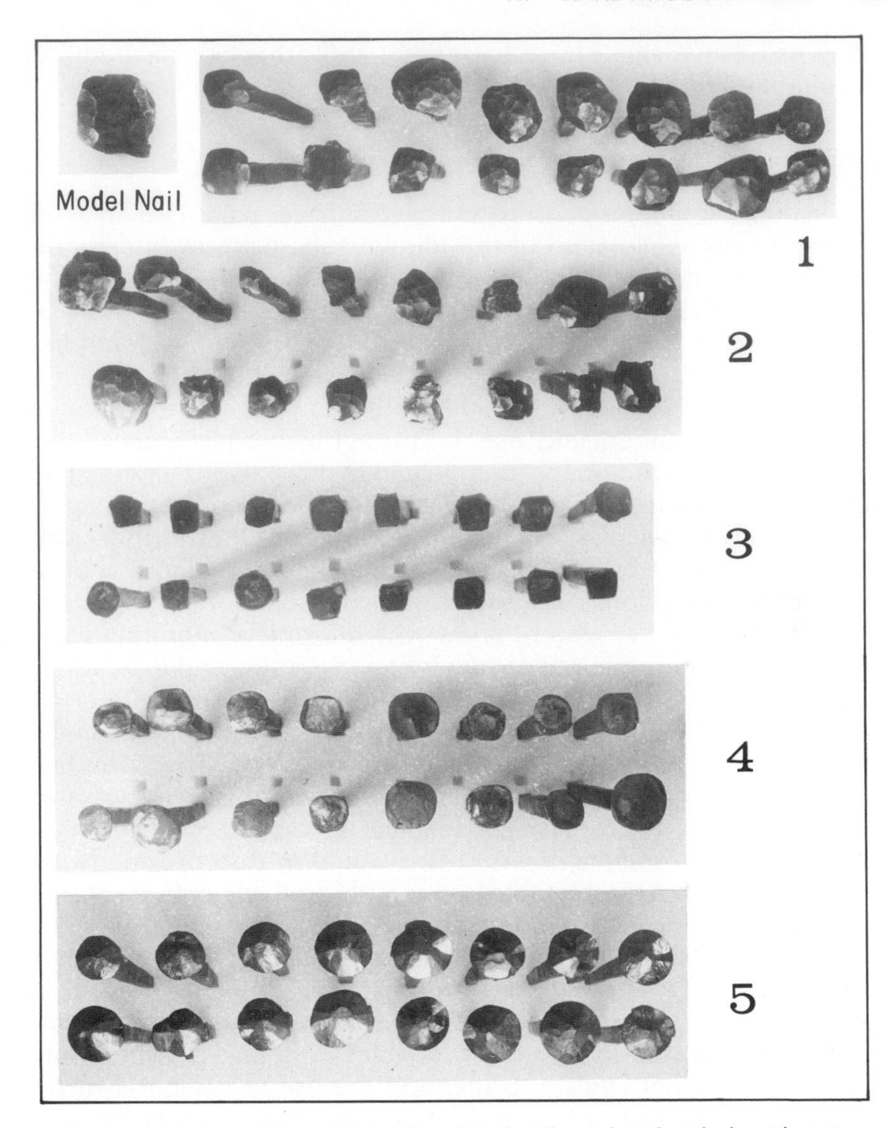

Figure 11.5. Head view of the model nail, and Nails 1 through 16 for Blacksmiths 1–5.

A further observation from Figure 11.3 is that spatial contiguity of blacksmiths may play a part in the production of nails that overlap in their range of variation. Blacksmith 2 utilized the tools and equipment of Blacksmith 1 in the production of his nails and had observed Blacksmith 1 in the production of nails. Blacksmiths 1 and 4, however, also knew each other and Blacksmith 4 produced nails in the presence of Blacksmith 1. Why Blacksmith 4's work should overlap with that of Blacksmith 2 (whom he did not know) is not immediately clear but may hinge upon factors of relative age, physical strength, and other personal attributes not controlled for in this experiment.

Significance of the Study for Historical Archeology

Archeological interests of recent years have paid ever-increasing attention to the exploration of the idiosyncratic patterns discernible in the archeological record, and reflect the generally high level of sophisticated data analysis and interpretation that are available to those who employ those techniques and approaches. It will seem no doubt ironic to many that the computer, whose main archeological application historically has been in the analysis and synthesis of large quantities of data relevant to the superorganic, may be turned with equal veracity to the assessment of such thoroughly unique and highly personal craft patterns. Such ability, valuable in its own right as a means of extracting new dimensions of knowledge from excavated artifacts, goes further. Armed with such knowledge, we should be able to gain a more thorough understanding of colonial proxemics and economics. As a hypothetical case in point, one may wish to know whether one or more blacksmiths were responsible for the iron products of a given site, and if so, whether the products were used within a restricted portion of the site or were combined with the products of contemporaneous blacksmiths. Similarly, one may wish to assess the spatial extent of the work of a given blacksmith. This approach has particular merit for town or village excavations. By employing such techniques, one may be capable of assessing the effective range of one man's work. This would in turn provide clues to economic aspects of blacksmithing previously available only via historical documents. Item specialization within the blacksmithing field itself should be detectable. It would also be informative to ascertain whether certain idiosyncratic attributes discernible in nails extend to other artifact categories as well or whether the technical demands of other artifacts call forth entirely new idiosyncratic variables. As a final possible application, one should not neglect to mention the use of computer-mapped idiosyncratic patterns as a key to the relative dating of structures and to comparisons of construction or remodeling sequences within a group of extant buildings.

The techniques and methodology used for this work are just beginning to be developed. The approach and its assumptions are not without their pitfalls. For instance, our assumption that *one* man is involved in the production of *one* nail is undoubtedly not historically valid at all times and places. Few one-to-one correlations between technical patterns and the wider cultural patterns in which our interest resides are to be found.

It is not the intent or purpose of this particular study to explore any or all of the possibilities outlined herein or to expand upon them. Rather, its significance lies in the exposition of both the idea and a suggested methodology.[3]

ACKNOWLEDGMENTS

The authors would like to express their gratitude to all those involved in the preparation of this chapter. Special thanks to Mr. Richard Barnhart, Jr., Mr. Frank Kracar, Mr. James Smalley, Mr. Carl Schultz, and Mr. Elmer Wessel, who either participated in the experimental aspects directly or aided in the arrangements necessary to such an undertaking. Also, to Dr. John M. Roberts, Mellon Professor, Department of Anthropology, University of Pittsburgh, we would like to express our sincere thanks for his encouragement and his advice.

APPENDIX A: WROUGHT NAIL ATTRIBUTE LIST

Column 1	*Blacksmith number:* 1–5
Columns 2–3	*Nail number:* in order of manufacture from 1 through 30, with the exception of Blacksmith 1 who made 31 nails. The thirty-first nail is the model nail shown to all participants in the project.
Columns 4–8	Overall length of nail including shank and head. This measurement is given in centimeters.
Columns 9–12	Maximum proximal width of nail. This refers to maximum shank width underneath the head of the nail. Measurement is given in millimeters.
Columns 13–16	Maximum distal width of nail. Refers to measurement taken 1 mm up the shank from the point of the nail; given in millimeters.
Columns 17–20	Minimum proximal width of nail in millimeters.
Columns 21–24	Minimum distal width of nail in millimeters.
Columns 25–29	Maximum diameter of head of nail in millimeters.
Columns 30–34	Minimum diameter of head of nail given in millimeters.
Columns 35–36	Head shape of nail as viewed from above. The code numbers are as follows:

01 Round
02 Oval
03 Rectangular
04 Square
05 Parallelogram
06 Trapezoid
07 Irregular oval with two adjacent perpendicular sides
08 Diamond shaped
09 Heart shaped
10 Irregular circle (with sprues of metal projecting from the sides)

[3] *Editor's note:* A paper on which this chapter was based has won the John M. Goggin Award for Method and Theory in Historical Archaelolgy, awarded in 1976 by the Conference on Historic Site Archaeology.

11 Irregular square (with sprues or "feet" extending from one or more sides)
12 Irregular parallelogram (with sprues or feet extending from one or more sides)
13 Irregular rectangle (with sprues or feet extending from one or more sides)
14 Irregular oval (with sprues or feet projecting from one or more sides)
15 Irregular head (with three straight sides joined by an excruved side)

Column 37 — Head shape profile:
1. Flat
2. Domed

Column 38 — Head position relative to shank:
1. Centrally positioned
2. Eccentric
3. *L* shaped

Columns 39–43 — Maximum overjet: the maximum spatial separation between the edge of the nail head and the shank; given in millimeters.

Columns 44–48 — Number of head facets: the number of identifiable head facets resulting from the formation of the nail head. Given as a real number, the result of averaging three separate counts of the integer number of facets.

Column 49 — Tip shape: the qualitative assignation of the tip of the nail as viewed from the side of the nail:
1. Flat
2. Rounded
3. Beveled
4. Flat, badly fissured
5. Spatulate, badly fissured
6. Pointed
7. Spatulate (i.e., a type of spoon-shaped or faceted-point type. Somewhat chisel- or "burin"-like)
8. Fractured

Columns 50–51 — Tip angle: where possible, whole degree deviations of the tip were calculated, particularly with regard to beveled types. Flat points are assigned a zero value.

Column 52 — See under column 53.

Column 53 — Header wear: number of surfaces or edges. Refers to one or more wear patterns represented on the shank of the nail as a consequence of the heading operation. The pattern results from abrasion of the header with the hot nail. Column 52 records the number of surfaces or edges upon which such wear is evident.

Columns 54–59 — Maximum length of header wear pattern on shank of nail: millimeter length as measured from beneath the head of the nail to the termination of the wear pattern coded in column 53. Represents the measurements of the *single* longest of such patterns.

Columns 60–61 — Number of head fissures: the integer number of fissures or "cracks" evident in the head of the nail.

Columns 62–63 — Number of shank fissures: the integer number of fissures or "cracks" evident in the shank of the nail.

Columns 64–65 — Number of head sprues: the integer number of metal sprues evident on the head of the nail.

Columns 66–67 Number of shank sprues: the integer number of metal sprues evident on the shank of the nail.

Columns 68–70 The angle (to nearest ½°) of taper of the shank of the nail.

Column 71 Phase relationship of the maximum and minimum shank widths: a phenomenon in which maximum proximal shank width may occur either on the same side of the nail as the maximum distal width or on the opposite side of the nail. If both proximal and distal maxima are achieved in the same plane, this is referred to as *in phase.* If the distal maximum occurs on the side 90° removed from the proximal maximum, this is called *90° out of phase.* If the proximal or distal measurements are identical or if the distal measurements could not be taken (e.g., because of crushing), the phase relationships do not apply.

1 = in phase
2 = 90° out of phase
3 = phase relations do not apply

Column 72 Evaluation of the cross-section regularity of the shank of the nail. Cross section may be *regular,* if basically symmetrical in square section from head to tip; or, the tip may evidence some crushing or rotation about this long axis of the nail.

1 = cross section regular
2 = regular near head but with tip crushing and rotation about the long axis of the nail

Columns 73–76 Head thickness: millimeter measurements of the thickness of the nail head.

Column 77 Nail edge evaluation (N.E.): a basic evaluation of the character of the edge of the nail (i.e., whether it is *straight* or *sinuous*). The evaluation refers to the entire nail, not to just one surface. Arbitrarily, it was decided that the evaluation of the nail would be determined by the character of the *majority* of the sides. Two straight and two sinuous sides were recorded as *sinuous.*

Columns 78–79 Distinguishing marks (D.M.): presence of certain distinctive marks on nails not generally included in any of the other categories:

01 Hardie marks on nail shank
02 Header indentation of shank of nail
03 Distinct facets present on shank of nail
04 Distinct *notch* on one or two *edges* of nail
05 Combination of 02 and 04
06 Rounded depression on one surface of the shank of the nail.
07 Excavated central pit or ringed head of nail
08 Combination of 04 and 07

APPENDIX B: RÉSUMÉ OF BLACKSMITHS INVOLVED IN THE PROJECT

Blacksmith 1 (16 years of age) had 2 years of blacksmithing expérience at the time of the experiment. Basic blacksmithing techniques, excluding the manufacture of nails, had been taught to him by another blacksmith not involved in the study. In addition to personal interest in the blacksmith's craft, Blacksmith 1 comes from a family with a pronounced interest in craft work in general. His older sister, a professional potter, is a frequent exhibitor in art and craft fairs and has served to interest her brother in such exhibits. The involvement of Blacksmith 1 extended from the apprentice/master form of instruction to the collection of a wide range of books and instructional pamphlets on the subject of blacksmithing. With the exception of occasional nails produced to complement other pieces (e.g., tacks to secure hooks to walls or posts) Blacksmith 1 had not previously engaged in the manufacture of nails on a regular basis. It should be noted that the model nail used in the experiment was itself manufactured by Blacksmith 1; however, he was not permitted to compare the ensuing 30 nails with the model.

Blacksmith 2 (26 years of age) was at an early apprentice level of proficiency at the time of nail manufacture. Previous blacksmithing experience extended only to the observation of the nail-making procedure carried out by others. Blacksmith 2 manufactured his complement of 30 nails under the instruction of Blacksmith 1 and used the equipment of that blacksmith. "Instruction" here denotes only information of the broadest, most general type necessary for personal safety. In most respects, Blacksmith 2 was permitted to experiment with the particular procedures employed in nail manufacture. In all save an intellectual understanding of the nail-making procedure, then, Blacksmith 2 may be considered the least experienced of the five blacksmiths involved in the project.

Blacksmith 3 (approximately 50 years of age) operates a metal redressing business in Pittsburgh, Pennsylvania. "Blacksmithing" as such is consequently but one facet of his customary working schedule. Previous experience in nail making was limited to occasional demonstrations for local craft interest groups. Blacksmith 3 has been involved with metal working all his adult life, as was his father before him. The nails were made in his shop and were heated in a gas rather than in the traditional coal-fired hearth. Only Blacksmith 3 used this alternative method of heating.

Since nail making is a remote aspect of this man's trade, he did not possess a heading device at the time that he was approached about the project. He subsequently manufactured a two-piece "mold" that could be inserted into a vise. The entire shank of the tapered nail was inserted and the head fashioned as described previously. The nail was removed from the heading device simply by opening the vise and allowing the two halves of the header to separate. This was the only two-piece header used in the project; all other smiths used single-piece heading devices of a type more commonly associated with handwrought nail manufacture.

Blacksmith 4 (35 years of age) is primarily a farrier. At the time that he was approached about the nail-making project, he had been active for only 6 months. He had no previous experience in the manufacture of handwrought nails and had not been shown the techniques by any other blacksmith.

Blacksmith 5 (72 years of age) is the most experienced blacksmith of those participating in the project. He is a native of Yugoslavia, where he and his father operated a wagon-making business. As a result of working with his father, Blacksmith 5 accumulated more than 50 years of blacksmithing knowledge. In addition to this great span of experience, he was the most practiced participant in terms of the manufacture of handwrought nails. This was a consequence of his employment as the blacksmith involved in the reconstruction of the sites of Fort Ligonier and Hanna's Tavern at Hannastown, both of which are situated in Westmorland County, Pennsylvania. He produced all the nails and hardware used at both these sites in addition to many other reconstruction projects.

The great experience possessed by Blacksmith 5 in the actual manufacture of wrought nails suggested that a time study of the steps employed by this artisan would be beneficial. The results of this study are presented in Table A.1. Blacksmith 5's facility in nail making was extraordinary. The entire process of making one nail consumed only 2 to 2½ min. The entire sample of 30 nails was completed in approximately 1½ hours. By comparison, Blacksmith 2 required approximately 8 hours to make the requisite number of nails.

TABLE A.1

Time Required to Accomplish Various Phases of the Nail-Making Process and the Number of Strokes Required to Taper and Head Nails (Blacksmith 5).[a]

	Time to heat stock (sec)	Strokes to taper nail	Time to taper nail (sec)	Strokes to cut nail on hardie	Reheating time	Number of strokes to head nail	Time to head nail (sec)
	90	80	30	5	35	43	30
	25	66		7	37	42	
	45	70		8	34	50	
		74	30	8	35	40	25
		71	32	8	25	43	20
		68	30	7		38	20
		72		7		47	18
		86		8			
		78		9	25	45	45
		85	40	11	35	30	10
		77		9	35	40	17
		97	40			47	20
	25	87	40	9	25	60	25
	17	75	40	10	25	42	15
	25	95		8	30	40	20
	25	88		10	26	41	15
	30	90	40	8	10	40	20
	30	81	35	9	30	34	15
		83		10	34	45	18
		82		8	35	37	
						44	15
						43	25
Total	312	1605	357	159	476	891	373
n	9	20	10	19	16	21	18
Mean	34.67	80.25	35.70	8.36	29.75	42.43	20.72

[a] The nail-making process proceeds from left to right.

APPENDIX C: NOMINAL AND CONTINUOUS ATTRIBUTES

A total of 26 nominal and continuous attributes were selected for study following the completion of the manufacture of the nails. In the statistical manipulations that followed, 17 continuous variables were chosen for analysis. These are marked with an asterisk in the following list of all considered attributes:

*1. Overall length (in centimeters)
*2. Maximum proximal width of nail shank (in millimeters)

*3. Maximum distal width of nail shank (in millimeters)
*4. Minimum proximal width of nail shank (in millimeters)
*5. Minimum distal width of nail shank (in millimeters)
*6. Maximum diameter of nail head (in millimeters)
*7. Minimum diameter of nail head (in millimeters)
8. Head shape of nail as viewed from above
9. Head shape of nail as viewed in profile
10. Head position relative to shank
*11. Maximum overjet of nail head with respect to the shank
*12. Number of facets present on the head of the nail
13. Tip shape
*14. Tip angle
15. Header wear patterns—number of surfaces or edges involved
16. Header wear patterns—surface or edge
*17. Maximum length of header wear pattern on shank of nail
*18. Number of head fissures
*19. Number of shank fissures
*20. Number of head sprues
*21. Number of shank sprues
*22. Angle (to nearest ½°) of shank taper
23. Evaluation of shank cross-section regularity
*24. Head height or thickness (in millimeters)
25. Nail edge evaluation
26. Presence of distinguishing marks on the nail

APPENDIX D: EXPLANATION OF NOMINATIVE AND CONTINUOUS ATTRIBUTES

The recognition of attributes in any particular artifact category must of necessity proceed from the nature of the artifact itself. The importance of certain attributes, specifically those pertaining to the general morphology of the artifacts (e.g., overall length and width) is so generally well known as to seem intuitively obvious. Other attributes, however, are more highly restricted in their distribution and therefore warrant a note of explanation in regard to both their derivation and their potential utility for idiosyncratic study.

The realization that the *awareness* of the full range of attributes that together come to characterize an artifact category is not a contemporaneous phenomenon is in itself a significant fact. In addition to the general attributes outlined, two other broad categories of attributes may be discussed with regard to the timing of one's awareness of their existence. Specifically, one may recognize a set of attributes that are distinguishable prior to the initiation of the experiment. This set includes a number of attributes deemed important by the investigator, based solely on visual inspection of the artifact or artifact group. Yet another set of attributes is distinguished processually—that is, their existence is most easily discerned via a personal acquaintance by the investigator with the actual *process* of artifact manufacture. The boundary between these groups of attributes is not immutable but varies with a number of parameters including the perspicacity of the investigator. What is discerned via inspection to one investigator is revealed to another only through actual participation in the process of artifact manufacture. Although it is not the purpose of this chapter to undertake an analysis of the pathways of artifact attribute discovery, suffice it to say that it is the authors' belief that a maximal delineation of attributes for a particular artifact category is attained only via integral participation by the investigator in the process of artifact replication.

The following division of attributes into categories is offered to demonstrate the actual chronological order in which particular attributes and their possible significance were perceived during the course of the experiment.

Attributes Selected prior to Actual Nail Manufacture

1. Overall nail length
2. Maximum and minimum proximal and distal widths of nail shank
3. Maximum and minimum diameters of nail head
4. Head shape of nail from above and in profile
5. Head position related to shank
6. Maximum overjet
7. Number of head facets
8. Angle of shank taper

Attributes Selected as a Result of Integral Participation in the Process of Nail Manufacture

1. Tip shape
2. Tip angle
3. Header wear patterns
4. Length of header wear pattern
5. Existence of head and shank fissures
6. Existence of head and shank sprues
7. Nail edge evaluation

During actual laboratory evaluation of the nails, three additional attributes were discerned. These attributes included the phase relationship of the sides of the nails, the evaluation of the cross section of the nail shank, and the presence of certain distinguishing marks on the shanks of particular nails.

REFERENCES

Adovasio, J. M., and J. D. Gunn
1974 Style, basketry and basketmakers. A paper prepared for the individual in Prehistory symposium at the 39th annual meeting of the Society for American Archaeology, Washington, D.C.
Dixon, W. J.
1974 Biomedical computer programs. (2nd ed.) *University of California Publications in Automatic Computation* No. 2.
Gunn, J. D.
1975 Idiosyncratic behavior in chipping style: Some hypotheses and preliminary analysis. *Lithic Technology: Making and Using Stone Tools.* Edited by Earl Swanson. The Hague, Netherlands: Mouton Publishers.
Jernberg, John
1927 *Forging.* Chicago: American Technical Society.
Nelson, Lee
1963 Nail chronology as an aid to dating old buildings. *History News* **XIX**(2):25–27.
Roberts, John M.
1971 Expressive aspects of technological development. *Philosophy of the Social Sciences* **1**:207–220.
Schwartzkopf, Ernst
1916 *Plain and ornamental forging.* New York: Wiley.

A Strategy for Getting the Job Done

ROBERT L. STEPHENSON

The reader of the earlier chapters of this book will have been impressed, I am sure, with the vast potential that has been developed for productive archeological research within the framework of a science of culture (White 1949:347–415). It may have eluded him, though, that this potential does *not* become reality merely by someone having the ideas and concepts for productive research. Indeed, it often eludes those who are actually doing such research that there is, and must be, an organizational structure supporting the work and making it possible to put those concepts into practice. The archeologist is unable to put research ideas and strategies, however sound, into effect if he does not have the tools with which to do it. This organizational structure must be more than simply the routine administration of a project. It must be an *organizational strategy* for getting the total systematic research job done (Stephenson 1963:277–291).

Strategy, as used here—despite how it may be used elsewhere—is defined as "the science and art of employing the political, economic, psychological, and military forces of a nation or group of nations to afford the maximum support to adopted policies in peace or war . . . the art of devising or employing plans or stratagems toward a goal [Webster 1971]." The goal is the successful achievement of the best research efforts. These research efforts are the adopted policies, and the science and art of supporting them with all possible forces is what we will, here, call a *strategy for getting the job done.* I shall, in this chapter, consider the means by which the archeologist can accomplish as much productive research as he is capable of doing, and the tools he must have to do the job.

These tools consist of a great deal more than the theoretical research concepts, the mechanical devices used in excavation, and the technical instruments for laboratory analyses. Of at least equal importance are such tools as a professional, scholarly climate in which to work; adequate time frames within which to operate; freedom of movement to work when and where the research problem requires; specialized assistants and consultants with whom to collaborate; scholarly direction toward long-range goals and objectives; long-range curation of collections and records with easy access to them; suitable office and laboratory space and facilities for maximum productiveness; and, of course, appropriate funds.

It is the organization of these tools into a systematic and cohesive program of research that will be discussed in this chapter—but some basic criticisms of present archeological procedures and of archeologists themselves will also be discussed. We, as archeologists, are not doing a very good job of exercising the great capabilities that we have developed and are continuing to develop. We speak of the "culture systems" that we wish to investigate but we seldom approach our discipline with anything like a systematic research program. If cultures exist as systems, and there is abundant evidence that they do (White 1975), then an investigation of those cultures can only be successful within a systematic research program. A system can hardly be understood piecemeal. Priorities must be sorted out and systematic goals and objectives of the discipline established. The value of intelligible public communication will also be discussed. Nearly all archeological funding comes from public sources, but archeologists seldom speak to the public in intelligible terms. We have not yet learned to communicate our accomplishments to those who can help us to accomplish even more. We often do not even communicate well with our colleagues (USGS 1949).

A CHOICE OF STRATEGIES

There is no single "correct" way to approach any research problem. Neither is there a single valid approach to a systematic program of research problems. There are always alternative approaches, alternative strategies. There are several valid strategies that can get the job of archeological research done within a framework of a systematic research program. In one set of circumstances, one strategy may be superior to another; in other circumstances, the reverse ranking may be appropriate.

We may group these strategies under three major headings. There is the Academic Department Strategy, the Private Enterprise Strategy, and the Institutional Strategy. Each is useful and effective within its own set of circumstances. All three are valid, and can be used in concert or separately. It is the third strategy, however, that appears to have the most potential for delivering the best tools for maximum capability in productive archeological research. The headlong rush to change the surface of the ground throughout every state, county, and municipality is requiring such accelerated archeological research that all these strategies will have to be used, and used to their fullest capability, throughout the foreseeable future (Lipe 1974; McGimsey 1972).

The Academic Department Strategy

This has been the standard operating procedure for archeological research in the United States since the early 1920's and it has been productive. It has provided a great deal of what is known today of American archeology. It is done by an archeologist in an academic department of anthropology at an institution of higher learning. It is a strategy of part-time research. The archeologist is employed to teach in an academic department and teaching is his first and foremost responsibility. For 9 months of each year regular classes are to be met at regular hours each week. Research is usually encouraged, in fact it is usually demanded if promotions are to be obtained. It is, though, treated as a spare-time effort.

Research can be done in the summers, if summer session classes are not taught. Occasionally a semester can be taken off for research, but that is still a part-time effort. The archeologist is usually without salary for those research months and must develop his own funding source. He is entitled to some vacation during this time and he ends up with 6 or 8 weeks, at most, devoted to fieldwork and that confined to the summer months only. He does not have the freedom to select the best season of the year for his work or to take a contract project that *must* be done during the fall, winter, or spring months. For the most part his research is done on grants rather than contracts. It may be called "leisurely" archeology as opposed to "emergency" archeology that is done on contracts with construction or other land-changing agencies. It does not *have* to be done within a tight time schedule set for nonarcheological reasons. Contract projects can be done within the Academic Department Strategy, but only if they can be fitted into the academic schedule of the archeologist rather than the schedule of the sponsor.

When the fieldwork is finished, the laboratory analyses and report preparation must be fitted into a full-time teaching schedule. The 3 to 4 weeks required for laboratory analyses and report preparation for every week of fieldwork are hard to find when you have a full teaching load and have to prepare for lectures, counsel students, serve on committees, and do the other academic chores for which you were hired. On this basis, the 6-weeks of summer fieldwork may, and often does, require several years for the completion of a report. Sometimes it simply never gets done.

There are advantages, of course, to this strategy. There is usually plenty of time to put together a sound research plan for the proposal for the grant and to have it reviewed by selected peers. There is usually ample time, too, to take excursions into experimental ancillary research that may prove highly productive. Even so, these are done in the archeologist's "spare time."

The archeologist has access to students who can assist in the field as well as in the laboratory, but they too are part-timers. They, too, have classes to attend and to prepare for. These students can do a great deal of the laboratory work and shorten the reporting time, especially if funding for them is built into the grant or if departmental funding is available. The administration is usually minimal because most of it is done by the department head or by the various university offices, and the number of concurrent research projects is usually low. The academic archeologist ordinarily has access to good library facilities and to numerous colleagues in his own or related disciplines upon whom he can call for specialized services, advice, or discussions in a consistently scholarly atmosphere.

There is also a certain advantage to spending several years working with a one-site research project in that there is time for revising and reorienting interpretations. This is offset, however, by the long delays in making the information available to the professional community and to the public. It also tends to keep the archeologist oriented to one site rather than to a broader program of systematic research in an ecological area, a culture period, or some similarly broad and systematic research program.

I must emphasize, though, that despite the disadvantages of part-time research in the academic department this is, will continue to be, and should be a major part of American archeology. We must use every archeologist who is competent and available to accomplish every bit of research that can be done. Furthermore, academe is beginning to accommodate itself in one way or another to the necessities of contract archeology, and this accommodation will increase as the already overwhelming contract load accelerates. Many, perhaps most, archeologists are trained with the intention of being teachers and prefer to teach; for them, research may be a secondary interest or even a necessary chore. For them the academic department strategy is the proper one. For others research is the primary interest and teaching the chore. For these there are other, more productive strategies (Redfield 1973:1–3).

The Private Industry Strategy

This is a new but growing strategy within which to do archeological research and it has great potential for productive professional results. It can be done in two ways; I will have to discuss both together since they are intimately related in overall concept. One is for the archeologist to be employed by a consulting firm as its staff archeologist. The other is for the archeologist to establish his own company as a private, profit-making archeological research firm.

This puts the archeologist in a position of full-time research with the capability to engage in any kind of research project at any time of the year as the needs arise. The time frame for the research can (or should) be set in archeological reality and still be capable of meshing with the time frame of the sponsoring agency's needs. This is an almost totally contract strategy where all or nearly all the research is done on an emergency basis. Yet the emergency nature of the work need not be on the basis of barely beating the bulldozer to the site. It is usually possible to plan the work in conjunction with the early planning stages of construction (Baldwin 1966).

There are advantages and disadvantages to this Private Industry Strategy. If the archeologist is working on the staff of a consulting firm he probably has access to good mapping, drafting, and photography but little else in the way of a supporting laboratory facility. He may have adequate field equipment and vehicles but few if any support personnel. He has a major problem in educating his employer to the various archeological needs, especially laboratory time and the need for full technical reporting of results of the research. Unless he has a rather strong and forceful personality he could easily be put in a position of being told how much archeology will be done or of being told not to find any at all. Again this is a matter of educating the employer to the realities of archeological needs, and it can be done.

If the archeologist is to establish his own company he avoids the problem of educating his employer and deals directly with the agency doing the construction. There are other problems here, though. To establish any company requires a capital investment. A building, laboratory facilities, field and laboratory equipment, working capital, and staff all have to be acquired. This, in most cases, would require a bank loan, probably of $100,000 minimum. Staff would include an accountant/business manager, photographer, illustrator, secretary, laboratory personnel, and however many archeologists the contract flow would require. The director—the person who does the decision making—*must* be an archeologist. The business manager cannot do that, though he is essential to the operation of the company. Sufficient profit, overhead, and fringe costs must be added to each contract to pay off the bank loan, pay salaries, maintain the facility, and show some profit above the expenses of each research project. This is the job of the business manager in conjunction with the director. The staff must include competent qualified archeologists who are geared to the same professional research goals as are the academic archeologists. The director must assure himself that he has this kind of staff.

A private research company simply cannot operate as a one-man operation working out of the archeologist's home with no capital investment. When that is tried the second contract received winds up paying some costs of the first and by the third or fourth contract, the archeologist has gone broke.

The Private Industry Strategy can work and, I venture to say, will be a part of the routine archeological scene in a few years. It must be operated as a business with full business principles being employed. I have argued for years that archeological research *is* a business and though it is a scholarly business it can operate best by the employment of good business principles, whether under the Academic Strategy, the Private Enterprise Strategy, or the Institutional Strategy.

Disadvantages of the Private Enterprise Strategy usually include a serious lack of library facilities, depending on the location of the business. Access to a good university library might be available, but probably would not be, and a working library would have to be purchased. Also, the private archeologist may not have access to student help unless he can hire students for summer work and this restricts his use of their talents the other 9 months. Nor is there much chance of access to colleagues in anthropology or related disciplines except on a paid consultant basis. The intellectual stimulation of day-to-day discussions with these colleagues would be sorely missed, especially by the archeologist on the staff of a consulting firm.

The Institutional Strategy

This is both an old and a new strategy for doing full-time research archeology. It depends upon some form of host institution, an integral part of which is an archeological research facility. The host institution provides the stability and basic support, and the research effort is funded by contracts, grants, and programs of federal, state, local, or private derivation. The Bureau of American Ethnology, the U.S. National Museum, the National Park Service, the American Museum of Natural History, and various state, local, and private museums have been doing archeological research within this framework for many decades. In the nineteenth and early twentieth centuries, before the development of anthropology departments in so many universities, this was the way much of the archeological research was done in America (Willey and Sabloff 1974). Many of these institutions have continued to provide this capability up to the present time.

Until recently these institutional research facilities have been a part of either a federal agency such as the Department of the Interior, a quasi-federal agency such as the Smithsonian Institution, a large or small museum complex, or an historical society. Now this concept is beginning to be linked to academic institutions with the university becoming the host institution. Examples are the Balcones Research Center at the University of Texas, the Arkansas Archeological Survey at the University of Arkansas, the Nevada Archeological Survey at the University of Nevada, and the Institute of Archeology and Anthropology at the University of South Carolina. Three of these four are direct developments from the Bureau of American Ethnology's River Basin Surveys program of the 1940s–1960s (Stephenson 1967). The Arkansas Archeological Survey developed somewhat differently but still within a framework of a full-time research facility as a part of a university.

Another, only slightly different, concept is the archeological research facility that is a part of a state Department of Archives and History. Examples are the facilities at the North Carolina Division of Archives and History and at the Florida Department of Archives and History. This kind of host institution provides nearly the same assets and liabilities to the archeological research as does the university host, with the obvious exception of the easy access to students and some of the varied resources of academic colleagues in a wide range of disciplines.

It seems to me that the Institutional Strategy has most of the advantages of the other two strategies with fewer of the disadvantages of either of them. In the first place there are full-time research archeologists working the year around without any necessary commitment to a teaching schedule. The Arkansas example is somewhat of an exception; some of the archeologists are required to teach part time but here the emphasis is first on research and second on teaching as opposed to the reverse in the academic department research. At South Carolina, Texas, and Nevada there is a freedom to teach if it does not interfere with the primary goal of research. This can be an asset to the research if viewed with the primary goal as being research.

The Institutional Strategy is very important to American archeology and will become more important as earth-moving construction projects continue to accelerate. We can no longer rely on the luxury of part-time leisurely archeology to do the whole job for us. It will always be a welcome and valuable supplement but it must become just that—a supplement to the full-time research programs that must develop throughout the nation. Full-time research facilities capable of using all the best research techniques available must be developed in strategic locations throughout the country. Perhaps in every state, certainly at least in every major geographic region, or perhaps at several locations in some states.

In addition to the full-time research capability, the research agency attached to an academic institution of higher learning has access to good library facilities and to a wide variety of colleagues in a range of related disciplines: botany, zoology, history, chemistry, geography, geology, and computer science, to name but some. There is the advantage of being located on a campus where a professional, scholarly climate exists in which to work. Seminars, discussions, visiting lecturers, student intellectual contributions, and the other routine aspects of a scholarly climate are all important in developing the best scientific approach to archeological research. This is especially important in developing a scholarly, scientific direction for long-range goals and objectives. Several archeologists working together with the assistance of colleagues from other disciplines are far better equipped to set these goals and objectives than is any one archeologist working alone or with few colleagues.

Long-range curation of archeological records and specimens is also best accomplished in this Institutional Strategy. These records and specimens are the heritage of the people of America and cannot become the private property of any individual or company merely because that individual or company paid for their recovery. They, therefore, must be curated by some public institution and the Private Industry Strategy is not very adaptable to this. Neither is the Academic Department Strategy. The department has space for students and for teaching and is not often amenable to providing space that appears to be storage. The Institutional Strategy provides for this curation at a university in public trust and makes it clear at the beginning that space for active files of specimens and records (this should never be referred to as "storage" because they are, or should be, active research tools) is a necessary part of the research facility. Both the records and the specimens must be easily accessible, systematically filed for easy retrieval, and maintained under conditions of temperature and humidity control.

The Institutional Strategy provides a sound financial structure within which to work. There is, first, a basic funding from the institution that stabilizes a working structure and makes the facility itself relatively secure in long-range planning. There is, also, a capability of doing as much contract work as the facility can accommodate with each contract paying the costs of the work done under that contract. To the contract costs are added the costs for overhead to the host institution and that eases some of the financial burden on the institution for space, utilities, accounting, and other indirect costs. This kind of funding structure provides the capability of doing both contract (emergency) archeology and grant (leisurely) archeology within the same institutional framework and, of even more importance, of meshing the two within broad regional frameworks of cultural studies.

Like nearly all "new" concepts, theories, methods, and strategies in American archeology, this Institutional Strategy is only a useful adaptation of old and well-tried ideas to a changing research climate and changing needs of the profession. Some "new" adaptations become so esoteric and even irrelevant that they are expensive wastes of precious research time and funds. Others are so realistic and relevant that they become major advances in the profession. I am convinced that the Institutional Strategy is well within the latter category. It does work. To demonstrate this, let us move, briefly, from the general concept to an examination of a specific example of this strategy.

The South Carolina Example

The Institute of Archeology and Anthropology is a research facility within the University of South Carolina. It was established first as a separate state agency known as the South Carolina Department of Archeology. This had no chance of success because it had no host institution for a budgetary umbrella nor did it have anyone to whom it answered for responsibility.

In 1967 it was transferred to the University of South Carolina with a line-item budget within the University budget, which provides the basic "hard" money platform from which to operate and the foundation upon which long-range planning and stability can be achieved. With one exception, this budget has increased every year. The Institute is a separate administrative entity within the university and reports directly to the Vice-President for Research. There are no administrative ties to any department or college, though close association and cooperation are maintained with the Department of Anthropology and other related departments such as history, geology, and computer science (Stephenson 1969:3–6).

The working funds of the Institute are derived from a combination of contracts and grants. The grants are from such usual granting agencies as the National Science Foundation; the contracts are from federal, state, local, and private sources and combinations of these. These combinations include funds from counties, municipalities, private industry, and private individuals as well as state and federal agencies. There is a program of Highway Archeology combining state and federal funds and a site inventory program from National Historic Preservation Act funds derived through the South Carolina Department of Archives and History. Contracts for environmental impact studies of very small to very large scale are developing from all of the funding sectors.

The basic facility is one floor of a building centrally located on the university campus. Space is provided for offices, laboratories, specimen and record files, darkroom, drafting room, and, in an adjacent building, storage space for field equipment. Staff includes a director and eight other archeologists, a conservator, a photographer, an illustrator, secretaries, an administrative clerk, a laboratory supervisor, a records clerk, six research assistants, and 6 to 20 part-time student assistants as well as the temporary field crews required from time to time. There is a substantial inventory of field and laboratory equipment. The Institute, thus, has the tools of space, staff, equipment, scholarly climate, library, consultants, and curatorial capability with which to work.

There are no teaching commitments by any of the Institute staff but any of the archeologists may teach an occasional course if desired if the teaching does not interfere with the research objectives and time. Field courses and related laboratory courses are taught as parts of research projects. On-the-job training is also available to the part-time student assistants as a part of their employment. The six research assistants, graduate students in archeology selected from all parts of the country, are in an internship for 1 year of nonclassroom training with the staff archeologists. The full-time research schedules that this system provides allow the archeologists freedom of time frames throughout the year and scheduling time within which to produce scientific, professional products.

This, then, is a valid, and I believe successful, example of the Institutional Strategy for accomplishing archeological research. It is a full-time research facility engaged in scientific archeological research within a systematic, long-range, regional program. There is no need to discuss here the philosophical and theoretical directions that this research takes; that is exemplified in other chapters in this volume. It may, though, be pointed out that the program does have a systematic, long-range direction toward which it is heading as discussed in its "Plan" for the coming decade (Stephenson 1975). This Institute is not a new concept. It is a direct outgrowth of the research strategy of the River Basin Surveys Program of the 1940's–1960's, adapted to the university situation and to the changing research climate and needs of the profession. It has a flexible base and can continue to adapt its procedures to the accelerating growth and maturing of American archeology (Lipe 1974).

This example incorporates elements of the Institutional Strategy that are basic to all strategies for doing archeological research. Some of these elements are so commonplace as to be overlooked or even avoided by many of our colleagues. For this reason their need for emphasis is pressing; I am convinced that such elements as administration, leadership, diplomacy, systematic research planning, and public responsibility are essential to the health of our profession. Let us, then, return from the specific to the generalized discussion of these elements and their application to any research strategy.

THE ELEMENTS OF ANY STRATEGY

Systematic Research Administration

Productive archeological research can be carried out within the framework of any of these strategies. There are problems, responsibilities, and obligations that are common to all three strategies. As mentioned in the first paragraph of this chapter, it is often the case that even archeologists themselves fail to recognize those problems, responsibilities, and obligations that do not directly pertain to their own immediate research. The problems, responsibilities, and obligations of setting the framework for and of administering the programs of those immediately-at-hand pieces of research are time-consuming and at least as complex as the archeology itself. These problems, though, are really challenges to move forward in our professional responsibilities; to make it possible for the greatest number of dedicated, competent, professional people to accomplish archeological research at their maximum capacity toward as full an understanding as possible of the cultural processes as reflected in archeological data.

This is usually called administration but I believe it is more than that. Certainly the elements of administration are a major part of making it possible to get the research job done. There are equally important elements of leadership, diplomacy, and overall research guidance that are necessary. And certainly there are the elements of responsibility and accountability, both to the profession and to the public, that must be carried out. Somebody has to answer for all that is done in the total research program, just as surely as the archeologist has to answer for what he says in his research monograph. This person is necessarily the program director in the Private Enterprise or Institutional Strategies and may be in the Academic Department Strategy as well. In the latter, though, the job often falls to the department head or the individual archeologist himself. In any event it usually centers in one person who must be willing and able to carry it out or the program will not succeed.

Archeologists are notoriously reluctant to assume administrative roles and to guide and direct long-range programs in a systematic attack on broad cultural problems—but only an archeologist can do it. I have referred to archeological research as a business, and I believe it is, but a business executive without training in archeology simply does not have the understanding of the archeological research requirements to direct and administer such a program. The archeologist who accepts this responsibility must understand good business practices and put them to use but it is his archeological training that provides the knowledge of what to apply the business practices to.

The archeologist who avoids this leadership role is missing much of the satisfaction and challenge that our profession offers. It is tremendously rewarding to be in a position of creating the climate and facilities within which a group of archeologists can accomplish a wide range of individual research projects within a systematic framework of integrated cultural studies. This leadership role may not permit the program director to have one of the specific research projects himself but it does permit him to develop an overview of all the research within the program. That in itself is a research accomplishment of value. It can far outweigh the routine tasks of administration (Gussin 1973:90–91).

There is no need to belabor these well-known tasks of administration. Staffing and personnel procedures, budgeting, purchasing and developing inventories of equipment, maintenance of equipment and facilities, planning and securing space, preparing proposals and contracts, scheduling of field and laboratory activities, and dealing with interpersonal staff problems and salary structures are all parts of the administrative responsibility. These are the routine, and often less than enjoyable, necessities of operating a research program. They are the tasks for which the administrator probably will never get any recognition or thanks if he does them well but for which he will bear the full blame if any of them goes wrong.

Systematic Research Goals

The elements of leadership, diplomacy, and research guidance are not so routine but they are at least as important as the purely administrative tasks. They include the actual development of the long-range goals and objectives of the program and the selection of the individual research projects that will best fit into those goals. It is, in a sense, a "super" research design that asks questions, poses hypotheses, provides for testing of the hypotheses, and develops syntheses for, not a single research project, but a whole complex of projects developed into a systematic research program. This design must include not only the known research projects that are anticipated but any remotely conceivable projects that might develop by contracts throughout any part of the research program area. It must be flexible enough so that, as goals and objectives are achieved or redirected and changed, these changes can be accommodated in the long-range program.

This research design or long-range plan can best be developed by all the archeologists in the program working together—not by the director alone, although he must provide the leadership and general guidance for it, as he will be responsible for its execution and results. He is the one who must ensure that its goals are realistic and that they are kept uppermost in each project of the program. He must be sensitive to the needs for changes of the goals and objectives but he must assure himself that these changes are not made frivolously.

This is the very heart of the whole program. Without this long-range plan the program may be merely an unconnected series of research projects without goals, objectives, or continuity. Such aimlessness has far too long been a weakness in American archeology. It is the one-site-at-a-time concept with too little coordination between the multiple parts of a cultural system as represented by a complex of sites. This long-range planning is often difficult within the Academic Department Strategy, especially when only one archeologist in a department is concerned with the archeology of a single large area. Often there is only one archeologist in a department and it is most difficult for him to coordinate his work with colleagues several hundred miles away in a "research plan." It may be equally difficult in a Private Industry Strategy with contracts developing from several parts of the country.

The Institutional Strategy is ideally designed to accommodate this kind of long-range planning. It would be for this reason alone, if for no other, that I am convinced that the Institutional Strategy is the most promising way to do American archeology in the future. It provides individual research freedom to do whatever research is called for within a professionally disciplined framework. It provides professional research standards with abundant capability for innovative variation in technique, method, and theory. It provides a systematic attack on broad problems of past human behavior. It provides standards of production within reasonable time frames. And there is a capability for curation of specimens and records that can bring about the institution's development into a major research center.

This whole concept of research direction is based on a systematic approach to goals and objectives. If we are studying cultures and cultures exist as systems, then the approach to a study of those cultures should certainly be systematic. This leads to the ultimate purpose of any system and that is the responsibility for results. The archeologist, though working with past cultures, is a part of his own culture and as such has obligations and responsibilities for productive results of his research. The responsibilities to professional colleagues have been discussed, but there is an equal responsibility for productive results to that segment of our own culture that pays the bills—the public.

Responsibility to the Public

There is hardly any aspect of American archeological research that is not financed totally by some segment of the American public. Federal and state appropriations and sometimes county appropriations are derived directly from tax dollars. Specific segments of the public, too, are becoming increasingly heavy investors in archeological research. These are the federal, state, county, and municipal agencies that are now obligated by law to support contracts for environmental impact studies. These are also the private corporations, businesses, and individuals that also must consider the cultural resources as they develop construction projects. Even these private companies and individuals are a part of the public since they are all involved without partiality. They are not archeologists. Archeologists do not finance archeology except to the extent that they, too, are taxpayers.

Cultural resources, like natural resources, are public property (Tilden 1957). They are the heritage of the people and they belong to the people. It is altogether fitting that the conservation and study of these cultural resources should be financed by the public (Udall 1963).

With this public support for archeological research there is the responsibility of the archeologist to make the results available and comprehensible to the public—to even the most disinterested member of the public because his tax dollars, too, are involved. As archeologists we are increasingly losing sight of this responsibility. We are accelerating our professional responsibilities to our colleagues as we should be but we are not talking to the public very well.

The archeological end product—the result of our well-planned and well-executed research—is the published report. This is generally all we have for a product. There are specimens for museums and sometimes there can be reconstructed, restored, or stabilized ruins, but usually the report is our only product. Certainly it is our primary one. And to whom do we write it? Ourselves. We write our archeological interpretations and explanations for other archeologists with the attitude of "the public be damned."

As new adaptations of our methodologies, philosophies, theories, and concepts overwhelm us with the great potential we have for doing better and better archeology, we become increasingly impressed with ourselves. We are led to feel that this is too "heady a brew" to be understood by the public and we create an accelerating jargon with which to write it (Mead 1976). Of course, with this jargon we make very sure that the public cannot understand it. Unfortunately it is not always understandable to our colleagues, either. We just are not communicating well. It is really *easier* to write plain, understandable English than to create a jargon and have to remember the nuances and implications of these new words as they are used in different contexts. I submit that it is no more scientific, scholarly, intellectual, or erudite to "engage in the operationalization of the quantification of a hypothesized, statistically significant ceramic sample" than it is to "count a large group of potsherds." Even our erudite colleagues appreciate good English and certainly our public audience is not going to develop any interest in our efforts if we do not use it.

American archeology today has more public support than it has ever had in the past. These supporters are not concerned about which strategy we use or what our theoretical approach is. They are concerned about the conservation, study, and understanding of their heritage and they are hiring us as archeologists to do these studies and to tell them about it so that they can understand it. The better we write for the public understanding of the achievements we are making, the more support we are going to get from the public (Mead 1976).

The Society for American Archeology has recognized this and established a Committee for Public Understanding of Archeology. The effort is certainly commendable but it cannot be successful until the individual archeologist becomes his own committee of one and speaks to his employer—the public—in a language that is clear and concise.

This can be done within any of the three research strategies that we have discussed, but it may be a little easier under the Institutional Strategy. It requires some self-discipline in writing technical reports for our colleagues so that, technical as they may be, they are written in the clearest English possible. To reach the general public well, though, will require the technical reports to be rewritten in modified form, in lay language, with the technical details relegated to the background. A series of such "popular" (and brief) reports of the work explained in long detail in the technical monographs would support archeological research to the public more effectively than a dozen times as many technical reports. Within the Institutional Strategy there could be a publication fund for just this kind of public communication.

American archeologists are confronted with a vast array of opportunities that appear to be accelerating tremendously. It is up to us to seize these opportunities and do our research within the framework that is best for our own individual productivity. Whether we labor in an academic department, a private archeological corporation, or an institutional research center we have limitless worlds to conquer. Our professional colleagues can bask in the glories of our achievements and proudly exhibit theirs to us. But if this exciting world is to continue and to capitalize on the advantages it now has we are all going to have to demonstrate its worth to Mr. and Mrs. American citizen.

REFERENCES

Baldwin, Gordon C.

1966 *Race against time.* New York: Putnam.

Gussin, Carl M.

1973 The "newly applied" anthropologist. In *Anthropology beyond the university,* edited by Alden Redfield. Southern Anthropological Society Proceedings, No. 7. Athens: Univ. of Georgia Press, Pp. 90–91.

Lipe, William D.
1974 A conservation model for American archaeology. *The Kiva* **39**(3–4): pp. 213–245.
McGimsey, Charles R.
1972 *Public archeology.* New York: Seminar Press.
Mead, Margaret
1976 Towards a human science. *Science* **191** p. 903.
Redfield, Alden
1973 *Anthropology beyond the university.* Southern Anthropological Society Proceedings, No. 7. Athens: Univ. of Georgia Press, Pp. 1–3.
Stephenson, Robert L.
1963 Administrative problems of the river basin surveys. *American Antiquity* **28**(3):277–291.
1967 Reflections on the river basin surveys program. Desert Research Institute, Univ. of Nevada, *Preprint Series* No. **48.**
1969 Background and current program of the institute. *The Notebook* **1**(1):3–6. Institute of Archeology and Anthropology, Univ. of South Carolina, Columbia.
1975 An archeological preservation plan for South Carolina. *The Notebook* **7**(3): Institute of Archeology and Anthropology, Univ. of South Carolina, Columbia. pp. 101–175.
Tilden, Freeman
1957 *Interpreting our heritage.* Chapel Hill: Univ. of North Carolina Press.
Udall, Stewart L.
1963 *The quiet crisis.* New York: Holt.
USGS
1949 *Suggestions to critics.* United States Geological Survey-Geologic Division Mineral Deposits Branch, Washington, D.C.
Webster, Noah
1971 *Webster's third new international dictionary, unabridged,* edited by Philip Gove. Springfield, Massachusetts: C. & G. Merriam.
White, Leslie A.
1949 *The science of culture.* New York: Farrar, Straus.
1975 *The concept of cultural systems.* New York: Columbia Univ. Press.
Willey, Gordon R., and Jeremy Sabloff
1974 *A history of American archaeology.* London: Thames & Hudson.

Index

G

O

P

Q

A
B 7
C 8
D 9
E 0
F 1
G 2
H 3
I 4
J 5